THE WORKERS' REVOLT IN CANADA, 1917–1925

Canadians often consider the Winnipeg General Strike of 1919 to be the defining event in working-class history after the First World War. This book, the collaboration of nine labour historians, shows that the unrest was both more diverse and more widespread across the country than is generally believed.

The authors clarify what happened in working-class Canada at the end of the war and situate 'the workers' revolt' within the larger structure of Canadian social, economic, and political history. They argue that, despite a national pattern, the upsurge of protest took a different course and faced a different set of obstacles in each region of the country. Their essays shed light on the extent of the revolt nationally while retaining a sensitivity to regional distinctiveness.

Drawing on the approaches of social history, this study moves beyond conventional labour history and its focus on the strike and union organization to re-examine what was once called the 'western revolt.' *The Workers' Revolt in Canada* combines insights from new archival research with the considerable body of secondary literature on the subject to produce a compelling new synthesis, which will be of great use to teachers and of interest to economists, sociologists, and historians.

CRAIG HERON is an associate professor in the Division of Social Science and the Department of History, York University. He is the author of *The Canadian Labour Movement: A Short History,* co-editor of the series Themes in Canadian Social History, and former co-editor of the series Studies in Gender and History.

EDITED BY CRAIG HERON

The Workers' Revolt in Canada, 1917–1925

UNIVERSITY OF TORONTO PRESS
Toronto Buffalo London

Toronto Buffalo London
Printed in Canada

ISBN 0-8020-4238-4 (cloth)
ISBN 0-8020-8082-0 (paper)

Printed on acid-free paper

Canadian Cataloguing in Publication Data

Main entry under title:

The workers' revolt in Canada, 1917–1925

Includes bibliographical references and index.
ISBN 0-8020-4238-4 (bound) ISBN 0-8020-8082-0 (pbk.)

1. Labour movement – Canada – History – 20th century.
2. Working class – Canada – History – 20th century.
I. Heron, Craig.

HD8106.W67 1998 331.8'0971'09042 C97-931686-3

This book has been published with the help of a grant from the Humanities and Social Sciences Federation of Canada, using funds provided by the Social Sciences and Humanities Research Council of Canada.

University of Toronto Press acknowledges the financial assistance to its publishing program of the Canada Council for the Arts and the Ontario Arts Council.

Contents

ACKNOWLEDGMENTS vii

Introduction 3
CRAIG HERON

The Great War, the State, and Working-Class Canada 11
CRAIG HERON and MYER SIEMIATYCKI

The Maritimes: Expanding the Circle of Resistance 43
IAN McKAY and SUZANNE MORTON

Quebec: Class and Ethnicity 87
GEOFFREY EWEN

Southern Ontario: Striking at the Ballot Box 144
JAMES NAYLOR

The Prairies: In the Eye of the Storm 176
TOM MITCHELL and JAMES NAYLOR

British Columbia and the Mining West: A Ghost of a Chance 231
ALLEN SEAGER and DAVID ROTH

National Contours: Solidarity and Fragmentation 268
CRAIG HERON

Conclusion 305
CRAIG HERON

BIBLIOGRAPHY 315
ILLUSTRATION CREDITS 356
CONTRIBUTORS 357
INDEX 359

Illustrations follow page 184.

Acknowledgments

The contributors to this book accumulated many debts to librarians, archivists, colleagues, and family. We all owe a special thanks to Gregory Kealey for a careful, helpful reading of the manuscript. Gerry Hallowell was a consistent source of encouragement and sound advice at University of Toronto Press, and Emily Andrew, Darlene Zeleney, and Sarah Robertson moved us efficiently through the editorial process.

THE WORKERS' REVOLT IN CANADA, 1917–1925

When our historians shall sit down to write the history of the present day it will, we believe, be all different from the history of bygone days. The industrial situation today, the social unrest existing, and the part labor is taking in the uplift of humanity through trade unionism will have to receive some consideration, otherwise that history will simply be a camouflage ...

Workers' Weekly (Stellarton), 19 December 1919

Introduction

CRAIG HERON

On 26 October 1996 a quarter of a million people thronged the streets of Toronto to protest the right-wing agenda of Ontario's Conservative government. Their 'days of action' continued a movement that had already shut down London, Hamilton, and Kitchener over the course of the preceding year. Collective memory of such struggles is usually weak enough that few would have realized that their determined action and their slogan 'Organize, Educate, Resist' placed them in a long tradition of similar working-class resistance. In particular, they would probably have heard little about a workers' revolt that had begun to gather steam across the country eighty years earlier.

The history of workers' protest has suffered in the wake of the abrupt end of the Cold War. It has become fashionable to dismiss the socialist experiment that began in the Soviet Union eight decades ago as some kind of aberration in human history. It is all too easy to forget that the Russian workers themselves, not a tiny revolutionary elite, propelled their country into a new age,[1] and that they were not alone in envisioning a new kind of society that promised a better life for workers. In 1919 the clenched fist of working-class solidarity was raised defiantly throughout the industrialized world. Never before had such a dramatic convergence of working-class discontent, militancy, and socialism been seen on an international scale. The Scottish Clydeside seethed with radical fervour and exploded into a strike for the forty-hour week. In Britain generally, the Triple Alliance of miners, railwaymen, and dockers threatened concerted industrial action, while a revitalized Labour Party championed a new, overtly socialist program. In France waves of general strikes rolled through the mining, metalworking, and construction industries. In Italy occupations of factories were under way in Milan and Turin. Workers' councils had already led revolutionary battles to implant socialism in Germany and Austria late in 1918, and a similar struggle erupted in Hungary a few months later. In the United States a general strike in Seattle, Washington, and a nationwide steel strike highlighted a massive wave of strikes and political agitation. Across the seas Australia and New Zealand were rocked by aggressive new labour movements. In 1917 the Russian Revolution provided the most famous and influential experiment in working-class power; by 1919 the country's revolutionary leaders were attempting to inspire and coordinate the international revolt. At few points in history had workers throughout the industrialized world marched across the political stage with such unity and determination.[2]

What was happening in Canada? For most of the eight decades since those turbulent years, Canadian historians have simply pointed to the general strike that erupted in Winnipeg on 15 May 1919. Little else has found its way into the textbooks that cover the period.[3] A number of Canadian writers have even used the strike as a dramatic setting for their novels.[4] It was, indeed, a remarkable event. The entire wage-earning force of the country's third-largest city – most of whose members did not even belong to unions – walked off the job in support of striking construction and metal workers. The six-week strike polarized a community along class lines as few events in Canadian history have ever done and left deep impressions on the public life of the city and province for decades afterwards.

In recent years scholars and writers have taken a closer look at the activities of Canadian workers during and immediately following World War I. They have concluded that the Winnipeg strikers were not alone in taking their unprecedented stand. In the years between 1917 and 1925 working-class defiance swelled up in industrial centres across the country. In major cities like Halifax, Montreal, Toronto, and Vancouver, as well as in such unlikely settings as Amherst, Nova Scotia, and Gananoque, Ontario, workers formed their own organizations, marched off the job in record numbers, engaged in defiant acts of solidarity, and made bold new demands.[5]

To date this wider story has appeared largely as a set of fragments, generally in the form of local community studies. The full dimensions of the remarkable working-class activity that took place in Canada at the end of World War I have never been drawn together and properly analysed. The authors of this book have undertaken to present a more integrated social history that both surveys the national picture and introduces a broader comparative perspective. We hope to make clear the depth and breadth of this working-class upsurge, its organizational and ideological complexity, its different expressions across the country, and the factors that destroyed it.

The many Canadian historians who have helped to bring the varied dimensions of the workers' revolt to light have not all agreed about what Canadian workers actually wanted and how they proposed to get there. We have long known that widespread fear of revolution gripped the minds of many political leaders, businessmen, and newspaper editors at the end of the war. In 1938 Sir Robert Borden described in his memoirs the kind of menace he believed had been facing Canada two decades earlier. 'In some cities there was a deliberate attempt to overthrow the existing organization of the Government and to supersede it by crude, fantastic methods founded upon absurd conceptions of what had been accomplished in Russia,' he wrote. 'It became necessary in some communities to repress revolutionary methods with a stern hand and from this I did not shrink.'[6] Early scholars of this phase of Canadian working-class history undertook to prove that such ruling-class hysteria was misplaced by arguing that, despite the strident rhetoric of working-class leaders, Canadian workers were organizing simply to win, within the context of the existing capitalist system, limited rights to which they were entitled. In the fullest scholarly treatment of the Winnipeg General Strike, David Bercuson sought to deflate the political overtones of the strike and to situate it more solidly within the longer-range patterns of industrial conflict in this western boomtown.[7]

In the 1970s a new crop of writers began to question previous interpretations of the Winnipeg General Strike. In a challenging introduction to a new edition of the strikers' own history, Norman Penner argued that the events surrounding the strike had more overtly political dimensions.[8] Gregory Kealey made the most commanding statement of an alternative perspective in a paper presented to a 1983 conference on the Winnipeg strike. He surveyed the speeches, writings, and activities of local working-class leaders across Canada and found what he believed was a consistent pattern: 'the message ... was the same across the country. The capitalist system could not be reformed; it must be transformed. Production for profit must cease; production for use must begin.'[9] Other writers also suggested that the workers' challenge went well beyond formal politics to encompass the 'politics of production.' Implicitly and explicitly, Canadian workers were promoting and defending rights in the workplace that could guarantee some kind of 'industrial democracy.'[10] In this light the broad patterns of working-class activity from 1917 to 1925 could legitimately be called a 'workers' revolt.'[11]

By the 1980s the degree and extent of the radicalism fuelling the revolt was at the centre of the debate. The role of socialists became a particularly contentious issue. Some writers argued that, notably in the One Big Union (OBU) in western Canada, left-wing leadership took angry workers along fruitless syndicalist paths, thereby depriving them of the opportunity to make more limited gains through more conventional organizations.[12] Subsequent research suggested that rather than manipulating western workers, the OBU's socialist leadership was swept along on a wave of militancy over which it had little control, and that in many communities across the country radicals helped to provide creative leadership in articulating the concerns of workers.[13]

Perhaps the most ink has been spilled on the question of how the working-class ferment was distributed across the country. Several western Canadian historians staked out the provocative claim that radicalism and militancy were much stronger west of the Lakehead as a result of the unique frontier environment in which western workers found themselves.[14] The first recent survey of Canadian labour history integrated that perspective by consigning labour's post-war upsurge to a chapter entitled 'The Western Revolt.'[15] Even that book's major Marxist competitor for a general readership incorporated the argument about the impact of an industrial frontier into a controversial analysis of that period of Canadian working-class history.[16] Historians of the working-class experience in Atlantic Canada, Quebec, and Ontario have responded with detailed local studies revealing the same indications of deep-seated disaffection and resistance. Some of these 'eastern' writers have acknowledged the unevenness of the revolt across the country, attributing it to the particularities of political economy, social structure, and cultural practices and institutions rather than to region per se. The patchwork of local studies that has emerged reveals both radicalism and moderation in all parts of the country.[17]

Far less attention has been paid to the social complexion of the revolt. A few writers have attempted to determine precisely which workers were at the forefront of the post-war upsurge and what factors accounted for their participation.[18] By focusing attention on the frequently active role of European and Asian immigrants in strikes, union organizing, and socialist politics, some writers have reminded us that not all Canadian workers swept up in this revolt were white, English-speaking males.[19] Others have shed some light on the participation of women in the workers' revolt.[20] All of these studies hint that the ferment ran deep in working-class communities. But the unacknowledged vantage point of almost all writers has remained the white, English-speaking male wage earner, and the real dimensions of gender and ethnicity have yet to be fully integrated into an analysis of the revolt.

The long-term impact of this remarkable episode in Canadian history has been no less controversial. For the most part, it has been drawn into the history of the left, setting the stage for both communism and social democracy. Communist sympathizers have tended to belittle the political 'immaturity' of working-class radicals and militants before the founding of the Communist Party of Canada, while their critics have been more likely to see such men and women as dupes of Moscow-based manipulators.[21] Social democratic writers have concentrated on the political survivors of the period in provincial and national legislatures, notably J.S. Woodsworth, in spinning their tales of the rise and consolidation of social democracy in Canada.[22] Too often the chroniclers of the left have been highly selective in their ransacking of the period and quickly dismissive in their rush to establish the legitimacy of the later radical organizations they are most interested in. They have seldom considered the workers' movements that emerged during and following World War I on their own terms.[23]

A few historians have sensed that the 1917–25 period was a great moment in the history of class relations in Canada. Never before had workers posed such a broadly based and potent challenge to the existing structures and ideologies of class rule in Canada. Some historians have tried to suggest the implications of the massive defeat that independent working-class organizations suffered in the early 1920s – the options that were stifled, the difficulties of rebuilding organizations, the vulnerability of Canadian workers, and the enhanced ability of Canadian capitalists to pursue their corporate strategies.[24]

The aim of this book is to clarify what happened in working-class Canada at the end of the war and to situate the workers' revolt within the larger structure of Canadian social, economic, and political history. One of our more specific objectives is to explore more carefully the dynamics of regionalism within the workers' revolt. We begin with the premise that the revolt was a cross-country phenomenon that emerged in similar ways across Canada but nonetheless took a different course and faced different obstacles in each region. We explore themes that surpass the boundaries of individual regions, but do not attempt simply to homogenize the rich local detail into a single national pattern. During the period in question, and arguably throughout its history, the 'Canadian working class' never existed as a coherent, self-conscious social force. Most often, workers' struggles have had no more than a local focus. What makes the 1917–25 period so unusual is the convergence of these struggles in regional labour movements that exerted influence at the national level immediately following World War I.

The book opens with an overview of the larger context within which the workers' movements emerged. We then proceed to individual essays on each of five major regions. (We regret that it was not possible to include Newfoundland, which had a rich and fascinating history of its own during the 1917–25 period, and northern Ontario, whose working class reflected many of the main currents of western Canadian militancy and radicalism.)[25] Finally, we sketch the common themes that emerged within the various workers' movements. Although individual authors or teams prepared each of the essays, we worked together on the central questions and issues to be addressed in order to shape as coherent an argument as possible about the nature of the workers' revolt in Canada.

In many ways, unearthing the story of the workers' revolt has been the collective project of a whole generation of labour historians. We are indebted to the many scholars and writers whose previous work, listed in the bibliography at the end of the book, enabled us to undertake this project. It is our intent not only to provide a synthesis of this huge body of research but also to encourage the investigation of hitherto neglected questions about the 1917–25 workers' revolt.

Notes

1 See Sirianni, *Workers' Control and Socialist Democracy*; and S.A. Smith, *Red Petrograd*.

2 Montgomery, *Fall of the House of Labor*, 370–410; Hinton, *First Shop Stewards' Movement*; Cronin, 'Labor Insurgency and Class Formation'; Wrigley, ed., *Challenges of Labour*; Geary, *European Labour Protest*, 134–78, and 'Radicalism and the German Worker'; Shorter and Tilly, *Strikes in France*, 122–7; Williams, *Proletarian Order*; Bertrand, *Revolutionary Situations*; Haimson and Tilly, eds., *Strikes, Wars, and Revolutions*; Carr, *Bolshevik Revolution*; Andrae, 'Swedish Labour Movement'; Nelson, 'Labour Insurgency in Norway.'

3 See, for example, Edgar McInnis, *Canada: A Political and Social History* (Toronto: Holt, Rinehart and Winston 1969), 514; Brown and Cook, *Canada, 1896–1921: A Nation Transformed*, 310–14; Desmond Morton, *A Short History of Canada* (Edmonton: Hurtig 1983), 158–60; Robert Bothwell, Ian Drummond,

and John English, *Canada, 1900–1945* (Toronto: University of Toronto Press 1987), 167; R. Douglas Francis, Richard Jones, and Donald B. Smith, *Destinies: Canadian History since Confederation* (Toronto: Harcourt Brace 1988), 196–8; Alvin Finkel, Margaret Conrad, with Veronica Strong-Boag, *History of the Canadian Peoples*, vol. 2, *1867 to the Present* (Toronto: Copp Clark Pitman 1993), 303–6.

4 The most recent (and poetic) treatment of the Winnipeg General Strike is Sweatman, *Fox*. Earlier novels that touch on the event include Connor, *To Him That Hath*; Durkin, *Magpie*; and Wiseman, *Crackpot*.

5 Bercuson, *Confrontation at Winnipeg*; Bright, '"We Are All Kin"'; Conley, 'Frontier Labourers' and 'Class Conflict and Collective Action'; Ewen, 'La Contestation à Montréal en 1919'; Hak, 'British Columbia Loggers'; Heron, 'Working-Class Hamilton', 'Great War and Nova Scotia Steelworkers,' and *Working in Steel*; Heron and De Zwaan, 'Industrial Unionism in Eastern Ontario'; Hogan, *Cobalt*; Gregory Kealey, '1919'; Makahonuk, 'Class Conflict in a Prairie City'; Mitchell, 'Brandon 1919'; Morton, 'Labourism and Economic Action'; Naylor, 'Toronto 1919' and *New Democracy*; Reilly, 'General Strike in Amherst'; Seager, 'Socialists and Workers' and 'Workers, Class, and Industrial Conflict'; Siemiatycki, 'Munitions and Labour Militancy' and 'Labour Contained.'

6 Borden, *Memoirs*, vol. 2, 972.

7 Masters, *Winnipeg General Strike*; Rea, *Winnipeg General Strike*; Bercuson, *Confrontation at Winnipeg*. For an extended discussion of the historiography on the Winnipeg General Strike down to the early 1970s, see McNaught and Bercuson, *Winnipeg General Strike*, 99–124.

8 Penner, ed., *Winnipeg 1919*.

9 Gregory Kealey, '1919,' 12. Bercuson's vehement rejoinder appeared in the form of an afterword to the 1990 edition of *Confrontation at Winnipeg*.

10 Frank, 'Class Conflict' and 'Contested Terrain'; Heron, *Working in Steel*; McKay, *Craft Transformed*, 68–74; Naylor, *New Democracy*.

11 These new historiographical perspectives paralleled new currents in the writing of working-class history in other countries. See, for example, Geary, *European Labour Protest*; Sirianni, *Workers' Control and Socialist Democracy*; Smith, *Red Petrograd*; Cronin, 'Labor Insurgency and Class Formation'; Montgomery, *Fall of the House of Labor*.

12 Bercuson, *Fools and Wise Men*; Morton with Copp, *Working People*. Bercuson has recently revised his assessment of the radicals' role; he now argues, in 'Syndicalism Sidetracked,' that they were not syndicalists at all. From a radically different perspective, Myer Siemiatycki agrees that the socialists had a limited bag of tactical tricks to offer workers; see 'Labour Contained.'

13 Friesen, '"Yours in Revolt"'; Frank, 'Class Conflict'; Heron, 'Great War and Nova Scotia Steelworkers'; Gregory Kealey, '1919'; Naylor, 'Toronto 1919'; Reilly, 'General Strike in Amherst.'
14 Bercuson, 'Labour Radicalism and the Western Industrial Frontier'; McCormack, 'Western Working-Class Experience'; Pentland, 'Western Canadian Labour Movement.'
15 Morton with Copp, *Working People*, 113–24.
16 Palmer, *Working-Class Experience*, 209–10.
17 Conley, 'Frontier Labourers'; Ewen, 'La Contestation à Montréal'; Frank, 'Class Conflict'; Heron, 'Great War and Nova Scotia Steelworkers' and *Working in Steel*; Heron and De Zwaan, 'Industrial Unionism in Eastern Ontario'; McKay, *Craft Transformed*; Naylor, 'Toronto 1919'; Reilly, 'General Strike in Amherst'; Seager, 'Workers, Class, and Industrial Conflict.'
18 Conley, 'Frontier Labourers'; Frank, 'Class Conflict'; Heron, *Working in Steel*; McKay, *Craft Transformed*.
19 Avery, *Dangerous Foreigners*; and 'Ethnic and Class Tensions'; Creese, 'Class, Ethnicity, and Conflict'; Heron, *Working in Steel*; Gregory Kealey, 'The State, the Foreign Language Press, and the Canadian Labour Revolt'; Knight and Koizumi, *Man of Our Times*; Radforth, 'Finnish Lumber Workers'; Seager, 'Finnish Canadians and the Ontario Miners' Movement' and 'Class, Ethnicity, and Politics.'
20 Bernard, 'Last Back'; Campbell, 'Sexism in British Columbia Trade Unions'; Creese, 'Politics of Dependence'; Frager, 'Class and Ethnic Barriers' and 'No Proper Deal'; Horodyski, 'Women and the Winnipeg General Strike'; Howard, *Struggle for Social Justice*; Linda Kealey, '"No Special Protection"'; Roome, 'Amelia Turner.'
21 The former group includes Buck, *Thirty Years* and *Yours in the Struggle*; and Communist Party of Canada, *Canada's Party of Socialism*. The latter group includes Avakumovic, *Communist Party in Canada*; and Rodney, *Soldiers of the International*. A somewhat more balanced view is available in Angus, *Canadian Bolsheviks*.
22 Avakumovic, *Socialism in Canada*; Caplan, *Dilemma of Canadian Socialism*; McNaught, *Prophet in Politics*; Mardiros, *William Irvine*; Steeves, *Compassionate Rebel*; Young, *Anatomy of a Party*.
23 For a more sensitive discussion of the evolution of socialist and communist strategy, see Peterson, 'Revolutionary Socialism and Industrial Unrest.'
24 See, for example, Naylor, *New Democracy*; Siemiatycki, 'Labour Contained'; and Heron, *Working in Steel*.
25 See McDonald, *'To Each His Own'*; McInnis, 'All Solid along the Line'; Hogan, *Cobalt*; Radforth, *Bushworkers and Bosses*; and Heron, *Working in Steel*.

The Great War, the State, and Working-Class Canada

CRAIG HERON and MYER SIEMIATYCKI

Wars in the modern world are never merely military campaigns. They are rare moments that allow national states to mobilize the resources and collective will of their citizenry to a degree seldom, if ever, attempted during peacetime. The self-interest that drives the capitalist economy and the social relations within in it are challenged by new ideologies of self-sacrifice and national service. At the same time, long-standing social antagonisms can be inflamed by the unusual economic, social, and political conditions of wartime society. In some countries revolutions have erupted. In Canada the First World War eventually disrupted the dynamics of pre-war working-class life and provided new pressures and opportunities that would fuel large-scale working-class organization, resistance, and radicalization across the country. It turned out to be quite a 'Great War' of class forces on the home front.[1]

The Great War in Canada

The European war that erupted in the late summer of 1914 never extended to Canadian soil, but Canadians nonetheless found it a profoundly disruptive event. Although it galvanized the country into a single national purpose and revitalized a sagging economy, it also transformed the role of the state and unleashed a new flood of protest from many sectors of Canadian society.

For Canadian industrialists, their employees, and thousands of primary producers, war would eventually become an economic godsend. Initially, however, it deepened the depression that had hung over the country since 1913 by restricting access to foreign capital and by disrupting some vital trade and commerce. Economic recovery was slow and uneven across the country. British officials delayed placing orders for military supplies in Canada because of worries about the ability of the Dominion's manufacturers to produce to the exacting specifications required. The cost and complications of retooling for uncertain war production gave many industrialists pause before they took war contracts. Not until mid-1915 did the increasing orders for food, lumber, munitions (mostly shells), uniforms, and other supplies for British and French troops bring fuller employment for factory workers in central Canadian cities, where the bulk of these contracts were filled. Eventually Canada supplied a huge proportion of the ammunition that the Allies fired at the enemy.

Other sectors of the economy got a similar boost. Miners began to feel the heavier demand for their labour power by early 1916. On the east and west coasts and on the Great Lakes, new shipbuilding operations drew together large new workforces. Prairie farmers quickly expanded their acreage in response to the voracious European demand for Canadian wheat. Certainly by the end of 1916, although construction and a few other sectors were still stagnant, unemployment had dried up virtually everywhere in the country. As more people found jobs, consumer spending at home also took off. The wartime boom nonetheless reinforced longer-term patterns of uneven development in the Canadian capitalist economy. The Maritime provinces shared least in the prosperity, while Ontario and Quebec probably enjoyed the most benefits. Manufacturing and agriculture got a far greater boost than most resource industries. On the whole, though, the massive death and destruction under way in Europe allowed the Canadian economy to surge to unprecedented heights of production and profit.[2]

First and foremost, of course, the war was a military event. Before the war, the dominant strain of English-Canadian nationalism had been 'imperialism' – a passionate identification with the Empire – and the previous half-decade had seen a flurry of military preparedness (militia reforms, cadet training, and the like) under the frenetic Minister of Militia, Colonel Sam Hughes. As the loyal administration of a colonial state within the British Empire, Robert Borden's Conservative government responded to Britain's declaration of war by organizing a contingent within the British armed forces known as the Canadian Expeditionary Force. What began as a jaunty little adventure that was expected to end by Christmas became more than four agonizing years of carnage and destruction. More than six hundred thousand Canadians would eventually don the khaki uniform of the Canadian Armed Forces during World

War I, while fifty thousand more served in other allied armies. In all, roughly a third of the male population at military age enlisted. Nearly one in ten did not return from the battlefields. Thousands more limped back with physical and psychological wounds.[3]

Initially, the federal government tried to carry out its responsibilities for the war effort overseas and at home with as much voluntary and philanthropic organization as possible. Private individuals and organizations took on responsibilities for recruitment (and, to some extent, equipping) of individual battalions, pro-war propaganda, munitions production, resource coordination, and assistance for soldiers' families and returned veterans.[4] Newspaper editors, Protestant clergymen, and school teachers whipped up jingoistic fervour. Local voluntary recruiting leagues organized parades and nabbed men for the army. Branches of the Canadian Patriotic Fund solicited donations to support soldiers' families. Women's organizations knitted socks for the men in the trenches. Schoolchildren collected scrap metal. Women volunteered to replace men in traditionally male jobs. At every turn in their daily lives, Canadians were exhorted to buy war bonds.[5] The passions aroused occasionally boiled over into violent attacks on German-Canadians and other 'aliens,'[6] but, on the whole, this was an orderly national moral crusade. Pacifists and others opposed to the war, especially radical labour leaders, were overwhelmed and isolated. The pre-war resolutions of the Trades and Labor Congress calling for a general strike in the event of war were quietly shelved. Even such traditionally cautious French-Canadian leaders as Sir Wilfrid Laurier and Henri Bourassa pledged their support for the cause. Few noticed the quiet indifference to all this hoopla in the Maritimes, Quebec, and much of the rural countryside generally.[7]

Wartime propaganda initially emphasized Canadian obligations to the British Empire, but calls for private sacrifice and public service increasingly highlighted a fight against 'Prussianism' or 'Kaiserism,' and the 'great war for democracy.' Paradoxically, by the end of 1916 such rhetoric stood in increasingly sharp contrast to life on the home front. Voluntarism was giving way to state compulsion and authoritarian restriction of civil liberties. The sweeping War Measures Act had made such moves possible since 1914, and some measures dated that far back. A press censor monitored and hectored the country's newspaper editors to avoid revealing such evidence of social discontent as strikes. (A press blackout became one of the more effective devices for undermining the first major wartime munitions strike.) Within the country's eastern-European immigrant communities, many men were loosely and often inaccurately branded 'enemy aliens' and interned or ordered to register each week with local police departments. Despite their lack of love for the Austro-Hungarian Empire, Ukrainians probably felt the fullest weight of these measures. The Dominion Police and Royal North-West Mounted Police also recruited spies to report on labour activities that looked threatening to the war effort. In 1916 strikes in war-related industries were brought under the regulatory mechanisms of the Industrial Disputes Investigation Act (IDIA), the pre-war federal labour legislation that required workers and their bosses in resource, transportation, and utilities industries to submit their demands to compulsory conciliation before initiating strikes or lockouts.[8]

In the first two years of the war, the state moved cautiously in expanding its traditionally limited role. In 1917, however, it became sharply more interventionist. The Director of Public Information took over coordination of propaganda activities. Most shocking for French Canadians, farmers facing labour shortages, and socialist labour leaders – all of whom were decidedly cool to this imperialist war – was the government announcement in 1916 that registration of all manpower would be necessary to deal with labour shortages at home and in the trenches. The National Service Board was put to work registering and classifying the country's workforce. Amid the steady pressure of rising casualty rates and imperial demands for more soldiers in the trenches, full-scale military conscription followed the next year. The state even invaded Canadians' leisure time. Beer drinkers found their supply cut off by provincial prohibition legislation in 1916 and 1917 and eventually by federal action in March 1918 – all in the name of a more efficient war effort. Everyone had to adjust their clocks in an unpopular new scheme, known as 'Daylight Saving,' aimed at more efficient use of light. Early in 1918 the federal government even went so far as to pass the 'Anti-Loafing Act,' which required adult males to make themselves available for wage-earning work or face criminal prosecution. A series of orders-in-council in September and October 1918 brought the heaviest repressive legislation, which outlawed several radical labour organizations (and their newspapers) and banned strikes. By this point the cabinet had become accustomed to ruling by order-in-council.[9]

The state had also entered into unprecedented economic regulation, though never on the scale that it would in World War II. As much as possible it recruited help from the private sector, rather than expanding the civil service. The Imperial Munitions Board, established late in 1915 to replace the much-maligned Shell Committee in administering war contracts, was like its predecessor a committee of industrialists and experts. The board set new standards for coordination of production across the country's metalworking plants, with centrally controlled inspection and factory-administration guidelines in some six hundred firms by 1917. The board also set up its own production facilities, known as National Factories, to manufacture shells, explosives, aircraft, and ships. In 1917 the federal government moved much more decisively into the economy: it established a Board of Grain Supervisors, a Coal Controller, a Canadian Wool Commission, and a Natural Resources Commission, and made its first moves to take over the floundering railways that would become the Canadian National Railways in 1919.

Meanwhile, public outrage over wartime 'profiteering' had not been placated by orders-in-council denouncing hoarding and price gouging or by the introduction of direct taxation in the form of a business war-profit tax in 1916 and a 'temporary' income tax the next year. The government therefore appointed a Cost-of-Living Commissioner in 1917 to investigate and report on price inflation (though not to prosecute). The food controller also undertook to investigate food prices; in 1918 his work was transferred to a Food Board with powers to fix prices and control supplies. Concerns about labour shortages brought campaigns to recruit more farm labour and eventually the creation of a nationally coordinated Employment Service of Canada. A new federal ministry was charged with the reintegration of returned soldiers into Canadian life. The War Trade Board created in February 1918 had sweeping powers to effect centralized co-ordination of the private-enterprise economy.[10]

As Canadian capitalists took on administrative roles in many of these new bodies, traditional liberal conceptions about the separation of capital and the state were eclipsed by a growing fascination with some kind of corporatist state (denounced on the left in Britain as the 'servile state'). State institutions would more directly sustain the capitalist economy, and the principles of efficiency and managerial expertise – the hallmarks of what is often called pre-war 'progressivism' – would prevail over narrow party spirit. The recently established National Research Council seemed a promising example of this new notion of capitalist collaboration within the state. The Board of Commerce, appointed in 1919 to deal with soaring price inflation, was another.[11]

It was the Conservative Party that presided over this more activist state apparatus at the national level and in five provinces at the beginning of the war (Nova Scotia, Quebec, Saskatchewan, and Alberta were the exceptions). The war did not eliminate the easy morals that had so often characterized Tory administrations. Sam Hughes and the 'minister of elections,' Robert Rogers, made sure that Tory supporters were well rewarded with jobs, commissions, and contracts, turning the war into what historian John English has called 'a massive Conservative rally.' By the end of 1915 newspapers were regularly publishing stories about the misuse of patronage and the serious flaws in military training and equipment. Abandoning the party truce, the Liberal opposition repeatedly attacked the government's apparent favouritism, corruption, and general mismanagement, especially in the distribution of war contracts through the hastily improvised Shell Committee, which was dissolved in November 1915. From press, pulpit, and Canadian Club auditoriums, the public outcry against narrow party allegiances grew louder.

The Conservatives eventually responded by creating the coalition Union government in October 1917. In the emotion-charged re-election campaign that followed, the Unionists rallied the country to the war effort, the Empire, and the Anglo-Saxon 'race,' and denounced their opponents with unprecedented rhetorical venom. The cynical, flagrantly corrupt procedures of that election – which included giving the vote to all soldiers and (for the first time) all their female relatives and taking it away from all those who had arrived from enemy countries since 1902, regardless of naturalization – were probably the most blatant example of the Tory willingness to give democracy short shrift. In December the Unionist forces won a smashing victory (outside Quebec) that consolidated the Tory hegemony and marginalized official Liberalism within national politics until after the war was over.[12]

Many other traditional threads of Canadian Toryism – elitism, imperialist jingoism, and bigotry, in particular – found their fullest expression in this context of single-minded national commitment. Official intolerance of ethnic minorities flourished. Anti-French sentiment once again broke through into Ontario politics, as the English-Canadian majority in the federal Parliament endorsed the provincial government's move to curb francophone schooling in 1916. Manitoba followed Ontario's example the same year. In the 1917 federal election French Canadians faced vicious attacks from Unionist candidates for their resistance to military conscription.[13] The government's campaign also fanned the growing resentment against European immigrants. Not surprisingly, 97 per cent of the 152 Unionists elected were white

Anglo-Canadian Protestant males from prosperous business or professional backgrounds.[14]

By 1917 workers were not alone in raising questions about the longer-term implications of wartime developments. The combination of war-induced moral fervour, strong inducements to subordinate private to public concerns, and popular outrage at the unsavoury practices of business and the state tore loose many groups of Canadians from their traditional social and ideological moorings and opened wide-ranging, intense debate about 'reconstruction' in post-war society. Numerous social movements presented their own agendas and competing visions, most of them projecting little confidence in the existing political and economic institutions. The moral energies of the Protestant churches' 'social gospel,' which had spilled over into patriotic passion for the war effort, were now focused as never before on the social and moral purification of Canadian society. Prohibition was the moral reformers' great wartime triumph, but they looked for more. In 1918 the Methodist Church of Canada went so far as to announce its commitment to production based on 'co-operation and service' rather than 'competition and profits.'[15] Many of the women involved in these campaigns were delighted that politicians were finally won over to the justice of giving them the right to vote in most provinces and at the federal level in 1918.[16] Intellectuals from many backgrounds looked for new solutions to the moral crisis; indeed, seldom had Canada seen such an outpouring of books prescribing remedies for all that ailed industrial capitalist society in Canada.[17] The farmers gave a far angrier edge to this ferment. Throughout rural Canada they were organizing against the erosion of their incomes and way of life, once again placing Canadian tariff policies at the centre of their demonology.[18] Veterans soon joined the chorus of angry voices. Returning from the trenches with their various scars and resentments, they became another volatile new force in Canadian society and politics – a force that found expression in spontaneous crowd action in the streets and, more persistently, through new organizations such as the Great War Veterans' Association.[19] All of this political turmoil spilled over into the months after the Armistice, when the restraints set by cries of support for the military effort had lifted. For many Canadians, much was at stake in 1919–20.

The third year of the war, then, proved a turning point, with the shift from voluntarism to more authoritarian state intervention, the growing popular uneasiness about private enterprise, the divisive political crisis over conscription, the take-off of retail price inflation, the increasing demoralization and disaffection of a war-weary population. It was in this broad context that the workers' revolt began to take shape in Canada.

Fuelling a Revolt

In the first two years of the war, working-class Canada showed considerable support for the war effort – sending sons to war, buying war bonds, holding back 'selfish' demands. But by 1917 workers' cynicism about the Great War was growing. A spirit of revolt was in the air, primarily as a result of the war's impact on working-class life.

The war economy had certainly shifted the balance of class forces in Canadian labour markets. At the outbreak of hostilities in 1914, Canadian workers had already suffered through more than a year of prolonged lay-offs, short time, and wage cuts in the deepest economic slump yet seen in the twentieth century. 'There have been other periods of depression in times gone by,' the executive of the British Columbia Federation of Labor noted that summer, 'but there has never been one so extensive and so entirely devoid of promise of improvement for years to come, as the present one.' Similarly gloomy comments were heard across the country. Many city councils had to face large demonstrations of jobless workers demanding 'work or bread.' It is not surprising, then, that the first military recruits were often the unemployed, particularly recent British immigrants. Indeed, during the early stages of the war few sections of Canadian society provided more soldiers than the labour movement. By the end of 1915 incomplete returns from unions in Canada showed that some thirteen thousand union members – one in twelve – had already enlisted. In many cases there was clearly more than patriotism motivating the decision to go to war. The sting of widespread unemployment and hunger 'conscripted' many. Since enlistment entitled the families of the recuits to support from the Canadian Patriotic Fund, and held the possibility of improving their eligibility for relief payments, many unemployed workers regarded overseas service as a means of providing for loved ones. As James McVety, president of the Vancouver Trades and Labor Council, reported in November 1914, 'Many of the families of the men who enlisted were so hard up that relief had to be given almost before the names were hardly dry on the enlistment roll.'[20]

Unemployment soon disappeared, however, as a result of both military recruitment and opportunities in the quickening industrial economy, especially munitions. The closing of immigration prevented the replenishment of pools of labour in the traditional way, and employers taxed their ingenuity to find workers and hold on to them. By the end of 1916 the Imperial Munitions Board was pushing employers to hire women workers for the shell plants. Perhaps thirty-five thousand ultimately worked in munitions. During the next year male labour shortages also brought women into such traditionally male jobs as bank teller and streetcar conductor. Far more of these female wage earners were married than ever before, though single women still predominated.[21] Youngsters were similarly pulled out of school and retired workers from old-age homes in the search for more wage earners.[22] 'Enemy aliens' were also shipped from internment camps to industrial centres where their labour was needed. European immigrants in general found their way into much better jobs than had been available to them in the ethnically stratified pre-war labour markets, which had typically left them on the lowest rungs of the occupational ladder.[23]

Free from the haunting fear of unemployment and bottomless poverty, Canadian workers showed a new confidence by 1916 that was in sharp contrast to their desperation in the pre-war slump. At home, working-class families in Canada began to feel the relief from economic insecurity that the bigger wage packets brought into their households. Families that had been doubled up in rented accommodation could now afford to rent their own places. They ate more meat. Player pianos and victrolas appeared in more working-class parlours. Some savings went into war bonds.[24] This was a familiar pattern from pre-war years – families taking advantage of economic upturns to clear away debts and take a few steps towards improving their living standards before another depression forced them back into a much more pinched existence.[25] On the job, wage earners also revived time-worn means of using the tighter labour market to their advantage. They could risk a cockier manner and thumb their noses at their foremen's efforts to get them to work harder. They could take an afternoon off work to enjoy a ball game or a movie, or even a move to another job, where the boss was probably willing to pay still higher wages to get help. They could even discuss unions more openly. 'Employment is so easily obtained that workmen change from one occupation to another for no apparent reason,' Nova Scotia's factory inspector reported in 1917, 'and employers complain that it is impossible to enforce discipline in their factories.' The same year, a Cominco official wrote from the other end of the country, 'Workers have been absolutely independent, knowing that if they were fired from one job they could get another immediately.' Toronto's John Inglis Company complained that it was '[a]lmost impossible to co-operate with present class of help as they appear to be getting too much money and don't want to work,' while Hamilton's National Steel Car plant bemoaned the difficulty 'to get our men to average 9 hours a day. It is not a question of too little money with them, but the trouble is they have too much. The surplus amount allows them to to take a great deal more time off than they ordinarily would.' Another manufacturer later complained, 'Taking a day off was a frequent occurence for many men who were receiving double, possibly treble, what they had ever done before.' By the end of the war, according to a government study, 'Turnover was universally high, many employers stating that 30 per cent of their staff was floating. Absence was also abnormal, amounting to 5 per cent per day and often running as high as 10 per cent.'[26]

These would hardly seem to be the conditions to promote a revolt. In fact, during 1915–16 most wage earners seemed more interested in making hay while the sun shone. Although union membership increased gradually and workers staged some significant confrontations (notably the 1916 strikes in the Thetford asbestos mines, Montreal shipyards, Hamilton munitions plants, Cobalt silver mines, and Alberta coalfields),[27] two features of working-class activity in the period predominated: the mobilization of as many able-bodied members of the household as possible to bring in wages; and the remarkable labour turnover, as workers jumped from job to job in search of better wages and less oppressive working conditions.

Yet the wartime boom was unsettling for workers at home and on the job. First, the newfound prosperity was soon threatened in many working-class households by the retail price inflation that began a dizzying four-year ascent in 1917. Canadian workers had already faced sharp price increases before the war, especially in the 1912–13 period, but no one could remember prices rising as fast or as high as they did in this new inflationary burst. An average weekly food basket for a family of five that had cost $10.11 at Christmas 1916 was fetching $12.25 the next Christmas (a jump of 20 per cent), and the addition of fuel, lighting, and rent brought the total increase to 31 per cent. By December 1918 the cost of this family budget had leaped by 46 per cent over the 1916 level and, at the peak of the inflationary spiral in July 1920, by 82 per cent. At that point the food basket cost a whopping 128 per cent more than it had on the eve of the war in 1914. (The European belligerents had much higher inflation rates, though Britain's was only moderately higher at 158 per cent; the United States was slightly lower at 115 per cent, and

Australia and New Zealand fell well behind at 94 and 67 per cent respectively.)[28] Almost every day, Canadian newspapers splashed stories across their front pages about the high cost of living, or 'H.C.L.' At a conference of international unionists held in 1917, delegates worried that Canadian workers were confronting a 'serious depression of their standard of living occasioned by the increase in the price of necessities of life.'[29] The problem was that wages were not keeping pace. All recent attempts to determine working-class income in Canada in this period have pointed to serious erosion of real wages after 1917 (although all these studies are marred by the use of the only available data, namely, the hourly wage rates of relatively skilled men, rather than their actual take-home pay or the earnings of the less skilled).[30]

Here was a family-based issue that irked the working-class housewife as much as her wage-earning husband.[31] Searching angrily for explanations for this injustice, workers invariably suspected that shady, unscrupulous profiteers were at work – in the words of the Regina trades council, 'feasting on the nation's suffering' and 'fattening on our soldiers' blood.'[32] Such highly publicized scandals as the revelations about the super-profits of pork-packer Sir Joseph Flavelle generated a deepening hostility towards the leading figures of Canada's business establishment. 'Having been engaged in recording Canadian political events for the past quarter century,' one veteran Conservative politician cautioned Prime Minister Borden in the wake of the Flavelle controversy, 'I can truly say that I never before met with such wide spread [*sic*] *rage* over any other scandal.'[33] In households and workplaces across Canada, deference to captains of finance and industry came unhinged as news of alleged corporate profiteering spread. As the federal government's numerous initiatives failed to curb the continuing price inflation through 1920, resentment at unknown profiteers who threatened rising working-class income raged across working-class dinner tables throughout the country. 'The authorities have had enquiry after enquiry made but they only show more clearly the gravity of the evil,' a Montreal commissioner reported in 1919. 'The masses understand nothing, they are driven mad for no remedy comes from anywhere.'[34] This 'madness' had prompted the Trades and Labor Congress, in 1917, to call for an end to 'gambling in foodstuffs by speculators' and to propose controls on (even the nationalization of) food-processing plants, coal mines, and railways.[35] From all parts of the country came demands for the 'conscription of wealth' as well as, or in preference to, the conscription of people (the new income tax was the government's reluctant and extremely limited response).[36] Workers also confronted the rising cost of living with a measure of self-help. Cooperative stores blossomed across the country – at least nineteen in British Columbia, more than one hundred on the Prairies, twenty in Ontario, and thirteen in the Maritimes – many of them in working-class communities.[37]

Workers became even more fearful about their household finances after the Armistice, when many lost their jobs in munitions work and unemployment rose steeply across the economy in the early months of 1919. In March unions reported levels of joblessness among their members that had not been seen since the end of 1915. Somewhat fuller employment returned during the next year and a half, broken by some slackness in the winter of 1919–20. Uncertainty hung over most industries, however, until the great crash in the winter of 1920–21, when enterprises closed or curtailed production drastically and thousands of wage earners were thrown out of work.[38] These could be the conditions that would allow employers to get the upper hand again, as they always had in previous economic downturns. So, through the lurching uncertainties and instability of the post-war era, wage earners and their families looked anxiously into the future and grasped at ways to build more collective economic security into their lives.

The wartime boom also had a disruptive effect on the capitalist workplace. In most industries employers accelerated production in order to meet the pressing demands for goods. Particularly in manufacturing, the high-volume production and the general labour shortage encouraged employers to cut costs and reorganize work to a degree unimaginable in the more limited pre-war markets. Workers in the busy clothing industry felt these pressures.[39] In munitions thousands of untrained workers were recruited to run narrowly specialized machines on piecework – a process soon known as 'dilution' of the crafts. The trend towards mass production that had begun at the turn of the century – the Second Industrial Revolution – was accelerating.[40] Craftsmen, especially in the metalworking plants, recognized that the prolonged attack on their crafts had intensified.[41] They resented losing more of the control they had long exercised over the labour process. Their craft pride was also offended by the erosion of the status hierarchy in their workplaces. The skilled workers who had so far survived the Second Industrial Revolution, such as the machinists, and those who had emerged within new work processes, such as the steelworkers, were disgruntled to see untrained, transient men (and sometimes women) taking home previously unimaginable wages earned on high-volume piecework, while their more skilled, longer-service workmates who set up and maintained the machinery enjoyed far smaller increases. The gap between skilled and unskilled was narrowing to the apparent detriment of the craft worker. 'It is true that young girls, with no experience ... [got] higher wages for doing soft snaps than skilled mechanics whose labor was indispensible to the proper carrying on of the work received,' one workman blustered in 1917.[42] 'The majority of the men on the plant did not share in these high wages, because they were kept in their old positions of skill and responsibility in order that the whole plant might continue to operate successfully,' Nova Scotia steelworkers complained three years later.[43]

The concern about disruptions in established workplace hierarchies extended to more workers as Europeans and Asians gained access to labour markets previously closed to them. To meet the chronic shortage of labour, many employers intensified the recruitment of non-Anglo-Canadian labour that they had begun before the war.[44] Now they drew in more European peasant-labourers from the resource industries of the north and west into the heavy secondary manufacturing of central and eastern Canada. The federal government even obliged by shipping interned enemy aliens, mostly non-Austrian citizens of the Austro-Hungarian Empire, to some large corporations short of less skilled labour, including railways, coal mines, and steel mills. In 1917 the *Canadian Annual Review* noted that 'the labour shortage everywhere [has] resulted in the employ of Austrian and German aliens in works of all kinds – the Imperial Munitions Board, the Lindsay Arsenal and many munitions and other industrial plants.'[45] Many Anglo-Canadian wage earners were outraged. The press heaped fuel on the fires of resentment with regular reports of high wages among these workers. White, English-speaking commentators also resuscitated pre-war fears of cultural degeneration they believed they saw in the immigrants' crowded-boardinghouse lifestyle, ignoring the reality that many of these men were simply biding their time until the re-opening of immigration allowed them to return to Europe or Asia.

By the end of 1917 returning soldiers had become the loudest and most belligerent critics of the employment of 'interlopers' and 'enemy aliens,' terms applied loosely to Europeans of many different backgrounds. Over the next two years the veterans often took to the streets to attack the men they alleged were stealing their jobs and to demand that the government intern or deport them. Early in 1919 there were violent assaults on eastern European immigrants in Calgary, Drumheller, Winnipeg, Port Arthur, Sudbury, and Halifax. Employers also felt the wrath of their workers, who demanded that the 'enemy aliens' be fired. Many companies complied to varying degrees. By 1919 this nativistic backlash was simmering in every part of the country where southern and eastern Europeans or Asians were working in large numbers.[46]

The huge strike wave that swept over all parts of the country after 1916 was also fed by the unflinching refusal of employers to deal with their workers collectively. In strike after strike, workers ended up on the picket lines because their bosses would not discuss the demands presented to them by workers' representatives. Capitalists dug in their heels to prevent wartime conditions from introducing any permanent changes in power relations in their enterprises. Workers who saw their employers profiting handsomely from big war contracts found their intransigence unfair and unacceptable: this was the issue that would ignite some of the biggest strikes in 1919, including the Winnipeg General Strike.

Part of what made these issues of shop-floor politics so unusually intense and widespread was the way in which the state was implicated, particularly the Borden government. Here was an administration that seemed to have lost its right to rule. For the thousands of families whose menfolk were dying in the trenches, grief mingled with bitterness at the apparent ineptitude and corruption in the prosecution of the war. Those working on the home front were no less outraged. The government had imposed rigid, authoritarian controls, from prohibition to national registration to restraints on strikes. It seemed to be protecting profiteers (the best known, Flavelle, was head of the Imperial Munitions Board). It offered no sympathy to workers who locked horns with their employers (indeed, in restraining strikes by means of the Industrial Disputes Investigation Act, it seemed to be tying the hands of unionists). And it refused to involve labour representatives in its wartime deliberations, in contrast to well-publicized initiatives in Britain and the United States.[47]

The creation of the Union government late in 1917 temporarily shored up the state's crumbling legitimacy, but the apparent insensitivity to working-class concerns continued into the post-war period. Many workers in Quebec and in the West were horrified by the heavy-handed use of the Military Service Act to impose conscription. Huge demonstrations and bloody riots broke out in the streets of Quebec.[48] In British Columbia draft dodgers were harassed and chased through the woods. Thousands of Vancouver unionists stopped work on 2 August 1918 to protest the fatal shooting of the fugitive draft dodger and radical unionist Albert 'Ginger' Goodwin.[49] The orders-in-council introduced in September and October 1918 to repress radical organizations and ban strikes were the final straw. Protest meetings against such attacks on civil liberties helped to radicalize the labour movement still further in cities as politically diverse as Toronto, Winnipeg, and Vancouver.[50]

The problem for this government was that the war had created new expectations of public morality among the mass of the population. Since 1914 workers had been urged to remember the men in the trenches and the cause they were allegedly fighting for and to hold their personal desires in check for the great crusade against 'Kaiserism.' From pulpits and street corners, on billboards and slips in their pay packets, workers had been asked to follow the banner of public service and self-sacrifice, ideals not often proclaimed in a capitalist society organized fundamentally on the basis of self-interest. By 1917 it appeared that many capitalists, especially their employers, were not showing the right spirit of self-denial. Nor were politicians and state officials themselves. In 1917 the constraining power of patriotic pro-war rhetoric began to fade and a deepening cynicism about the war effort spread. The last time patriotism was used to effect was in the 1917 federal election, but the elitism of the Union government and the flagrant electoral abuses left a foul odour.

A few months later the Imperial Munitions Board's director of labour reported a 30 per cent drop in productivity in war plants; 'all the enthusiasm and all the idea that munitions are vitally essential had gone out of the minds of the workpeople,' he noted, 'and ... today they take the War, and the work related to it, as they take the sunrise – an incident of the day.'[51] That summer the government's own security adviser, Montreal lawyer C.H. Cahan, reported that workers' discontent stemmed from 'the weakening of the moral purpose of the people to prosecute the war to a successful end,' a deepening awareness of 'the bloody sacrifices and irritating burdens entailed by carrying on the war,' and 'the growing belief that the Union government is failing to deal effectively with the financial, industrial, and economic problems growing out of the war.'[52] The country had been saturated with the rhetoric of service and the noble goal of fighting to defend 'democracy,' and workers now bitterly threw these words back at those in power. In 1918 Sydney's labour paper stated, '[T]he people of Cape Breton have suffered too dearly on the fields of Flanders and at home to be ruled by an autocracy [in the local steel plant].'[53] Western labour leaders similarly viewed the government's draconian labour legislation in the fall of 1918 as 'Prussianism at home.'[54] Democracy had become the new touchstone of industrial relations and politics.

Workers and their leaders could take heart that other Canadians – farmers, clergymen, intellectuals, veterans, women, and more organized groups – had similar concerns. Labour activists were also increasingly aware that they were part of an international working-class ferment. In scattered parts of the globe workers were challenging established political and economic power with bold new programs, and they were winning. Almost every day, there appeared in the press stories of massive strikes in Britain, Europe, and the United States. Canadian labour papers reported favourably on the British shop stewards' movement and 'Triple Alliance' (of coal miners, railwaymen, and transport workers), as well as on the new industrial unionism in Australia, especially the One Big Union. Labour Party breakthroughs in Australia also attracted much attention, as did the decision of England's revitalized Labour Party early in 1918 to transform its program from a weak labourist project into an overtly socialist vision.[55] These international working-class challenges were further legitimized when delegates at the post-war peace conference in Paris felt compelled to issue a set of principles governing industrial relations that guaranteed workplace standards and rights to organize.[56]

The pockets of socialist activists across Canada received even more inspiration from Russia's fragile new experiment in workers' power. Some of the European immigrant communities, especially the Ukrainians, Russians, Jews, and Finns, were particularly excited about the new radicalism in Eastern Europe. The Edmonton socialists even named their new newspaper *The Soviet* early in 1919. For socialists in Canada, Russia was a shining example rather than an ideological reservoir, since Bolshevik theoretical work had scarcely touched North America at this stage. The left in Canada soon found surprisingly large audiences for its efforts to educate Canadian workers on the emerging soviet system. Montreal's Tom Cassidy spoke for many long-time socialist activists in crowing that, since the Bolshevik revolution, Canadian workers were far more interested in socialism than in 'the days when we stood out on the bald prairies howling and lonesome like a native coyote.'[57] What many Canadian workers drew from the Bolshevik experience was a boundless belief that what could be yearned and struggled for could also be achieved. For one Winnipeg labourer, the Russian example promised a resolution of all working-class problems: 'equal rights for men and women, no child labor, no poverty, misery and degradation, no prostitution, no mortgages on farms, no revolting bills for machinery to keep peasants poor till the grave, no sweatshops, no long hours of heavy toil for a meagre existence but an equal opportunity for all, a life made worth living with unlimited possibilities to all, aided by splendid machinery to make [the] earth a real paradise where nothing but happiness can prevail ... this is Bolshevism.'[58] The Canadian government's decision to send troops to join the military invasion of the Soviet Union in 1919 brought cries of protest from the left of the Canadian workers' movements. Labour newspapers and socialist rallies regularly drew connections between all these dramatic international developments and the aspirations of Canadian workers.

The workers' revolt in Canada at the end of World War I, then, was not the desperate cry of a downtrodden and poverty-stricken proletariat. Rather it grew out of a newfound confidence in working-class power, a profound sense of injustice, and a determination that society could run differently. It was fuelled by a volatile mixture of those factors that had prompted working-class resistance in Canada for more than half a century and some special wartime conditions. Labour struggles over living standards in working-class households and wage earners' rights on the job were hardly new. But the prosecution of the war and the (mis)management of the wartime economy, which gave the national state such prominence, had unified many previously fragmented struggles around the country and given them some common focus. Wartime ideals, especially the fight for democracy, had also injected into public debate in Canada and abroad a moral fervour that piqued workers' imagination and heightened their expectations about the future. Old ways of viewing (and justifying) social relationships in capitalist society were dissolving. The wartime convergence of material and ideological forces thus facilitated the creation of the most broad-based, anti-capitalist workers' movements that had ever appeared in Canada. And, as the revolt took shape, workers inspired each other; the remarkable success of working-class mobilization in the final years of the war bred a heady confidence in the potency of workers' collective action.

The Limits of a Labour Movement

In 1914 working-class organizations in Canada were in no shape to face the shock waves that the Great War would send through Canadian society. They included two distinct and often hostile camps on the industrial front: craft unionism and industrial unionism. At the turn of the century the craft unionists had hitched their star firmly to the new narrowly focused, bureaucratically structured 'international' unions based in the United States and affiliated with the American Federation of Labor (AFL). For the most part, the craft unionists sought from their employers nothing more than a regularized contractual relationship that would protect their craft status and workplace power, in return for labour peace and wage stability.[59] Despite an effort at revival in the pre-war boom, the craft unionists had been driven out of most of the major urban industries. Local trades and labour councils across the country nonetheless still tried to represent the collective interests of these skilled workers. Their national organization, the Trades and Labor Congress of Canada (TLC), continued to pose as the central 'House of Labour' in the country, despite its acceptance of the autonomy of the big internationals and of the right of the American Federation of Labor to mediate jurisdicational disputes, and despite its weakness in the Maritimes and the West.

In those regions in particular, many workers had turned to new industrial unions that signed up everyone in one workplace. Some leaders of these organizations hoped to rally Canadian workers for a general assault on the capitalist system. In western Canada some of them had organized for the colourful Industrial Workers of the World, which had been launched in 1905 and had made its greatest impact among more transient workers in the region between 1909 and 1912.[60] Less flamboyant versions of industrial unions put down roots among coal miners, longshoremen, textile and clothing workers, and a few other groups, and just before the war led these workers out in some of the biggest, most bitter strikes in living memory.[61] Employers attacked the new unions with the same tactics they had used against the craftsmen – strike-breakers, special police, industrial spies, and blacklists. By 1914 industrial unions had carved out a place for themselves within the various workers' movements in the country, but few of them had much numerical strength or bargaining clout. Nor had they overcome the divisions along lines of race and ethnicity and gender; both craft and industrial unionists were predominantly white, male, anglophone and francophone Canadians. In Quebec the Roman Catholic clergy were promoting a less aggressive form of unionism based on clerical supervision of the workers' movement and Franco-Catholic solidarity across class lines, but by 1914 they too had only limited success to report.[62]

There were further splits in the Canadian workers' movement by the outbreak of the war. Industrial struggles had become rigidly separated from political campaigns, and, within the realm of independent working-class politics, two ideological tendencies – labourism and socialism – confronted each other. Both groups had a tiny handful of their standard-bearers elected to provincial legislatures and municipal councils, but their overall impact on Canadian politics was extremely limited.[63]

Although the workers' movements in Canada had undergone some important changes in structure and ideology since the turn of the century, by 1914 they were still fragmented by occupation, industry, locality, race and ethnicity, gender, and ideology. Within working-class communities they represented an extremely limited force (the 166,000 unionists reported in 1914 amounted to barely 10 per cent of all wage earners in the 1911 census and were confined principally to railways, coal mining, and skilled urban trades). Their economic and political power had been shattered by employers' attacks and the devastating depression of 1913–15. Traditions of solidarity had been either seriously weakened by these assaults or not yet fully developed in communities overwhelmed with newcomers.

Some of the first stirrings of a collective working-class response to the new wartime conditions came from craft-union officials, particularly the Trades and Labor Congress of Canada. The new importance of the Canadian state put pressure on the Congress to intervene as the major working-class lobbying agency at the national level. For this task the organization had only two permanent officers: the president since 1910, former British Columbia miner and socialist James Watters, and the secretary since 1900, printer Paddy Draper, once described as a 'straight line "pure and simple" trade unionist.'[64] Rounding out the Congress executive were three additional members, elected by convention, who remained on staff with their respective unions (provincial executives also maintained relations with their respective governments). In its dealings with the state, the Congress confined itself strategically to traditional lobbying methods, eschewing any attempts at mass mobilization to advance its claims. Its officers preferred personal correspondence and private meetings, asserting the urgency of concessions by the state and capital lest rank-and-file militancy escalate beyond union officials' restraining capacities.[65] Labour's lobby, however, proved ineffectual. As Borden confided to his diary, the Congress's annual meetings with the federal cabinet took on an inert ritual of their own. After both the 1914 and 1915 meetings, the prime minister noted that the views expressed by Watters and Draper were both moderate and sensible, and his own cautious, non-commital response brought an end to their consideration for another year.[66] Labour's inability to lobby its way to redress would be part of the alchemy of the rising working-class revolt.

During the first three years of the war, the Congress's weakness was starkly exposed by its failure to make a dent on government policy in three prime areas of concern. First, the Congress pressed the Borden government repeatedly to alleviate the hardship of early wartime unemployment through more generous relief programs and an expansion of public works. It got neither.[67] Second, as the war economy took off in 1915, the Congress and its affiliates spent over a year pleading with the Borden government and the Imperial Munitions Board to impose fair wage clauses on military production in order 'to protect our people from extortion on the one hand and grinding poverty on the other.'[68] Instead, Ottawa extended the discredited Industrial Disputes Investigation Act to wartime industries, thereby imposing compulsory conciliation against strike attempts by discontented workers. Across the country labour's frustration at this outcome was vented not only at the government but also at the Congress leadership, condemned by the Toronto District Labor Council for not exercising 'the proper vigilance and care ... when a measure of the character referred to has been allowed to become law.' At the TLC convention in September 1916, a majority of delegates voted for the act's repeal. Over the next two years, however, the federal government turned ever more frequently to IDIA boards, special royal commissions, roving labour department troubleshooters, and threats of coercion under the War Measures Act (seldom actually used) to head off strikes and maintain industrial peace.[69]

Third, the Congress failed to influence the conduct of the war itself, an issue that proved highly divisive within the house of labour. Before 1914 no representative body in Canadian society had developed a stronger anti-war position than the Congress. In 1913 it had even reaffirmed its willingness to call a general strike in the event of hostilities. Canadian labour, however, proved no more capable of preserving its pacifist principles than its European counterparts. At its September 1914 convention, the Congress reiterated its abhorrence of war but voted to support a war effort now characterized not as an internecine conflict among the capitalist classes of Europe, but as principled struggle pitting British and French democracy against German autocracy. The organization's position was not so surprising. Most unionists undoubtedly supported the Allied cause at this point; nor could there be any doubt that to persist with resistance might result in mass arrests, possibly culminating in an outright ban on unions. Besides, support for the war might enhance unions' legitimacy with both government and employers. A similar resolution in support of 'the cause of freedom and democracy' passed in 1915, though this time with a larger chorus of dissent.[70]

The creation of the National Service Board in October 1916 to undertake a compulsory national workforce registration placed the Congress leadership in a delicate position. Not only was labour characteristically excluded from board representation, but the whole procedure appeared to be at odds with the 1915 Congress resolution that emphatically declared 'unchangeable opposition to all that savours of conscription.' Many in the labour movement regarded registration as a prelude to military conscription and regimentation at work. Yet, after meeting with Borden in December and receiving his word that registration was unconnected to any specific plans for conscription, the Congress executive issued a statement recommending that all affiliated workers complete their registration forms. Labour leaders in Quebec and the West immediately denounced the statement. When conscription was introduced the following spring, Borden noted cheerfully that Canada's house of labour would mount only ritualistic opposition to the measure it had decried for years. 'They were very receptive and good natured,' he observed after meeting with the Congress executive, 'but we may have a good natured tilt with them as they said.'[71]

The Congress leaders were clearly attempting to barter their services to the state in return for recognition. Thus, immediately after signing on for registration, they urged Borden to bring a labour representative into the cabinet. (Watters had already begun quietly promoting himself for the job, to the prime minister's great exasperation.)[72] A campaign of resistance to military conscription was more important as leverage in pressing for greater recognition of organized labour by the Borden government. Accordingly, the summer of 1917 witnessed the Congress's most energetic anti-government campaign yet. In early June it convened a four-day conference to discuss problems confronting the labour movement. Delegates from across the country, representing eighty different affiliated unions, participated in wholesale condemnation of the Imperial Munitions Board, the high cost of living, and conscription itself. The Congress leadership stepped up the call for labour representation in policy development and demanded that wealth be conscripted before lives. Yet once conscription received parliamentary assent, the Congress executive faithfully fell into line, recommending to the September 1917 convention that Canadian labour not oppose the government's forced call to arms. At this point, however, they faced a large minority in opposition, which unleashed a torrent of passionate rhetoric against conscription and in favour of a general strike against the policy.[73] In this context, it is not surprising that the Congress leadership endorsed the creation of a Canadian Labor Party as a safer channel into which to direct this working-class anger over state policy.

Borden's government also sensed the dangers in continuing to ignore or deflect the labour leadership. As the December 1917 federal election approached, appointing a labour minister seemed essential to conferring greater legitimacy and workers' support on the new Union cabinet and its labour policies. Borden's choice was inspired. Gideon Robertson was Canadian vice-president of one of the country's consistently 'safe and sane' railway brotherhoods, the Order of Railroad Telegraphers. He already sat in the Senate and privately admitted to Borden to having 'done all possible since 1914 to maintain industrial peace in Canada, which is essential to efficient results in our war work.' He promised 'to support [the Borden government's] war policy, [and] to promote industrial peace in Canada.' Robertson's appointment to the cabinet as minister without portfolio was followed by a decided shift in state labour policy, no doubt inspired by the new tripartite structures recently introduced by the American government. In January 1918 four cabinet ministers held extensive discussions with fifty-six labour leaders carefully selected by Congress officials from forty different unions. For the first time, labour received representation on a host of state regulatory bodies and, most important, the Labour Sub-Committee of the cabinet's Reconstruction and Development Committee. Moreover, the Congress executive triumphantly informed its affiliates, all such labour appointees would have to be recommended by, or acceptable to, 'the recognized heads of our movement.' As a symbol of the new openness to labour, AFL President Samuel Gompers was invited to address Parliament. According to James Watters, the war showed 'the necessity of co-operation, not alone on the actual field of battle, but in every industrial activity associated with the prosecution of the war ... Competition has, therefore, given place to co-operation – co-operation between the State and Capital and Labor.' Here were the terms of the social contract that labour leaders hoped to establish. In exchange for their commitment to harmonious workplace relations and production, these officials expected the quid pro quo of reciprocal recognition from the state and capital.[74]

Pursuing such a course inevitably drove Canada's top union leadership towards intensified commitment to the government's industrial agenda. The Congress endorsed a second registration campaign for a further inventory of the country's labour force. More important, labour officials accepted the government's apparent commitment to conciliation of industrial disputes (including some of their proposed amendments to the IDIA) and worked assiduously to prevent strikes. Union staff and structures were mobilized to restrain working-class militancy. In two critical sectors – coal mining and shipbuilding – unions participated in tripartite forums with employers and state officials to discuss means of averting strikes and boosting production.[75] A national strike of thirty thousand railway shop workers was averted only by the threats of charter revocation from international headquarters. The use of the 'big stick,' as one labour paper termed it, brought compliance from the Canadian bargaining committee representing the rail workers and the imposition of a collective agreement patterned on a recent American rail settlement.[76] In a number of instances, such international union directives against strike action in Canada were prompted by a direct federal government appeal. Watters himself became something of a roving troubleshooter acting on government request to curb militancy, as in the Nova Scotia steel industry in the spring of 1918.[77] In the same year, on at least three occasions during 1918 Gideon Robertson called on AFL President Sam Gompers and Secretary Frank Morrison to prevent strikes of Cape Breton coal miners and British Columbia shipbuilders and electrical workers.[78]

During 1918, however, it became apparent that the state was dictating the terms of its rapprochement with labour and that the new relationship produced no demonstrable advances in state labour policy. In fact, in both its legislative and employer roles, the federal government showed renewed intransigence in its dealings with labour. Although it announced a policy endorsing unionization that summer, the government provided no enforcement mechanisms and, in fact, enacted its most coercive labour legislation of the war during 1918 – first the infamous 'Anti-Loafing Act' in April and then the orders-in-council outlawing radical organizations and banning strikes in the fall. On none of these measures was labour consulted. An order-in-council in July announcing the terms of employment that workers had a right to expect, including collective bargaining, lacked any enforcement mechanism and therefore had no significant impact on labour relations in the country. The Trades and Labor Congress leadership had been incorporated into the state apparatus not to shape policy, but to enhance the legitimacy of coercive measures deemed necessary by the Borden government.

Nor did the new ties to the Congress transform the federal government's treatment of its own employees. Public-sector employees had been particularly victimized by wartime inflation. At the federal level wage restraint was the byword of a government straining to meet its wartime expenditures. Indeed, federal intransigence in the face of wage appeals from letter carriers brought western Canada to the brink of a massive general strike in the summer of 1918. When a paltry government wage offer was rejected in July, letter carriers went off the job in six centres, and within forty-eight hours widening strike action left twenty centres with no mail service. In contrast to their coverage of most other wartime strikes, the country's press was uniformly sympathetic to the aggrieved strikers. The *Calgary Herald* branded Ottawa 'utterly careless and lacking in the first principles of common decency as employers.'[79] When letter carriers in thirteen western cities rejected a new settlement negotiated by their leaders, the postmaster general instructed local postmasters to begin hiring strike-breakers and served notice that all strikers would be dismissed unless they returned to work within twenty-four hours. Several unions in the West threatened sympathy strikes, and a settlement was quickly negotiated to restore mail service by 1 August.[80]

The 1918 postal strike revealed two problems that confronted labour officialdom in its new relationship with the state – first, persistent tendencies to intransigence and coercion in state labour policies and, second, a union membership no longer willing to accept its leadership's restraining hand. The workers' movements that were taking shape across the country would not be tied down to the narrow project of corporatist accommodation among state, labour, and capital. 'The fact is they have got beyond our control,' one union official lamented in the summer of 1918.[81] The chapters that follow make clear that, despite the machinations of national labour leaders in and around Ottawa, workers wanted a labour movement that was more flexible, more militant, and often more radical: it was a challenge as much to their established leadership as to capital and the state.

The Iron Fist and Velvet Glove

The Canadian state never flinched in the face of the escalating, widely based labour revolt. However much the legitimacy of the Borden government had been undermined in the popular mind, state institutions in Canada had not crumbled as they had in Germany, Austria-Hungary, or Russia, and political leaders and officials moved quickly to fashion new tools of statecraft to curb the working-class challenge. The federal government shared business fears about the post-war economy and the need for restraint on labour demands. Borden told a national audience in September 1919 that the challenge was to foster greater production, efficiency, and cooperation in industry while avoiding measures that would 'drive away capital, restrict industry or hinder development.' But the government's concerns were also political. Now guided in its response to the revolt by the rigidly conservative Arthur Meighen, the government recoiled in horror at the size and radical overtones of the workers' movements in Canada, especially those in the West. Since September 1918, when a secret report on mushrooming radicalism in Canada crossed the cabinet's desks, politicians and state officials had been aware that more was at stake than wages and working conditions. The secret security apparatus of the Dominion Police and the Royal North-West Mounted Police was strengthened to allow the placement of spies inside labour organizations. The spectre of Bolshevik-style revolutions hung over the cabinet table as these agents' reports inflated the radical undercurrents in strike settings where workers took direction from leaders with a long-term anti-capitalist agenda. According to the labour minister, the government was also deluged with 'insistent inquiries and requests ... that something be done immediately or that Bolshevism may prevail, property and life held lightly, and the country be destroyed.' Although it still hoped to direct workers' aspirations into safe channels until the normal market mechanisms of peacetime could tame them, the government was even more determined to show that radical options were not necessary and would not be tolerated.[82]

The infamous orders-in-council in September 1918 – the first effort to stifle the new radicalism, especially in the immigrant communities and in the West generally – had been followed by several arrests. 'Alien' internment and press censorship (now aimed at socialist, not anti-war, ideas) continued for more than a year after the Armistice. The secret security reports advised that the spirit of revolt was continuing to spread in all parts of the country. The Western Labour Conference of March 1919 seemed particularly menacing. In this context, the well-established machinery of industrial conciliation was set aside in favour of blunt coercion. Winnipeg workers became the first post-war strikers to confront the full state arsenal of weapons for strike-breaking and repressing radicalism. Troops and 'special' police were deployed to harass strikers and to take back control of public space. Arrests were made under a hastily legislated measure for deporting immigrants ('alien' or British) who were deemed seditious. (The strike leaders were ultimately tried under preexisting criminal law against seditious conspiracy; immediately after the strike, the Criminal Code's definition of sedition was broadened through the addition of the infamous Section 98.)

Winnipeg's workers were not the last to face such measures. In a similar effort to control the streets, the military clamped down on all public working-class gatherings during the subsequent Vancouver general strike. Four years later in Sydney, steelworkers were hit with similar military and legal repression, as were the Nova Scotia miners in 1925, this time at the hand of the provincial government. After crushing the Winnipeg strike, the federal government collaborated in the anti-radical Red Scare that businessmen and conservative journalists were promoting across the country. The workers' revolt had thus pushed the state to create more powerful, centralized mechanisms for combatting radicalism than had existed in pre-war Canada.[83]

Borden's government was astute enough to realize that repression alone could have backfired had the outrage it prompted unified all labour leaders in opposition. It therefore made conciliatory gestures to the voices of caution and moderation in the labour movement. First, in the spring of 1919 a royal commission on industrial unrest – chaired by Justice T.G. Mathers and including Trades and Labor Congress President Tom Moore and another reliable union leader, John Bruce – visited twenty-eight centres across the country to allow for an airing of grievances and a show of official concern, just at the height of militancy within the workers' revolt. In September there occurred the most remarkable public dialogue ever held between capital, labour, and the state – the National Industrial Conference. Convened in the Senate Chamber in Ottawa, this tripartite domestic peace conference was modelled on a similar gathering in Britain a few months earlier: a labour representation of eighty-eight 'responsible' men and women, carefully handpicked by the TLC leadership, faced an equal number of employers (chosen by the Canadian Manufacturers' Association and assorted trade associations) and thirty-four public representatives nominated by the government.

The results of both the royal commission and the conference were inconclusive. Neither body straightforwardly endorsed the eight-hour day or the right to organize and bargain collectively. Both endorsed industrial councils but never clarified whether these were to include unions. Precisely the same stand-off on important issues developed when the government sent representatives of labour and capital to the recently established International Labour Organization. Within a year these conciliatory gestures were no longer felt to be necessary, and labour requests that the industrial conference be reconvened were politely ignored. Having beaten labour into submission on the picket lines, neither capital nor the state felt the need for concessions in the name of stability. Fifty years later John Bruce recalled his experience with the Mathers Commission as 'one of the bitterest lessons that ever I learned about political chicanery.'[84]

The Great War transformed the social relations of production in Canada. Workers gradually developed a measure of material and ideological confidence in wartime society, but also the grounds for a deep-seated sense of injustice. Their outrage was vented at shadowy profiteers, intransigent employers, and, to an unprecedented degree, an insensitive state. The national labour leadership never managed to defend workers' interests effectively and fell victim to the national government's determined efforts to derail the workers' revolt. These common features of the Great War experience in working-class Canada were played out in particular ways in each region of the country.

Notes

1 On the impact of war on the home front, see Marwick, *War and Social Change*; Fussell, *Great War and Modern Memory*; Winter, *Great War and the British People*; Eksteins, *Rites of Spring*; Read, ed., *Great War and Canadian Society.*

2 Shortt, 'Economic Effects of War'; R.T. Naylor, 'Canadian State'; Norrie and Owram, *History of the Canadian Economy*, 411–40; Thompson, *Harvests of War*, 50–6.

3 The course of the Canadian military effort can be followed in Morton and Granatstein, *Marching to Armageddon*. The plight of the Canadian soldier in this war is sensitively treated in Morton, *When Your Number's Up*.

4 Corry, 'Growth of Government Activities.'

5 On social life in Canada during the war, see Read, ed., *Great War and Canadian Society.*

6 For example, coal miners in western Canada's District 18 of the United Mine Workers used a strike in 1915 to get 'enemy aliens' removed from the mining operations where they worked. In April 1917 the office of a German newspaper was ransacked in Regina. Avery, 'Ethnic and Class Tensions,' 80, 89. See also Wilson, *Ontario and the First World War*, lxx–lxxxiv.

7 Socknat, *Witness against War*, 43–59.

8 Steinhart, *Civil Censorship*; Cole, 'War Measures Act'; Keshen, 'All the News'; Siemiatycki, 'Munitions and Labour Militancy'; Peter Melnycky, 'The Internment of Ukrainians in Canada,' in Swyripa and Thompson, eds., *Loyalties in Conflict*, 1–24; Gregory Kealey, 'State Repression.'

9 Corry, 'Growth of Government Activities'; Smith, 'Emergency Government in Canada'; Thompson, *Harvests of War*, 27–44; Boudreau, 'Western Canada's

"Enemy Aliens"'; Swyripa and Thompson, eds., *Loyalties in Conflict*; Rasporich, *For a Better Life*, 75–92; Craven, *Impartial Umpire*; Granatstein and Hitsman, *Broken Promises*, 22–104; Spence, *Prohibition in Canada*; Hallowell, *Prohibition in Ontario*, 7; Forbes, 'Prohibition and the Social Gospel'; Heron, 'Daylight Savings'; Reilly, 'General Strike in Amherst.'

10 Corry, 'Growth of Government Activities'; Smith, 'Emergency Government in Canada'; Brown and Cook, *Canada, 1896–1921*; Cuff, 'Organizing for War'; Morton and Wright, *Winning the Second Battle*.

11 Hinton, *First Shop Stewards' Movement*; Owram, *Government Generation*; Thistle, *Inner Ring*; Traves, *State and Enterprise*, 55–70; Struthers, *No Fault of Their Own*, 16–43.

12 English, *Decline of Politics*, 88–221; Brown, *Robert Borden*.

13 Armstrong, *Crisis of Quebec*.

14 English, *Decline of Politics*, 136–203; Brown, *Robert Borden*, 83–125; Graham, *Arthur Meighen*, 145–210; Granatstein and Hitsman, *Broken Promises*, 70–83.

15 Bliss, 'Methodist Church'; Allen, *Social Passion*, 63–103; Thompson, 'Beginning of Our Regeneration'; Gray, *Booze*; Hallowell, *Prohibition in Ontario*.

16 Cleverdon, *Woman Suffrage Movement*; Bacchi, *Liberation Deferred?*

17 See, for example, Miller, ed., *The New Era in Canada*; Bland, *The New Christianity*; Irvine, *Farmers in Politics*; King, *Industry and Humanity*; Leacock, *Unsolved Riddle*; MacIver, *Labor in the Changing World*. For a discussion of this intellectual ferment, see Owram, *Government Generation*, 80–106.

18 Thompson, *Harvests of War*; Morton, *Progressive Party*; Wood, *History of Farmers' Movements*; Young, 'Conscription, Rural Depopulation, and the Farmers of Ontario.'

19 Morton and Wright, *Winning the Second Battle*; Morton, *When Your Number's Up*, 253–75.

20 *BC Federationist*, 3 July 1914; Siemiatycki, 'Labour Contained,' 10–15; Roy, 'Vancouver: "The Mecca of the Unemployed,"' 400–2; Matters, 'Public Welfare Vancouver Style'; Schulze, 'Industrial Workers of the World'; Goeres, 'Disorder, Dependency and Fiscal Responsibility,' 39; Avery, 'Ethnic and Class Tensions,' 80; Heron, 'Working-Class Hamilton,' 206; Piva, *Condition of the Working Class*, 76–82; Larivière, *Albert Saint-Martin*, 109–18; Ewen in this volume; Canada, Dept. of Labour, *Labour Organization in Canada*, 1915, 17; UBC Archives, Vancouver Trades and Labor Council Minutes, 19 November 1914; Morton and Granatstein, *Marching to Armageddon*, 7–8; Morton, *When Your Number's Up*, 278–9. According to Morton's calculations, nearly two-thirds of the Canadian Expeditionary Force counted in March 1916 had been manual workers.

21 Price, 'Changes in the Industrial Occupations of Women'; Ramkhalawansingh, 'Women during the Great War'; Lowe, *Women in the Administrative Revolution*; Linda Kealey, 'Women and Labour during World War I'; Naylor, *New Democracy*, 130–6; Piva, *Condition of the Working Class*, 40–3; Heron, 'Working-Class Hamilton,' 388–90.

22 Copp, *Anatomy of Poverty*, 56; Piva, *Condition of the Working Class*, 40–3; Heron, 'High School and the Household Economy'; and 'Working-Class Hamilton,' 29.

23 Bliss, *Canadian Millionaire*; Carnegie, *History of Munitions and Supply*; Avery, '*Dangerous Foreigners*'; Andrij Makuch, 'Ukrainian Canadians and the Wartime Economy,' in Swyripa and Thompson, eds., *Loyalties in Conflict*, 69–78; Heron, 'Working-Class Hamilton,' 319–24 and *Working in Steel*, 140.

24 Heron, 'Working-Class Hamilton,' 237–8.

25 See Bradbury, *Working Families*; Synge, 'Transition from School to Work' and 'Self-Help and Neighbourliness'; Abella and Millar, eds., *Canadian Worker in the Twentieth Century*, 76–150; Copp, *Anatomy of Povery*; Piva, *Condition of the Working Class*; and Heron, 'High School and the Family Economy.'

26 Nova Scotia, Factories' Inspector, *Report*, 1917, 6; Naylor, *New Democracy*, 34; Siemiatycki, 'Labour Contained,' 111; NAC, MG 30, A16 (Sir Joseph Flavelle Papers), Vol. 2, File: Department of Labour, Basil Magor to J. Flavelle, 7 June 1916; 'The Industrial Slacker,' *Canadian Foundryman* 9, no. 5 (May 1918), 105; Piva, *Condition of the Working Class*, 106; Carnegie, *History of Munitions and Supply*, 252–3; Heron, 'Working-Class Hamilton,' 238–9 and *Working in Steel*, 114–16.

27 Ewen in this volume; Hogan, *Cobalt*, 24–31; Siemiatycki, 'Munitions and Labour Militancy'; Seager, 'Proletariat in Wild Rose Country.'

28 *Labour Gazette*, September 1917, 736–7; January 1918, 48–9; August 1919, 1004–5; July 1921, 972. Calculations of percentages are ours.

29 Canada, Dept. of Labour, *Labour Organization in Canada*, 1917, 38–9.

30 Naylor, 'Canadian State,' 83–7; Piva, *Condition of the Working Class*, 27–59; Copp, *Anatomy of Poverty*, 30–43; Bartlett, 'Real Wages and the Standard of Living,' 57; Sutcliffe and Phillips, 'Real Wages and the Winnipeg General Strike'; Makahonuk, 'Class Conflict,' 98–100; Heron, *Working in Steel*, 139.

31 See Frank, 'Miner's Financier.'

32 Quoted in McCormack, *Reformers, Rebels, and Revolutionaries*, 127.

33 Bliss, *Canadian Millionaire*, 329–62; NAC, MG 26, H 1(a) (Sir Robert Borden Papers), Northrup to Borden, 21 July 1917.

34 Quoted in Copp, *Anatomy of Poverty*, 134.

35 Canada, Dept. of Labour, *Labour Organization in Canada*, 1917, 38–9; McCormack, *Reformers, Rebels, and Revolutionaries*, 121–3.

36 Robin, *Radical Politics and Canadian Labour;* McCormack, *Reformers, Rebels, and Revolutionaries,* 128–9.

37 MacPherson, *Each for All,* 63–66. Working-class consumer co-ops are discussed in Heron and De Zwaan, 'Industrial Unionism,' 169, 172; and Heron, 'Working-Class Hamilton.'

38 *Labour Gazette,* 1919–20.

39 Steedman, 'Female Participation in the Canadian Clothing Industry'; Ewen in this volume; Heron, 'Working-Class Hamilton,' 422.

40 In the decade before the war many of Canada's new corporate employers, both domestic and foreign, had begun to reorganize their work processes with more centralized, authoritarian managerial structures and new labour-saving technology. The transformation of their workplaces was most evident in such central Canadian cities as Montreal, Toronto, and Hamilton, where trend-setting American managerial styles had their greatest impact, but was far from complete in most industries by the outbreak of the war. Heron, *Working in Steel* and 'Second Industrial Revolution'; Heron and Palmer, 'Through the Prism of the Strike'; McKay, 'Strikes in the Maritimes'; Lowe, *Women in the Administrative Revolution;* Armstrong, 'Quebec Asbestos Industry'; Stacey, *Sockeye and Tinplate;* Rajala, 'Managerial Crisis' and 'Rude Science'; Hovis, 'Technological Change and Mining Labour'; Babcock, 'Saint John Longshoremen'; Foster, 'On the Waterfront'; Steedman, 'Skill and Gender'; Tuck, 'Union Authority'; Marshall, Southard, and Taylor, *Canadian–American Industry.*

41 Heron, 'Crisis of the Craftsman'; Roberts, 'Toronto Metal Workers.'

42 *Industrial Banner* (Toronto), 7 September 1917.

43 Quoted in Heron, *Working in Steel,* 140.

44 Avery, *'Dangerous Foreigners'*; Andrij Makuch, 'Ukrainian Canadians and the Wartime Economy,' in Swyripa and Thompson, *Loyalties in Conflict,* 70; Wickberg, ed., *From China to Canada.*

45 Makuch, 'Ukrainian Canadians and the Wartime Economy,' 71; Peter Melnycky, 'The Internment of Ukrainians in Canada,' in Swyripa and Thompson, eds., *Loyalties in Conflict,* 14–15; Morton, *Canadian General,* 343; Avery, *'Dangerous Foreigners'*, 32.

46 Bradwin, *Bunkhouse Man;* Harney, *Gathering Place;* Ramirez, *On the Move;* Heron, *Working in Steel;* Avery, 'Ethnic and Class Tensions,' 79–98 and *'Dangerous Foreigners'*, 73–89; McCormack, *Reformers, Rebels, and Revolutionaries,* 121; Heron, 'Working-Class Hamilton,' 320–7; Wickberg, ed., *From China to Canada,* 120–2; McKay, 'The 1910s,' 222.

47 Robin, *Radical Politics and Canadian Labour;* McCormack, *Reformers, Rebels, and Revolutionaries,* 122–3.

48 Provencher, *Québec sous la loi des mesures de guerre*; Armstrong, *Crisis of Quebec*; Ewen in this volume.
49 Mayse, *Ginger*; Hanebury, *Ginger Goodwin*.
50 Naylor in this volume; Robin, *Radical Politics and Canadian Labour*, 163–9; McCormack, *Reformers, Rebels, and Revolutionaries*, 152–4.
51 NAC, MG 30 (Sir Joseph Flavelle Papers), A16, Vol. 38, File 1918–19, March Irish to Flavelle, 20 June 1918.
52 Quoted in Robin, *Radical Politics and Canadian Labour*, 165.
53 Quoted in Heron, *Working in Steel*, 142.
54 Quoted in Bercuson, *Fools and Wise Men*, 71.
55 Bercuson, *Fools and Wise Men*, 75–8.
56 The leadership of the Winnipeg General Strike made much of this declaration. See Penner, *1919*, 40–1; and McKay and Morton in this volume.
57 Public Archives of Manitoba, Robert Russell Papers, Cassidy to Stephenson, 19 January 1919.
58 McCormack, *Reformers, Rebels, and Revolutionaries*, 139–43 (quote at 141); Avery, *'Dangerous Foreigners'*, 70–6; Krawchuk, *Ukrainian Socialist Movement*; Laine, 'Finnish Canadian Radicalism.'
59 Babcock, *Gompers in Canada*.
60 McCormack, *Reformers, Rebels, and Revolutionaries*; Leier, *Where the Fraser River Flows*.
61 McKay, 'Industry, Work, and Community'; MacEwan, *Miners and Steelworkers*; Seager, 'Proletariat in Wild Rose Country'; Foster, 'On the Waterfront'; Rouillard, *Les travailleurs du coton*; Steedman, 'Female Participation in the Canadian Clothing Industry.'
62 Rouillard, *Les syndicats nationaux*.
63 Robin, *Radical Politics and Canadian Labour*; McCormack, *Reformers, Rebels, and Revolutionaries*; Frank and Reilly, 'Emergence of the Socialist Movement'; Krawchuck, *Ukrainian Socialist Movement*; Laine, 'Finnish Canadian Radicalism'; Frager, 'Radical Portraits'; Heron, 'Labourism and the Canadian Working Class.'
64 Wisconsin State Historical Society, American Federation of Labor Papers, Flett to Gompers, 3 October 1916.
65 Siemiatycki, 'Labour Contained,' 51–6.
66 NAC, MG 26, H 1(a), Borden Diaries, 5 June 1914; 15 June 1915.
67 Siemiatycki, 'Labour Contained,' 25–8.
68 NAC, MG 30, A16, Watters to Borden, 22 November 1915.
69 NAC, Toronto District Trades and Labor Council, Minutes, 6 April 1916; Siemiatycki, 'Munitions and Labour Militancy'; Tucker, 'World War I and the Post-War Labour Revolt.'

70 Canada, Dept. of Labour, *Labour Organization in Canada*, 1914, 18–19; Socknat, *Witness against War*, 37; Trades and Labor Congress of Canada (TLC), *Proceedings*, 1914, 20; 1915, 14, 91.

71 TLC, *Proceedings*, 1915, 15; NAC, MG 26, H 1(a), Borden Diaries, 21 May 1917.

72 Siemiatycki, 'Labour Contained,' 153–4.

73 Ibid., 155–8.

74 NAC, MG 26, H 1(a), Robertson to Borden, 23 August 1917; Watters and Moore, 'To Organized Labor in Canada' (undated circular); TLC, *Convention Booklet, 1918*.

75 *Halifax Herald*, 26 February 1918; *Machinists' Monthly Journal*, May 1918, 455.

76 *Labor News*, 26 July 1918.

77 Heron, 'Great War and Nova Scotia Steelworkers,' 17.

78 Siemiatycki, 'Labour Contained,' 216–17.

79 *Calgary Herald*, 23 July 1918.

80 Siemiatycki, 'Labour Contained,' 203–4.

81 *Toronto Telegram*, 23 July 1918.

82 Canada, National Industrial Conference, *Report*, 6; Graham, *Arthur Meighen*, 211–44; Horrall, 'Royal North-West Mounted Police'; Gregory Kealey, 'State Repression of Labour'; Canada, Senate, *Debates*, 2 April 1919, 194.

83 Mitchell, 'To Reach the Leadership'; Bercuson, *Confrontation at Winnipeg*, 115–75; Macgillivray, 'Military Aid'; Frank, 'Trial of J.B. McLachlan'; Seager and Roth in this volume. On federal collaboration in the Red Scare, see Canada, Department of Labour, *Information Respecting the Russian Soviet System and Its Propaganda in North America* (Ottawa: King's Printer 1920). Before the war radicalism that seemed menacing was simply repressed in an ad hoc fashion. Local municipal police forces would simply lock up soapbox socialists who caused a seditious nuisance. Any combination of large-scale militancy and radicalism would generally result in the mobilization of the militia to occupy the streets. Leier, *Where the Fraser River Flows*; Schulze, 'Industrial Workers of the World'; Frank and Reilly, 'Emergence of the Socialist Movement,' 89–90; McCormack, *Reformers, Rebels, and Revolutionaries*, 105–7; Heron, 'Working-Class Hamilton,' 654–55; Morton, 'Aid to the Civil Power.'

84 Canada, Royal Commission on Industrial Relations, *Report* (Ottawa: King's Printer 1919) (the unpublished testimony is available in the Labour Canada Library in Hull); Canada, National Industrial Conference, *Report*; Siemiatycki, 'Labour Contained,' 355–67; Naylor, *New Democracy*, 188–214 and 'Workers and the State,' 28–35; Gerber, 'United States and Canadian National Industrial Conferences'; Hucul, 'Canada and the International Labour Organization'; NAC, John Bruce Papers, Interview, 30 March 1963.

The Maritimes: Expanding the Circle of Resistance

IAN McKAY and SUZANNE MORTON

This is how one pictures the angel of history. His face is turned towards the past. Where we perceive a chain of events, he sees one single catastrophe which keeps piling wreckage upon wreckage and hurls it in front of his feet. The angel would like to stay, awaken the dead, and make whole what has been smashed. But a storm is blowing from Paradise; it has caught in his wings with such violence that the angel can no longer close them. This storm irresistibly propels him into the future to which his back is turned, while the pile of debris before him grows skyward. The storm is what we call progress.

Walter Benjamin, 'Theses on the Philosophy of History'

Throughout 1919 and 1920 the traditional power bases within Maritime society appeared to be breaking apart. Working-class men and women across the region offered their communities an alternative vision of economic, political, and social reality. Between 1917 and 1925 Maritimers rose in their thousands to demand radical change, creating a successful third party and fighting some of the most spectacular and savage strikes ever seen in Canada. The great revolt of 1917–25 will always confound those who try to create a one-dimensional image of an unchanging, innately conservative Maritimes. However, unlike the Winnipeg General Strike or the On to Ottawa Trek of 1935, the fact that this regional labour revolt could be largely extinguished in collective memory tells us something about the success with which bourgeois hegemony was restored. Class struggle and progressive politics did not disappear in the Maritimes after 1925, but those who fought labour's battles did so against an ideologically well-armoured opponent.[1]

Any movement for radical social change in the Maritimes confronts three kinds of serious obstacles. First, there is the lasting legacy of early capitalist development and the uneven, fragmented economy that it bequeathed to the twentieth century. In effect, there were at least two distinct, if related, socio-economic regions within the Maritimes: one, heavily industrialized and urban, peopled by immigrants as well as by the native-born, encompassing the coalfields and the port cities; the other, underdeveloped, rural or small-town, and more uniformly Canadian by birth, embracing the great remainder of the region. In the 1921 census Prince Edward Island, Nova Scotia, and New Brunswick all reported that over 90 per cent of their respective populations were native-born.[2] This did not entail homogeneity. Even within the 'homogeneous' rural areas, one found important but diverse pockets of Acadians, blacks, and native peoples.[3] In 1919 most Maritimers lived in a rural environment, and many were engaged in petty commodity production, often part-time or seasonally in fishing, farming, lumbering, or available labouring jobs.[4] We therefore confront two social regions within one: industrial and commercial communities set within, and interacting with, resource-based rural capitalism.[5] The fundamental problem this social configuration has always posed for radical movements in the Maritimes is that of bringing together rural primary producers – men and women on the farms, in the fishing villages, on the woodlots – urban workers, and progressive intellectuals. This problem was and is both economic and geographic. There was no single regional metropolis, no great centre radiating its influences throughout the hinterland. Even so great a social upheaval as a general strike might echo but quietly in the surrounding countryside.

Second, this economic legacy formed the vital nucleus of a tenacious sociocultural pattern of paternalism, that complex and often reciprocal process through which producers and patrons honoured each other and affirmed personal and political ties, thereby 'transcending' (and mystifying) class positions and interests. If, in some places, these processes of deference and reciprocal recognition of social place had become outmoded by 1900, they were deeply implanted elsewhere. The outmigration of the young to the United States or central and western Canada, the cumulative weight of poverty, the seemingly effortless imposition of cultural authority on the part of businessmen and professionals, the existence of sharp divisions between craft workers (the 'labour aristocracy) and the less skilled[6] – these are among the factors that have weighed heavily against movements of resistance. Deeply rooted in dense networks of reciprocal interest and patronage, and drawing nourishment from a sense of tradition, the two-party tradition, although shaken in the 1920s, has never been broken – a political pattern that sets the Maritimes apart from all other regions in Canada.

Finally, there was the fundamental fact of gender inequality – a universal phenomenon with particular importance in a region where the most powerful and influential wage earners came from the all-male preserves of the shipyards, the steel and lumber mills, the coal mines, the waterfront, and the fishing fleets. Unless the region's radicals looked beyond the articulate, organized wage earner to the whole society, and specifically addressed questions of gender, racial, and linguistic oppression, they risked both isolating themselves and avoiding issues that were as fundamental as class. These three obstacles by no means precluded the emergence of powerful radical movements in the region, but they have tended to limit and localize their impact.

Herein lies the tragic radiance of the years 1917–25 in regional history. For the first time, radicals overcame many of these obstacles. Primary producers and workers did make common cause. The country and the city started to share the same universe of radical opinion. Acadians rejected the call of their elites to join Catholic unions and in towns such as Bathurst composed a large component of the pulp and paper workers' union.[7] The coal miners, whose distinctive workplaces and struggles could so easily lead to their isolation within the broader community, or to a simplistic perception of Cape Breton as the region's 'one pocket of radicalism,' were integrated within a much wider social and political movement. Women wage earners joined the revolt, and housewives, hitherto excluded from the left, were included within the framework of protest. And then the moment faded. The liberating, exhilarating strikes were succeeded by the dull compulsion of daily labour, wage cuts, and a mass exodus from the region. The alliances fell apart, and new ideologies of consumerism proved more attractive than those of labour to a new generation of women workers.

A right-wing populist revolt reaped where labourism had sown, restoring bourgeois hegemony by naturalizing a notion of Maritime traditionalism and unfurling the dazzling flag of Maritime Rights.[8] To the extent that this bourgeois offensive succeeded in changing 'common sense' – and one should not imagine a total victory that wiped out the memory of the struggle – the idea of Maritime conservatism has a certain validity, not as some unchanging regional 'essence,' but as the successful outcome of a conscious, complex, and subtle struggle to reimpose bourgeois hegemony in a society rife with dissension and rebellion. The regional labour movement, as a radical force contesting capitalism, was defeated in the 1920s. Notwithstanding moments of resistance from the 1930s to the 1970s, Maritime labour radicalism has never recovered from the catastrophe of 1922–25.

Our exploration of the Maritime workers' revolt will proceed in three stages. The first section will explore the revolt's most dynamic phase, from 1917 to 1920. In this period workers across the Maritimes made a number of triumphant breakthroughs in organizing trade unions, labour parties, and direct action. The key to this period was the consolidation of a working-class consciousness. The tone of the workers' movement was one of social polarization, anti-capitalism, and immense optimism; its ideology was that of labourism. In the transitional period from 1920 to mid-1922, the workers went on the defensive, as the region entered into a profound economic and social crisis. Suddenly, as the economy fell apart, so did much of the labour movement. Workers suffered one immense defeat after another. Labourism and more radical ideologies contended for influence, and in the ranks of the coal miners, who had retained their capacity to fight, the radicals gained power within the miners' union. The third period, from mid-1922 to 1925, saw the last stand of these now quite isolated radical miners, who were undermined from outside their ranks by state violence, new forms of regionalist populism, by the logic of deindustrialization, and, from within their own ranks, by the evolution of industrial legality (that is, trade union law armoured by bureaucracy). The revolt came to a halt with a tragic, crushing finality, when the miners were defeated in their most desperate struggle in 1925. Defeated virtually everywhere, some workers began to listen to the arguments of a Maritime Rights movement dominated by the forces of business and the traditional parties, the very forces so many of them had earlier rejected.

The Rising of the Workers, 1917–1920

Earlier than in most other regions, the coming of the war brought economic prosperity and full employment to the Maritimes. Coal, steel, gypsum, and the construction trades expanded rapidly. Partly because of this wartime prosperity, pre-war social conflict was replaced by an unusual degree of social harmony and cohesiveness. Yet over and above the impact of full employment was the force of patriotism. Workers supported the war effort and the incidence of strikes was greatly reduced.

Following the outbreak of war there appear to have been no strikes at all in 1914, eleven in 1915 (none major), and just three in 1916, the lowest regional total in the twentieth century.[9] In December 1915 the *Halifax Herald* noted that industrial peace was unprecedented in the fifteen years covered by the Department of Labour's records – a remarkable finding given that full employment generally promotes strikes.[10]

The mood of social peace quickly evaporated. By 1917 many workers had distanced themselves from the bourgeois 'common sense' that demanded they place patriotism ahead of their economic interests. Despite an increasingly repressive climate, culminating in an order-in-council in October 1918 threatening those who organized strikes or lock-outs with forced military service,[11] the number of strikes more than doubled, from eleven in 1917 to twenty-seven in 1918, and the number of striker days represented by wartime strikes soared from 12,549 to 84,121. There were a further seven strikes in 1918 after the Armistice on 11 November.

The strength of the strike wave made it seem more like a mass uprising than a set of discrete strikes. In 1919 there were at least thirty-eight strikes, with 123,847 striker days, including seven small strikes in Saint John, six in Halifax, and five in Sydney. The same year witnessed the region's epic strikes: the Hants County gypsum quarrymen's battle for union recognition, a large general building strike in Halifax (which in turn brought the whole city close to a general sympathetic strike), and the Amherst general strike – in all three communities, the largest strikes recorded to date. The strikers generally met their objectives. Of the strikes for which a clear result is known, workers won eighteen and employers six; five ended in compromise. In 1920 there were a record fifty-five strikes, accounting for 174,325 striker days. Seven of these were in Glace Bay, six in New Waterford, five in both Springhill and Halifax, and four in each of Amherst, Sydney, and Saint John. Yet by 1920, even before the end of the revolt, the tide had already begun to turn against the workers. Of the strikes for which a clear result can be recorded, fifteen were won by workers and twelve by employers; eleven ended in compromise.

The soldiers returning from the front added their own contribution to this explosive atmosphere, viewing their non-combatant employers with scarcely concealed contempt. Although returned soldiers and labour supporters had not been friends during the 1917 conscription crisis, they afterwards often found common ground. In Cape Breton veterans and workers jointly protested the activities of immigration agents.[12]

In Halifax the Great War Veterans' Association and the labour movement easily cooperated in investigating shipyard conditions and came close to concluding an official political alliance.[13] This common ground was discovered in part through a shared rhetoric. For four years both soldiers and civilians had been saturated with a fervent progressivism that stressed individual sacrifice in the interests of collective welfare. Why, then, should capital not follow suit? Indeed, some workers believed that some such notion was embodied in the Treaty of Versailles. In 1920 the organizer of Saint John machinists who had been locked out and replaced accused their employers of 'refusing us the rights which are guaranteed by the Peace Treaty, and sealed with the blood of millions of workers.'[14] J.A. Gillis, secretary of the Sydney steelworkers' union, similarly concluded that the rights of collective bargaining and union recognition were 'covered by the labor provisions in connection with the peace treaty.'[15] Throughout the 1917–25 revolt the seismic shocks unleashed by the war unsettled the minds of workers and bourgeois alike. There was a sense that social relations could never again be the same.

The labour revolt was a broad social protest. It affected workers outside of unions, like workers at a Buctouche, New Brunswick, sawmill who, when they walked off the job, were simply called 'the crowd.' Yet at its core was the newly invigorated trade union movement. The most dramatic breakthrough in organization came in the coalfields.[16] Before the war the miners had been split between adherents of the local Provincial Workmen's Association (PWA) and the international United Mine Workers of America (UMW). The numerous socialists among the miners had aligned themselves with the UMW but were unable to unseat the more traditionalist PWA in a series of bitter pre-war strikes. By 1916 dissatisfaction with the old union had revived the fortunes of the UMW. On 13 October 1916 J.B. McLachlan, the miners' leader, wrote to John P. White, president of the UMW, urging him to revive at least the local union in Dominion. The miners, he reported, thought that the UMW could move in and reorganize Nova Scotia without spending any money. From McLachlan's perspective, the workers were ready to move. Six days earlier, the Casino Theatre in Glace Bay had been packed, and four or five hundred men had been unable to get inside thirty minutes before the advertised time for the meeting. They demanded a 30 per cent wage increase in defiance of the 6 per cent increase stipulated in the two-year contract signed by the PWA.[17]

Elsewhere in the wartime coalfields, strictly local organizations emerged as an alternative to the PWA. In 1917 miners in Springhill achieved something that had eluded them over the course of a savage strike that had extended from 1909 to 1911 – namely, a tacit recognition of their right to collective bargaining.[18] In response to miners' protests, the federal government announced in April 1917 the first of the major royal commissions whose reports punctuate a history of almost constant turmoil in the coalfields from 1917 to 1925. This commission recommended a wage increase and, significantly, amalgamation of rival unions. Accordingly, representatives of the PWA and the UMW of Nova Scotia met in Sydney in June 1917 and agreed to the formation of a new union, the Amalgamated Mine Workers of Nova Scotia (AMW), with the stipulation that it would have no ties outside the province.[19] 'As a whole the miners of Nova Scotia are organized today to the last man,' J.B. McLachlan reported in August 1917. '[Ten thousand] of them with us and 3000 [in Pictou and Inverness] with the A.F. of L. I may also state that our union has the check-off and complete recognition. The three thousand men simply tell us that they will join us, when we go into the U.M.W. of A.'[20] It was an astonishing comeback for the coal miners.

Throughout 1918 the coal miners moved steadily to the left, protesting the provincial legislature's rejection of the eight-hour day and, in July 1918, negotiating the last substantial increase in the miners' wages until 1920. The fundamental issue of the right to be represented by the UMW remained unresolved until February 1919, when delegates to the AMW convention voted unanimously to dissolve the AMW and accept a new charter for District 26 of the United Mine Workers of America. The emergence of District 26 was a startling sign of the miners' new power. What had been violently repressed ten years earlier, now was handed to UMW supporters by state bureaucrats and company officials who feared the spectre of massive unrest more than they despised the international union.[21] Many coal miners would later rue the day they joined the United Mine Workers, but their decision made sense in both pragmatic and socialist terms. Rallying to the cause of the continent's largest and most successful industrial union was a logical response to the continental imperatives of monopoly capitalism, and, for socialists, the UMW represented both internationalism and the heroic legacy of the 1909–11 strikes. District 26, with over thirteen thousand members from Minto, New Brunswick, to Louisbourg, Nova Scotia, ultimately became the dominant force in the regional labour revolt.

The years 1917–20 formed a distinctive period in the history of the organized coal mines – a period of rank-and-file democracy, ideological ferment, and boisterous working-class power. There were no great strikes, not because the miners were weak, but rather because their strength enabled them to force one concession after another from the coal companies and the government. The union itself was young in the sense that it had yet to attain the levels of institutionalization and bureaucracy that later developed in the wake of written contracts and the automatic deduction of union dues. The early District 26, like the One Big Union (OBU) in western Canada, was very much an agent of working-class democracy. Although the emergence of District 26 was of seminal importance, what was distinctive about the first phase of the revolt was that thousands of workers far removed from the coalfields responded with as much enthusiasm as the miners to the ideals of trade unionism. By 1920 at least forty thousand Maritimers had signed on as union members, more than four times the number reported in 1915.[22] They included not only the coal miners, steelworkers, and metalworkers of the heavy-industry towns and the craft and industrial workers of the cities, but also pulp and paper workers, clerks, teachers, mail carriers, municipal employees, and, in Sydney and Saint John, law-enforcement officers.[23] 'Casting the mind's eye over the Canadian field of labor,' stated a contented *Eastern Federationist* in 1919, 'in no part does it look more bright than in Nova Scotia ... The entire province is organized ... and they are all affiliated in the Provincial Federation so that no union stands isolated.'[24]

The labour revolt would not have occurred without dramatic breakthroughs in organization and leadership. The labour movement had a depth and élan never known before or since. Before the war working-class leaders such as Robert Drummond, John Moffat, and John Joy had been little known outside the organizations with which they were affiliated. Now a crowd in Pictou County would flock to hear such orators as Red Dan Livingstone, Silby Barrett, Robert Baxter, J.B. McLachlan, and C.C. Dane, who became, at least in Nova Scotia, widely admired labour celebrities.

Because Maritime labour organizations did not generally follow those of the West in breaking with American international trade unions, their position has been misinterpreted as one of hidebound, parochial conservatism.[25] Yet this dismissal misses two vital points. First, Maritime support for the One Big Union was stronger and more deeply rooted than is often remembered. In the mid-1920s the OBU was able to capitalize on sympathies developed earlier in the coal communities of Thorburn, Westville, and Minto.[26] Second, broad support for OBU-style trade unionism – direct action, solidarity across the lines of industry and class, unified collective bargaining, and general strikes – found expression within the established trade union movement. Instead of standing by tried-and-true craft union methods, Maritime workers – influenced by such leaders as the UMW's James B. McLachlan, Scotsman and socialist, and the AFL's Clifford C. Dane, Australian boilermaker and self-proclaimed Bolshevist – developed a Maritime variant of socialist trade unionism. The districts, councils, and federations of labour associated with the new unionism all grouped masses of workers together in large, effective, and politically active bodies. In many places federations of labour, not individual craft unions, became the principal organizing mechanism. Unions in Halifax, Pictou County, Amherst, Moncton, and around the Miramichi River in New Brunswick conducted joint bargaining within industrial sectors such as the building, metal, and marine trades.[27]

A driving force behind the new forms of unionism was C.C. Dane. Dane began his impressive career in organizing in 1913 as secretary of the newly organized car workers in Pictou County. Eventually, his activities spread to Amherst, Sydney Mines, Inverness, and Halifax/ Dartmouth.[28] Described by Scotia Steel's general manager as 'a ticket-of-leave Australian convict agitator,'[29] Dane was free to devote all his efforts to organizing federal labour unions when, after being fired and blacklisted, he was employed by the AFL. The Pictou County Trades and Labor Council, along with seven branches of the Federation of Labor throughout Pictou and a similar 'industrial union' of workers at Canadian Car and Foundry in Amherst, were eloquent testimonials to Dane's extraordinary energy and talent as an organizer.[30] In Halifax Dane organized another OBU-style Federation of Labor, which claimed a membership of three thousand and included men employed by Consumer's Cordage and the sugar refinery who would normally be excluded from any craft union.[31] The careful Dane always publicly claimed that he would not accept craftsmen in his theoretically short-term federal labour unions. Some suspected, however, that Dane had already compromised the principles of craft unionism. Although the Pictou County Trades and Labor Council explicitly rejected the OBU in April 1919, the council itself raised suspicions of syndicalism by speaking for organized labour far more powerfully and visibly than any of its constituent unions.[32] Much the same accusation could be brought against the forceful local industrial union that Miramichi woodworkers called the Independent Labor Alliance; by June 1920 this union had incorporated twenty-five hundred workers in lumber camps along the river, longshoremen, and industrial workers in the sawmills and pulp and paper factories in Chatham and Newcastle.[33]

Workers across North America were experimenting with new forms of unionism, but they had a particular significance in the Maritimes. Less structured organizations spoke directly to the needs of the workers who might, in the course of a year, undertake a variety of occupations as small independent commodity producers and wage earners. They also spoke to the evident uselessness of dividing the workforce of small communities into tiny craft unions. This compromise formula allowed workers in medium-sized communities to sustain a dynamic yet stable movement – something that the craft and even the industrial forms of organization made difficult.

Even places where more conventional unions continued to dominate experimented with new forms of organization. In the spring of 1919 Halifax building workers put aside tradition and separate wage levels to launch a massive strike for one unified set of wage demands. In Pictou County the formation of a metal trades council in October 1919 was similarly seen as a modern tactic to meet the increased strength of capital.[34] National unions such as the Canadian Brotherhood of Railway Employees were strengthened as many semi-skilled railway workers responded to their industrial unionist appeal. It seems apparent that the OBU was weak in the East not because of eastern conservatism, but primarily because other organizations had undercut its appeal by promoting their own innovative and radical models of organization and politics.

The new labour organizations were all the more prominent because of the emergence of the first effective labour federations in the region. The associations formed in New Brunswick in 1913 and Nova Scotia in 1919 united a variety of labour leaders from across the political and geographic landscapes.[35] In addition, provincial federations were supported by local unions and district councils. Councils were generally affiliated with the AFL, but in the Maritimes only the Nova Scotia districts of Halifax, Sydney, and Pictou County held a single charter. Allegiance to the AFL-TLC was far from unreflecting. Halifax trade unionists openly disobeyed the TLC when they elected a member of a disbarred union as president in 1921.[36] In the rest of the region Saint John and Moncton possessed dual charters, Fredericton remained completely independent, and Amherst was affiliated with the OBU.

Evidence that the labour movement often thought in regional terms is plentiful. Plans for the 1919 Labour Day celebrations in Moncton had a regional scope, as invitations to participants in the parade were 'extended to unions in all sections of the Maritimes.'[37] Labour supporters from Amherst, Springhill, and Sussex were represented. In November 1920 the Moncton Amalgamated Central Labor Union and the Halifax Trades and Labor Council received correspondence from the Saint John council asking the organizations' opinion on 'the advisability of forming Provincial and Interprovincial Federations in the Maritime Provinces.'[38] The formation of interprovincial labour councils and such tentative attempts at regional unity suggested that labour was seeking to overcome the legacy of fragmentation.

Union recognition and the high cost of living were the two basic issues in the first years of the revolt. Labour unrest was attributed to inflation, which swallowed wages and made it even more difficult for adult males to support families.[39] Union recognition was an even more explosive demand. During the 1917 strike over the right of Saint John plumbers and steamfitters to control those working on union sites, an employer's summer home had been burned down, a man accused of strike-breaking had been killed on the street, and several strikers had been arrested for intimidation.[40] In 1918 Saint John was again in an uproar over the lockout of unionizing police.[41] Pictou miners, steelworkers, and car workers fought for union recognition and in 1918 united behind their own version of the OBU, a monster Federation of Labor representing about five thousand men. The refusal of the employers to recognize this massive federation sparked a strike in April.[42]

The region's 'red years,' 1919 and 1920, were times of millennial fervour and excitement. Crowds flocked to hear news of the Russian Revolution, broadcast at meeting after meeting by Roscoe Fillmore, a prominent activist in the Socialist Party of Canada whose career suggested the revived fortunes of the left in the region. Fillmore had been thoroughly demoralized by the war, and particularly, one suspects, by the cracks it opened in the Socialist Party of Canada in the region (Fred Hyatt and Colin McKay of Saint John were merely the most prominent local Socialist Party members to succumb to patriotism). Reactivated by the Russian Revolution, Fillmore, who would later travel to Siberia to help build Soviet horticulture, spread the Bolshevik message wherever he could. In Amherst, in February 1919, he twice addressed large audiences on the topic 'The Truth about Russia.'[43]

It was in Amherst, in fact, that the purest expression of the hopes and dreams of 1919 blossomed. The organizational forms were the most experimental. The Amherst Federation of Labor, known locally as the

OBU, grouped together unions of various kinds and bargained collectively with all the town's major employers. On 19 May 1919 workers at Canadian Car and Foundry struck for the eight-hour day and recognition of the federation. This action was endorsed by the other units of the labour centre, and the town of Amherst skidded to a stop with a three-week general strike.[44] Amherst workers demonstrated their support for the OBU in June 1919 when the Amherst Federation of Labor voted to affiliate with the OBU by a majority of 1185 to 1.[45] The decision to rally to an alternative vision of industrial order – beyond craft organization – suggests the extent to which Amherst workers had constructed a new framework for seeing their problems and were willing to experiment with new methods for solving them. To the large majority of Amherst workers, this new vision and its new tactics brought at least temporary success. As a result of the strike, most employees were granted a shorter workday with no reduction in wages.[46]

At its height the workers' revolt fused economic demands and political radicalism. In 1920 Amherst men and newly enfranchised women combined with Springhill's working-class movement to elect Archie Terris – an Independent Labor Party candidate and Springhill miner – as their member of the provincial assembly. The experiment of mixing politics with union work usually took the form of a labourism sufficiently vague and flexible to incorporate both pre-war members of the Socialist Party of Canada and temporarily disillusioned adherents of the traditional political parties. Hitherto intermittently organized and politically marginal, labourists mounted a serious struggle for power during the 'red years.'

Independent labour parties (ILPs) were locally based and eventually loosely affiliated with one another within New Brunswick and Nova Scotia. Labour candidates did quite well in the 1917 election. The most complete breakthrough came in Cape Breton where a party established in November 1917 achieved municipal success in New Waterford, Sydney, and Glace Bay the following year. The transformation was most complete in Glace Bay: in 1917 there was one coal miner on town council; by 1919 the same council was composed of two machinists and seven coal miners.[47] The provincial ILP was launched at the January 1919 founding convention of the Nova Scotia Federation of Labor. By mid-April 1920 labourists had concluded an alliance with the politicized farmers and were searching for common ground with the veterans' movement. In the provincial election held on 27 July 1920, the Farmer-Labour-Soldier ticket swept Cape Breton County, and three Cape Breton labourists and one Cumberland County Labor Party supporter (out of ten labour candidates) sat among the eleven Farmer-Labour supporters to make up the official opposition. There were municipal breakthroughs in Pictou County and Halifax. Provincial labour success in New Brunswick was concentrated in the north, in Moncton and in Saint John. The Moncton Labor Party, formed in 1919, achieved considerable municipal success and prided itself on a slate carrying a French-speaking candidate.[48] Labour parties also appeared in Saint John, Albert County, Newcastle, and Sackville.[49]

What did all this labour party activism represent? In New Brunswick local labour parties emerged piecemeal, in some cases (as in Saint John) building on extensive pre-war experience in struggles for factory and workers' compensation legislation. They adopted the general framework of the political program announced by the Trades and Labor Congress of Canada in 1917, but added their own emphases. The overall orientation of the party in the 1920 provincial election was towards concrete immediate matters, with stress given to such practical questions as the storing of food products, sanitary plumbing, and free school books.[50] Nova Scotia labourism had a different, more radical flavour. The party always represented the distinct, competing, and shifting perspectives of socialists, labourites, and the traditional Liberal-Labour coalition. Until the formation of the Nova Scotia ILP, the various labour parties all interpreted the TLC program in their own idiosyncratic ways. By 1920, however, the party had evolved its own highly original interpretation of socialism. Its election manifesto began with the assumption that the first duty of the state was to ensure proper shelter, food, and clothing for the people; it also advocated more radical guild socialist ideas: housing construction by workers' guilds, state-encouraged cooperatives, workers' democracy in industry, and proportional representation in Parliament.[51]

Moderate and conservative trade unionists were caught up in the excitement and joined with socialists and reformers in an imprecise but compelling vision of a better day heralded by the local labour parties. Labourists did not emphasize the expropriation of capital or the redistribution of wealth or property. Rather they demanded, rather naively, that labour be given its fair share of political power. The message was even more cautious among some at the local level. The Pictou County ILP embraced a platform with which many workers in the Liberal Party could identify.[52] Moderates and conservatives, with links to existing political parties, could accept vague labourist demands for 'justice' and 'equality.' Radicals could use the Labor Party as a vehicle for disseminating socialism. Many rank-and-file workers also experienced the party as a social institution by attending its numerous dances, basket socials, mock parliaments, and lectures.

Labourism's explicitly political tactics were limited, but its cultural and intellectual activities reached beyond social democracy in an attempt to remould the opinions of the working class. Labour's electoral campaigns thus drew in a wide range of issues – housing, medical care, women's rights, temperance, public transit – and analysed them from a class perspective. The establishment of a vigorous and combative alternative working-class press represented the clearest attempt to articulate a distinctive view of the world. Labour papers such as the *Labor Leader* (Sydney), the *Union Worker* (Saint John), the *Citizen* (Halifax), the *Eastern Federationist* (New Glasgow), and *Workers' Weekly* (Stellarton) were all-important in putting labour's viewpoint before the public. This had a special significance in the Maritimes, for outside the larger centres, where newspapers dwelled on the labour revolt at length, often sensationalizing its radical aspects, the local press tended to understate the extent of labour unrest in the interests of preserving small-town harmony.[53] In light of geographic distances and an uncooperative local press, communication among community-based labour parties was remarkable. H.H. Stuart was among those who brought experience and broad contacts to the new movement. The New Brunswick-based school principal and ILP stalwart had helped form a pre-war branch of the Socialist League in Cape Breton, had acted as editor of the *Union Advocate* in Newcastle between 1907 and 1910, had sat on the Newcastle town council from 1911 to 1919, and had been a member of the Socialist Party of Canada until 1916.[54] Similarly, the temporary relocation to Moncton of blacklisted Halifax labour alderman E.J. Rudge after the 1920 Halifax Shipyards strike probably assisted the city's already dynamic labour movement to adopt such innovations as the institution of Labour Open Forums.[55]

Labourism could at times seem organizationally inchoate and ideologically confused, but in this time and context it could also represent a profoundly productive pluralism, a discursive context within which identities and subject-positions could be both distinctive and combined with each other in a broad-left alliance. Here labourism was symptomatic of the most interesting aspect of the revolt from the Maritime perspective, namely its tendency to break down 'natural' social divisions and categories. A good example was the unprecedented spread of unrest to middle-class occupations. In Moncton local nurses addressed the local trades council requesting its cooperation in an organizational drive. Public school teachers were successful in forming unions and making demands on their government employers. Teachers in Fredericton and Prince Edward Island received salary increases after setting strike dates. Rarely did professional organizations resort to a work stoppage, although teachers at Prince of Wales College in Charlottetown were victorious after a two-week strike in October 1920. With the active support of the miners, the less socially elevated clerks who worked for Dominion Coal mounted a major struggle for better wages, and tried to join the UMW. Similarly, clerks at Dominion Iron and Steel Company were assisted by members of the Amalgamated Association of Iron, Steel and Tin Workers.[56] Although professionals were cautious in adopting the language of labour, the strike and the principle of solidarity clearly had appeal far beyond the working-class base. Among the prominent middle-class figures recruited to the radical movement were A.T. McKay, a Pictou County lawyer, and Joe Wallace, a leading Halifax Liberal and future Communist poet. In the buoyant years of 1919 and 1920, middle-class activists were not 'experts' to whom workers deferred, and they were not necessarily moderates. They gravitated to a working-class counter-hegemony and worked as 'organic' intellectuals of what appeared to be the emerging dominant class. Only later would traditional middle-class intellectuals begin to re-establish hegemony over workers in the populist Maritime Rights movement.

An equally striking example of the boundary-breaking originality of the early years of the labour revolt was the prominence given to women. Women in the region composed less than 15 per cent of wage earners.[57] Most of women's labour was hidden in the household and in petty commodity production, especially farming and fishing. In spite of their limited numbers, female industrial workers were mobilized in the general labour upsurge of 1919. In Truro and Amherst, women were prominent in textile mills and played an active role in the union. Amherst employees of Stanfield's struck in April 1920, the third time within three years, in reaction to an unfair dismissal.[58] In New Glasgow female wage earners formed their own branch within the Federation of Labor. In May 1919 unorganized 'girls' employed in Moirs' chocolate works in Halifax struck successfully for the eight-hour day. The following May, women box makers at the same company struck for higher wages.[59] The labour revolt also affected the more numerous female workers in the service sector. Clerks in both New Glasgow and industrial Cape Breton, some of them women, organized unions, and those in Cape Breton conducted a major strike against Dominion Coal. Halifax waitresses struck in October 1920 to support a provincial minimum wage.[60] Perhaps most remarkably, domestic servants in Sydney attempted to organize, and apparently even went on strike over low wages.[61]

Just as most men participated in the labour revolt as married men with the heavy responsibility of supporting a family, most women participated not as paid labourers but as workers' wives. Running parallel to efforts to organize women as workers were attempts to organize women as spouses. Such organizations as the Women's Auxiliary of the Brotherhood of Locomotive Engineers, organized in Truro in May 1919, reinforced and extended workplace loyalties into the home.[62] These loyalties were important because wives and children were often situated as pawns in the midst of industrial strife. During the Amherst general strike the *Daily News* stood on both sides of the fence by claiming that families needed a quick settlement while admitting that one of the problems addressed by the strike – long hours – 'infringed on family life.'[63] In fact, the support of wives was regarded as critical to the success of the strike by its organizers. 'The women were the best stickers among the fighters in the present struggle,' one Amherst leader claimed.[64] In a similar manner, the leadership of the Halifax Shipyards strike of 1920 assured the striking men that 'their wives and families know their husbands and fathers are out fighting for better conditions.'[65]

Wives' interests extended beyond their husbands' workplace as women and labourists linked such issues as temperance to women's economic welfare, violence against women within the family, and the immorality of profiteering. The temperance issue was in a sense owned by middle-class progressives, but radicals like J.B. McLachlan did not hesitate to denounce the liquor trade.[66] Nor were female labourists reticent about placing the bone-dry position before a labour movement more inclined to the softer options of government control through licensing. Working-class women organized more independent campaigns on such issues as the quality and price of milk. In 1918, for example, an appeal from 'the Ladies of Springhill' convinced the miners' union to pursue 'the milk question' with their town council.[67]

Labourism had an appeal to women that the radical left has seldom been able to duplicate. Joan Sangster has suggested that labourism could complement maternal feminism in such matters as the desire for female minimum-wage law and mothers' pensions.[68] Furthermore, labourists took care to include women in their organizations, platforms, and rhetoric. Bertha Donaldson, one of the first female candidates to seek election to the Nova Scotia House, ran for the Labor Party in Pictou in the 1920 election.[69] The initial program of the Halifax Labor Party included a number of platforms specifically directed towards women such as the promise of political, social, and industrial equality and the guarantee that every child be provided with 'the material necessities of life, medical supervision, and unlimited education until *it* becomes self-supporting'[70] (emphasis added). Likewise, as its masthead proudly declared, the Halifax *Citizen* was '[a] Journal Devoted to the Interest of the Working Class – Male and Female.' The labourist world extended beyond the shop floor, the coal mine, the shipyard, and the construction site into the home.

In contrast, the more coherent, if rigid, ideology of the radical left was more likely to locate the class struggle explicitly in the waged workplace at the point of production. This political understanding of a primarily male class struggle was reinforced by definitions of masculinity that were closely tied to the work itself. Steven Penfold has argued that in communities such as the Cape Breton coal towns, where the radical left would find its greatest support, 'masculinity was thought to dispose one naturally toward loyalty to the working class ... [and] miners did not fully integrate the radical efforts of women into their view of class militancy.'[71] The 'soft left' of labourism seems to have given greater prominence to women in its organizations and political statements than did the more radical left of socialists and communists emerging in the cities and in Cape Breton. Elsewhere in Canada a few women played prominent roles in the leadership of the Workers' or Communist Party, but significantly the Maritimes produced no equivalent to Rose Henderson, Annie Buller, or Becky Buhay. This is not to say that women did not participate in the region's radical left. A women's auxiliary was associated with the Halifax Workers' Party and Women's Labor Leagues became powerful radical voices in industrial Cape Breton. Women in Cape Breton took 'hard left' positions – for example, on the question of accepting Soviet relief money and as participants in pickets, demonstrations, and riots.[72] Notwithstanding, these actions could be overlooked in a worldview focused so closely on the male-only mine or mill.

Yet another 'natural' division – the division between country and city – began to erode in 1919 and 1920. The significance of this division in an underdeveloped region can hardly be overstated. Confined to urban, industrialized areas, the regional working-class movement could only be a minority movement in a region in which primary production and rural lifestyles were crucial.[73] The key challenge to be addressed in 1919 and 1920 was the creation of an alliance between rural workers, primary producers, urban workers, and progressive intellectuals.

There were reasons to believe that subordinate classes in the country and the city could find common ground, since they confronted a common economic catastrophe. The region's dependence on primary resource industries made it particularly vulnerable to the post-war tumble in commodity prices. The value of the fisheries in Nova Scotia fell from $15 million in 1919 to less than $10 million in 1921.[74] Added to the instability of collapsing prices was the transition from salt to fresh fish and from inshore to offshore production – a transition that restructured the industry by making it more capital and technologically intensive.[75] In New Brunswick sawmills cut less than half the number of board feet in 1921 as they had in 1915.[76] Like fishing, lumbering was also undergoing pressures other than the decline of market prices. Large tracts of land were being taken over by consolidated pulp and paper companies backed by American and central Canadian capital, a development that increased production levels in northern New Brunswick.[77] Farmers had enjoyed wartime prosperity, but agriculture was also entering a period of capitalist restructuring, highlighted by the extension of potato monoculture under the aegis of merchants' capital in New Brunswick.[78]

Could the post-war revolt reach the countryside? The answer in 1919 and 1920 was deeply ambiguous. Fred Winsor argues that the 1920 extension of workers' compensation to offshore fishers in Nova Scotia, most of them from rural areas, was probably the result of general labour pressure, since the fishers themselves were not sufficiently organized to make such a demand.[79] Perhaps the most moving voices of all in the 'red years' came from the rural areas where workers had long fallen silent in their quiet misery. And perhaps the deepest failure of the working-class movement in 1919 and 1920 was its inability to cement an alliance with primary producers. Here was one boundary that the labour revolt only temporarily and partially crossed.

In the rural Maritimes the largest strikes mounted by waged workers had the character of stirring rebellions by the powerless and unorganized against indignities too long endured. A general strike on the Miramichi started spontaneously at Robinson's Mill in Newcastle in August 1919 and spread throughout the region to include longshoremen who left work to join mill workers. And so, without a union and without an 'outside agitator,' fifteen hundred workers spontaneously and successfully struck for the nine-hour day and the sixty-five-cent hour.[80] But it was Hants County that became a symbol of these rural struggles. In 1919 even these Nova Scotia quarrymen, far removed from the main trade union centres, stood alone no longer. They were pitted against a classically autocratic employer, the Wentworth Company, which had used its domination of company housing and the company store to overturn a 1912 agreement with the international union and lock out its men in April 1918.[81] The strike was marked by a high level of violence. Union men were successful stopping the flow of strike-breakers armed with revolvers, axes, knives, and razors into the quarries, but not before thirty-five men were arrested.[82] One strike-breaker met 'a shower of sticks and stones' from a number of black women sympathetic to strikers and avoided hurting them only because his gun misfired.[83] A demonstration and parade in Windsor were followed by a jury discharging thirty-one of the men and bringing a verdict of 'disagreed' in the case of the remaining four.[84] In the end the quarry workers carried the day, and the strike was won.

It was one thing to extend the struggle to waged workers in the countryside, another to find common ground with the primary producers. There were some indications that labour models could be adopted by primary producers. A 'milk strike' of dairy farmers near Halifax in protest against a reduction by city dairies in the price paid for milk was one such example.[85] By and large, however, primary producers remained outside the reach of the labour movement. Discontented offshore fishers – many of them technically 'co-adventurers' in the schooners that took them to the Grand Banks – turned to rum-running or left the region. Rumours that a wave of trade union organization was poised to sweep up from the United States and transform the Nova Scotia fishery remained unfounded.[86] Dispersed, isolated, often identifying themselves with potent myths of independence, rural fishers and lumbermen proved difficult indeed for urban workers to reach.

Farmers were far better organized, and a political alliance with them was concluded by labour in 1919 in New Brunswick and Nova Scotia. Special mention was made of farmers and veterans in the call for the Pictou County ILP Convention where they were represented by a 'workingman farmer,' perhaps one of the many people in the region who mixed small independent production with waged labour.[87] The foundation of the United Farmers of New Brunswick (UFNB) in January 1918 was in part inspired by the model of farm groups in the West and Ontario. On 27 October 1919 T.W. Caldwell, president of the UFNB in Victoria-Carleton, was elected in a Dominion by-election under the farmer banner. (He would be re-elected in 1921.) In the 1920 provincial election twenty-six UFNB candidates were nominated and six were elected.[88] The foundation of the UFNB was both an importation of an external, Ontario-based model and an indication that domestic class relations in agriculture had changed.

The United Farmers of Nova Scotia (UFNS) emerged from meetings in January 1920, at the close of the convention of the Nova Scotia Agricultural Association. During a meeting in April about three hundred farmers adopted the constitution of the UFNB and the *United Farmers' Guide* of Moncton as the official organ.[89] Farmers also organized on Prince Edward Island and offered three candidates in the 1921 federal election.[90] The positions adopted by the three farmers' movements were moderate, reflecting an influence of like organizations in Ontario and the West that was so strong it may have undermined the local producers' capacity to craft original and indigenous responses to their situation comparable to those evolved by Maritime labour.[91] The 1920 Nova Scotia election was a success for the United Farmers, who nominated sixteen candidates and elected seven.[92] Together with the ILP, the Nova Scotia United Farmers won 30.9 per cent of the popular vote, elected eleven members, and pushed the Conservatives out of the position of official opposition.[93]

Although the labour movement and the farmers did begin to collaborate, and although the Farmer-Labour 'party' had enjoyed considerable success, in a fundamental sense the primary producers represented a problem labour was never successful in understanding. Labour never had a theory of regional transformation or a strategy for the rural producers, and it was here, perhaps, that the weight of conventional trade union assumptions derived from other regions exacted its heaviest toll. Although potentially providing a program founded on working-class hegemony through which a category of 'the people' could have been naturalized and radicalized, the Farmer-Labour formula in fact left both parties in the coalition autonomous, thereby encouraging not their organic unity but rather a growing sense of their irremediable differences. Had the massive organization of workers in 1919 and 1920 encompassed certain of the more dependent primary producers, such as the fishers, and crystallized in a different structure, the rural–urban divide might have been overcome.

The standings in provincial legislatures give us one measure of the impact of Farmer-Labour ideas at the end of the decade. In New Brunswick two Labourists and nine United Farmers were elected in 1920, in a house dominated by twenty-four Liberals and thirteen Conservatives.[94] In Nova Scotia Farmer-Labour, an uneasy alliance of oppositional interests, formed the opposition with four Labour members and seven Farmers, in a House made up of thirty Liberals and just two Conservatives. This was an impressive indication of how far the labour revolt had carried into politics, yet it was misleading as a sign of producer–worker unity. The third-party opposition in New Brunswick was inchoate and rudderless, and the more developed opposition in Nova Scotia was still a marriage of convenience that could easily fall apart with the emergence of an issue on which farmers and workers had different class interests.[95]

No balanced account of the vibrant years from 1917 to 1920 can fail to note both weaknesses and strengths in the popular movement. The weaknesses were the clear and predictable consequences of the region's particular social and economic history, including political fragmentation, the gulf between industrial centres and resource hinterlands, the paternalist nexus, and the different subject-positions of men and women. What seems remarkable were the achievements of the popular movement. Age-old obstacles to effective popular mobilization had been weakened and traditional divisions eroded, while new alliances had been conceptualized and, to some extent, transformed into political realities. Then, slowly at first and then with remorseless speed, the tide turned against the working-class movement.

A Crisis of Labourism, 1920–1922

The recession that hit the Maritime provinces so severely in the 1920s was first evident in the late spring of 1920. The collapse in the price of primary products was reinforced by an economic downturn that brought construction and manufacturing to a virtual halt and created high levels of unemployment. In the coalfields loss of St Lawrence markets, competition from other producing areas and fuel sources, and an extravagant merger placed the industry in crisis.[96] Communities outside the coal towns were also devastated by this economic crunch. In 1922–23 the shipyard at East River in Pictou, which had employed five hundred men, was dismantled. In April 1921 amalgamation within the Canadian National Railway cost over six hundred men their jobs in the Moncton shops. Sydney Mines lost its steel mill in a similar rationalization of the Nova Scotia steel industry.[97]

Across the region the economic crisis meant wage reductions and the lengthening of hours. Workers had known economic recessions before, but nothing on this scale since the 1870s. An effective response to deindustrialization eluded them. Strikes had worked brilliantly at a time of labour scarcity, but now seemed only to hasten the pace at which capital was closing factories and mines. Many workers faced an unpleasant choice: they could relinquish the gains they had made over the past decade, or they could leave. As early as 1919 workers in certain pockets were turning to the traditional remedy: outmigration.[98] The post-war slump in Sydney prompted hundreds of young men, including the leader of the steelworkers, to seek employment in the West, Halifax, and other areas.[99] Throughout the region there was a rapid decline in the number of trade unionists. In 1922 the total membership reported by 172 unions in the region was twenty thousand, only half the figure reported three years before.[100]

Workers who a year before had struck for increases and shorter hours now confronted wage reductions and lay-offs. A minor disagreement at the Amherst woollen mill gave management an opportunity to close the mill 'for repairs,' at the same time as the town's moulders were driven by the threat of a shutdown into an open-shop arrangement.[101] On the Miramichi the Fraser Companies simply closed their mill shortly before Christmas 1920 and posted a notice that it would reopen under a 20 per cent wage reduction. It did so the following June.[102] Some workers fought back. In the winter of 1921 pulp, sulphite, and paper mill workers in Chatham struck to prevent a decrease in wages and the reintroduction of the ten-hour day throughout the northern part of the province. Such conflicts persisted into 1924.[103]

In the period after 1920 strikes were much less common and generally aimed at defending workers against wage reductions. Of the eight strikes recorded by the Department of Labour in 1922, the four largest – the massive province-wide coal strike, the weavers' strike in Saint John, the tailors' strike in Charlottetown, and the plumbers' strike in Fredericton – were sparked by attempts to reduce wages. In not one case did the workers win a clear victory. In 1924 five of seven strikes – all in coal-mining communities – were caused by employers' attempts to discharge workers. Only one of these strikes ended in victory for the workers. Clearly and emphatically, the initiative had passed from labour to its opponents.

Bourgeois hegemony was reconstituted in company unions and corporate welfare schemes. Workers in the Saint John Sugar Workers' Union, who struck in October 1919, were simply informed that the company would not recognize outside (that is, independent) unions.[104] A group insurance plan was established in 1920 by the Cosmos Cotton Mill of Yarmouth, and in September 1919, following a strike at the St Croix cotton mill, the workers were offered a profit-sharing plan as part of the settlement.[105] In 1920 the Marysville cotton mill offered workers supervised recreation with a company athletic director appointed in 1920; workers not interested in sport were invited to attend the local movie theatre, also thoughtfully provided by Canadian Cotton.[106]

Imperial Oil's massive new refinery at 'Imperoyal,' located on the shores of Halifax Harbour, was another integrated attempt to apply a corporate welfare policy. Residential, educational, health, recreation, and transportation needs were all met by the company on site. On the subject of labour relations, an admiring contemporary reported, '[There is] no labour unrest or dissatisfaction – the scale of wages is generous and adequate, and the general atmosphere of the place radiates peace and goodwill.' Imperoyal established an industrial representation plan under which each craft annually elected representatives to a board that comprised an equal number of company appointments and was responsible for the resolution of employee grievances and matters relating to wages and working conditions.[107]

Company unionism and a revived paternalism were potent weapons turned against the working-class movement. So too was the anti-red campaign, which steadily gained in influence and venom as the 1920s progressed.[108] J.B. McLachlan's unsuccessful attempt to win a Cape Breton seat in the 1921 federal election was probably frustrated in part by a campaign of anti-red hysteria, as well as by the brazen forgery of a letter that misrepresented his position in internal District 26 affairs. (It is telling that McLachlan still managed to carry the industrial area of the riding.)[109] Labour candidates in Moncton and Saint John–Albert, Northumberland, and Halifax were also defeated in 1921. Attempts at cooperation between Farmer and Labour groups in the political sphere were generally unsuccessful. In the 1921 federal election, labour candidates formed a Farmer-Labour ticket in Westmorland and Saint John-Albert, hoping to reap the labour support in the urban centres; Farmer candidate A.E. Trites of Moncton and F.A. Campbell (street railwayman and president of both the Saint John Trades and Labor Council and the Union Bus Company) lost their deposits.[110]

What had been a labourist consensus – admittedly one masking profound differences – disintegrated under the twin pressures of general socio-economic crisis and internal factionalism. Outmigration not only had a generally demoralizing effect, but removed key labour radicals from the region. Factionalism intensified as a number of labour radicals turned to communism and their opponents to business unionism.

Halifax in 1919 and early 1920 could boast of a labour movement that stood comparison with Cape Breton's in terms of militancy, organization, and radicalism.[111] Then, in fifty-two short days in 1920, the world of Halifax labour came crashing down. In the largest and most important strike in the city's history, two thousand industrial workers at the Halifax Shipyards were taught a bitter lesson in the new regional realities.[112] The shipyard workers were defeated by an unusually hard-nosed employer, Roy Wolvin, in the first of his celebrated appearances in regional labour history. They were thwarted by the courts, in the first application of a sweeping general injunction against picketing.[113] They were also defeated by the inability of the rest of the labour movement to grasp sufficiently the signal importance of this strike, despite the best efforts of shipyard workers (duly recorded by the RCMP's spy) to persuade the local labour council to declare a general sympathetic strike.[114] Yet what contributed most to their loss was the sudden and catastrophic collapse of their ability to exert economic pressure on the employer. In a sense Halifax labour never recovered from this debacle in 1920, and down to 1925 remained helpless, polarized, and weak. The central problem it confronted after 1920 was the organization of the unemployed.[115] In May 1922 the Labor Party lurched to the left and affiliated with the Workers' Party of Canada (the public face of the underground Communist Party of Canada). Ultimately, the Communists would achieve power within the local labour council, but in a city whose labour movement had been reduced to a mere shadow of its former glory, their victory was a hollow one indeed.[116]

While the Halifax Shipyards strike was the turning point for the broad regional movement, labour did not readily admit defeat. In June 1921 street railway workers in Saint John struck over the wages and introduction of one-man cars. The 230 employees accepted the decision of the conciliation board but their employer, the New Brunswick Power Corporation, locked out all employees, replaced the union men, and refused any further negotiation. Striking workers led by F.A. Campbell started their own bus company, which operated into the winter of that year in order to compete with the city streetcars. Both the weakness and tenacity of labour's position was demonstrated in the Department of Labour reports, which reported regularly through to December 1925 that the strike had never lapsed.[117]

The Miners' Armageddon, 1922–1925

The restoration of bourgeois hegemony in the coalfields proved, predictably, to be a much tougher assignment. In Saint John and Halifax the flame of 1919 had sputtered out by 1920–21, but in the coalfields it burned brightly, defiantly on. Unable to tame the coal miners in 1920, the coal companies were forced to concede a contract (called the Montreal Agreement) that preserved the miners' wartime wage gains. Yet this first district-wide agreement between the UMW and the coal companies was not a clear-cut victory. The one-year contract traded away the right to strike during the life of the agreement in exchange for a favourable wage settlement.[118] Furthermore, grievances would not be heard if miners suspended work. Problems not resolved by the union executive and the company superintendent were to go to binding arbitration. While many rank-and-file miners saw in these clauses a threat to their independence, the union gambled that relatively high wages, union recognition, and the check-off of union dues would more than make up for the loss of local autonomy. As later conceded by J.B. McLachlan, the miners' most influential leader, even the wages provision, seemingly the most attractive aspect of the deal, left the workers unprotected against reductions in rates affecting a wide range of mining work and allowed the coal company to lay off 'surplus' miners at will.[119] The owners' desire for industrial stability aimed directly at the spontaneous, unofficial work stoppages that had long characterized work relations in the mines.[120] This concession represented the beginnings of a crucial development within the miners' movement, namely, the gradual substitution of the contract for rank-and-file democracy.

The Montreal Agreement was thus partly an impressive victory, in which miners defied the wage-cutting logic of the recession, and partly a subtle and far-reaching accommodation that ultimately proved to be the undoing of the UMW's radical left. The expiration of the first Montreal Agreement on 31 December 1921 precipitated the coal miners' struggle in the spring and summer of 1922 – the last, brilliant flash of the labour revolt – in the sense that, in the coalfields at least, many workers still thought in terms of going on the offensive against capital.

By the end of 1921 it was clear that the company intended massive wage reductions and the abolition of local contracts. In January 1922 a conciliation board recommended a 30 per cent wage reduction, which a pithead vote rejected. An attempt to work out a compromise divided the District Executive, with three out of four senior officers believing that the deal was the best obtainable under the circumstances. Their extraordinary will to fight, not to mention a remarkable ingenuity and cunning, allowed some Cape Breton miners to meet the proposed wage reduction with a cutback in production, a form of direct action critics denounced as unmanly and unworthy of British subjects. The coal miners proved to be exceptions in that, when all around them workers were making substantial concessions to capital, they were successful in limiting the extent of the concession demanded by the British Empire Steel Company (Besco).[121]

Yet, at the same time, District 26 exemplified a regional pattern of class fragmentation that went well beyond the left–right splits on the executive. As unemployment worsened, locals began to demand that jobs be restricted to men from their own area. Further undermining the unity of the District was the widespread feeling that the agreement accepting rates below the 1921 level was a betrayal. Because the District Executive had favoured a compromise, it fell into disrepute. After months of applying an ingenious strike-on-the-job strategy, District 26 struck on 15 August 1922. The troops arrived soon afterwards. The agreement negotiated by the provincial government restored some of the reduced wages and dropped the 'peace obligation' from the two-year contract. Interpretations of these developments varied within the District. McLachlan's strike-on-the-job policy was not generally adopted and, at least in some areas, did little to diminish the feeling that the union had betrayed the membership. After McLachlan and Dan Livingstone, the two leading leftists, joined the Workers' Party of Canada in 1922, there was also a sharper ideological cleavage within the District, although 'left' and 'right' issues could be significantly complicated by local loyalties, rank-and-file hostility to any compromise, and the manoeuvres of ousted UMW bureaucrats to get back into office.

The battle between labourists and revolutionaries in District 26 came to a climax at its June 1922 convention in Truro. President Robert Baxter appealed desperately to the lost labourist consensus, expressing bemusement at 'elements within our own ranks ... inspired or hypnotized by the rhetoric of some impractical person or persons, who persuade themselves to be able to revolutionize after the fashion of Lenin.' No, he truly could not understand the angry, resolute mood of the convention. It voted in favour of a notorious resolution put forward by Delegate A.A. McKay, who represented Local Union 4530. It is customary to quote only the thunderous conclusion of this famous resolution; here we provide a more complete (and unedited) version:

If the miners of Nova Scotia must now accept a thirty per cent cut in their wages and almost a fifty per cent cut in the available working time, thus plunging them into the direst poverty what is going to happen to us when the 600,000 striking miners in the United States go back to work? If a super abundance of coal NOW spells wage cuts, idle time and poverty what in heaven's name shall happen to us when the super abundance of coal is augmented by the labors of 600,000 more miners than are now employed?

Keeping in mind the present state of the coal business, the poverty into which our people have been sunk, and the grudging and clownish efforts of the Government to bring relief, two ways are open for the mine workers of this Province to follow:

a) Accept the present conditions with all their humiliation and poverty, and repudiate the sacred obligations which every sire owes to his son; or

b) Reject and fight with all the power that is in us the present conditions and make one bold attempt to hand down to our children something better than a slave's portion.

Believing that this convention shall accept the last of these alternatives your committee proposes the following policy for the adoption of this convention:

a) No contract shall be signed by the officers of this district which does not carry with it the wage rate that prevailed in December 1921.

b) That this convention now hold out its hand to any and all workers in Canada, and declare it is prepared to sign an agreement with any other organized body of workers, such as agreement to cover

(1) an obligation on each party to the agreement to do their utmost to create one united front of all the workers in Canada. In the first instance this invitation is extended to the coal miners in the west

(2) Such agreements to cover the joint action to be taken to secure for the workers of this country a living, such action to be taken either with or without the consent of the Government.

(3) Over the heads of Governments we appeal to all soldiers, and minor law officers that they join with us in our attempt to secure for our class and their class, the working class of Canada, a living and free access to all the means of life in this country. To all soldiers and minor law officers we appeal, and when you are ordered to shoot the workers, don't do it. When you are asked to arrest the workers, don't do it, when you are asked to spy on the workers, don't do it. But rather use your position and all the facilities your position affords you to help the workers in their mass fight against all the exploiters of labour.

4) The Dist. No. 26, U.M.W. of A., at once apply for membership in the Red

Internationale [*sic*] of Trades Unions and that a delegate be appointed from this convention to represent us at next convention of the Red International of Trade Unions held in Moscow.

5) That we proclaim openly to all the world that we are out for the complete overthrow of the capitalist system and capitalist state, peaceable if we may, forceable if we must, and we call on all workers, soldiers, and minor law officers in Canada to join us in liberating labour.[122]

This remarkable document shows us the strength of a radicalism fused with down-to-earth, economic concerns: from consideration of the immediate problems of survival in the coalfields and the 1921 wage cuts, we pass swiftly to an urgent call for a global revolution. The resolution's weakness as rhetoric (no really rousing manifesto can successfully incorporate the phrase 'minor law officers'!) suggests its roots in the daily struggles of rank-and-file miners. The working-class language nevertheless conveys a sophisticated sense of the balance of class forces in 1922. Yet also inscribed within this extraordinary resolution are indications of the radical left's underlying strategic weakness. Alliances are sought in the West, but there is nothing concrete for workers and primary producers closer to home. And 'the sacred obligations which every sire owes to his son' takes us back to patriarchal traditions of fathers teaching their sons how to mine; we are in a single-gender discourse of protest, in which women do not really exist. There was revolutionary breadth but also an unconscious narrowness of vision in this most famous document of the Maritime labour revolt.

The resolution that helped to catapult District 26 – the region's largest and most powerful union – into virtually permanent crisis from 1922 to 1925 gave rise to a number of key questions. How could a trade union that negotiated with employers on a regular basis simultaneously be a revolutionary movement? How could it intend to survive within an increasingly centralized and conservative international union? Was the lurch to the left a Communist gamble that the international revolution was imminent? If so, why prepare for it within the UMW? For all its bravery and its eloquence, the 'left turn' of 1922 seems to have lacked a strategic sense. If it was part of a strategy to found a separate revolutionary union or join the OBU, neither option was pursued by the left leadership. (Indeed, McLachlan would advocate continued support for the UMW long after other Communists had opted for dual unionism.) Probably a majority of miners were unable to negotiate as rapid and extreme a turn to the left as that contemplated on 25 June 1922. Outside Cape

Breton, the left turn was not understood. Springhill in particular became a bastion of UMW traditionalism.[123]

The demise of the UMW revolutionaries, from the left turn of 24 June 1922 to the revocation, of the District 26 charter on 17 July 1923, is usually portrayed in terms of stereotypically earnest and radical Nova Scotia miners confronting a brutal, distant, and arrogant American union leadership.[124] In fact, the idea of lifting the District charter seems to have come from the miners themselves. On 30 August 1922 the Springhill local took the fateful step of demanding the resignation of the executive officers, and asked John L. Lewis, the international president, to take over the District.[125] Indeed, there was throughout the period of the left turn considerable opposition to the left executive, especially President Red Dan Livingstone and Secretary-treasurer J.B. McLachlan. There is little reason to suppose that District 26 was converted, as a body, to revolutionary politics. Both a restive rank and file and the deposed 'right' viewed the left executive with some suspicion, the first because it had 'sold out' the miners by accepting a wage reduction in 1922, and the latter because it opposed communism and wanted its jobs back within the UMW machine. Some responsibility for their demise rests with the left leaders themselves.

By raising the idea of affiliating with the Red International, the radicals threw down a gauntlet before the leadership of the UMW. But did they themselves perceive it that way? The tone of McLachlan's letter to John L. Lewis in early January 1923 was that of someone who believed he shared at least some assumptions in common with his correspondent. Asked to define the objectives of the Red International, McLachlan wrote that the program was one of 'direct revolutionary mass action of the workers of the world for the complete overthrow and ending of all capatalist [*sic*] exploitation of Labour.' Capitalist societies, McLachlan maintained, now had 'unprecedented POWER' to overproduce and 'unprecedented IMPOTENCE' to sell these goods, a combination that meant unemployment 'midst of plenty and wars and mass murder of the workers between Capitalist countries for possession of such markets as are to be had.'[126] These were the words not of someone writing to an arch-enemy, but of someone who hoped to persuade a potential ally (if not Lewis personally, then at least others on the UMW Executive).

One is also struck by the unpreparedness of Red Dan Livingstone when he was brought before the UMW International Executive Board to explain the position of District 26. It was a fierce, unrelenting interrogation by people who sensed a threat to their power and who had already exercised discipline over districts in western Canada and Kansas. Asked about the Red International, Livingstone responded that he did not 'know very much about [it].' But there was an eloquent, magnificent courage in his proud stand before the UMW bureaucrats. 'I told your International President when I came here first that I was a radical,' he proclaimed. 'I am a radical yet. I have been a radical since I was that high. I have seen the beast of capitalism in all its horrors before I was nine years old. I hate the capitalist class of this and all countries, and I would kill capitalism tomorrow.'[127] Courage notwithstanding, there was arguably little strategy. How did Livingstone expect the international union and John L. Lewis, that Republican exponent of industrial legality, to react to so strong a challenge to their underlying principles? Livingstone evidently saw no contradiction between the UMW's doctrine of the 'sanctity of the contract,' and the Red International's view of collective bargaining as something 'propagated by the opportunists of all countries,' and as 'nothing more than an armistice.' Philip Murray, vice-president of the International Executive Board, declared that it was 'ridiculous to the extreme' that Livingstone, a UMW district president, 'should come before the Members of this International Executive Board seeking affiliation with another organization that is seeking the destruction of the Union that [he] belong[s] to.'[128] The board's handling of Livingstone was aggressive and brutal, but there was a logic in its position. How could one enjoy the benefits of UMW respectability, founded on the sanctity of the contract, and at the same time embrace the revolutionary socialism offered by Moscow?

In sum, the 'left turn' in District 26 was something of a pyrrhic victory for the socialist miners. Although it showed that the ideals of revolutionary socialism still had a mass base, it also set in motion a destructive polarization within the union, alienated large numbers of miners who had received no warning of the proposed affiliation with the Red International, and brought District 26 into direct conflict with the parent international. If, as David Frank suggests, the affiliation proposal was 'a flamboyant, largely symbolic gesture,'[129] rather than a serious proposition (a suggestion that seems to be supported by Livingstone's vagueness during his stormy interview with the executive board and by McLachlan's subsequent willingness to withdraw the idea), it was nevertheless a damaging development – one that advised the UMW's conservative leadership that District 26 posed a threat and left the District quite defenceless in the event of a decision by the international union's bureaucracy to defend itself. More generally, the 'peace obligation' –

which was dropped from the two-year contract of 1922 but reinstated in the highly controversial agreement of 1924 – promoted the centralization of power within the union by removing from local unions the right to go on strike over day-to-day issues. While the District was in radical hands, there was little risk that this diminution of rank-and-file power would lead to a mushrooming of bureaucracy, but the odds against the radicals holding their position were huge. District 26 was part of an international union that was dedicated to the 'sanctity of the contract,' highly bureaucratic in its procedures, and, under the autocratic leadership of John L. Lewis, fully committed to accommodation with capital in the interests of rationalization.

The 'left turn' within District 26 from 24 June 1922 to the suspension of District autonomy on 17 July 1923 was the high point of the labour revolt in the region. Containing and ultimately reversing this movement was the task of capital, the state, and the international union. That the conventional forms of unionism could, at least in the short term, shelter a far more radical concept of labour strategy was proved by the coal miners' heroic efforts to support the Sydney steelworkers in their battle for a trade union. (One official from the Department of Labour who visited Sydney in March 1923 reported that the miners and steelworkers appeared to have formed 'something like a local One Big Union.')[130] Rejecting a scheme for a 'plant council,' floated by the notorious Roy Wolvin, the president of Besco, the steelworkers pressed for their own union throughout early 1923. They encountered the gamut of anti-labour tactics: an intensification of spying, the blacklisting of union militants, the expansion of the provincial police with a view to 'eradicating Bolshevism,' and, in late March 1923, a pre-emptive wage increase. By late June the company had rejected all the union's demands and there ensued a vigorous battle for control of the plant and coke ovens. On 1 July 1923 – 'Bloody Sunday' – a mounted squadron of provincial police attacked a crowd on Victoria Road in Whitney Pier, the working-class neighbourhood adjoining the steel plant. The following day a mass meeting called by the Phalen Local of District 26 resolved that the executive should call a general strike if the provincial police were not withdrawn from Sydney. On 3 July, McLachlan and Livingstone urged all locals to go on strike in sympathy with the steelworkers and in protest against the tactics of the provincial government. That day a sympathetic strike stopped work in the Cape Breton mines.

The state and the international union were not slow to respond. For months the provincial attorney general had been contemplating legal action against the 'reds,' whom hostile factions within the UMW were also planning to overthrow. The state used to its advantage McLachlan's inflammatory letter to UMW locals after Bloody Sunday. McLachlan and Livingstone were arrested, Livingstone turned King's evidence, and only McLachlan was tried, convicted, and sentenced to two years in Dorchester Penitentiary for seditious libel.[131] The international union vindictively used this opportunity to suspend the District's charter, remove its executive officers, and order its members back to work. The steel strike ended on 2 August, without achieving its objectives.

The termination of the steel strike marked the end of the proactive, creative phase of the labour revolt – the phase in which workers took the initiative, made new and far-reaching demands, and sought a different kind of society. Now the initiative clearly resided with the enemies of the left. From mid-1923 to November 1925, the old world of capital and privilege battled the new world of labour and socialism, and won. In 1924 the right-wing leadership of a 'provisional' District 26 won a victory when it managed, over the outraged objections of rank-and-file miners, to ram through a collective agreement that gave the miners a wage increase in exchange for a 'peace obligation'; the end of 100 per cent strikes, which included vital maintenance men; and, perhaps most significant in terms of restoring bourgeois hegemony, the withdrawal of UMW funding for J.B. McLachlan's ultra-radical *Maritime Labor Herald*. Although some of these remarkable provisions were unenforceable, the agreement was a significant victory for the right. A more direct assault on the left was probably behind the burning down of McLachlan's newspaper in September 1924 (it would burn again in 1925). In early 1925 the left succeeded in winning back the District (whose autonomy was officially returned on 10 September 1924), regained the key executive positions (although not with McLachlan or Livingstone, who were banned from holding such office), and won a mass endorsement of 100 per cent strikes. In early 1925 Besco counter-attacked with an explosive proposal to impose a 20 per cent wage reduction. Material force was added to this demand by the company's starving out of militant locals, its eventual restriction of credit at company stores, and its appeal to local civic leaders and authorities to rout Bolshevism once and for all.

In March 1925 District 26 felt compelled to call a strike, the fourth 100 per cent strike in four years. It was to be the most bitter, violent, and destructive strike of all the years of the Maritime workers' revolt. In essence, it was a small civil war, in which whole communities were placed on the front lines of state and corporate violence. The strike was not entirely one-sided. With profound creativity and resourcefulness, workers began to control, under self-management, some of the institutions of civil society. There was a finely honed strategic intelligence at work in the seizure of power plants, which were then run in such a way that the hospital could function, but not the mine pumps. By June the battle for the New Waterford power plant was being waged in earnest. On 11 June 1925 miner William Davis was killed in a battle with company police. There followed two wild weeks of burning and looting during which the wash-house in New Waterford was attacked, along with Besco stores in Caledonia, New Aberdeen, Reserve, Dominion, No. 11, No. 6, and Sydney Mines, and the surface workings at No. 2 colliery. Besco added new demands: the abolition of the check-off, blacklisting of those involved in 'disorderly conduct,' the removal from the union of fifteen hundred men in various job categories, and the end to negotiations with Communists. On 5 August the recently elected Conservative premier offered a six-month contract – a compromise that removed the 1924 wage gains – a royal commission, and a referendum on the check-off. District 26 voted in favour of acceptance. It was a crushing defeat. For five months the workers had been plunged into utter poverty, reduced to relying on Dominion-wide appeals for relief. The socialist demand for a new coal industry structured on entirely different lines, already heavily qualified by UMW labourists and moderates, would be muffled altogether in the ensuing royal commission on the coal industry, which adroitly combined a critique of Besco's intransigence vis-à-vis its employees with support for the underlying logic of the company's wage reductions.[132]

So ended the Maritime workers' revolt, not in jubilant bonfires signalling the destruction of the old, corrupt world of capitalism, but rather in grinding despair, petty betrayals, and state violence that proclaimed the death of the new social order so many had glimpsed, with so much hope, in 1919 and 1920. The defeat of 1925, accompanied as it was by such depths of suffering and violence, was long remembered, although often in sentimental and populist ways that lost the sense of the internal debate and minimized the possibilities of choice. It was widely believed that John L. Lewis had single-handedly betrayed the miners. That Lewis had been in the midst of a drastic campaign for union centralization does merit attention. But Lewis did not invade District 26; he was invited to suspend the District's autonomy by Nova Scotia miners opposed to the left turn. The District's internal dynamic was one of both radicalism and increasing bureaucratization. The key instruments (especially the check-off, shrewdly preserved by the provincial state in 1927, and the abrogation of the local right to strike) that later UMW conservatives were to use against the left were evolved under a left leadership that, for all its courage and creativity, had made serious strategic errors. Perhaps the leftists simply misread the UMW, seeing in the union not the conservative, bureaucratic body it had become, but the animated, militant body they had originally fought for. From the initial flawed choice of a UMW District as a quasi-revolutionary instrument came the tragic confrontations and betrayal of 1923–25, in which the left was devoured by the very organization it had done so much to create.

A Balance Sheet

By 1925 the workers' revolt was over everywhere in the Maritime region. Only a few of its achievements could withstand the reimposition of bourgeois hegemony. Many people left the region, driven out by high unemployment, factory shutdowns, and the decline of the resource sector. Others meekly returned to the old habits of deference and patronage that had chained them in the past. In October 1925, for example, the *Labour Gazette* reported that the employees of James Pender and Co. Ltd., a Saint John–based subsidiary of Besco, 'recently agreed to work extra time each week without pay in order to enable the company to export its products to Jamaica in competition with products from Europe.'[133] Maritime workers began to accept working conditions and wages inferior to those offered elsewhere, on the understanding that if they did not, they would have no work at all.

The workers' revolt of 1917–25 both refutes and confirms the idea of Maritime conservatism. It refutes the suggestion that it is some timeless essence in confirming the notion that it was patiently reconstructed and reimposed in the wake of labour's defeat in the 1920s. Were other outcomes possible? The Maritime terrain is a difficult one for mass organizations on the left. The dispersed, heterogeneous character of the settlement patterns, the sharp cultural and economic divisions between primary producers and wage earners (often bitterly resentful of the rural population's threat to wage levels), the patchwork of ethnic traditions and local identities, at times in bitter conflict[134] – all these (the legacy of the region's eighteenth- and nineteenth-century history) pose obstacles for popular organizations. Neither the labourists nor the radicals seem to have addressed, in a serious and sustained way, the problem of building a counter-hegemonic movement in so divided and heterogeneous a region. There were tantalizing moments – Farmer-Labour cooperation, rural donations of food to the miners – that remained, in the press of events, undeveloped. Ironically, the importance of working with local primary producers was recognized more clearly by the Catholic Church: the Antigonish cooperative movement would later illustrate both the possibilities of social struggle in the countryside and the potential for rural struggles to be undermined by a liberal agenda. But, unlike the pragmatic Catholic Church, both 'lefts' – the labourists of 1919–20 and the radicals of 1920–25 – adopted a somewhat abstractly internationalist approach, rather than developing their own original strategies to cope with regional issues. In truth, neither movement had time to work out an analysis of paternalism or a more subtly crafted radicalism appropriate to the Maritimes. This made them particularly vulnerable to a right-wing regionalist and populist movement that seemed to provide just such an analysis.

The crisis of the 1920s and the rise of class-based movements of opposition loosened the grip of traditional hegemonic strategies, but one could argue that the immediate beneficiaries of the labour revolt were not the workers, but the Conservative proponents of Maritime Rights and regional populism generally. In 1925, in a stunning reversal in provincial politics, the Nova Scotia Conservatives wrapped themselves in the flag of Maritime Rights and gained all but three seats. All through the Maritimes a new conservatism, draped in right-wing populism and based on a perception of regional grievances, took hold. Sponsored particularly by the *Halifax Herald*, this conservative neonationalism was subtle, many-sided, and potent. The great myths of consolation – the myth of the Golden Age and the myth of the Maritimes as an unsophisticated folk society – emerged during this period, along with such cultural symbols as the *Bluenose*. So widespread and systematic was this counter-revolution of ideas that only the most dramatic aspects of the Cape Breton story remained in popular memory.

Under the guise of the Conservative Party, Maritime Rights usurped the labour movement and deftly redirected the focus of discontent. In this discourse of regionalism the enemy was not capital, but rather the non-Maritime big shot. Both the labourists and the socialists might have undermined this powerful revision of social reality had they, at an early stage, developed a regional analysis. But explicitly regional concerns were rarely addressed by either movement. The community focus of labourism and the absence of any real national ties made the post-war labour movement an obvious candidate to incorporate the concerns of Maritime Rights. A labour-dominated Maritime Rights movement could have posed a very substantial challenge to the social order. It might have united workers and primary producers in defence of regionalist objectives. Questions raised by the powerless and having to do with the speed of social change could have been answered more effectively within the language of class.

Instead, labourism was swallowed and radical socialism was marginalized by the resurgent right-wing populism exemplified by Maritime Rights. This was less a question of 'co-opting' leaders than of creating a vivid new subject position, 'the Maritimer,' where once 'the Worker' had stood. True, there were some prominent labour leaders in Maritime Rights, and connections between labour and Maritime Rights clearly strengthened as the 1920s progressed.[135] But more important were the efforts to win over the rank and file of the labour movement as a whole. In the fall of 1924 a Halifax/Dartmouth association for the unemployed, the United Workmen of Nova Scotia, was irrevocably linked with Maritime Rights when H.S. Congdon, the most prominent spokesman of the regional movement, was named treasurer. Shortly thereafter the organization changed its name to the Maritime Progressive Workmen's Association.[136]

The chosen name reminds us of the inability of the region's labour movement to reach out and truly incorporate women. Maritime men may have claimed to desire a new vision of the world, but it was essentially one in which they remained economically, politically, and socially privileged over their mothers, wives, sisters, and daughters. Deindustrialization and new workplace technology fostered a crisis of masculinity, and many working-class men derived comfort and a sense of power, albeit limited, from their ability to support a family. In promoting themselves as breadwinners, men reinforced the role of their wives and mothers as domestic-based consumers, thereby excluding them from class-based movement. Working-class daughters who traditionally composed the most important group of wage-earning women were also alienated as they entered new female job ghettos in retail and clerical work. Given that working-class identity remained largely synonymous with being a man, it was impossible for an all-encompassing class-based movement to persist, particularly in a region where industrial opportunities for women were limited and where the strongest voices of labour were so closely identified with masculinity.[137]

From 1917 to 1925 the Maritimes witnessed the rise and fall of a progressive labour movement, the most important left-wing movement in the region's history. Industrial capitalism prompted a powerful movement of reform, and society appeared to be on the brink of a great renewal. After 1925 attention shifted from utopia to survival. What deindustrialization started, an aggressive right-wing regionalism completed: the marginalization – but never the elimination – of the dream of a new social world. Workers who had once conceived of themselves as progressive members of an industrial society were reduced to begging various levels of government to keep their mines and factories open. Not everything achieved in the labour revolt was lost. Collective bargaining rights were not destroyed in the mines; however bureaucratized, undemocratic, and inwardly focused, industrial trade unions survived in the coalfields, as a limitation to the power of capital and, ultimately, as an inspiration to a later generation of workers. Yet it is fair to measure these partial and limited working-class achievements against the ideal of a new world that suffused the radical 1920s: truly, the old world could not die, and the new world could not be born.

The angel would like to stay, awaken the dead, and make whole what has been smashed. But a storm is blowing from Paradise; it has caught in his wings with such violence that the angel can no longer close them. This storm irresistibly propels him into the future to which his back is turned, while the pile of debris before him grows skyward. This storm is what we call progress.[138]

Notes

Our thanks to David Frank for comments on an earlier draft of this chapter.

1 For an excellent overview of the history of the region in the 1920s, see Frank, 'The 1920s.'
2 Canada, *Census*, 1921, Vol. 1, 3, 245, 360–91.
3 Ibid.; Forbes, *Maritime Rights Movement*, 8–9.
4 Canada, *Census*, 1921, Vol. 4, 10–35.
5 For an analysis, see Samson, ed., *Contested Countryside*.
6 See Latta, 'Labour Aristocracy.'
7 Léger, 'L'évolution des syndicats au Nouveau-Brunswick,' 27–8.
8 See Baker, 'Drawn to Hegemony.'
9 McKay, 'Strikes in the Maritimes,' 3–46.
10 *Herald* (Halifax), 27 December 1915.
11 Ibid., 12 July, 16 October 1918.
12 *Sydney Daily Post*, 11, 18 August, 14 December 1917.

13 *Herald*, 14 February, 11 July, 3 December 1919.
14 *Saint John Standard*, 7 May 1920.
15 *Herald*, 14 May 1919.
16 On the coal miners in the Maritimes, see Cameron, *The Pictonian Colliers*; Frank, 'Class Conflict,' 'Cape Breton Coal Miners,' 'Trial of J.B. McLachlan,' 'Tradition and Culture,' 'Contested Terrain,' 'Election of J.B. McLachlan'; MacEwan, *Miners and Steelworkers*; Macgillivray, 'Military Aid to the Civil Power'; MacIntosh, 'Boys in the Nova Scotia Coal Mines'; McKay, 'Industry, Work, and Community,' 'Provincial Workmen's Association,' 'Realm of Uncertainty'; Mellor, *Company Store*; and Muise, 'Making of an Industrial Community.'
17 UMW Archives (Alexandria, Virginia), President's Correspondence, District 26, 1916–19, J.B. McLachlan to John P. White, 13 October 1916.
18 Angus L. Macdonald Library, St Francis Xavier University, Antigonish, Springhill Local of the Amalgamated Mine Workers of Nova Scotia, Minutes, 10 May, 14 July, 11 August, 6, 13 October 1917.
19 Frank, 'Cape Breton Coal Miners,' 298.
20 UMW Archives, J.B. McLachlan to John P. White, 24 August 1917.
21 Frank, 'Cape Breton Coal Miners,' 307.
22 Forbes, *Maritime Rights Movement*, 40; source is Canada, Dept. of Labour, *Labour Organization in Canada*, 1916, 1920.
23 Forbes, *Maritime Rights Movement*, 40; source is Canada, Dept. of Labour, *Labour Organization in Canada*, 1916 (206–7), 1920. On specific occupational groups, see *Herald*, 24 November 1919 (Sydney policemen); *Herald*, 19 November 1919 (PEI mail carriers); and *Canadian Annual Review*, 1919, 725 (PEI teachers). See also the following local studies: Heron, 'Great War and Nova Scotia Steelworkers'; Lambly, 'Canada's Street Railways'; McKay, *Craft Transformed*; Morton, 'Labourism and Independent Labour Politics'; Reilly, 'Emergence of Class Consciousness' and 'General Strike in Amherst.'
24 *Eastern Federationist* (New Glasgow), 29 March 1919.
25 Robin, *Radical Politics and Canadian Labour*; Bercuson, 'Labour Radicalism and the Western Industrial Frontier'; Pentland, 'Western Canadian Labour Movement.'
26 Seager, 'Minto'; Canada, Dept. of Labour, *Labour Organization in Canada*, 1924, 'Affairs of District 26,' 175–84.
27 *Eastern Federationist*, 11 October 1919; Trueman, 'New Brunswick and the 1921 Federal Election'; McKay, *Craft Transformed*, 69; NAC, RG 27 (Department of Labour, Strikes and Lockouts Files), Vol. 320, Strike 148, Building Trades, Moncton, New Brunswick, May 1920.
28 Heron, 'Great War and Nova Scotia Steelworkers,' 13.

29 Thomas Cantley, MP, Pictou County, quoted in Sandberg, 'Deindustrialization of Pictou County.'

30 How much of the extraordinary breakthrough of 1917–19 should be attributed to Dane is not easily determined. Dane was something of a one-man labour movement. In 1919 he not only organized thousands of workers in Halifax but also investigated conditions at the Eureka Woolen Mills and addressed mass meetings in Cape Breton on the failure of the Eight Hours' Bill. First President of the Nova Scotia Federation of Labor and an AFL organizer, Dane was not a typical representative of Samuel Gompers' trade unionism. Dane positioned himself to the left of McLachlan, whom he severely criticized for having signed a royal commission report that, in Dane's opinion, 'sold out' Pictou County workers. He electrified the Mathers Commission by proclaiming himself to be a 'Bolshevik' at its Nova Scotia hearings. Then, paradoxically, in the fall of 1919 he took a job with the Department of Labour, reportedly as a fair wages officer. For references to Dane, see *Eastern Federationist*, 8 March, 12 and 26 April, 27 September 1919; and Heron, 'Great War and Nova Scotia Steelworkers,' 15.

31 Rose, *Four Years with the Demon Rum*; *Eastern Federationist*, 24 May 1919; *Chronicle* (Halifax), 15 May 1919.

32 *Eastern Federationist*, 26 April 1919.

33 Trueman, 'New Brunswick,' 346; *Daily Times* (Moncton), 10 June 1920.

34 *Eastern Federationist*, 11 October 1919.

35 Trueman, 'New Brunswick,' 72; *Chronicle*, 1 March 1919.

36 Canada, Dept. of Labour, *Labour Organization in Canada*, 1920, 97; *Citizen* (Halifax), 14 January 1921.

37 *Daily Times*, 24 June 1919.

38 Ibid., 25 November 1920; *Citizen*, 10 December 1920.

39 Heron, 'Great War and Nova Scotia Steelworkers,' 22–3.

40 *Saint John Standard*, 21 April 1917; *Herald*, 10 August 1917.

41 Nelles and Armstrong, 'Great Fight for Clean Government,' 55.

42 NAC, RG 27, Vol. 308, Strike 77, 'Steelworkers, New Glasgow, 1918'; Heron, 'Great War and Nova Scotia Steelworkers,' 17–18.

43 Nicholas Fillmore, *Maritime Radical*. On pre-war socialism in the region, see Frank and Reilly, 'Emergence of the Socialist Movement'; Roscoe Fillmore, 'Early Socialism in the Maritimes'; and Chapman, 'Henry Harvey Stuart.'

44 Reilly, 'General Strike in Amherst,' 56.

45 The OBU was also popular among skilled union men in New Glasgow and Maritime railwaymen. According to one charter member of the Firemen's Brotherhood in Moncton, even though the organization was not recognized by the railway authorities, it had the support of the majority in the district.

These were the comments of Charles Lockard. No naive supporter of the syndicalists, Lockard predicted that the OBU would be short-lived, for the 'OBU and the internationalists were checkmating each other.' *Eastern Federationist* 25 October 1919; *Daily Times*, 26 February 1920; Reilly, 'Emergence of Class Consciousness,' 256.

46 Reilly, 'General Strike in Amherst,' 76.

47 Frank, 'Cape Breton Coal Miners,' 161–2; and 'Company Town/Labour Town.'

48 *Daily Times*, 26 January, 7 October 1920, 31 January 1922.

49 Ibid., 3 June, 24 August 1921.

50 *Canadian Annual Review*, 1920, 715.

51 Ibid., 682–3.

52 *Eastern Federationist*, 15 March, 26 April 1919. 'Liberalism will contend with Labor by promulgating a policy more progressive than that advocated by the Union men.' Mr. R. Graham, MLA, Pictou County.

53 For example, the *Sackville Tribune*, only a short distance from Amherst, made no mention of the Amherst general strike until 26 May. The same paper alluded very generally to the national labour revolt in observing, 'There has been a little industrial unrest in Sackville, as well as other parts of Canada, but fortunately everything appears to have been settled to the mutual satisfaction of the employers and employees.' *Sackville Tribune*, 15 May 1919. The stove moulders' struggles in Sackville were, in fact, to become a regional cause célèbre in the early 1920s.

54 Frank and Reilly, 'Emergence of the Socialist Movement,' 91–7; Chapman, 'Henry Harvey Stuart.'

55 *Daily Times*, 24 September 1920.

56 Ibid., 27 January 1920, 7 February 1919; *Canadian Annual Review*, 1919, 725; *Charlottetown Guardian*, 7, 9 October 1920; *Mail* (Halifax), 7 October 1920; NAC, RG 27, Vol. 312, Strike 115, 'Dominion Coal Clerks Strike,' May 1919; Heron, 'Great War and Nova Scotia Steelworkers,' 19.

57 Canada, *Census*, 1921, Vol. 4, 10–35.

58 Reilly, 'General Strike in Amherst,' 77; NAC, RG 27, Vol. 103, Strike 103.

59 Heron, 'Great War and Nova Scotia Steelworkers,' 16; *Eastern Federationist*, 10 May 1919; *Citizen*, 7 May 1920.

60 *Mail*, 13 October 1920, cited in Lambly, 'Towards a Living Wage,' 16.

61 *Eastern Federationist*, 26 April 1919.

62 *Daily News* (Truro), 7 May 1919.

63 *Daily News* (Amherst), 23 May, 2 June 1919.

64 Ibid., 10 June 1919.

65 *Citizen*, 18 June 1920.

66 *Herald*, 19 October 1920: 'I have been actively engaged in the labor movement for the last thirty years, and know of nothing that is better calculated to upset the best efforts of labor men and labor unions than a drinking member.'

67 Springhill Minutes, 5, 12 October 1918.

68 Sangster, *Dreams of Equality*, 19.

69 MacKenzie, 'Farmer-Labour Party,' 98. A second female candidate, Grace McLeod Rogers, was nominated by the Conservatives in the labour centre of Amherst.

70 *Citizen*, 19 September 1919.

71 Penfold, '"Have You No Manhood in You?"' 30.

72 *Ibid.* J.B. McLachlan tended to be relatively sensitive to the inclusion of women in the revolt, or at least realized the important role they played in determining household finances. He even urged they be given the right to vote in UMW contract negotiations. See Frank, 'Miner's Financier.' The financial support of the UMW freed the *Maritime Labor Herald* from the need to attract women and the important advertising dollars that accompanied their readership. The masculine bias could emerge unmeditated by consumer appeals to housewives. As a result, women played a very limited role in the newspaper until the spring of 1924. Readers were addressed as 'working men,' and men's clothing, cars, and pipes dominated the advertised products. The paper's masculine bias was further revealed in such headlines as '"Pappa, We're Hungry" Sobbed Little Children' (8 April 1922). The *Maritime Labor Herald*'s interest in women coincided with the UMW's withdrawal of financial support and also with McLachlan's rise to the position of editor. Suddenly appeals for assistance read 'Workers: Miners, Steelworkers, Housewives' (22 March 1924).

73 See McKay, ed., *Towards a Working-Class Culture*, chapter 2, for a sophisticated contemporary analysis of this issue by the region's leading Marxist theorist, Colin McKay.

74 Canada, *Canada Yearbook, 1922–23* (Ottawa 1924), 'Total Value of Fisheries by Province in the Calendar Years 1917–1921,' 352.

75 Barrett, 'Development and Underdevelopment,' 21; Colpitt, 'Alma, New Brunswick,' 55.

76 Barrett, 'Development and Underdevelopment,' 1; MacNeil, 'United Maritime Fishermen,' 11.

77 Colpitt, 'Alma, New Brunswick,' 73; Parenteau, 'Woods Transformed.'

78 One Nova Scotia farmer noted that the years 1916 to 1920 were 'the only time we ever made much money on the farm.' Cf. Mackenzie, 'Farmer-Labour Party,' 10; Trueman, 'New Brunswick,' 61. Between 1910 and 1921

potato acreage more than doubled in Carleton, Victoria, and Madawaska counties.

79 Winsor, '"Solving a Problem,"' 74–5.

80 *Daily Times*, 21 August 1919.

81 NAC, RG 27, Vol. 315, Strike 205, 'Hants County, 1919.'

82 *Herald*, 21 June 1919.

83 *Hants Journal* (Windsor), 21 May, 25 June 1919.

84 *Windsor Tribune* (Windsor), 23 May 1919; *Herald*, 21, 30 May 1919; NAC, RG 27, Vol. 315, Strike 205, 'Hants County, 1919,' E. McG. Quirk to Hon. G.D. Robertson, 3 June 1919.

85 *Herald*, 1 June 1921.

86 Barrett, 'Development and Underdevelopment,' 73–4.

87 *Eastern Federationist*, 26 April 1919.

88 Trueman, 'New Brunswick,' 29.

89 *Canadian Annual Review*, 1918, 659; 1920, 677.

90 Robb, 'Third Party Experience on the Island.'

91 See Forbes, *Maritime Rights Movement*, 43–51.

92 Rawlyk, 'Farmer-Labour Movement,' 34.

93 Mackenzie, 'Farmer-Labour Party,' iii, 195–8.

94 See Frank, 'The 1920s,' 236–7, 517.

95 *Herald*, 22 May 1920. Farmers and Labour were unable to resolve their differences on the issue of the eight-hour day.

96 Frank, 'Cape Breton Coal Industry'; Forbes, *Maritime Rights Movement*, chapter 4; McKay, *Craft Transformed*, 74–5.

97 Cameron, *Industrial History of New Glasgow District*, 21; Trueman, 'New Brunswick,' 9, 22; Heron, 'Great War and Nova Scotia Steelworkers,' 31.

98 Thornton, 'Out-Migration from Atlantic Canada'; *Eastern Federationist*, 8 March, 6 September 1919.

99 *Eastern Federationist*, 13 September 1919.

100 *Labour Organization in Canada*, 1922, 36.

101 *Herald*, 16 April 1920; *Amherst Daily News*, 25 June 1920.

102 W.G. Stevens to K.G. Christie, RG 27, Vol. 324, File 20 [400]. Emphasis not in the original.

103 *Daily Times*, 24 March 1921, 11 July 1923.

104 NAC, RG 27, Vol. 318, Strike 362.

105 NAC, RG 27, Vol. 317, Strike 355; Lambly, 'Towards a Living Wage,' 43.

106 Pond, *History of Marysville*, 116, 151.

107 *Herald*, 26 March 1920; *Canadian Annual Review*, 1918, 328.

108 *Eastern Federationist*, 19 April 1919, citing *Halifax Herald*.

109 Frank, 'Working-Class Politics,' 197.

110 Trueman, 'New Brunswick,' 73, 252; *Daily Times*, 26 September 1921; Morton, 'Labourism and Economic Action,' 118.

111 See, for example, 'The Great Debate,' *New Maritimes* 3, no. 7 (April 1985), 4–10.

112 Morton, 'Labourism and Independent Labour Politics,' 73–4.

113 *Montreal Gazette*, 26 July 1920.

114 NAC, RG 27, Vol. 321, Strike 198, 'Halifax Shipyards, June 1920,' Extract from the Report of the Royal Canadian Mounted Police, week ending 24 June 1920.

115 In July 1922 the Springhill UMW received, and endorsed, a resolution from the Unemployed of Halifax suggesting a Dominion-wide demonstration day on 2 August 1922. Springhill Miners' Museum, Minutes of Local 4514, United Mine Workers of America, Springhill, 22 July 1922.

116 Manley, 'Communists and the Canadian Labour Movement,' 25.

117 NAC, RG 27, Vol. 327, Strike 161, 'Saint John Street Railway Employees, 1921'; Lambly, 'Canada's Street Railways,' 155–60.

118 Frank, 'Cape Breton Coal Miners,' 235–6, 249.

119 Nova Scotia, Royal Commission to Inquire into the Coal Mining Industry of the Province of Nova Scotia, Minutes of Evidence, Evidence of J.B. McLachlan, 258, microfilm, Public Archives of Nova Scotia (PANS).

120 Frank, 'Cape Breton Coal Miners,' 235–6.

121 Frank, 'Class Conflict,' 171–7.

122 United Mine Workers of America, District 26, *Proceedings of the Third Annual Convention of District 26 United Mine Workers of America Held at Truro, Nova Scotia June 20th, 1922 ... With Financial Statement from August 1st, 1921 to April 30th, 1922*. Subsection 4 was subsequently amended to read, 'That Dist. 26 U.M.W. of A., at once apply for membership in the Red International of Trade Unions and that a delegate be appointed from this convention to represent us at the next convention of the Red International of Trade Unions held in Moscow. And that this convention send a delegate to Dist. No. 18 to hear their voice re sending a delegate to Moscow.'

123 McKay, 'Industry, Work, and Community,' chapter 7.

124 In the index of John Mellor's popular account, *Company Store*, a subentry under Lewis's name reads 'treachery (coal and steel strike of 1923).'

125 Local 4514 Minutes, 30 August 1922. The militant Phalen Local also circulated a resolution critical of the agreement, but it is not clear that it called for the suspension of District autonomy. 14 October 1922.

126 UMW Archives, J.B. McLachlan to John L. Lewis, 2 January 1923, in U.M.W. Executive Minutes, 1923, 9–13.

127 UMW Archives, U.M.W. Executive Minutes, 2 January 1923, 23.

128 Ibid., 57.
129 Frank, 'Trial of J.B. McLachlan,' 210.
130 Ibid., 210.
131 Frank, 'Trial of J.B. McLachlan'; Cahill, 'More "Echoes from Labor's Wars,"' 9.
132 The summary of events in Cape Breton in the preceding paragraphs is drawn principally from Frank, 'Cape Breton Coal Miners,' chapter 5.
133 *Labour Gazette,* October 1925.
134 As Frank, 'The 1920s,' reminds us, the 1920s were also years of Ku Klux Klan activity in New Brunswick and sharp ethnic cleavages (evidenced, for example, in the 1925 provincial election).
135 The president of the Moncton ILP addressed the inaugural meeting of the Moncton Maritime Club in June 1923. Labour was also present when the Halifax Maritime Club was formed in February 1924. In 1925 Saint John longshoremen's leader James Tighe represented labour in the 'Great Delegation' to Ottawa. Labour journalists such as C.W. Lunn of the *Eastern Federationist* and Rev. Neil Herman of the *Citizen* jumped on the Maritime Rights bandwagon by presenting a regional critique centred on outmigration. *Daily Times* 7 June 1923; PANS, Congdon Papers, MG 2, Vol. 1096; Forbes, *Maritime Rights Movement,* 40; *Citizen,* 4 May, 2 November 1923.
136 *Citizen,* 31 October 1924, 7 January 1925.
137 Morton, *Ideal Surroundings.*
138 Walter Benjamin, 'Theses on the Philosophy of History,' in Hannah Arendt, ed., *Illuminations: Essays and Reflections* (New York, 1969), 257–8.

Quebec: Class and Ethnicity

GEOFFREY EWEN

Quebec has generally been ignored in previous discussions of the workers' revolt even though Quebec workers organized unions and went on strike to an unprecedented degree in the 1914–23 period. Their fierce combativeness and the tangible community support that they received reveal that workers wanted greater influence in politics, more control over the shop floor, and a new relationship with the economic and political elites.

If the Quebec labour revolt has been neglected, it is partly because Quebec labour historians have focused on the emergence of the Catholic labour movement.[1] By competing for the allegiance of francophone workers, the Catholic unions posed a real threat to the American Federation of Labor (AFL). Indeed, the 1914–23 period is characterized by an intense rivalry between international unions affiliated with the AFL and Catholic organizations. Yet Catholic unions contributed relatively little to the militancy of the revolt, especially in the peak year of 1919. Their role was primarily to act as one of the factors that undermined the revolt and the international unions in many of Quebec's industrial centres outside of Montreal. A study of the revolt in Quebec must focus primarily on secular unions, both international organizations affiliated mostly with the AFL and federal labour unions directly chartered by the Trades and Labor Congress of Canada (TLC). It was through these organizations that Quebec workers participated in the revolt. In Montreal the greater religious and ethnic diversity of the working class meant that Catholic unions had less impact than elsewhere in Quebec. Nevertheless, the fragmentation of the labour movement within the international unions was strikingly evident. Throughout Quebec ethnic, religious, political, and gender divisions, which were often closely related, made the revolt more limited than in other regions.

The Fragmentation of Working-Class Quebec

Any consideration of Quebec labour must take into account three obstacles to the formation of a unified and effective challenge to the social order. First, there were regional divisions within the province's economy. Montreal held a dominant position because of the size of its industrial and commercial output. While Quebec City and the urban areas of the Eastern Townships focused mostly on light manufacturing, elsewhere industrial centres based their development on resource-extractive industries. Second, there were specific ethnic mixes within particular regions and industries. Third, distinct organizational and ideological positions within the labour movement reflected and were reinforced by demographic and occupational differences.

The labour revolt occurred during a period of rapid urbanization and industrial development in Quebec. In 1911, 48 per cent of the population was urban, a trend accelerated by the war so that by 1921 the figure had reached 56 per cent. With a population of 618,506 in 1921, Montreal accounted for over a quarter of the province's population and, with its suburbs, for over half of all industrial production. An important commercial and financial centre, it had a diversified manufacturing sector with a large number of labour-intensive light industries such as textiles, clothing, food processing, and tobacco, as well as some heavy industry such as the production of transportation equipment. This growth and the concentration of people and production meant that construction was also an important employer. The second-largest centre, Quebec City, was much smaller, with a population of 95,193, but it was the centre of a still-important boot and shoe industry. Among the much smaller industrial centres were Sherbrooke, Trois-Rivières, and Hull, each with over 20,000 inhabitants. An abundance of hydroelectricity attracted pulp and paper mills to Hull, the Saguenay region, and Trois-Rivières, where electrochemical plants were also being established. Asbestos was extracted at the one important mining centre around Thetford. In the Eastern Townships light manufacturing was most common; textiles, furniture, rubber and metal working plants could be found in Sherbrooke, Drummondville, and Granby. The importance of light industries, especially textiles, garments, leather, rubber, electrical appliances, confectionery, and tobacco, account for the employment of a large proportion of women in Quebec's paid labour force. In plants in some of these industries women made up more than half of the employees. In 1911, 27 per cent of the workers in manufacturing were female, and women were also entering clerical and retail employment at a growing rate.[2]

Quebec's ethnic groups were not evenly distributed across the province. Eighty per cent of the population was francophone in 1921, but anglophones were concentrating increasingly in Montreal, which also attracted most of the province's immigrants and had significant Jewish and Italian communities. While francophones made up only 60 per cent of the population in Montreal, they constituted almost 70 per cent of the population in the region around Hull, 77 per cent in the industrial areas of the Eastern Townships, over 90 per cent in Quebec City, and 95 per cent in the St Maurice Valley, the region that included Trois-Rivières.[3] In all centres except Montreal the proportion of francophones was increasing. It was Montreal's larger proportions of non-Catholic, non-francophone workers that would hinder attempts there to establish Catholic unionism, a more viable option in Quebec City given its relatively homogeneous working class.

Ethnicity also influenced the division of labour, and this too had an impact on union organization. Anglo-Celts tended to hold a privileged position in the labour market. They predominated in many kinds of office work (especially in firms owned by anglophones) and in supervisory factory positions. The iron and steel industries had a mixed workforce but anglophones held more skilled positions than francophones. Some employers, such as the giant Canadian Vickers shipyards and the Canadian Pacific Railway's Angus workshops, gave preference to job applicants from Great Britain, often apprenticeship-trained workers who were knowledgeable about new technology imported from Great Britain or the United States. Skilled craft workers from outside Quebec, generally Americans, were hired in the new pulp and paper mills, while unskilled labour came from nearby villages and farms. There were more anglophones than francophones, both skilled and labourers, in the printing, publishing, and bookbinding industry. Francophones accounted for the majority of skilled and unskilled boot and shoe workers, and predominated in the textile mills, in the tobacco industry, in woodworking and logging, in municipal employment, and in asbestos mining. The latter industry also employed significant numbers of eastern European immigrants. While Jewish workers were employed in a wide range of trades and workplaces, there were large concentrations of these workers in the garment trades. Italians generally worked on railway and street railway construction or in short-term labouring jobs (in the railway shops, for example).[4]

The ethnic division of labour meant that many unions had mixed memberships. In some unions particular groups predominated. For example, most members of the British-based Amalgamated Society of Engineers (ASE) were anglophones. Overall, francophones made up three-quarters of Montreal's international union membership in 1918.[5] Montreal's police, firefighters, tramway workers, boot and shoe workers, and tobacco workers, just to name a few, had predominantly francophone organizations under French-Canadian leadership. Francophones probably accounted for an even higher proportion of members in such organizations elsewhere in the province. The concentration of Jewish immigrants in certain sectors of the clothing industry, such as men's ready-made clothing, meant that the garment unions were important institutions in the Jewish labour movement and the Montreal labour movement as a whole. Within the garment unions ethnic locals were also set up for French Canadians and Italians.[6] The concentration of Italians in poorly organized sectors such as street-railway construction and labouring explains why so few members of this group were organized.[7]

Working-class communities in each of the industrial centres had distinctive histories. Both Montreal and Quebec City had a proletariat with a tradition of organization and established working-class institutions. Anglo-Celtic and European immigrants often arrived with experience of socialist or labour activities. Migrants from the rural parishes with little or no previous exposure to unions supplied much of the labour in most cities but may have accounted for a much larger proportion of the workers in newer industrial centres such as Shawinigan, Cap-de-la-Madeleine, Grand-Mère, and La Tuque in the Mauricie region near Trois-Rivières, and Chicoutimi, Jonquière, and Kénogami in the Saguenay–Lac Saint-Jean region. There was a split between the older and newer industrialized centres, similar to the one between industrialized and rural parts of the Maritimes.[8] Workers from rural parishes were harder to organize and were eventually more susceptible to Catholic unionism. The best-organized workers were in metalworking, railway running trades, construction, printing, the garment industry, boot and shoe production, cigarmaking, and longshoring. There had been repeated but unsuccessful attempts to organize textile workers.

By 1921 over three-quarters of the unionized workers belonged to international unions, most of which were affiliated with the American Federation of Labor and to the Trades and Labor Congress of Canada.[9]

Although there was a Quebec provincial executive of the Congress, its activities were limited to an annual pilgrimage to lobby the provincial government. Local trades and labour councils were much more active and influential. In fact, the influence of the Montreal Trades and Labor Council reached into numerous other industrial centres, reflecting Montreal's industrial and commercial dominance, and the weakness of the international movement outside the metropolis. The only council with a viable newspaper, *Le Monde ouvrier/The Labor World*,[10] it often initiated or participated in organizing efforts outside Montreal. The council's leaders in this period, such as president J.T. Foster and secretary Gustave Francq, were craft unionists who were dedicated to international unionism and closely associated with the policies and positions of the Trades and Labor Congress of Canada. They were labourists who insisted on a separation of economic and political action – a position that precluded any political use of the strike weapon. They also dominated the Quebec Labor Party, which had been established in 1904. While the membership of international unions was perhaps three-quarters French Canadian,[11] the international movement included workers from numerous religious and ethnic backgrounds. For this reason leaders such as Francq opposed appeals to the national interests of any particular community. They also believed that a separation of economic and religious matters was necessary to ensure the unity of a working-class movement that included significant numbers of Catholic, Protestant, and Jewish members. It was the diverse composition of the working class that led craft union leaders in Montreal to oppose appeals based on the ethnic nationalism of any particular community. This position explains why the Montreal Trades and Labor Council opposed the French-Canadian nationalist campaign for official recognition of St Jean Baptiste Day as a legal holiday.[12]

The international unions faced two kinds of rivals. First, there were the national unions, many of which had been expelled from the TLC as dual unions in 1902; based largely in Quebec City, their strongest organizations were among workers in the boot and shoe industry.[13] Second, there was the emerging Catholic labour movement, which was motivated by concern for the plight of industrial workers and by fear of both socialism and the secularism of religiously neutral international unions. Before the war only a few small Catholic unions had been established by interested clergy.

There was another distinctive form of working-class organization in Quebec – the labour clubs. Established in the 1890s, these neighbourhood political organizations provided a forum in which members of both national and international unions could meet with unorganized workers to socialize, discuss current issues, pass resolutions asking for government action, and organize political campaigns for candidates they had chosen or endorsed. Since only a small proportion of workers belonged to unions, some of these clubs provided a larger basis of support for the Labor Party. By the start of the First World War, however, all but two of the clubs in Montreal had severed links with the party.[14] This division followed an alliance between the Labor Party and a municipal reform movement that included important elements of the business community whose aims were to administer the city rationally and in a businesslike manner, put an end to corruption and patronage, and reduce taxes. A broadly based coalition that hoped to cross ethnic and class lines, the reform movement had endorsed francophone labourist and carpenter Joseph Ainey for election to the powerful new Board of Control. The reform movement won the 1910 municipal elections, but changes in the way street-paving projects were paid appeared to favour wealthier western wards and alienated francophone workers in eastern sections of the city. In the 1912 elections an opposition group led by cigar manufacturer Médéric Martin emerged to challenge the reform majority on city council.[15] Although Ainey remained popular, most labour clubs abandoned the Labor Party before the 1912 elections so that they could support candidates not endorsed by the party. The breakaway clubs formed a federation that in 1914 took the name of the Fédération des clubs ouvriers municipaux de Montréal (FCOM).[16] During the war the FCOM presented itself as representing the class and national interests of French-Canadian workers. Ainey, on the other hand, represented the current within the Labor Party that opposed appeals on ethnic or national lines, and that was willing to join coalitions that included the anglophone business community.

The labour clubs had a diverse composition and reflected a wide range of positions, particularly as many more clubs were established in 1919 and 1920. Most of the clubs affiliated with the Labor Party were francophone organizations, but some had a mixed membership that included anglophones. The Saint-Louis Labor Club served workers in the heart of the Jewish garment district. Some clubs restricted membership to workers to prevent them from being taken over by members of the liberal professions. Among the few clubs that crossed class lines was the Longueuil Labor Club, which drew together farmers, workers, shopkeepers, and professionals.[17] Its membership included the mayor, a manufacturer, and most of the aldermen who were local merchants.[18] Despite such exceptions as the Verdun Labor Club and the Saint-Louis Labor Club, which had large socialist memberships, most clubs were labourist organizations that denounced monopolies and desired more working-class influence and participation in government, but did not proceed to a systematic denunciation of capitalism. Some of the clubs provided a base for radicals; Alfred Mathieu of the Montreal Trades and Labor Council and Henri Julien of the Sainte-Marie Labor Club were among those working-class French-Canadian nationalists who were opposed to the socialists but prepared to advocate militant, direct action to achieve political ends.

Montreal also had a significant socialist movement, represented by members of the Social Democratic Party of Canada and the Socialist Party of Canada. The Montreal Trades and Labor Council did not reflect socialist strength in the labour movement, since large numbers of socialist garment workers were members of the Amalgamated Clothing Workers (ACW), an organization excluded from the council because it was not a member of the American Federation of Labor. Similarly excluded from the council were socialist machinists who belonged to the Amalgamated Society of Engineers. Most socialists were Anglo-Celtic and European immigrants. Indeed, socialism was particularly important in the growing Jewish immigrant community.[19] In the 1916 Montreal municipal elections in St Louis, the heart of the Jewish garment district, both the Social Democratic Party and Poale Zion (Labour Zionists) presented candidates. Joseph Schubert of the International Ladies' Garment Workers Union ran for the SDP, while Hananiah Meir Caiserman, who later founded the Canadian Jewish Congress, ran for the Labour Zionists.[20]

There was also a French section of the Socialist Party, led by Albert Saint-Martin. Despite the energetic leadership of Saint-Martin and L.G.N. Pagé (the president of the barbers' union), who were able to help mobilize large numbers of workers around such issues as unemployment, socialist parties attracted few French-Canadian members.[21] This failure was probably due to the long-standing hostility of the Catholic clergy. French-Canadian socialists tended to hold unorthodox religious views, while most French-Canadian workers remained practising Catholics.

The ethnic divisions within the working class were extremely deep and entrenched organizationally. Anglo-Celts, French Canadians, and Jewish workers often predominated in different unions, although there was some contact through the Montreal Trades and Labor Council. Even within the same union, workers were often divided into separate locals that split along language lines. Ethnicity also divided workers on the political front, as socialists who were predominantly immigrants also organized along ethnic or linguistic lines. Among francophone labourists in Montreal there was a serious disagreement about whether to use ethnic bonds to advance workers' interests at city hall. The French-Canadian working-class nationalism of the Fédération des clubs ouvriers municipaux, while an effective source of militancy, was at odds with the view among Labor Party leaders that nationalist appeals were divisive. Throughout the province francophones were also seriously divided on the question of whether to support international or national unions. At the same time, Catholic social activists were attempting to lure francophone Catholics into unions established along religious lines. A factor that favoured national and Catholic unions outside of Montreal was that only a few of the larger international unions had francophone or bilingual business agents. Local unions often had to deal with international representatives and undertake their correspondence with headquarters in English.[22]

Many of the organizational differences within the Quebec working class were played out during the severe crisis of unemployment that gripped the country in 1914 and lasted through the first year of the war. Trade unions in Quebec, both national and international, retreated in the face of attacks by employers. Mounting unemployment meant that few strikes succeeded, little organizing was possible, wages were cut, and many locals struggled for survival or disappeared altogether. Towards the end of 1913 shoe manufacturers in Quebec City locked out more than four thousand national union members and forced them to accept a contract with a no-strike clause that stipulated fines against the unions for any transgression.[23] In September 1913, 350 garment workers in Montreal struck against a pay cut and were then replaced.[24] In 1914 the carpenters' union in Montreal suffered a serious defeat after employers broke an agreement to reduce hours and increase wages.[25] Large-scale unemployment also meant massive poverty for large numbers of working-class families from 1913 until the onset of a recovery based on munitions production. Although its impact varied depending on the location and on the sector of the economy, this economic revival relieved much of the distress through late 1915 and early 1916.

The incidence of strikes in Quebec gives some indication of labour's weakness at the start of the war. Disputes involving all types of unions numbered twenty-six in 1912, nineteen in 1913, and only six in each of 1914 and 1915. Of the six strikes in 1914 all but one involved fewer than forty workers. Five of the strikes in 1914 involved attempts to improve wages and conditions, while one was a defensive struggle against a wage decrease; the results were a single victory, four losses, and a compromise in the form of a reduced wage decrease. Two of the strikes in 1915 were sympathetic actions, one by papermakers in Donnacona, the other by Montreal ironworkers in support of fellow union members in the United States. Both strikes, along with those waged by Montreal tailors and unorganized munitions workers in Sherbrooke, resulted in losses for the workers. A walkout by some two thousand Thetford miners, without benefit of a union, won a wage increase and better conditions. At Montreal's Canadian Vickers shipyards the organized trades won wages increases, but those without a union failed to do so. Three of the disputes in 1915 involved industries engaged in war-related production – industries in which either unions had not yet been formed or organization was incomplete; in two of these disputes, however, there was a measure of success.[26] The improving economy of 1916 was evident in the increased number of disputes (fourteen in all), the increased number of strikers (most disputes involved several hundred workers), and the improved results (workers won or accepted a favourable compromise in twelve cases).

Until the economy picked up, the most important expression of working-class militancy was a massive movement of the unemployed in Montreal. Among Canadian cities Montreal had the largest number of unemployed workers, an estimated fifty thousand.[27] From April 1914 until June 1915 large numbers of jobless workers, mostly men, appeared regularly at city hall to demand work. Workers directed their demands at Montreal's municipal government not only because both the federal and provincial governments left responsibility for unemployment relief to municipalities, but also because Liberal Médéric Martin had just been elected mayor in a campaign in which he had promised to complete public works and provide employment. Martin's victory marked a break in the traditional alternation of English- and French-speaking representatives in the mayoral office. It also signalled the growing political weight of French-Canadian workers, whose numbers were being augmented through rural–urban migration and Montreal's annexation of several of the surrounding working-class suburbs. The mass demonstrations began when Martin, on taking the oath of office, invited Montreal's unemployed to report to city hall for work the following Monday morning. The twelve thousand people who showed up surpassed both the mayor's expectations and the city's ability to provide jobs; only some twenty-five hundred workers were temporarily engaged on public works.[28] Crowds numbering from scores to thousands appeared time and again for well over a year to demand work.

Championing the demands for work on the part of Montreal's French-Canadian workers was the Fédération des clubs ouvriers municipaux, which claimed that Martin owed his election to the federation's support and that his pledge of employment was made specifically to its members.[29] Initially elated by Martin's victory, by 1915 the FCOM was criticizing him for his inability to fulfil his election promise. When Martin arrogantly demanded that the unemployed no longer annoy him at city hall, the FCOM sought a candidate who would be able to defeat him in the 1916 elections. One newspaper, *La Patrie,* saw this move by the FCOM as a critical loss of support for Martin.[30] According to Alfred Charpentier, a labour club member who would later become a leading figure in the Catholic union movement, the FCOM dominated municipal politics in 1915.[31] The federation tried to recruit Adélard Fortier, president of the Montreal Dairy Company, as their candidate for mayor.[32] As military contracts began to have an impact in reducing unemployment in late 1915, this campaign collapsed and Fortier declined to run.

The Socialist Party, which had initially organized the crowds that appeared at city hall, also played a major role in mobilizing the unemployed. Locals of the Social Democratic Party, organized on language lines, were active as well in mobilizing immigrants hard hit by the crisis.[33] Among a crowd of seven thousand unemployed assembled at city hall were several thousand Italian, Jewish, Polish, and Russian workers.[34] While newspaper reports do not always identify the leadership of protests by immigrant workers as socialists, it is clear that immigrant workers organized numerous demonstrations to demand an end to their exclusion from job sites by city foremen. In March 1915 Italian workers occupied city hall and a week later demonstrated outside the Italian consulate.[35]

The mobilization of the unemployed revealed a number of characteristics of Montreal's working class. In a period of high unemployment and with a weakened union movement, French-Canadian workers in Montreal expected to use their political clout to exert greater influence over the allocation of jobs and services at the municipal level. Médéric Martin was able to secure his election in 1914 with an appeal that combined class and ethnic solidarity. The strength of the ethnic ties was such that the FCOM turned to a prominent member of the francophone business community when seeking a challenger to Martin. International union leaders, on the other hand, usually opposed appeals based on ethnic solidarity that divided anglophones and francophones, such as those made by both Martin and the FCOM. Leaders of the Montreal Trades and Labor Council also opposed Martin and challenged his claim to represent the working class. The council and Martin, who had defeated a Labor Party candidate in a federal by-election in 1906,[36] differed on a number of issues. The council had less influence in municipal politics than the FCOM, however, and played a less active role in the unemployment movement than either the FCOM or the socialists. The council believed that the federal government should take responsibility for unemployment, a problem too large for local governments. The council was also reluctant to mobilize the unemployed, fearing the rowdy demonstrations that could result would be used by socialists to attack the moderation of council leaders. At the onset of the war, then, workers' movements in Quebec were deeply divided by ethnicity, ideology, and organizational structure.

The New Militancy

As military production increased and unemployment diminished, militancy among workers grew. In munitions industries union leaders complained frequently about poor working conditions and low wages. Demands for a fair wage clause in contracts issued by the Imperial Munitions Board were presented to the federal government.[37] From 1916 until the end of the war, international unions led a succession of disputes and strikes, most notably in asbestos mining, garment production, metalworking, and shipbuilding. Many of these major disputes involved workers who were recently organized in industrial unions or joint councils that united the skilled and the unskilled, men and women, in struggles over economic demands and control of the work process. Striking workers also engaged in often pivotal struggles for community support. Their militancy mounted despite efforts by some international unions and Montreal Trades and Labor Council leaders to prevent work stoppages in the interest of the war effort.[38]

The new militancy was often a rank-and-file affair tempered by a cautious leadership. One of the first large strikes in munitions production occurred at Montreal's giant Canadian Vickers shipyards in February and March 1916, when between three hundred and five hundred shipwrights walked off the job for over a month. While many of the details of this dispute for fair wages are obscure because of effective censorship by a federal government fearful of sympathetic action by other workers, it may have been the international union leaders themselves who kept the strike from spreading. Certainly, Montreal Trades and Labor Council leaders were blamed for its failure.[39] This incident may have produced a legacy of bitterness and suspicion against the council executive (which was headed by the machinists' business agent, J.T. Foster) that was to last into 1919.

An even larger strike in a war-related industry occurred in August 1916, when some nine hundred members of the Western Federation of Miners (WFM) downed their tools at five mines at Thetford.[40] This dispute demonstrated that ethnic diversity did not necessarily lead to division. The success of the union in uniting much of an ethnically diverse workforce made up of francophones, anglophones, Russians, and Italians led one employer to turn to a new pool of labour. Just before the strike, the government had furnished Asbestos Corporation with 140 German and Austrian internees, a move that the union claimed was meant to intimidate its membership. Initially, the internees got a hostile reception that included a protest meeting and calls from the *Labor World* for their removal.[41] The indignation of the local community, home to some two hundred citizens who had joined the army to fight in Europe, led Narcisse Arcand, Quebec organizer for the United Brotherhood of Carpenters and Joiners, to declare that 'the men might just as well get their guns and fight against alien enemies at home as go to Europe to do their fighting.'[42] Yet sympathy soon developed between union members and the prisoners, many of whom carried union cards and did not want to scab. The company responded to this newfound solidarity by threatening to withhold food from internees if they joined the union. Nor did the internees want to work in Thetford's mines. Dissatisfied with dangerous working conditions that resulted in at least one death, the men wanted to return to the internment camp.[43] In this case workplace contact and the shared experience of obnoxious company tactics and dangerous working conditions combined to produce solidarity across ethnic lines. The Thetford strike – which was defeated after several weeks due largely to employer intransigence and the organization of a rival Catholic union that supplied strike-breakers to the companies[44] – was like the 1916 Hamilton machinists' strike in that militancy peaked early and never fully recovered after the defeat.

The sector with the most frequent and the largest strikes in Quebec during the war was the garment industry. Based primarily in Montreal, this sector depended heavily on immigrant and female labour. Many of the workers in the garment factories and shops, especially in men's clothing, were Jewish immigrants, although there were also significant numbers of French Canadians and Italians. The garment unions were the most important organizations in Montreal's Jewish labour movement. While aspiring to organize all garment workers regardless of gender, ethnic origin, or religion, the leadership and the membership of the recently organized Amalgamated Clothing Workers and of the International Ladies' Garment Workers Union (ILGWU) consisted mainly of Jewish immigrants.[45] Both these industrial unions were socialist in their politics and committed to the class struggle. The ACW in particular was opposed to the conservative craft unionism of the American Federation of Labor.

In the early months of 1917 a wave of strikes hit all sectors of the garment industry. In January the ACW declared a two-month general strike of some forty-five hundred workers in the men's clothing industry.[46] The enthusiasm that accompanied this walkout encouraged other garment unions to take similar action. One thousand ILGWU members struck two weeks later, followed by fur workers and journeymen tailors in March.

The ethnic composition of the strikers immediately became an issue in the strike when one gentile employer in the men's clothing industry tried to arouse anti-German and anti-Semitic sentiment against strikers and union representatives. Realizing that the strike drew its strongest support from Jewish immigrants, Alfred Wood, vice-president of Semi-Ready Company, argued that the 'German-Jewish' strikers were disloyal, and that the dispute was caused by German agents bent on hindering the production of military uniforms.[47] Wood's anti-Semitism found a receptive ear in Montreal's judiciary. When three young picketers charged with disturbing the peace were acquitted after witnesses gave contradictory testimony, the court recorder (the city's chief magistrate) declared that the accused and union representatives had not told the truth, unlike the police constables who testified against them and who 'know what it is to perjure themselves, and are, at least, Christians.'[48] Most employers in the men's clothing industry were also Jewish and were appalled by such inflammatory and racist statements, preferring instead to attack the American leadership of the union. The Clothing Manufacturers' Association took out full-page advertisements in

Montreal newspapers denouncing the union leaders from outside the country who wanted control over their operations.[49] The Ladies' Clothing Manufacturers' Association was less scrupulous about inciting ethnic divisions and issued an official statement that 'every French-Canadian and Italian-Canadian is now at work in the shops in the number of several hundreds. The only workers who still in part remain out in the cold of winter are the Jewish-Canadians.'[50] Throughout the strike the employers hoped to mobilize public opinion in their favour.

Jewish employers also hoped that their community ties would help to diminish class antagonisms. Clothing Manufacturers' Association President Lyon Cohen, prominently identified with the Jewish Federation of Charities, claimed that he had agreed to head the association because he believed his work in the community would help in dealing with the union.[51] The union won some public support, however. Lyon W. Jacobs, a lawyer and municipal councillor for Saint-Louis ward in the heart of the garment district, established a Businessmen's Strike Relief Committee to provide moral and financial support to the strikers.[52] It was through the efforts of Jacobs and Peter Bercovitch, Liberal Member of the Legislative Assembly for Saint-Louis, that the strikers were able to counter the employers' massive and hostile publicity campaign. They organized support meetings and convinced Mayor Médéric Martin to attempt to mediate. When his efforts proved unsuccessful, Martin came out four-square behind union demands for recognition.[53] The community support and the widespread attention that this strike received helped the Amalgamated Clothing Workers secure a satisfactory settlement.

Shipbuilding was an other industry affected by growing militancy. In 1918 the Marine Trades Federation was formed among craft workers in an attempt to establish collective bargaining on an industry-wide basis and uniform conditions over all the shipyards of eastern North America. This joint council had a significant impact in the shipbuilding centres of Montreal, Trois-Rivières, Sorel, Quebec, and Lévis. In 1918 several disputes erupted in Quebec shipyards. In Montreal there was a strike of ships' carpenters at Frazer-Brace in May 1918. In another dispute at the John McDougall Caledonian Iron Works, forty-three machinists stayed out from March until October. A ten-day dispute involving fifteen hundred workers occurred at another yard in Montreal at the end of July 1918. In July the Department of Labour also received from shipyards across the province numerous requests for boards of conciliation. International union leaders wanted throughout the whole industry uniform wages and hours similar to those introduced in the railroad shops.[54] Instead of forming a board under the Industrial Disputes Investigation Act to deal with each request, the government appointed a royal commission with the power to determine the bargaining agent and wage scales in all the disputes. Many of the shipyards in question, notably those in Trois-Rivières and Lévis, were also the scene of rivalry between international and Catholic unions. The majority report of the royal commission ignored the demands of the Marine Trades Federation for a uniform settlement and recommended different scales in each locality. It also decided that Catholic unions would be recognized at two companies in Trois-Rivières and at the Davie shipyards at Lauzon, where a strike of 239 men had erupted when the employer declared that he would hire only Catholic union members and fired seventeen Marine Trades Federation militants.[55] The federation also believed that the commission had been surreptitiously influenced by the Catholic unions in Trois-Rivières. A delegation of international union leaders was reportedly ready in October 1918 to threaten a general strike in shipyards on the St Lawrence from Toronto to Quebec City if the Davie dispute was not settled to its satisfaction.[56] While it is unclear why the delegation backed down, it did so just days before orders-in-council prohibited strikes in all wartime industries.

During the war municipal employees and tramway workers across Quebec also organized and fought on an impressive scale for the right to bargain collectively. There were often expressions of solidarity between these two groups of workers. Police and firemen struck in Sherbrooke in 1916.[57] During a dispute that same year Quebec City firemen stationed at the city hall attacked passing streetcars run by scabs.[58] Tramway workers in Montreal organized and secured a contract after a strike threat in 1918. Municipal workers insisted on forming or joining larger movements. Montreal's civic workers organized in September 1918, joined the trades and labour council, and then formed a common front of police, firemen, waterworks engineers, and incinerator workers before going on strike in December 1918. Although the tramway union threatened sympathetic action to support the municipal workers, in some cases the split within the workers' movement kept civic workers apart. For example, in Quebec City firemen organized a national union while the police formed a Trades and Labor Congress Federal Union.

In December 1918 some fifteen hundred municipal workers in Montreal went on strike. The dramatic, two-day walkout erupted against a background of hostility towards an undemocratic civic administration imposed earlier that year by the provincial government. After decades of growth and the annexation of smaller and indebted municipalities, the City of Montreal was heavily in debt. To ensure fiscal restraint the provincial government placed the city under a five-man administrative commission. This action was taken at the behest of the Bank of Montreal, the city's principle creditor and a powerful symbol of English-Canadian financial capital at a time when French-Canadian workers expected to exert considerable influence over municipal authorities. To head the trusteeship Liberal Premier Jean-Lomer Gouin chose Ernest Décary, a notary who administered the investments of wealthy families.[59] Liberal MP Alphonse Verville, a former Trades and Labor Congress president and Member of Parliament for the Labor Party, was named to the administrative commission to represent the working class. What little influence Verville had among workers was rapidly lost following his appointment.[60] In a city where Mayor Médéric Martin won the support of most francophone workers by appealing to their nationalism and by promising to promote their class interests, many French-Canadian workers were convinced that the trusteeship left them without any effective representation at the municipal level.

Montreal municipal workers organized their unions just as the civic administration was reorganizing the civic employees and municipal services with the help of efficiency experts who redefined job assignments, delineated lines of authority, determined wage scales, and participated in labour negotiations.[61] The new police chiefs imposed by the administrative commission were hired from outside the force; one did not speak French fluently, and all three were accused of corruption by reform groups.[62] Just before the strike was declared, the unions added the removal of the new chiefs to demands for increased wages and shorter hours.[63]

The administrative commission refused to negotiate on most issues and prepared for a showdown with the unions. Décary appealed to the Montreal business community to support his plans to break the strike. The city began to hire strike-breakers and to organize volunteer forces to replace the strikers. Many of these volunteers were from the large companies, such as the Canadian Pacific Railway, and the utility and insurance companies.[64]

The two-day strike, which erupted on 13 December, was likened by one reporter to a civil war.[65] Fire alarms began ringing as soon as the strike began and continued through the rest of the day until 304 had been set off. Scabs were booed as they appeared in answer to the calls.

Crowds gathered around firehalls to direct their anger at the replacement firemen. In working-class districts volunteer firemen were either not allowed to leave their stations or were forcibly ejected. Some firehalls were sacked.[66] Most of the violence, however, was directed at strike-breakers. In only one instance did the collective sense of outrage spill over into random looting (involving a store and a cinema), and striking police soon intervened. In addition, most observers agreed that the violence was initiated by sympathizers rather than strikers.[67] Martin had few powers under the trusteeship, but there were still clear benefits in having a mayor who wished to be identified with workers. Martin had encouraged civic workers to unionize and refused to read the Riot Act, declaring that he would not call out the army for a few black eyes.[68] Such crowd actions were hardly new: the previous year had witnessed anti-conscriptionist riots against a law considered undemocratic because it had been passed by a parliament that had exceeded the normal five-year term.

The municipal workers' walkout forced Premier Gouin and Catholic Archbishop Bruchési of Montreal to participate in the negotiations. Both figures were influential in securing or conceding some of the unions' demands. The settlement included a major victory in the dismissal of the new chiefs of police, as well as a double shift for firemen.[69] All other issues were referred to arbitration.[70] Initially, many of the strikers and civic union leaders were euphoric and considered the outcome a total victory, one that expressed the power of the new municipal unions.[71]

The settlement came as a shock to leaders of the Montreal Trades and Labor Council, who had been actively engaged in their own mediation efforts when the settlement was announced. Arbitration had been accepted on the terms offered by the Committee of Public Safety of the Citizens' Protective Association, which had been organized by the Board of Trade on the first day of the strike. The fifty-member committee was composed almost entirely of members of the English business community, and included only a few representatives of the French-Canadian bourgeoisie.[72] The Committee of Public Safety issued an ultimatum threatening to take 'legal and military steps' if its offer of a 'fair, square deal' for the unions was rejected. Under the conditions of this offer all five members of the arbitration board were to be chosen from the employer-based Committee of Public Safety.[73] In this case Montreal workers faced resistance from employers in the form of a united front similar to the one that emerged during the Winnipeg General Strike. The Citizens' Protective Association chose Grant Hall, a vice-president of the

Canadian Pacific Railway, and Alfred Lambert, a manufacturer. The unions chose F.W. Stewart (a manufacturer and director of the City Improvement League) and Adélard Fortier (the president of the Montreal Dairy Company who had been courted in 1915 by the Fédération des clubs ouvriers municipaux de Montréal as a candidate for mayor). An executive member of the firemen's union said that the union's choices would ensure that they received 'entière justice.'[74] In accepting arbitration by a board consisting entirely of employers, the civic unions displayed a remarkable degree of deference, but they may also have believed that the business community had the authority to guarantee that the funds would be found for the wage increases. There was greater confidence in members of the business elite, especially when one of them was French Canadian, than in working-class organizations such as the Montreal Trades and Labor Council. The astonished council leaders attributed the confidence expressed in the Committee of Public Safety to the inexperience of civic union leaders who were new to the labour movement.[75] The arbitration board's final settlement was a disappointment: wage increases were held down, and civic unions were required to sever all ties with each other and with any other organization, such as the trades and labour council. The latter stipulation came as a particular shock to the municipal workers and their unions, which ignored it.[76]

The last months of the war had marked the beginning of a massive union recruitment campaign that by 1919 extended throughout Quebec. Montreal's meat packers organized a local in 1918. The next year rubber workers formed unions in Montreal, Granby, and St Jérôme. There was a renewed effort to organize and gain recognition for the employees of Dominion Textile in Montreal, Magog, and Montmorency. The garment unions tried to organize shops that had been established outside Montreal to avoid unionization. The ILGWU tried to organize shirtmakers. The Teamsters established four new locals in Montreal in 1918 and added another one in 1919. Among the many new groups of workers that joined the labour movement in 1919 were seamen, gas workers, and laundry workers.[77]

Strikers often received tangible and open support in the community. Several shops in Montreal refused deliveries by strike-breakers during a dispute in April 1919 at the Dominion Express Company.[78] During a strike of eight hundred employees of the Montreal Light, Heat and Power Company in the same month, strike sympathizers disarmed the private detectives who had been hired to protect strike-breakers.[79]

A qualitative change was evident in workers' aspirations, which went beyond demands for a better and more secure standard of living to include a redistribution of power in the workplace and in society. Workers challenged economic and political elites from a keen sense of their exploitation and of the disparities in wealth and influence that it produced. This workers' offensive clearly encouraged established craft union leaders. J.T. Foster, president of the Montreal Trades and Labor Council and the machinists' business agent, declared that workers were increasingly discontented because employers were making enormous profits by exploiting them.[80] Benjamin Drolet, a cigarmaker and labour columnist for *La Patrie*, wrote that 'la classe ouvrière ne retournera plus aux conditions d'avant guerre: elle veut avoir son mot à dire dans la direction des industries.'[81] Even Gustave Francq, in a vehemently anti-Bolshevik diatribe, declared that workers were on the threshold of a 'transformation des masses.'[82] Francq believed that the proletariat would no longer tolerate their servitude to capitalists as they had in the past.[83] The war had accelerated the class struggle, giving rise to '[une] irrésistible poussée des consciences justement révoltées par un régime par trop inégalitaire. Peu à peu la lumière se fit dans les esprits et les conditions économiques dans lesquelles l'ouvier languissait lui apparurent de plus en plus intolérables. Dès ce jour, la lutte des classes commença et c'est cette lutte qui se continue aujourd'hui, plus âpre que jamais.'[84] The working class now wanted 'a share in the management of industries,'[85] to deal with capital as an equal, and to receive its legitimate share of the national wealth.[86] And workers through their unions were asserting their right to a share of influence in parliament and to legislation that reflected their interests.[87]

The organization of large numbers of women workers was equally significant. Some industrial unions in the garment trades had already made major advances in this area during the war. In 1917 women made up about 40 per cent of the forty-five hundred striking Amalgamated Clothing Workers and half of the five hundred striking fur workers. The ACW noted how women maintained the picket lines during the bitterly cold and long winter strike. During one day of confrontations with scabs and police, nine women were arrested.[88] After the strike the ACW described the women as being more active than men in rank-and-file affairs, and much more active than women in other clothing centres.[89] Indeed, largely due to the efforts of activist Jewish women, women in the garment industry were more militant than those in other sectors.[90] The organization of the men's ready-made clothing sector was the most successful campaign to incorporate women into the labour movement during the war. It was also significant for having united Jewish and French-Canadian workers of both sexes.

Women's organization in the garment trades was uneven, however. Three-quarters of the ILGWU strikers in 1917 were male cutters in the cloak and suit trade. Organizing efforts apparently concentrated on these workers because they were alleged to be the most solid union supporters. This was a case in which ethnicity and gender combined to hinder greater unity. The organized cutters were mostly skilled Jewish men, while the women were predominantly French Canadians who were considered less skilled. The male unionists considered gentile women more difficult to organize.[91] Skill may also account for the stronger support that men gave to the ILGWU, a union in which it was much harder to replace skilled workers who played a key role in the production process. The women were much more vulnerable to being fired and replaced by employers.[92] Male ILGWU members were ambivalent when women initiated strike action, as they did over the uneven distribution of work in a shop later in 1917. Having initially supported their female co-workers, the men returned to work three days later, only to be ordered out again by the union.[93]

If the organization of women was viewed positively by many needle trade unions – the ACW in particular – the entry of women into wartime industries was considered a serious threat by other international unions. Thousands of women were hired during the war to produce munitions, including explosives and fuses, and the federal government encouraged their employment. Women also entered a wide range of jobs in a number of industries, not all engaged in war work, that had been previously occupied almost exclusively by men. For example, women replaced men in the hose room and in the moulds and roll departments of rubber-goods factories, in some furniture and upholstery concerns, and in a number of areas in electrical factories. In the large railway shops women ran light machines and lathes, and toiled as general carpenters, painters, mattress makers, armature winders, and unskilled labourers.[94]

Labour leaders in Quebec suspected that women were being hired not so much to meet a labour shortage as to release more men for military service. In 1916 the Montreal Trades and Labor Council objected to this hiring trend on the grounds that there were still men out of work.[95] While every other province suspended the enforcement of provisions in their factory acts that restricted the employment of women, the Montreal Trades and Labor Council convinced the Quebec government to enforce the regulations that limited the hours of work for women, that prohibited night work, and that allowed government inspectors to decide on the suitability of various kinds of work for women. The result was that in munitions factories where there was twenty-four-hour production many women were thrown out of work.[96] The conservatism of the Quebec government on this issue bolstered the ability of male trade unionists to exclude women from employment. Nor were attempts to prevent the entry of women into new areas restricted to wartime industries; in 1918 Montreal's cigarmakers struck a number of times in response to the increased hiring of women workers.[97]

The expectation of an imminent transformation of society was not accompanied by a questioning of the sexual division of labour. Male trade unionists viewed women as secondary wage earners and feared that they would remain in jobs that had been monopolized by men before the wartime influx of women into the workforce. In February 1919, when the first women delegates (from the waitresses union) arrived at the trades and labour council, the painters' union introduced a resolution asking the federal government to fire and replace all women working in enterprises where men had previously been employed. The council endorsed the resolution (widows and women with dependents were excepted), thereby denying women their right to compete for jobs with men in order either to live independently or to supplement an inadequate male wage.[98] The council recognized that some women were the main breadwinners, whether for themselves or their families, but affirmed the ideal of the family wage. The restrictions on women's employment were enforced during and after the war in Montreal's two large railway shops. As one contemporary observer explained, '[O]rganized labour insisted that no man's work be given to a women unless she was in need for her own subsistence or for the support of dependents.' The latter group referred mostly to widows who supported families or soldiers' wives who supported sick husbands. In the railway shops most women fell into this category, as reflected by the unusually large proportion of married women who made up 75 per cent of the total female workforce in the shops in 1919.[99]

Despite the hostility to women's employment in non-traditional jobs, efforts to recruit women and to encourage their participation in labour organization reached a new peak in 1919. Large numbers of women joined unions as efforts were renewed in the textile, garment, and shoe industries, and campaigns were undertaken in previously little-organized sectors represented by rubber workers, meat packers, waitresses, and office workers. In all of these industries record numbers of women were elected to local executives or selected as delegates to conventions or the Montreal Trades and Labor Council. Sometimes women formed separate locals, as was done among fur dressers and dryers, ladies' clothing workers, and tobacco workers. Labour men and women offered organizing support, and unions made serious efforts to recruit women wage earners. Business agents in some unions were hired specifically to work among female workers. In early 1919 the ILGWU made a serious attempt to bridge ethnic and gender divisions. First, it hired Joseph Métivier, a veteran of the stonecutters' union, to organize francophone women.[100] The need for a female organizer was acknowledged a few months later by the ILGWU when Anita Gastonier was named to organize shirt workers.[101] The cap makers also appointed a francophone organizer, Mme Rompré.[102] Some unions had female international organizers. The cap makers sent Carolyn Wolfe from New York to help during a lockout in late 1919.[103]

Strike and lockout files compiled by the federal Department of Labour reveal that women were involved in at least twenty-seven of the seventy-nine strikes on which it kept records. This is almost certainly an underestimation. Men and women usually took strike action together and frequently supported each other's struggles. Female telephone operators at police headquarters walked off the job during the 1918 municipal workers' dispute.[104] There was one glove workers' strike that involved only women,[105] and in several garment, textile, and rubber strikes women predominated. There was a women's strike involving seventy-three women and three men in the shirt department of John W. Peck.[106] At Royal Silk Dress 121 women and 11 men walked out before a union was formed.[107] At the Acme Glove Company employees (250 women and 150 men) were satisfied with the company's offer but went on strike in sympathy with workers at another company where two-thirds of the strikers were women.[108] There was a strike at the Adanac Glove Company over the discharge of two women for union activity.[109] In another glove workers' dispute thirty-seven women and four men, without authorization or approval from the union, demanded the discharge of a foreman for intimidation.[110] The largest strikes involving women were in the textile and rubber industries.

Organization was not restricted to wage-earning women. The wives and other female relatives of male union members organized auxiliaries to help support union activities. In 1918 the carpenters' local 134 in Montreal established a women's auxiliary that renewed its activity during the building trades strike in the fall of 1919.[111] In October 1919 the Ligue auxiliaire des femmes d'unionistes (an organization parallel to the Women's Labor Leagues in other parts of the country) was formed. Its purpose was to support the union label, to see that the wages of organized workers were spent on union products, to promote unionism, and to investigate and denounce profiteering merchants.[112] Members studied how they could help their husbands' trade union activities. In particular, women were asked to encourage their husbands to attend union meetings.[113] Labour journalists often placed an emphasis on the moral support that women could provide:

> L'aide morale que la femme peut donner à l'homme dans sa lutte pour le bien-être des siens est certainement une des forces les plus profitables pour l'organisation. Le mari, le père, qui se sent soutenu par les siens dans la lutte qu'il doit entreprendre et mener à bonne fin pour obtenir les améliorations qui lui sont nécessaires dans sa situation, est un grand facteur. Au contraire, lorsque l'ouvrier trouve chez lui, dans la personne des êtres qui lui sont chers, des ennemis de son organisation ou des indifférents, ça le décourage et il devient insouciant aux intérêts de son local. Le mal est pire quand la femme, craintive de nature, combat les idées du mari.[114]

Male trade unionists recognized the need to include female family members in their struggles, and promoted the Ligue as a means of improving the working conditions of family members. The Ligue also served as a social organization for women (much as the labour clubs did for men), with entertainment, music, and song used to attract participants to evenings featuring labour speakers.[115] A request by the Ligue for affiliation with the Montreal Trades and Labor Council was met with the suggestion that they affiliate instead with the Women's Trade Union Label League of the United States and Canada.[116] Although the organization of more women in trade unions reduced the male exclusivity, the council insisted on admitting only wage-earning workers. The Ligue's activities included lobbying. For example, a delegation of forty women led by Ligue president Emma Bouchard protested before civic authorities both the lack of water and the refusal to negotiate during a waterworkers' strike. In 1921 the Ligue was active in campaigning for a legislated eight-hour day for women,[117] and in organizing women workers.[118]

As the wave of militancy rolled through industrial Quebec, strikers were sometimes accompanied by violent crowd actions that erupted during struggles against unpopular governments or private-sector employers. In the opinion of the Montreal Trades and Labor Council, such actions had no place in the labour movement. When a strike of some four thousand teamsters was declared, the strikers took control of the streets of Montreal to stop all deliveries. Working carters were forced to stop, told of the strike, and accompanied to the Labor Temple to join the union. If a driver resisted, he was pulled down from his rig, his horses were unleashed, and his cargo was unloaded onto the streets.[119] Such tactics were condemned by union and council leaders who commonly argued that the labour movement promoted discipline and directed workers' grievances into acceptable channels. In this case the council reaffirmed its insistence on the rule of law and defended the police who accompanied strike-breakers on deliveries on the grounds that they were doing their duty to protect property and persons.[120]

Growing labour militancy was also reflected in expressions of socialist sentiment. At the 1918 Labor Party convention, delegates expressed their support for the October Revolution and, to the horror of *Labor World* editor Gustave Francq, discussed the use of violence.[121] On May Day in 1919 some three thousand people singing the Internationale marched down St Catherine Street. Among the marchers was a large delegation of men's clothing workers who had won the eight-hour day through contract negotiations rather than a strike. Although the Montreal Trades and Labor Council remained dominated by conservative craft union leaders throughout 1919, socialists were stronger in the local labour movement than their presence on the council would indicate. Not represented on the council were large numbers of socialist garment workers and machinists in the Amalgamated Society of Engineers. This organization was the backbone of the Montreal branch of the One Big Union, which was established in 1919 and, after disintegrating, revived the following year.[122] The eight hundred members of the ASE joined the OBU when the international union dissolved union its North American locals in 1920.[123]

In Quebec the labour revolt took on new proportions at the start of June 1919. Leading the strike movement in Montreal were the workers at the Canadian Vickers shipyards. The Vickers dispute was part of a larger strike movement in the shipbuilding industry and would be the core of the general strike movement in Montreal, one that trades and labour council executive members attributed not only to radical elements but also to 'outsiders.'[124] There was some truth to this claim: one of the principle promoters of the sympathetic strike movement was

R.J. Johns, an OBU supporter from Winnipeg who was in Montreal to participate in the negotiations involving Division 4 of the American Federation of Labor's Railway Employees Department.[125] The Vickers strike began days after a general strike in support of striking metalworkers was launched in Toronto on 30 May. On 2 June, when Harry Kirwin (the president of the Marine Trades Federation and a member of the Toronto General Strike Committee) arrived in Montreal, the members of the Marine Trades Federation at the Vickers shipyards walked off the job.[126] One of the unifying themes in the general strike movement was the strikers' demand for an eight-hour day.

The strike movement quickly gathered momentum. On 3 June some eighteen hundred boilermakers at Vickers voted to lay down their tools.[127] The same day, 500 barbers, 40 glassworkers, and 2300 workers at the Canadian Consolidated Rubber also went on strike. The next day all the other trades at the Consolidated Rubber plant left work.[128] OBU supporter William Baugh, president of the Marine Trades Federation in Montreal, assumed the presidency of a general strike committee that was formed to coordinate action among the striking workers at Vickers. Committee members distanced themselves from the business agents who answered to the international unions' head offices by stating that the strike was 'the affair of the men on the job and the union officers have nothing to do with it.'[129] The strike movement continued to gather strength as 300 glovemakers went on strike on 6 June, followed by 355 employees of the Columbus Rubber Company the next day.[130] By mid-June the momentum was increasing. On 15 June 3500 textile workers went on strike, followed by 200 meat cutters and 360 electricians the next day.[131] The 'Federation of militants,' as one activist described the general strike committee at Vickers, established links with the textile workers as well as with the 150 employees of Jenkes Valve Company. This cooperation resulted in the production of a joint publication for six weeks.[132] The Building Trades Council was also considering strike action to secure the eight-hour day. The workers in Division 4 of the AFL's Railway Employees Department were unhappy at the slow pace of negotiations and wanted to show their support for workers in Winnipeg.[133] Union leaders and the strike committee in Montreal made plans to call a strike on 18 June without waiting for approval from international union headquarters.[134] By mid-June no less than twelve thousand workers in Montreal were on strike and another fifteen thousand were ready to walk out if their demands were rejected.[135]

The momentum of the labour revolt began to falter on the issue of the general strike, which involved a serious disagreement over tactics as well as fundamental ideological differences. International unions and the leaders of the Montreal Trades and Labor Council opposed a general strike and looked to their own 'outside influences' as AFL union roadmen arrived in Montreal in an attempt to counter the expansion of the movement. At a council meeting in early June, when the issue of support for the Winnipeg General Strike came up, council president J.T. Foster maintained that only individual unions, not the council, had the authority to call a strike.[136] This argument was based on an insistence that each union had complete autonomy with respect to job actions and that, if required by a union's constitution, strikes could not be called without the sanction of the international headquarters. General strikes were also rejected because they challenged the sanctity of contracts; the orderly collective bargaining system desired by council leaders required the observance of agreements.

Council leaders in Montreal were uneasy about the situation in Winnipeg. *Labor World* advised withholding judgment until all the facts were known but stated that Winnipeg workers could not be blamed for defending their right to bargain collectively against intransigent employers.[137] Foster feared that the Winnipeg strike was being used to destroy the whole labour movement.[138] He was convinced that a defeat for workers in Winnipeg would soon be felt in Montreal. In the face of mounting pressure to show solidarity with Winnipeg workers, the council found a resolution that did not offend the AFL or craft unions, and that would carry all factions within its ranks. It voted its support for all workers striking for the forty-four-hour week as well as for the principle of collective bargaining.[139]

Fundamentally, however, the craft union leaders were opposed to general strikes. Debate was not limited to union meetings. As the strike wave gathered strength in June, *La Patrie* printed numerous interviews with francophone union leaders who denounced the OBU, Bolshevism, and the general strike. Many of the denunciations came from council executive members and from the leaders of many of the newly organized unions that had recently engaged in strike action, including the teamsters and the municipal workers.[140] Conservative international union leaders also used xenophobic statements to distinguish themselves from socialists in the labour movement. Both Foster and cigarmaker Benjamin Drolet argued that Bolshevism and radicalism were supported primarily by European immigrants.[141] According to Foster, Bolshevism had little attraction among French-Canadian workers who were 'loyaux et respectueux [des] lois.'[142] Foster used this argument to call for more restrictive immigration policies.[143]

The craft unionists' hostility towards socialists intensified when socialists promoted the general strike or gave open support to the OBU. The general strike tactic threatened craft unionism because it amounted to a unilateral setting aside of some of the rules and conventions that bound locals to their international headquarters. The craft unionists refused to abandon structures that had taken years to build – and that, in their view, had proven effective – for a new and untried form of organization. Like their counterparts in Toronto, Montreal craft union leaders preferred closer cooperation through joint councils, which allowed for a united front within an industry while respecting craft jurisdictions.[144]

There was mounting pressure from the international unions for an end to the strike movement in Montreal. Charles Dickie, the secretary of Division 4 of the railway shop workers, ordered the Montreal leaders to await his return from a conference in Atlantic City before calling a strike. On his return Dickie announced that a strike would be postponed for another three weeks.[145] On 18 June council leaders intervened in several disputes, in an attempt to bring them to an end. Foster convinced the Building Trades Council to postpone its walkout until Labour Day. On 19 June the council deplored the arrest of strike leaders in Winnipeg, but again refused a request by the Vickers shipyard workers for a general strike in Montreal.[146] While many of the strikes continued, the momentum of the movement had been halted.

Although Montreal was the centre of most strike activity, there were disputes across the province. In June 1919 firemen in Hull struck in an effort to win the right to belong to an international organization.[147] Some 850 shipyard workers went on strike in Trois-Rivières on 17 June, while another 900 walked out in Lévis in July. Strike activity reached its peak in June but continued through the rest of the year and into 1920. Troops were called in when eleven hundred workers at the Dominion Textile plant in Montmorency walked out in support of some six thousand striking textile workers in Montreal and Magog. There were also strikes by about two thousand rubber workers in Granby, St Jérôme, and Montreal in September and October 1919.

The record of strike activity indicates a high level of labour militancy in Quebec, but what conclusions can be drawn about the attachment of Quebec workers to craft unionism? International craft unions certainly played a role in undermining the strike movement. In June 1919 support for the general strike was much weaker in Montreal than in Toronto or many western centres. But Quebec workers also showed a desire to establish organizations that could bargain more effectively than craft unions and that would include unskilled workers. Often these larger bodies took the form of joint councils that respected the integrity of individual crafts while serving as an industrial union. The large Angus and Point Saint Charles railway shops achieved such an arrangement in 1917, with the establishment of Division 4. Similar initiatives could be found throughout Quebec shipyards as a result of action by the Marine Trades Federation. There were also more informal common fronts such as the one that united Montreal's municipal workers. During the war some of the most notable strikes were undertaken by industrial unions such as the Western Federation of Miners and the Amalgamated Clothing Workers.

Craft unionism nevertheless remained a strong force that could undermine attempts to establish effective joint councils. On Labour Day in 1919 the Montreal Building Trades Council, revived after years of inactivity, declared a general construction strike in an effort to win recognition as the bargaining agent for the whole industry. A number of member locals, apparently unhappy at the timing of the walkout (the building season was about to close), voted to ignore the council's directive.[148] Only the strongest international building trade unions – the carpenters, plumbers, and electricians – hoped to secure an industry-wide agreement. Most bricklayers belonged to a secular national union that was not supportive of industry-wide struggles.[149] Several weeks into the strike each of the unions signed separate agreements either with individual employers or with the Builders' Exchange.[150] In the metal trades in Montreal, a Metal Trades Council was established only at the Canadian Car and Foundry Company; rivalries and craft particularism helped to undermine the establishment of a council for the whole industry. The boilermakers stuck to policy established by their international headquarters and refused to join a federated council. The moulders would not act in unison with other crafts because they felt bound by a collective agreement that ran until September 1919. The International Association of Machinists was ready to participate but remained weak in Montreal since its rival, the Amalgamated Society of Engineers, represented a large number of machinists. Faced with these difficulties, Montreal's pattern makers abandoned efforts to form a joint council and decided to fight for the eight-hour day on their own.[151] In Winnipeg and Toronto, by contrast, general strikes were called to support metal trades councils, while in Amherst, Nova Scotia, there was a strike in support of a general metalworkers' union.

Yet circumstances could lead Montreal workers to threaten a general strike. The second major confrontation with the undemocratic administrative commission since the end of the war – a strike of some 250 workers in the waterworks department – rallied Montreal workers to threaten such a move despite the reluctance of the Montreal Trades and Labor Council leadership. The main issues were wages and classification. (Work was being reorganized by a firm of experts.) Rather than negotiate, the administrative commission tried to bypass the union. Its presentation of an ultimatum to the workers provoked them to walk out at midnight on New Year's Eve, leaving parts of the city without water for up to ten days. Once again it was with the assistance of the Canadian Pacific Railway, the utility companies, and several engineering firms that Commissioner Décary gradually restored order, replacing the strikers and refusing to take them back.[152]

On 11 January 1920 several hundred delegates attended one of the largest meetings ever held by the trades and labour council to consider the possibility of a general strike if the provincial government did not intervene to reinstate the strikers. The same council that had refused to consider sympathetic action during the Winnipeg General Strike now proposed to take a vote on a general strike involving all the organized workers in Montreal.[153] The vote was averted when Premier Gouin established a royal commission that included two council representatives,[154] and that eventually led to the reinstatement of all but one of the strikers.[155]

The strike threat highlighted some of the complex divisions within the Montreal labour movement. The call for an immediate general strike was led by Alfred Mathieu and Henri Julien, both leading figures in the labour clubs. In February 1920 Alfred Mathieu had strongly criticized the council executive for having attempted to avert a strike vote. Mathieu declared that the immediate call of a general strike would have forced Commissioner Décary and Premier Gouin to take organized labour seriously. Mathieu clearly favoured using the general strike as a political weapon for teaching the provincial Liberal government a lesson.[156] The most militant proponents of a general strike directed their hostility at the administrative commission and the provincial government for having deprived Montreal of its autonomy. In contrast with these French-Canadian workers, who felt that the undemocratic trusteeship was aimed directly at reducing their influence and control at city hall, some of the anglophone socialists who had supported the OBU and the general strike movement in May and June (including William Baugh, who had led the Vickers general strike committee) sided in January with Foster and those who wanted to avoid direct action.[157]

In 1919 workers won almost twice as many disputes as they lost.[158] Many of the victories, however, involved smaller groups of strikers. The results in the largest strikes – those involving over a thousand workers – were less encouraging. There were two early victories: one for the carters (although they had difficulty enforcing the agreement given the multitude of employers involved), and one for the Metal Trades Federation at Canadian Car and Foundry. Vickers shipyard workers, the leaders of the general strike movement, returned to work with very minor gains,[159] while rubber workers, textile workers, and wire workers were roundly defeated. In the general construction strike in September, the defection of some locals and the employers' refusal to deal with the Building Trades Council dashed hopes for uniform conditions, although some of the stronger building trades did sign a contract with the Builder's Exchange for the first time since 1914. In the region around Quebec City, workers confronted the militia in disputes at the Davie shipyards in Lauzon and Dominion Textile in Montmorency. Despite these reverses, in January 1920 Montreal workers had the self-confidence to threaten to take a vote on a general strike in support of striking waterworks workers, raising fears among international union leaders that Montreal would witness a conflict similar to the Winnipeg General Strike.[160]

The Defeat of the Strike Movement

Strike activity continued at a high level into 1920, until the recession that started in the summer brought soaring unemployment, wage reductions, longer hours, and an anti-union offensive by employers. Competition for work was intensified in the early 1920s when New England textile and shoe factories began laying off workers, thereby marking the end of a source of employment that had attracted men and women from Quebec since at least the middle of the nineteenth century. Now the trains were filled with families from New England mills returning to Quebec, a devastating problem for rural areas that depended on earnings from the United States.[161]

The turnaround in labour's fortunes came quickly and without a dramatic confrontation on the scale of a general strike. As late as July 1920, recently organized workers in Montreal still hoped to make gains.[162] A strike involving some four hundred steelworkers failed, and the union collapsed in the face of employer resistance. One employer, the Steel Company of Canada, refused arbitration and offered to meet with its own employees, but only if they abandoned their union and returned to work.[163] Many other unions of newly organized workers also collapsed. Soon employers were repudiating contracts that had been won by some of the stronger, more established organizations. In April 1920 the Metal Trades Council at Canadian Car and Foundry negotiated a new agreement that included a closed shop for most trades,[164] but under new American management, the company locked out its three thousand employees in August 1920. The lockout was the result of an unauthorized strike by thirty-four rivet heaters that was quickly repudiated by the unions.[165] The company ignored offers from the Metal Trades Council to replace the strikers and reopened as an open shop, giving workers a verbal assurance that the company would observe the other terms and conditions of the now-defunct collective agreement.[166] Other employers, such as those engaged in job printing, joined the open-shop campaign in 1921. Starting in 1920 striking workers, particularly those in construction and garment making, faced the increased use of injunctions to curb picketing.

Wage reductions were imposed on unionized workers in October 1920 and they continued through the next several years. In 1921, Montreal meat packers, boot and shoe workers, garment workers, Vickers shipyard workers, structural ironworkers (in Montreal and Quebec City), and papermakers (in Jonquière, Kénogami, Cap-de-la-Madeleine, and Hull) struck over wage reductions but returned on their employers' terms.[167] Other workers accepted wage reductions without a fight. Railway shop workers accepted wage cuts in 1921 and 1922 following the recommendations of a government conciliation board.[168] Under these circumstances it is not surprising that the number of strikes declined dramatically, and that there were fewer attempts to organize new groups of workers until the recession lifted in 1925.

One of the significant aspects of the labour offensive had been the organization of public-sector workers. These unions now came under fierce attack. Montreal's lay Catholic schoolteachers were among the first to be targeted. Complaining of nepotism, political interference, and patronage in hiring and promotion, and earning wages that had been substantially eroded by inflation during the war, they joined the American Federation of Teachers and the Montreal Trades and Labor Council in September and October 1919.[169] Although both the public and some newspapers were strongly supportive,[170] the Montreal Catholic School Commission – an appointed body whose members were named by the archbishop, the provincial government, and the City of Montreal – was immediately hostile. Union members were subjected to a vicious campaign. Their faith was questioned, they were accused of Bolshevism for having joined the trades and labour council, and the archbishop publicly declared that teachers should not form a labour organization. The union collapsed in June 1920 when sixty-eight teachers – the most active union supporters – were fired. The Catholic Church's interest in, and control over, education precluded it from tolerating a Catholic teachers' union of any sort, let alone a secular international one.[171]

Montreal municipal unions also came under attack. Montreal workers who had objected to the undemocratic trusteeship and hoped for better treatment from the new council elected in November 1921 were sorely disappointed when it emerged that the majority of aldermen were decidedly hostile to organized labour. City officials objected to the unionization of police, firefighters, and aqueduct workers.[172] The police union bore the brunt of an anti-union assault that was fuelled by business leaders who feared that unionized police would sympathize with other workers during industrial disputes.[173] The city government's campaign against the police union spanned several years and included the dismissal of union officials, an order to quit the union, and a court battle – that lasted until 1927 – over the right of police to organize. The police union resisted this campaign by maintaining close ties with the labour movement and by retaining its TLC charter and membership in the Montreal Trades and Labor Council.[174] Some unions established during the heady organizing years of 1918 and 1919 endured but not without a number of battles.

Outside Montreal a major impediment to militancy was the emergence of the Catholic union movement.[175] Although small before 1917, this movement grew to significant proportions in the last years of the war when it attracted most of Quebec City's national unions, including their strongest organizations in the boot and shoe industry. These national unions were attracted by the advantages offered by a close relationship with the Church, including the moral authority of the Church hierarchy over employers, a large and influential Catholic press, and financial and human resources reaching into every parish in the province. In return the Church was able to shape a movement that discouraged class conflict, preferred arbitration over strikes, emphasized workers' duties to their employers, and opposed independent political activity on the part of workers. Catholic unions held annual conferences starting in 1918, but until the creation of the Canadian Catholic Confederation of Labour in 1921, there was no central organization to represent this movement.

The Church and French-Canadian intellectuals promoted Catholic unions because they feared the militancy and secularism associated with international unions. It is no accident that the Catholic press – *Le Devoir, Le Droit, L'Action catholique,* and *L'Action française* – began an active campaign to promote Catholic unions when the post-war strike wave gained momentum in April and May 1919.[176] Some of the older national unions that joined the Catholic movement (especially those in the shoe industry) had a history of shop-floor militancy, but such activism was mostly absent from the Catholic union movement during the years 1917–19. A review of federal Department of Labour records reveals that there were few Catholic union strikes in 1917–18, a period of renewed strike activity.[177] In 1918 there was one strike by boot and shoe machine operators in Quebec City. In 1919, of the seventy-seven disputes in which the union can be identified, three were led by a Catholic union.[178]

Catholic unions could prove attractive to employers because some of their leaders opposed the eight-hour day.[179] Catholic union promoters also tried to reconcile the idea of a closed shop with the principle that employers should be free to employ whom they wished, and that workers had the right to refuse to join a union. A closed shop was acceptable if the purpose was to raise the craft by improving apprenticeship and helping to train honest and competent workers. As practised by international unions, the closed shop was tinged with socialism because it was used to swell the number of union members, to ostracize non-union workers, and to control the workplace.[180] According to international union leaders, the Marine Trades Federation suffered setbacks at shipyards in Trois-Rivières and Lévis in 1918 largely because employers actively supported Catholic unions.[181] In 1919 strikes were needed to regain exclusive recognition of the federation at two shipyards in Trois-Rivières.[182] At the Davie shipyards in Lévis a second determined strike of nine hundred workers in July and August 1919 was defeated because, in addition to employer intransigence, the strikers faced the active hostility of local clergy, threats from the courts against those arrested in picket-line clashes, and the use of troops.[183] These were key conflicts in which Catholic unions accepted lower wages than international unions were demanding. During the 1919 dispute at the Davie shipyards, Catholic union leaders declared that they were satisfied with existing wages.[184]

In 1919 Catholic unions were established in numerous smaller industrial centres, such as Granby, Sherbrooke, Lachine, and Saint-Hyacinthe, in the hope of undermining the expansion of international unions.[185] Catholic unions were generally established after international union organizers appeared on the scene (or at the beginning of a strike), and almost always among workers of the same occupations. For example, a Catholic union was established immediately after the start of a strike by rubber workers in Granby in June 1919. The local curate boasted that it did such good work that the strike failed and the international union disappeared.[186]

Strike activity continued through 1920, although there were fewer disputes than in 1919. Most of the disputes in 1919 occurred in Montreal, but the following year a much larger proportion took place in other parts of the province. The strikes during this period also began to involve more Catholic unions. Of the seventy-nine strikes that occurred in Quebec in 1920 at least eleven were by Catholic unions. These shop-floor disputes involved a wide range of issues (including discrimination in response to union activity), demands for increased wages, and, in the case of Quebec coal carters, opposition to the use of a three-ton truck for deliveries.[187] In 1921, in Quebec City, a civic workers' strike led by a Catholic organization drew considerable community sympathy.[188] But Catholic unions also helped employers play one group of workers off against another, thereby diluting the potential for wider class battles. In Thetford, where a Catholic union had supplied scabs to help defeat the Western Federation of Miners' strike in 1916, the legacy of bitterness was such that there was no solidarity forthcoming from workers in other mines when the Catholic union appealed to them to support their own struggle in 1920.[189] In the same year, the Master Plumbers' Association in Montreal, in a bid to undermine the international union, signed an open-shop agreement with a Catholic plumbers' union that represented few workers. This agreement extended the work day to nine hours and established a three-tiered wage scale with a maximum equal to the minimum wage accepted by the international union in the previous year. The result was a prolonged strike.[190]

The plumbers' dispute signalled the start of an aggressive Catholic union campaign to replace international organizations in their stronghold of Montreal. Starting in August 1920 numerous new Catholic unions were established among already well organized workers, including tramway workers and railway carmen at the CPR Angus shops.[191] Coinciding with the arrival of depression and unemployment, this campaign threatened to further weaken workers' bargaining power. This is not to say that all Catholic organizations acted to support employers, or that Catholic union promoters did not have a genuine desire to protect workers' interests. However, during the workers' revolt they often defined those interests primarily as being served by avoiding class conflict and by replacing secular international unions with national and Catholic unions. Clearly, the Catholic unions played a role in defeating the labour revolt. If they gained opprobrium for being a passive and quiescent movement, willing to cooperate with employers, it may have been particularly as a result of their actions during this period.

Political Action

The workers' revolt in Quebec was further limited by the inability of Quebec workers to put forward an effective and unified voice at the political level. There were three factors that were particularly important in defining the nature of Quebec labour politics at this time. First, political ideology sometimes divided workers along ethnic lines. While French-Canadian workers had a tradition of labourism, few became socialists. Most socialists were Anglo-Celtic and European immigrants. Second, although labourists insisted on keeping politics and unionism separate, when craft integrity was challenged by industrial unionism in the form of support for the One Big Union, they fought socialist influence within both their unions and in the Labor Party. Third, labourism in Quebec was characterized by close links with the Liberal Party.

Conscription produced a massive extra-parliamentary opposition movement in Quebec. French Canadians of all political stripes, and from all classes, were virtually unanimous in their opposition to the measure. At large anti-conscriptionist rallies held throughout Quebec in May and June 1917, union leaders appeared alongside both Liberal politicians and nationalist leaders such as Armand Lavergne.[192]

In Montreal socialists and the labour clubs played a much more active role than the trades and labour council in mobilizing working-class opposition to conscription. Violent opposition went on night after night through the summer of 1917. Some public demonstrations involved as many as fifteen thousand people. There were occasions when demonstrators attacked soldiers in the streets and broke the windows of pro-government newspapers.[193] Speeches by anti-conscriptionist orators in Montreal became increasingly vehement. Constitutional Club orators such as Paul-Émile Mongeau and Alphonse Bernier rose briefly to prominence on calls for armed resistance and a general strike to resist the Military Service Act. These men had links to the Fédération des clubs ouvriers municipaux rather than a base in the trade unions. Mongeau and Bernier were joined by francophone socialists in urging a general strike against conscription to start on Labour Day. When the strike did not materialize, they denounced those international union leaders, such as Gustave Francq and Joseph Ainey, who opposed the measure.[194] Arguing that it wished to maintain working-class unity, the Montreal Trades and Labor Council did not even permit the conscription issue to be expressed in the Labour Day parade. The council limited its participation in the anti-conscription movement to a strongly worded resolution expressing its opposition and to the organization of a single large rally in cooperation with Mayor Médéric Martin.[195]

Violent demonstrations were not confined to Montreal. For two weeks in September 1917 several hundred people made their way through working-class Shawinigan to protest against the Military Service Act.[196] Resistance did not end with the 1917 federal elections. To avoid the draft many men ignored the act, some fleeing into the woods. In Quebec City, in early spring 1918, attempts by the Dominion Police to enforce the Military Service Act and to look for draft resisters provoked three days of riots in the working-class districts of Saint-Rock and Saint-Sauveur. The federal government further inflamed passions by sending a battalion of Toronto soldiers to quell the riots, killing four civilians in the process.[197]

Quebec delegates to the 1917 Trades and Labor Congress convention, like their western counterparts, were fiercely critical of the Congress executive recommendation not to oppose the Military Service Act. These was, however, considerable ethnic division on the issue. Anglophone socialists from Montreal, such as journeyman tailor George Sangster and machinist Tom Cassidy, voiced support for the Farmilo amendment, which called for the conscription of wealth before the conscription of manpower. French Canadians opposed this win-the-war proposal because it gave conditional support for conscription of men. Carpenter Narcisse Arcand proposed an alternative amendment that called for a delay in the application of the Military Service Act until after the federal elections in December 1917, and for a campaign to get candidates to promise to vote for repeal. Although defeated, Arcand's proposed amendment was supported by most francophones who spoke during the debate. There was also some support among Quebec francophones for a general strike. Boot and shoe worker and FCOM president Gédéon Martel, together with Armand Néagle of the Brotherhood of Railway Carmen, declared that their locals wanted a general strike.[198] *L'Unioniste*, the organ of the Quebec and Lévis Trades and Labor Council, also appeared to approve of a general strike;[199] in fact, although one council officer advocated the measure, it did not have the support of the council as a whole.[200]

Not all francophone workers supported a general strike over the conscription issue. Gustave Francq summed up the reasons for the opposition. First, he argued, international union leadership in the United States would oppose such action. (AFL leaders, including Samuel Gompers, had taken a firmly pro-conscription stand.) Second, it would be unwise for workers to squander their economic power on a political matter, especially since some of the most vocal promoters of direct action in Montreal were not workers but professionals and merchants; these proponents were asking wage earners to pay the price for opposition to compulsory enlistment but were not at risk of suffering any economic hardship themselves.[201] And finally – in a statement that underlined the trades and labour council's preference for orderly, legal, and peaceful opposition – Francq stressed that once a measure was passed into law it should be obeyed.[202] Francq, alone among francophone delegates, also declared his support for conscription, an action that so infuriated the members of his International Typographical Union local that they removed him as their labour council delegate, forcing him to resign as council secretary.[203]

As Leo Roback has stated, the anti-conscriptionist movement 'never joined' with the industrial militancy of the revolt.[204] Conscription did, however, have a political impact. The shape of post-war labour political action in Quebec was largely decided by the 1917 Trades and Labor Congress of Canada convention when it came out against a general strike and voted to support the formation of a Canadian Labor Party. By 1917 the old Quebec Labor Party was largely ineffectual, without much influence in elections or the various levels of government. In office it had only Joseph Ainey, a francophone carpenter who had been returned as controller in Montreal since 1910. Alphonse Verville, a former TLC president who had been elected federally for Maisonneuve since 1906, ran as a Liberal during the 1917 election. The Quebec Labor Party was dominated by Montreal Trades and Labor Council leaders who shunned any attempt at cooperation with socialists. In 1912 the labour clubs that formed much of the party's base switched their allegiance to the Fédération des clubs ouvriers municipaux de Montréal.[205] It was because of the TLC resolution calling for cooperation among a wide range of working-class institutions and organizations that trade unionists, socialists, members of the cooperative movement, and labour club representatives from most of Quebec's larger and smaller industrial centres met to establish the Quebec Section of the Canadian Labor Party (QSCLP) at the end of 1917. The founding convention adopted a platform that included various social reforms (including a government monopoly over banking and the nationalization of utilities and natural resources) and allowed for direct affiliation of trade unions, labour clubs, and socialist parties.[206] The program was essentially that of the old Quebec Labor Party with some additional policies inspired by the platform of the Independent Labor Party of Ontario. Party officials reported considerable enthusiasm and a growing membership in the months following the convention.[207] The QSCLP represented a remarkable and unprecedented level of cooperation among working-class groups from across the province. Erstwhile political foes were brought together in a fragile coalition. For example, Joseph Ainey was chosen as president, while Joseph Schubert (a member of the Social Democratic Party) was elected treasurer.[208] When the Montreal Labor Party was formed in May 1918, a trade unionist acceptable to all factions, Joseph Métivier, became president, while the rest of the executive was distinctly socialist. Other table officers included Adélard Lanouette of the People's Power League, Bella Hall, Rose Henderson, and Ulrike Binette, later the OBU's paid organizer in Montreal.[209]

With only an embryonic organization, and perhaps realizing that the Laurier Liberals would take most of the anti-conscriptionist vote, the QSCLP did not contest the 1917 federal elections. The FCOM, on the other hand, perhaps hoping to capitalize on its prominence in the anti-conscriptionist movement, initially refused to join the new Labour Party and intended to run a number of its own labour candidates, including Alphonse Bernier, Alfred Mathieu, and FCOM president Gédéon Martel.[210] Faced with unexpected hostility from Liberal organizers, Martel alone remained in the race, only to receive a devastating 3 per cent of the vote.[211] The poor showing in these elections irreparably damaged the prestige of Martel and the FCOM. Martel soon resigned as president; once a force in municipal politics, the FCOM remained neutral in the 1918 municipal elections, and soon afterwards, in April 1918, joined the Labor Party, which was growing and gaining support.[212]

Political activity flourished during labour's industrial offensive in 1919 and 1920 as new labour clubs were established in many working-class neighbourhoods and suburbs around Montreal. At the municipal level labour representatives were elected in such places as Thetford, Sorel, and Montreal.[213] When provincial elections were held in June 1919, at the height of the workers' revolt, Labor Party candidate Adélard Laurendeau, a painter at the CPR Angus shops, was elected in Maisonneuve. Laurendeau was not the only trade unionist to gain election. Aurèle Lacombe, the president of the tramway workers' union in Montreal, won a seat as an independent labour candidate. Nor were the national and Catholic unions averse to political action in the 1919 elections. Despite some opposition within its ranks, the Conseil central national des métiers du district de Québec, held a convention in the working-class riding of Saint-Sauveur; it chose E.A. Lortie, a vociferous opponent of international unionism, as a candidate, and contributed funds to his campaign. Lortie and his supporters sought the endorsement of Liberal Premier Taschereau on the grounds that there should be a working-class representative within the government, but Taschereau refused. Lortie narrowly lost to the Liberal incumbent.[214]

The modest labour victories in Quebec and larger ones in other provinces encouraged workers to believe that they could challenge the established parties. To that end they sought closer links with other organized groups such as farmers. Cooperation between workers and farmers was discussed at the Maisonneuve Labor Club in 1919.[215] In June 1920 M Sauvage, the secretary of the Fermiers unis du Québec, addressed the Sainte-Marie Labor Club on the farmers' program and the desire of farmers to work with the Labor Party. The address led to a request to the executive committee of the QSCLP to study the possibility of a campaign involving field workers and farmers.[216] In 1920 the *Labor World* expressed the hope that in the forthcoming federal elections workers and farmers in Quebec would work together to defeat the old parties.[217] Despite the worker–farmer contacts, there is no indication that the hoped-for cooperation ever developed.

The unity of labourists and socialists in the QSCLP was fragile, however. The new structure of the QSCLP meant that leaders of the Montreal Trades and Labor Council could no longer play the dominant role they had assumed in the old Quebec Labor Party. While the council condemned the OBU in May 1919 by an overwhelming vote of seventy-three to three, the Montreal Labor Party endorsed the OBU on 1 June 1919. Thus began a bitter factional dispute between socialists and conservative craft unionists that was to harden over the next two years.[218] International union leaders opposed the OBU not only because they saw it as a secessionist movement that threatened to divide workers, but also because joining the OBU meant abandoning organizations that had proven their effectiveness and that had taken great efforts to establish. They complained that support for the OBU in the Labor Party came not from organized workers but primarily from socialists who were not trade union members. Moreover, they argued that the Labor Party had no right to vote on trade union matters. But support for the OBU, even among council members, was reported to be growing at the height of the strike wave in June. Through the summer and fall of 1919 international unions mounted a successful campaign to have the Montreal Labor Party censured at the QSCPL convention in November for having supported the OBU; their anti-OBU campaign continued into 1920.[219] Most OBU support came from immigrant socialists, and, despite OBU promoter Rose Henderson's optimism that there was a great potential for a breakthrough among francophones, the OBU attracted few French-Canadian members.[220]

Labourists such as Francq began to lose interest in political action when the Labor Party was not closely controlled by conservative international union leaders. In 1921 the Montreal Trades and Labor Council was quick to follow the new line of the Trades and Labor Congress of Canada and to distance itself from the Labor Party. While Francq expressed an implicit preference for working closely with the Liberal government, the *Labor World* officially took a Gompersite position and advised workers to vote for the candidates holding union cards.[221]

Another division within the fragile Labor Party coalition emerged over the question of working with the Liberal government. Many labourists in Quebec had a long-standing affinity for the Liberal Party, and close ties persisted into the post-war period.[222] In the 1918 Montreal municipal elections, the QSCLP chose to pit its president, Joseph Ainey, against incumbent mayor Médéric Martin. The campaign soon took on the appearance of a feud within the Liberal Party. Martin, a Liberal who campaigned on the theme that he too was a worker who still carried his cigarmakers' union card, directed his attacks as much against Premier Gouin's government – for having placed Montreal under trusteeship – as against his opponent. Ainey, considered the only candidate who could compete for the working-class votes that were needed to defeat Martin, received the backing of Premier Gouin's organization. While Ainey promised to work constructively with the appointed administrative commission, Martin claimed to represent the French-Canadian working class against the trusts, the English minority, and the provincial government. This appeal to the nationalism of the working class helped

Martin win re-election by a vote of 42,857 to 35,587. Even though the contest was between two francophone candidates, voters appear to have divided roughly along ethnic lines as French-Canadian wards voted largely for Martin while Ainey carried most of the predominantly anglophone ones.[223]

After the provincial elections of 1919, independent labour MLA Aurèle Lacombe and Labour Party MLA Adélard Laurendeau sat on the government benches with the Liberals. When Joseph Gauthier, vice-president of the Montreal Trades and Labor Council, and president of the Jacques Cartier International Typographical Union local 145, won a provincial by-election in Sainte-Marie in 1921, it was with the active support of Médéric Martin on a Liberal-Labour ticket. Later in 1921 Aurèle Lacombe was rewarded with a seat in the provincial cabinet as a representative of the working class, a move that was welcomed by Montreal labourists. Council leaders were clearly pleased at the election of representatives who would sit with the ruling Liberals. In the opinion of Gustave Francq, it was possible to be a good trade unionist without faithfully supporting the Labor Party.[224] J.S. Woodsworth, labour MP for Winnipeg North Centre, criticized the 'vicious practice' of negotiating and working with established political parties. Woodsworth believed that political action in Quebec was being compromised because the province's labour leaders were not very advanced in their ideals, and because labour candidates often ran on little more than a desire for more working-class representation.[225] Indeed, beyond the insistence on this representation, there was little to distinguish some labourists from progressive liberals. Establishing a separate identity became even more difficult in 1919 when the federal Liberal Party added to its platform a number of social reforms long sought by labourists.[226] During the 1920 federal by-election, Labor Party candidate Alphétus Mathieu went so far as to declare that there was no difference between the federal Liberal and Labor Party platforms.[227]

The alliance with the Liberals proved disastrous for labourism in Quebec. As unemployment mounted during the depression of the 1920s, the provincial Liberal government, which was primarily concerned with fiscal responsibility, did little for workers. When an International Typographical Union strike in 1922 interrupted the publication of the legislature's daily working papers, Liberal Premier Taschereau denounced international unionism and resorted to the use of strikebreakers supplied by a Catholic press.[228] Organized labour's few representatives were neither forceful nor very influential critics within the

Liberal Party during a period when provincial government policies were alienating workers. By the 1923 provincial elections Quebec workers were so displeased with the governing Liberals that Conservatives swept most urban ridings, although Premier Taschereau remained in power with the support of rural voters. Conservatives won thirteen of the fifteen seats on the Island of Montreal,[229] defeating not only Joseph Gauthier, Aurèle Lacombe, and Adélard Laurendeau but also two additional QSCLP candidates. One observer noted a decline in urban voter turnout, a trend that probably hurt labour candidates.[230]

'Lib-Labism' did not go unchallenged within the Labor Party. Anti-Liberal feeling within some of the labour clubs stemmed in part from the Gouin government's establishment of the trusteeship for the City of Montreal. Alfred Mathieu, who had been critical of the Montreal Trades and Labor Council leadership during the waterworks workers' strike in 1920, was a determined opponent of the provincial Liberal government. It was Mathieu's Sainte-Marie Labor Club that was most critical of the pro-Liberal stance of Labor Party MLA Adélard Laurendeau. Mathieu, president of the Montreal Trades and Labor Council in 1921 and now president of the Sainte-Marie Labor Club, ran on a QSCLP ticket against Liberal-Labour incumbent Joseph Gauthier in the provincial election of 1923. To the dismay of Gustave Francq, Mathieu was able to draw enough votes away from Gauthier to ensure the victory of Conservative Party candidate Camillien Houde, his opponent in Sainte-Marie who would in later years serve as leader of the Quebec Conservative Party and mayor of Montreal.[231] Socialists also disdained Lib-Labism. In the 1918 mayoral contest, socialist Michael Buhay was as unenthusiastic about the moderate Joseph Ainey as he was about Médéric Martin.[232] Buhay objected when the trades and labour council congratulated Premier Gouin for promoting Aurèle Lacombe to the cabinet.[233]

By 1921 the One Big Union had faltered, but many socialists regrouped with the establishment of Communist Party of Canada (CPC). First established as an underground organization, in 1922 the CPC formed the above-ground Workers' Party of Canada. The Workers' Party attracted many former members of the Socialist Party and the Social Democratic Party in Montreal, including Michael Buhay, Becky Buhay, Bella Hall, and Ulric Binette. Montreal remained a centre of CPC activity despite a small membership of about a hundred. In 1920 Annie Buller and Bella Hall opened the Labour College, which provided a forum for Communists and other reformers.[234] During the 1920s the

Workers' Party devoted its energies to mobilizing Montreal's unemployed and supporting the Trade Union Educational League (TUEL). The TUEL, an organization that sought Canadian autonomy from the American international unions along with the amalgamation of craft unions and industrial unions, focused primarily on railway shopmen and the garment industries.[235] The Communists in Montreal were mostly immigrants, largely from the Jewish community; the Workers' Party failed to recruit many French-Canadian members.[236]

In 1923 a small group of francophone socialists associated with Albert Saint-Martin tried to affiliate with the Communist International. Refused on the grounds that there already was a Communist Party in Canada, Saint-Martin's group then affiliated with the Worker's Party, but soon left. Saint-Martin preferred to keep his distance and to work independently.[237] In 1925 he established l'Université ouvrière, which hosted conferences on themes ranging from communism to literature. Few French Canadians joined Saint-Martin's group, and even fewer joined the CPC. Those who did had generally experienced a loss of faith accompanied by an abandonment of religious practice.[238] Communists tended to encounter considerable hostility from francophone workers who remained practising Catholics.

There was a close link between ethnicity, political divisions, and the failure of labourism in Quebec. When J.S. Woodsworth campaigned for the QSCLP in 1923, he cited the ethnic divisions between English, French, and Jewish workers that made cooperation difficult and brought about defeat.[239] Among French-Canadian workers, labourism – a significant force in Quebec since the beginning of the century – was clearly in decline by 1923 and disappeared altogether by the end of the decade. The case of Alfred Mathieu is representative of this decline and of a shift to right-wing populism: by the mid-1920s the former labourist was appearing on Conservative Party platforms and was later elected to city hall as a Houdiste alderman.[240] In the growing immigrant community, however, socialism remained alive and vital. In the Saint-Louis ward, in the heart of the Jewish garment district, Michael Buhay – the SDP's candidate for councillor in 1918 – took 38 per cent of the vote.[241] It was in the same ward that the Montreal Labor Party elected Joseph Schubert – a socialist identified with the right wing of the needle trades, and a leading figure in both the Saint-Louis Labor Club and the ILGWU – to city council in 1924.

Quebec labourists supported a number of measures that could appeal to women, including suffrage, a mothers' allowance, and a minimum wage. One of the strongest voices for these reforms was Eva Circé-Côté, a francophone feminist and assistant librarian who wrote a weekly column in the *Labor World* under the pseudonym 'Julien Saint-Michel.' Circé-Côté fought women's economic exploitation by calling for protective legislation, better working conditions, and more educational opportunities for women. Her male pseudonym allowed her to identify in her column with men and with organized labour, but she also assumed the voice of the young modern woman worker, defending women's right to work, denouncing sexual harassment in the workplace, and challenging the notion that men should be head of the household. Her commitment to equality and democracy led her to answer an article attacking women's suffrage written by Henri Bourassa, the influential editor of *Le Devoir* and a conservative Catholic. As her biographer has noted, she was a modern figure in a Quebec usually depicted as wedded to conservative, rural values.[242] Within the Labor Party Rose Henderson, a veteran of the suffrage movement, provided a link with anglophone women's groups. The party was sufficiently interested to send a representative to a Quebec women's conference in 1921.[243]

The women who were most prominent in left-wing organizations in Montreal were at odds with conservative international union leaders in the factional disputes of this period. Among these women, most of whom were socialists, were Annie Buller and Mrs Ray Mendelssohn, members of the Social Democratic Party; Becky Buhay, an organizer for the Amalgamated Clothing Workers during the war; and Mrs S. Larocque, who addressed a meeting of the unemployed in 1919 and presided over May Day celebrations; and Rose Henderson and Bella Hall, who were on the first executive of the Montreal Labor Party. These women, who assumed prominent public roles during the labour revolt, were strong supporters of industrial unionism, the general strike, and the One Big Union. Buhay, Mendelssohn, and Henderson all addressed a rally in support of the Winnipeg General Strike, and Buhay became a member of the defence committee established to raise funds for the arrested leaders in Winnipeg. Henderson campaigned for the OBU, while Buhay and Buller were secretary and vice-president respectively of the General Workers Unit in Montreal.[244] At the Labor Party meeting in June 1919, Henderson, Buhay, Larocque, and Mendelssohn all spoke in favour of the motion supporting the revolutionary industrial union.[245]

International union leaders who supported political action tended to view women in the Labor Party with suspicion, whatever their politics. Many believed that political action should be conducted and controlled by organized labour and that candidates for office should be chosen from among those who had made their mark in labour organizations over long years – a standard few women could meet given that women had been poorly organized and inadequately represented in union hierarchies even when they formed a large part of the membership. Rose Henderson, the only woman who ran for the Labor Party in the 1921 federal election, was the only labour candidate who was not an established member of an international union and a delegate to the Montreal Trades and Labor Council.

Most labourists were similarly reluctant to encourage women to participate in electoral action. The fact that Quebec was the only province in Canada to refuse to grant women's suffrage until 1940 might explain why there was no broad-based attempt by labour to mobilize working-class women for the provincial elections in 1919. But even with women's enfranchisement for federal elections, the Labor Party made little effort to secure their support. During a 1920 federal by-election in Saint-Jacques in Montreal, the *Labor World* questioned labourist indifference to the organization of women, and appealed to women in the riding to present 'la discussion avec courage sur le terrain ouvrier.' Even this concern seems to have been prompted mostly because the Liberal candidate was working to secure the support of women's groups.[246]

Few of the socialist women were francophones. Participation in labour politics may have been more difficult for francophone Catholic women who faced hostility from within the Church hierarchy to feminism, the Labor Party, and international unionism. Eva Circé-Côté, for instance, came under attack in the Catholic press, particularly in the pages of *L'Action catholique*.[247] Outside of trade unions, francophone women were active in the Ligue auxiliaire des femmes d'unionistes whose purpose was to support the union label and promote unionism, and whose political activity extended no further than lobbying.

Conclusion

The post-war labour revolt in Quebec resembled the upsurge in other parts of Canada in a number of ways. Quebec workers from all ethnic backgrounds demonstrated the same desire to organize unions, and to act in concert by establishing joint councils, by undertaking simultaneous strike action, and by threatening a general strike. There was an unprecedented level of strike activity that revealed a remarkable degree of solidarity. Crowd actions suggest that this sentiment was shared by those outside the membership of labour organizations. There was renewed political activity aimed at extending these struggles in order to increase political influence. But the labour revolt in Quebec was ultimately unsuccessful, a failure attributable to employer intransigence, high levels of unemployment during the depression of the 1920s, and profound divisions within Quebec's working class.

As in other regions, although not of the same proportions, there was a division between craft unionists who favoured American Federation of Labor organizations and supporters of the One Big Union. There was discord, as well, over the issue of support for the 1919 general strike. In politics there was a bitter antagonism between labourists and socialists and between those who hoped to gain influence by working with the governing Liberals and those who wanted to avoid such an alliance. The inability to present a unified, distinct, and independent voice at the political level also contributed significantly to the decline of labourism.

In Quebec divisions within the working class – divisions based on complex combinations of gender, ideology, religion, and language – played a key role in the failure of the revolt. While women organized and engaged in militant action on a new scale, male workers seem to have been more overtly hostile to women's paid work, at least in non-traditional areas, than were their counterparts in other regions. Perhaps the strength of conservative nationalist ideology regarding women's proper sphere, as proscribed by the Church and Catholic intellectuals such as Henri Bourassa, explains why male workers in Quebec took fewer pains to integrate women into the revolt.[248] Among women, there was a division between Catholic francophones in the Ligue auxiliaire des femmes d'unionistes and anglophone and Jewish women who were more actively engaged in socialist politics and the promotion of the One Big Union.

In Montreal ideological, political, and ethnic divisions further fragmented the labour movement. Many French-Canadian workers demonstrated an aversion to socialism. The left wing of the labour movement was made up largely of anglophone and European immigrant workers. But while French-Canadian workers on the whole did not espouse socialism, and while those in Catholic unions were quiescent, francophone members of the international unions in Montreal demonstrated a militant streak – a militancy evident during the civic workers' strike in 1918 and the waterworkers' strike in 1920. Francophone workers in Montreal tended to focus on a provincial government that was depriving Montreal workers of their political rights and influence, whereas anglophone socialists focused on the general strike movement in May and June 1919. Led by a secondary leadership of socialists who had little influence at the Montreal Trades and Labor Council, the general strike movement was part of a wider attempt to confront capital. Clearly, it was both these groups – the militant francophone labourists and the socialist advocates of a general strike – that posed a threat to council leaders who insisted on the separation of industrial action and political action.

While more limited than elsewhere in Canada, the workers' revolt in Quebec is nevertheless significant. The organizational vehicles for the revolt were secular international unions. It was this labour movement – associated with class conflict and considered militant towards employers – rather than the Catholic unions, that attracted most francophone Catholic workers and that remained the predominant expression of Quebec labour. The Catholic union movement was least successful at attracting support in Quebec's main industrial centre of Montreal, whose working class included large numbers of Protestant and Jewish workers. In smaller, more ethnically homogenous industrial areas, however, organizations based on the solidarity of Catholic workers seriously undermined the international unions. Most large strikes outside Montreal involved interunion rivalry.

The workers' revolt is also essential to an understanding of why the fledgling Catholic unions received such massive backing from the Catholic Church during this period. The revolt provided the impetus for a counter-attack by the Catholic unions that helped to defeat the strike wave outside of Montreal. And while its initial success in establishing unions and attracting workers was moderate, Catholic union activities in this period laid the groundwork for later growth.

Notes

1 There is an extensive literature on national and Catholic unions. The best recent histories are Rouillard, *Les syndicats nationaux* and *Histoire de la CSN (1921–1981)*. See also Parisé, *Le fondateur du syndicalisme catholique*; Isbester, 'History of the National Catholic Unions'; Têtu, 'Les premiers syndicats catholiques canadiens.' A Catholic union leader has left an important memoir: see Charpentier, *Cinquante ans d'action ouvrière*. On Charpentier, see Rouillard, 'Les écrits d'Alfred Charpentier.' On the response of the American Federation of Labor to Quebec workers before 1914, see Babcock, *Gompers in Canada* and 'Samuel Gompers and the French Canadian Worker.'

2 Dales, *Hydroelectricity and Industrial Development*; Roby, *Les Québécois et les investissements américains*; Linteau, Durocher, and Robert, *Histoire du Québec contemporain*, 351–427. On women workers, see Marie Lavigne and Jennifer Stoddart, 'Ouvrières et travailleuses montréalaises, 1900–1940' in Lavigne and Pinard, *Travailleuses et féministes*, 99–114; and Price, 'Changes in the Industrial Occupations of Women,' 52.
3 Keyfitz, 'Population Problems,' 73.
4 Roy, 'French–English Division of Labour'; McCormack, 'Cloth Caps and Jobs'; Reynolds, *British Immigrant*, 157–89; Rudin, *Forgotten Quebecers*, 201–14; Tulchinsky, 'Contours of Canadian Jewish History,' 48. On Italian workers, see Ramirez, 'Workers without a Cause.'
5 This estimate was made by Catholic union activist Alfred Charpentier. Jacques Rouillard also believes that the same estimate holds true going back to the start of the century. Rouillard, *Les syndicats nationaux*, 36, n. 89.
6 Rosenberg, *Canada's Jews*, 177; Tulchinsky, 'Third Solitude,' 99–100.
7 Ramirez, 'Workers without a Cause,' 119–34.
8 The latter split is described by McKay and Morton in this volume.
9 Rouillard, *Les syndicats nationaux*, 233–4. Rouillard estimates that in 1921 there were 72,761 organized workers, 17,600 of which belonged to Catholic unions.
10 See Leblanc, '*Le Monde ouvrier/The Labor World*.'
11 Rouillard, *Les syndicats nationaux*, 36, n. 89.
12 *Labor World*, 7 February 1925.
13 See Babcock, 'Samuel Gompers and the Berlin Decisions'; and Rouillard, 'Le Québec et le congrès de Berlin.'
14 On the labour clubs, see Rouillard, 'L'action politique ouvrière.'
15 Gauvin, 'The Reformer and the Machine,' 21.
16 Groupe de chercheurs de l'Université du Québec à Montréal sur l'histoire des travailleurs québécois, *L'action politique des ouvriers québécois*, 23, 71, 73.
17 *La Patrie*, 3 November 1921.
18 Ibid., 14 February 1920.
19 Tulchinsky, 'Contours of Canadian Jewish History,' 46; 'Third Solitude,' 100.
20 *La Patrie*, 4 April 1916.
21 On Albert Saint-Martin, see Larivière, *Albert Saint-Martin*.
22 Roback, 'Quebec Workers in the Twentieth Century,' 167.
23 *La Patrie*, 12, 20 January, 16 February 1914; *Labour Gazette*, February 1915, 932–3.
24 *Labour Gazette*, February 1915, 934.
25 *La Patrie*, 15 July, 26 December 1914.

26 *Machinists' Monthly Journal* (henceforth MMJ), August 1915, 746; September 1915, 837; Dumont, 'Histoire du syndicalisme,' 126–7; *Le Canadien*, 21 October 1915; *Blacksmith's Journal*, August 1915, 17.
27 *Blacksmith's Journal*, 17 April 1914, 27 February 1915.
28 Nagant, 'La politique municipale à Montréal,' 253; *La Patrie*, 17 April 1914; Rumilly, *Histoire de Montréal*, vol. 3, 458–60.
29 *La Patrie*, 25 September 1915.
30 Ibid., 14 May 1915.
31 Charpentier, 'Le mouvement politique ouvrière de Montréal,' 161.
32 *La Patrie*, 29 September 1915.
33 For example, a local of the Ukrainian Social Democratic Party organized demonstrations of unemployed Ukrainians in Montreal. Krawchuk, *Ukrainian Socialist Movement*, 44.
34 *La Presse*, 21 April 1914.
35 *La Patrie*, 3, 10 March 1915.
36 Rouillard, 'L'action politique ouvrière,' 281–2.
37 See, for example, NAC, MG 30 A16 (Sir Joseph Flavelle Papers), Vol. 6, File 64, G.H. Vickers to Crothers, 13 November 1914.
38 *Labor World*, 9, 18 March 1916.
39 There were 500 strikers according to the District Council of the United Brotherhood of Carpenters and Joiners, and 294 according to the company. NAC, RG 27 (Department of Labour, Strikes and Lockouts Files), Vol. 305, Strike 65, W.J. Jeffers to Department of Labour, 2 March 1916; *Labor World*, 18 March, 8 April 1916.
40 For an account of this strike, see Dumont, 'Histoire du syndicalisme.'
41 *Labor World*, 15 July 1916.
42 Trades and Labor Congress (TLC) *Proceedings*, 1916, 111.
43 Ibid., 107–9.
44 Dumont, 'Histoire du syndicalisme,' 128–34.
45 Rouillard, 'Les travailleurs juifs,' 257; International Ladies' Garment Workers Union, *Proceedings*, 1918, 14–16.
46 NAC, RG 27, Vol. 306, Strike 34; Tulchinsky, *Taking Root*, 215, 218.
47 *Montreal Star*, 15 January 1917.
48 *Labor World*, 10 February 1917.
49 See *La Patrie*, 25 January 1917, for an example.
50 *Montreal Gazette*, 23 February 1917.
51 Ibid., 13 January 1917.
52 *La Patrie*, 1, 15 February 1917.
53 *Advance*, 9 March 1917.
54 'Report of Royal Commission Appointed to Inquire into the Alleged Unrest

Existing in the Shipbuilding Industry in the Province of Quebec,' *Labour Gazette*, November 1918, 964–7.

55 *Labour Gazette*, November 1918, 955–9; NAC, RG 27, Vol. 309, Strike 125.

56 *Labor World*, 12 October 1918.

57 Lavoie, *Les débuts du mouvement ouvrier à Sherbrooke*, 97.

58 *La Patrie*, 30 August 1916.

59 Rumilly, *Histoire de la Province du Québec*, vol. 23, 49–50, 139. On the importance of municipal governments to workers, see Heron, 'Working-Class Hamilton.'

60 *La Patrie*, 5, 6, 7, 8 May 1919.

61 Ibid., 14 May 1918; *Montreal Star*, 2, 24, 29 January 1920.

62 *La Patrie*, 31 July, 10 September 1918.

63 Ibid., 5 December 1918.

64 *Le Devoir*, 10 December 1918; *Montreal Gazette*, 12, 13 December 1918; *La Patrie*, 13 December 1918.

65 *La Patrie*, 13, 14 December 1918.

66 *Le Devoir*, 13 December 1918; *Montreal Gazette*, 13 December 1918.

67 *Montreal Gazette*, 13 December 1918.

68 Copp, *Anatomy of Poverty*, 133; *La Patrie*, 13 December 1918; *Le Devoir*, 13 November 1918.

69 *La Patrie*, 16 December 1918.

70 *Montreal Gazette*, 14 December 1918.

71 Ibid., 14 December 1918; *La Patrie*, 18 December 1918.

72 *La Patrie*, 13 December 1918.

73 *Montreal Gazette*, 14 December 1918.

74 *La Patrie*, 18 November 1918.

75 *Labor World*, 21 December 1918.

76 The complete report issued by the arbitration board is in *La Patrie*, 3 February 1919.

77 On meat packers, see *Labour Organization in Canada*, 1919, 128; on rubber workers, see *Montreal Gazette*, 3 June 1919; *Labor World*, 21 June 1919, and NAC, RG 27, Vol. 318, Strike 391; on textile workers, see *Labor World*, 5 April 1919, 24 May 1919, and *Deux grèves de l' 'International',* 3–4; on garment workers, see *Advance*, 5 December 1919; on shirtmakers, see *Labor World*, 21 June 1919; on teamsters, seamen, gas workers, and laundry workers, see Canada, Dept. of Labour, *Labour Organization in Canada*, 1919, 130, 1920, 172–7.

78 *Montreal Gazette*, 15 April 1919.

79 Ibid., 14, 15 April 1919.

80 *La Patrie*, 7 July 1919.

81 Ibid., 26 March 1919.

82 Francq, *Bolchévisme ou syndicalisme, lequel?*, 31.
83 *Labor World*, 26 April 1919.
84 Ibid., 8 March 1919.
85 Ibid., 12 April 1919.
86 Ibid., 22 March 1919.
87 Ibid., 8 March 1919.
88 *Montreal Gazette*, 2 February 1917.
89 *Advance*, 23 November 1917.
90 Frager, *Sweatshop Strife*, 99; Linda Kealey, 'Women's Labour Militancy,' 6.
91 ILGWU, *Proceedings*, 1918, 14–16. For a discussion of ethnic and gender divisions among garment workers in Toronto, see Frager, *Sweatshop Strife*.
92 Ibid., 102–3.
93 NAC, RG 27, Vol. 306, Strike 41.
94 Price, 'Changes in the Industrial Occupations of Women,' 53–4, 74–5.
95 *Labor World*, 18 November 1916.
96 NAC, MG 30 A16, Vol. 38, File 1918–24, Mark Irish to Flavelle, 3 May 1918.
97 NAC, RG 27, Vol. 308, Strike 42, clipping from correspondent's report, n.d.
98 *Labor World*, 8 February 1919.
99 Price, 'Changes in the Industrial Occupations of Women,' 39–40.
100 *Labor World*, 12 April 1919.
101 Ibid., 21 June 1919.
102 Ibid., 19 March 1921.
103 *Montreal Star*, 1 December 1919.
104 *Le Devoir*, 13 December 1918.
105 The twenty-five workers involved in this strike were attempting to force an employer to honour an agreement. See NAC, RG 27, Vol. 317, Strike 289.
106 NAC, RG 27, Vol. 311, Strike 49.
107 *Labor World*, 17 May 1919.
108 Ibid., 31 May 1919. For the number of strikers, see NAC, RG 27, Vol. 313, Strike 154, J.A. Demers to Department of Labour, 31 May 1919, and Hudson Bay Knitting Co. to Department of Labour, 31 May 1919.
109 *Labor World*, 21 June 1919.
110 NAC, RG 27, Vol. 315, Strike 215, J.A. Demers to Department of Labour, 8 July 1919.
111 *Labor World*, 4 May 1918; *La Patrie*, 25 October 1919.
112 *La Patrie*, 25 October 1919.
113 *Labor World*, 13 August 1921.
114 Ibid., 28 August 1920.
115 See, for example, ibid., 1 May 1920.
116 Ibid., 22 November 1919.

117 Ibid., 8 January, 19 February 1921.
118 Ibid., 7 May 1921.
119 *Montreal Gazette*, 16, 22, 24 April 1919.
120 Ibid., 19, 23 April 1919.
121 *La Patrie*, 16 December 1918.
122 Bercuson, *Fools and Wise Men*, 160–1.
123 NAC, MG 27 II D19 (Arthur Sifton Papers), Vol. 9, RCMP Report, C.I.B. Division, 21 October 1920, 18–19.
124 *Montreal Gazette*, 4, 11 June 1919. In May 1919 Welland and Toronto experienced strikes in shipbuilding. Naylor, *New Democracy*, 50. Shipyard workers in Trois-Rivières walked off the job in June 1919, while those in Lévis did so in July.
125 *Montreal Gazette*, 24, 28, 31 May 1919; *Montreal Herald*, 3 June 1919; Gregory Kealey, '1919,' 28.
126 *Montreal Herald*, 3 June 1919.
127 *Montreal Gazette*, 24, 31 May 1919; Gregory Kealey, '1919,' 28; *Montreal Herald*, 3 June 1919.
128 *Montreal Gazette*, 4, 11 June 1919.
129 *Montreal Star*, 4 June 1919; *Montreal Gazette*, 12 July 1919.
130 *Labour Gazette*, July 1919, 779; NAC, RG 27, Vol. 314, Strike 188.
131 *Labour Gazette*, July 1919, 798–9.
132 Alex Gauld in *The Worker*, 5 September 1923.
133 *La Patrie*, 21 May 1919.
134 *Montreal Star*, 18 June 1919; AFL, Railway Employees Department, *Proceedings*, 1920, 69.
135 *La Patrie*, 16, 17 June 1919.
136 *Montreal Gazette*, 6 June 1919.
137 *Labor World*, 24 May 1919.
138 Ibid., 21 June 1919.
139 *Montreal Gazette*, 5, 6 June 1919; *Labor World*, 7 June 1919.
140 See, for example, *La Patrie*, 2, 3 June 1919.
141 *La Patrie*, 27 March, 17 April 1919; *Montreal Star*, 4 June 1919.
142 *La Patrie*, 18 January 1919.
143 Ibid., 27 March, 17 April 1919; *Montreal Star*, 4 June 1919.
144 Naylor in this volume.
145 *Montreal Star*, 18 June 1919; *La Patrie*, 25 June 1919.
146 *Montreal Gazette*, 20 June 1919.
147 *La Patrie*, 2 June 1919.
148 *Montreal Star*, 9 September 1919.
149 *Montreal Gazette*, 6 September 1919; Logan, *Trade Unions in Canada*, 94.

150 *La Patrie*, 6, 8 July 1919; *Montreal Star*, 11 July, 9 September 1919; *La Presse*, 3 September 1919.
151 *Pattern Makers Journal*, May 1919, 14–15.
152 *Montreal Star*, 11 November, 2, 12 January 1920.
153 Ibid., 12 January 1920; *La Patrie*, 12 January 1920.
154 *Montreal Gazette*, 22 January 1920.
155 *Montreal Star*, 29 January, 24 February, 8 May 1920.
156 Ibid., 6 February 1920.
157 Ibid., 12, 16 January 1920; *La Patrie*, 12 January 1920.
158 According to figures compiled from the *Labour Gazette* and the Department of Labour's Strikes and Lockouts Files.
159 The workweek was reduced from 50 to 47.5 hours, while skilled workers received a wage increase of seven cents an hour. *Ottawa Citizen*, 12 July 1919, in NAC, RG 27, Vol. 314, Strike 189; *Montreal Star*, 14 July 1919; W. Baugh to Department of Labour, 9 August 1919 in NAC, RG 27, Vol. 314, Strike 189.
160 TLC, *Proceedings*, 1920, 113.
161 *Labor World*, 30 July 1921; Lavoie, 'Les mouvements migratoires des Canadiens,' 79–80; Roby, *Les Franco-Américains de la Nouvelle-Angleterre*, 286–7; Rouillard, *Ah Les Etats!*, 79–80.
162 NAC, RG 27, Vol. 322, Strike 293.
163 *Labor World*, 21 August 1920; Heron, *Working in Steel*, 133–4.
164 *Montreal Gazette*, 24 August 1920.
165 Naylor, *History of Canadian Business*, vol. 2, 293; *Windsor Star*, August 24, 1920 in NAC, RG 27, Vol. 323, Strike 324; *Montreal Star*, 20 August 1920.
166 NAC, RG 27, Vol. 323, Strike 324, Theo. Bertrand to Department of Labour, 11 September 1920.
167 *Labour Gazette*, 1921.
168 Ibid., July 1922, 771–2, April 1923, 404; Logan, *Trade Unions in Canada*, 129.
169 For an account of these early organizing efforts, see Chartrand, *Une certaine alliance*, 15–25. On the grievances over hiring and promotions, see *La Patrie*, 11, 12 December 1919; also Archives de l'Université du Québec à Montréal, Fonds de l'École Normale Jacques Cartier, Correspondence avec divers particuliers et organismes, 1918–1921, 'Nos instituteurs ont-ils des griefs?' (anonymous mimeograph, n.d.). For an account of wage increases during the war, see *La Patrie*, 18 October 1919; *Factum. Respectueusement dédie à l'Honorable Premier Ministre Sir Lomer Gouin*, n.d., in Montreal Catholic School Commission Archives (MCSCA), Associations syndicales et autres, Association du Bien-être des instituteurs et institutrices de Montréal, 1919–1920, 3.

170 Over ten thousand people expressed their support for the teachers' demands by signing a petition that the teachers submitted to their employers, the Montreal Catholic School Commission (MCSC). Eudore Gobeil to MCSC, n.d., in MCSCA, Associations syndicales et autres, Association du Bien-être des instituteurs et institutrices de Montréal, Généralité, 1919 à 1920. Among the newspapers offering encouragement was *La Patrie*. See, for example, *La Patrie*, 9 October 1919.

171 *Labor World*, 5 June 1920.

172 *La Patrie*, 21 February 1923.

173 Ibid., 20 March, 15 July 1922.

174 Ibid., 14 April, 6 June, 29 and 30 November, 3 December 1923; Canada, Dept. of Labour, *Labour Organization in Canada*, 1923, 217; 1925, 204–5; 1927, 235; TLC, *Proceedings*, 1927, 135.

175 The following interpretation differs significantly from that of Jacques Rouillard who maintains that the Catholic unions in the post-war period were less fearful of striking and more focused on defending workers' interests. Rouillard, *Les syndicats nationaux*, 232.

176 Ibid., 224.

177 These figures are based on a review of files in NAC, RG 27, Strikes and Lockouts Files.

178 Two of the Catholic union strikes involved the union representing carriage makers in Montreal, while the third was declared by roofers and plumbers in Quebec City. *Labour Gazette*, March 1920; NAC, RG 27, Vol. 317, Strikes 316, 317.

179 For an example, see Labour Canada Library, Royal Commission on Industrial Relations, Evidence, Quebec City, 11 June 1919, 4051.

180 On the attitude of Catholic unions towards the closed shop, see *Programme Souvenir du Premier Congrès de la Confédération des Travailleurs Catholiques du Canada*, 11–13; and Logan, *Trade Unions in Canada*, 592–3.

181 'Report of Royal Commission Appointed to Inquire into the Alleged Unrest Existing in the Shipbuilding Industry in the Province of Quebec,' *Labour Gazette*, November 1918, 955–9; *Labor World*, 12 October 1918.

182 NAC, RG 27, Vol. 316, Strike 248.

183 *Le Soleil*, 6 August 1919; *Blacksmith's Journal*, September 1919, 35; *Quebec Chronicle*, 2 August 1919; Doré et al., *History of the Quebec Labour Movement*, 84.

184 *Quebec Chronicle*, 12 August 1919.

185 Maltais, *Les syndicats catholiques canadiens*, 82–101.

186 *Programme Souvenir du Premier Congrès de la Confédération des Travailleurs Catholiques du Canada*, 63.

187 The figure for the number of disputes in 1920 is from Gregory Kealey, '1919,' 17; NAC, RG 27, Vol. 319, Strikes 35, 41, 43, 65, 77; Vol. 320, Strikes 134, 135; Vol. 322, Strike 299; Vol. 323, Strike 360; *Le soleil*, 1 May, 15 November 1920.

188 On the Quebec civic workers strike, see Rouillard, *Histoire de la CSN*, 95–6.

189 On the Western Federation of Miners' strike, see Dumont, 'Histoire du syndicalisme,' 128–9. On the 1920 strike, see NAC, RG 27, Vol. 323, Strike 360; *Sherbrooke Record*, 11 November 1920.

190 NAC, RG 27, Vol. 323, Strike 351.

191 *Programme Souvenir du Premier Congrès de la Confédération des Travailleurs Catholiques du Canada*, 31.

192 *La Patrie*, 25 May 1917.

193 Armstrong, *Crisis of Quebec*, 168–79. On the conscription crisis in Montreal, see Dansereau, 'Le mouvement ouvrier montréalais.'

194 *La Patrie*, 4 September 1917.

195 *Labor World*, 16 June 1917; Roback, 'Quebec Workers in the Twentieth Century,' 170; Dansereau, 'Le mouvement ouvrier montréalais,' 76, 84.

196 Provencher, *Québec sous la loi des mesures de guerre*, 31.

197 Ibid., 41–140; Armstrong, *Crisis of Quebec*, 226–30.

198 TLC, *Proceedings*, 1917, 142–9.

199 *L'Unioniste*, 30 June 1917.

200 *Labor World*, 7 July 1917.

201 Ibid., 29 September 1917.

202 *La Patrie*, 21 September 1917.

203 *Labor World*, 13 October 1917; Dansereau, 'Le mouvement ouvrier montréalais,' 95.

204 Roback, 'Quebec Workers in the Twentieth Century,' 171.

205 Rouillard, 'L'action politique ouvrière,' 286.

206 On the constitution and program of the QSCLP, see *Labor World*, 10 November 1917; and *L'action politique des ouvriers québécois*, 98–101.

207 *Labor World*, 19 January 1918.

208 Ibid., 10 November 1917.

209 Ibid., 18 May 1918.

210 *La Patrie*, 15, 22 October 1917; Le groupe de recherches sur l'histoire des mouvements politiques ouvriers de l'Université du Québec à Montréal, *Chronologie*, 238.

211 Liberals decided that they had been mistaken in tolerating the anti-conscriptionists' attacks on Laurier and Premier Gouin in the preceding months. *La Patrie*, 15 October 1917. In a bizarre incident Alfred Mathieu's campaign manager, Paul-Émile Mongeau, claimed to have been drugged to

prevent him from depositing Mathieu's election papers. Around the same time, Mathieu issued a statement denying that he had been paid to withdraw from the race. *La Patrie*, 22 November 1917; *La Presse* 18 December 1917; *Le Devoir*, 20 December 1917.

212 Le groupe de recherches sur l'histoire des mouvements politiques ouvriers de l'Université du Québec à Montréal, *Chronologie*, 239, 242, 244.

213 At Thetford J. Lacasse Rousseau, secretary of the Western Federation of Miners, was mayor from 1920 to 1923. On 1 May 1920 *Labor World* noted that organized labour had three representatives at city hall in Sorel.

214 *Le Soleil*, 4, 9, 10, 13, 18, 24 June 1919.

215 *La Patrie*, 6 November 1919.

216 *Labor World*, 19 June 1920.

217 Ibid., 17 April 1920.

218 Ibid., 7 June 1919.

219 For a report on this convention, see *Labor World*, 22 November 1919.

220 Bercuson, *Fools and Wise Men*, 118–19, 160–1.

221 *Labor World*, 4 December 1921.

222 On the ties between labourism and liberalism, see Heron, 'Labourism and the Canadian Working Class.'

223 *La Patrie*, 1, 4 March, 1, 3 April 1918.

224 *Labor World*, 8 October 1921.

225 *Worker*, 1 March 1923.

226 *Labor World*, 3 April 1920.

227 *La Patrie*, 1 April 1920.

228 This incident is examined in Rouillard, *Les syndicats nationaux*, 299–302.

229 Rumilly, *Histoire de la Province de Québec*, vol. 26, 228–9.

230 *La Patrie*, 6 February 1923.

231 *Labor World*, 3 February 1923.

232 Ibid., 9 March 1918.

233 Ibid., 8 October 1921.

234 Fournier, *Communisme et anticommunisme au Québec*, 13–16; Watson, *She Never Was Afraid*, 11–14.

235 *Worker*, 3 October 1925.

236 Fournier, *Communisme et anticommunisme au Québec*, 14; Larivière, *Albert Saint-Martin*, 137; Communist Party of Canada, *Proceedings of the 5th Convention of the Communist Party of Canada*, 1927, 5; *Worker*, 22 October 1927, 1 June 1929.

237 Larivière, *Albert Saint-Martin*, 135–6; Fournier, *Communisme et anticommunisme au Québec*, 21; Buck, *Thirty Years*, 29–30.

238 Fournier, *Communisme et anticommunisme au Québec*, 22–8.

239 *Worker*, 1 March 1923.

240 Rumilly, *Histoire de Montréal*, vol. 4, 113, 141.

241 *La Patrie*, 3 April 1918.

242 Lévesque, 'La citoyenne selon Eva Circé-Côté,' 47–66; on Henri Bourassa, see Trofimenkoff, 'Henri Bourassa and "the Woman Question,"' 104–15.

243 *Labor World*, 22 January 1921.

244 Linda Kealey, '"No Special Protection"'; on Mrs Larocque, see *Labor World*, 25 January, 3 May 1919.

245 *Labor World*, 7 June 1919.

246 Ibid., 20 March 1920. The Liberal candidate, Fernand Rinfret, had earlier given a conference on women's emancipation; see *Labor World*, 10 January 1920. During the election Rinfret was supported by the Club Libéral des Femmes and its president, Mme F.L. Béique. Rumilly, *Histoire de la province de Québec*, vol. 24, 203.

247 See her reply in *Labor World*, 16 August 1919.

248 On Henri Bourassa, see Trofimenkoff, 'Henri Bourassa and the Woman Question,' 104–15; on the Church's attitude towards feminism, see Marie Lavigne, Yolande Pinard, and Jennifer Stoddart, 'La Fédération nationale Saint-Jean-Baptiste et les revendications féministes au début du 20e siècle,' in Lavigne and Pinard, eds., *Travailleuses et féministes*, 199–216.

Southern Ontario: Striking at the Ballot Box

JAMES NAYLOR

'The Spirit of Revolt is Everywhere Apparent' declared Ontario labour journalist Joseph Marks in the *Industrial Banner* in the midst of the First World War.[1] Growing anger at a government that protected profiteers and patronage machines, he argued, had thrown the old political parties into disrepute. Defying censorship regulations, Marks pointed to the massive strike of munitions workers in Hamilton as a sign both of state and employer arrogance and a working-class challenge to the old social order. By the signing of the Armistice in Europe, others had come to share this appraisal. The newly appointed federal labour minister, Gideon Robertson, told his colleagues that 'there [is] greater fear of the Labour situation in the City of Toronto than in any other spot.'[2] In the spring of 1919 that city was on the verge of a general sympathetic strike. By autumn the combined forces of workers and farmers had won a startling victory in the provincial legislature; Ontario was in the vanguard of labour electoral action.

Images of the Winnipeg General Strike and the formation of the One Big Union (OBU) in western Canada dominate our view of the post-war working-class upsurge in Canada. While historians have debated the depth of radicalism reflected in such movements, participants had little doubt that they were engaged in challenging an inequitable social order dominated by capitalists and the politicians who protected them. Central and eastern Canada seemed to be out of step with such developments. To the historians who wrote of the 'western labour revolt,'[3] and no doubt to western workers as well, Ontario appeared to be a conservative monolith. At the end of each summer, as unionists met at the Trades and Labor Congress (TLC), Ontario delegates, with the force of numbers behind them, solidly defeated westerners' attempts to guide the labour movement towards socialism and industrial unionism. Throughout the war the Hamilton-based *Labor News* repeatedly declared in its statement of policy that socialism was 'impractical,' and defended the modest goal of 'a wage system based upon a just return for services offered.'[4] In the early spring of 1919 the geographical character of this political division was apparently confirmed at the Western Labour Conference held in Calgary. Western radicals would go their own way; the TLC was abandoned to the conservatives.

Is it possible to reconcile these starkly opposed images? Was Ontario a centre of labour conservatism or was it, as Marks and Robertson seem to suggest, caught up in a wave of social revolt not unlike that of the West? Strong cases can be made for either argument. The self-confidence and security created by high levels of employment in the war economy spurred organization and created a political space within which workers could voice, debate, and, it was hoped, implement their visions of a better society. Wartime rhetoric of democracy and service validated a working-class critique of a class-divided society. Yet the Ontario labour movement was deeply divided, reflecting both the strong values of pre-war craft unionism and the catalyst of wartime pressures. The extent of working-class activity in Ontario was unprecedented, but in retrospect the goals of this movement appear meagre in comparison with the passion with which workers fought for them. Workers' deeply rooted belief in the dignity of labour and their uncompromising faith in democracy were reinforced by the war. Such ideals provided a strong impetus to activity, but supplied few strategic pointers for working-class activists. Both the character of the Ontario labour movement and, as we shall see, the concatenation of struggles on different fronts at the end of the war help to explain this incongruous aspect of working-class activity. Finally, in contrast with the West, the lack of dramatic confrontations in Ontario and the paucity of material gains for labour eventually combined to blur the memory of a widespread working-class revolt in the province.

The Challenge

By late 1915 the pre-war economic depression had given way to an economic boom as millions of dollars were poured into the economy for munitions and war supply production. Sixty per cent of Canadian war production, organized under the Imperial Munitions Board (IMB), was concentrated in Ontario. Several factors placed labour and the state on a collision course. An overheated economy and domestic commodity shortages fuelled inflation. Rents escalated towards the end of the war. The creation of the IMB placed a vast amount of power and money in the hands of a small group of businessmen led by Toronto millionaire meat packer (and accused profiteer) Joseph W. Flavelle. Unlike its American and British counterparts, the Canadian government excluded even conservative labour leaders from wartime planning, while the IMB ignored the trade union movement.[5]

Not surprisingly, the initial working-class response came from a trade union movement that immediately recognized a threat to the position of its skilled members in war-related industries. Metal trade workers, particularly machinists and moulders, had been at the forefront of union battles during the industrial transformation of central Canada in the preceding two decades. As such industries grew and merged, and as employers sought to introduce new machinery and managerial systems aimed at undermining workers' autonomy and control on the shop floor, these workers clung tenaciously, if often unsuccessfully, to a proud craft ideal that combined notions of skill, equality and independence on the shop floor. Canada's concentration on producing shrapnel shells for the war meant that a large proportion of Ontario's metalworkers were set to work producing long runs of standardized products. The possibilities of deskilling were readily apparent to employers, and 'specialists,' including women, were soon introduced into these shops.[6]

Pressed by an increased pace of work and uncontrolled inflation, and emboldened by the high demand for metalworkers' labour, the industry exploded. In June 1916 some two thousand Hamilton munitions workers struck. The essential features of this strike demonstrate that workers in Ontario could respond to the challenges of the war economy in a militant manner much the same as the rest of the continent. The conflict immediately revealed the depth of working-class support for trade unionism, as hundreds of organized and unorganized workers joined the strike called by the metal trades unions. Moreover, organizational and jurisdictional differences dissolved as members of the machinists' union and the British-based Amalgamated Society of Engineers joined ranks. A further sign of working-class anger was the ineffectiveness of employers' appeals to patriotism; these workers took the war emergency seriously, but they were not about to sacrifice their own class interests.[7] As one Toronto metal polisher commented during a 1918 strike, he was striking 'so that when the boys return they will not have to submit to a starvation wage, but will be given at least the right to a fair wage and a decent living for themselves and their families.'[8]

A crucial feature of the Hamilton strike was noted by a federal labour department official, who reported that workers were beyond the control of their union officers who had urged restraint.[9] In contrast with the dynamics of pre-war conflicts, the goals of union militants and officers began systematically to diverge. Leaders of the Trades and Labor Congress and the international unions set their sights on the growing number of administrative bodies in Ottawa, and demanded labour representation upon them to ensure that the interests of unionists were not overlooked. While not entirely averse to wartime strikes, the leadership recognized that an ability to control its membership was a key bargaining chip in such a demand. For many workers, however, such a strategy paid few dividends, and increasingly workplace disputes led to strikes. In southern Ontario alone, the number of days lost in strikes grew from 25,000 in 1915, to 77,000 in 1916, to over 120,000 in the final year of the war.[10] As presaged by the Hamilton strike, a common sense of grievance against employers and the federal government was reflected in growing numbers of industry-wide and sympathetic strikes. Increasingly, militants gained the leadership in local conflicts that transgressed the bounds of established unions.

While further confrontations of the scale of the Hamilton munitions strike would await the end of the war, union membership soared in the final years of the war and into 1919. Established craft unions in the metal and building trades found themselves, often for the first time, capable of exercising some real control over the labour market. In London fewer than one in ten carpenters had been organized early in the war; by 1919 70 to 80 per cent were members of the United Brotherhood of Carpenters and Joiners. In Toronto the Amalgamated Clothing Workers grew from two hundred to thirteen hundred members during the war; by 1919 it had three thousand members in the city. In Hamilton the same union organized seven hundred of the eight hundred workers in the trade in 1919. Even the long-defunct coopers' union was briefly resurrected.[11]

A mere growth in membership, however, understates the development of organized labour. For the first time since the heyday of the Knights of Labor in the 1880s, unionism ceased to be the preserve of skilled men. New unions such as those of bank clerks, firefighters, building labourers, rubber workers, civic workers, retail clerks, and domestics emerged at a staggering rate. Some of the new unions included workers (such as the teamsters) who had struck before, but who had never been able to form and sustain a union. Women telephone operators who had organized and struck unsuccessfully a decade earlier were again organized, forming part of a union movement that was undergoing a profound transition. The willingness of the machinists' union to organize women specialists – and, in at least one highly publicized case, to strike in defence of women unionists – suggests that some ideas about the role of women in the workforce and in unions were being debated. This debate was the product of both the suffrage movement and the entry of large numbers of women into non-traditional jobs during the war.[12]

More substantial, in terms of the number of new unionists, were workers from eastern and southern Europe. Previously, Jewish workers were the only non-British or non-Canadian-born workers to establish a stable tradition of trade unionism in Ontario. In this new situation an Italian organizer was summoned from the United States to help organize building labourers;[13] an organizer of the Amalgamated Association of Iron and Steel Workers in Hamilton reputedly spoke seven languages. The Amalgamated Association was a former craft union that had widened its jurisdictional boundaries to admit unskilled workers, resulting in rapid growth during the post-war upsurge.[14] Such developments were even more dramatically apparent in the province's meat packing plants. The Amalgamated Meat Cutters and Butcher Workmen, for example, grew from a nucleus of twenty-two members in 1918 to over, thirty-nine hundred a year later, becoming Toronto's largest union local – one that included large numbers of women and immigrant (including, to the amazement of many, Chinese) workers.[15] Fuelled by long-standing animosities and official nativist justifications for the war (it was characterized as a war pitting 'British democracy' against the 'Hun'), differences of national origin continued to divide workers. Indeed, major nativist demonstrations occurred in both Toronto and Hamilton in 1918.[16] Nevertheless, in particular unions (including the meat packers' and steelworkers' unions), and in the speeches of radicals across the province, the labour movement increasingly symbolized working-class unity across craft and ethnic lines.

With the exception of steel and meat packing – and to a certain extent the garment industry, where erstwhile craft unions appeared to be transforming themselves in the direction of industrial unionism – the established structures of the trade union movement had difficulty accommodating the less skilled. In the American Federation of Labor (AFL) and the Trades and Labor Congress of Canada, union membership was determined by the particular skill a worker possessed. Craft unionists were concerned about the 'dilution of labour' that would result from hiring increasing numbers of unskilled workers in the context of industrial expansion during the war.[17] The debate over the role these workers should play in an expanded labour movement further divided unions, with radicals, attracted to ideals of a more inclusive industrial unionism, championing the cause of the unskilled within the established unions. Well into the post-war upsurge, large groups of unskilled workers (including 450 rubber workers in 1920) challenged their employers in strikes initiated without the aid of a union.[18] For the moment, until jurisdictional differences could be resolved, hundreds of unskilled workers were organized into 'Federal Labor Unions' that were directly chartered by the AFL or TLC. At the Imperial Oil refinery in Sarnia, for instance, those workers who did not qualify as boilermakers formed a 'Fed.' In Kitchener labourers from several factories joined the Fed; two hundred joined in Orillia, while the London Federal Labour Union could claim twice that number.[19]

Leadership of these new unions often came from socialists who viewed the organization of the entire working class as key to the success of labour. President Louis Braithwaite of the meat packers' union rapidly became a recognized leader in the Toronto socialist movement. At a meeting over a thousand members of the Toronto Federal Labor Union elected to the executive Isaac Bainbridge, the leader of the Social Democratic Party (SDP) who had been jailed during the war for his anti-war views; his union soon grew to over two thousand members.[20] By 1919, then, the union movement in Ontario had been transformed in several ways. Once a movement of craft workers who had banded together to defend their control over their skills and workplace, unionism was increasingly reaching out to workers of all types, including the semi-skilled and unskilled. That this trend occurred unevenly across the province and across different sectors of the economy was reflected in conflicts within the labour movement. Industrial unionists and socialists gained respected places within both the new and established unions, but beyond a militancy that seemed to pervade every corner of the union movement, little consensus existed as to which the direction to follow.

Toronto, with its well-established socialist movement – the Social Democratic Party had boasted a thousand members before the war, and had elected James Simpson to the city's Board of Control by a huge majority in 1914 – soon epitomized the tensions developing in the labour movement.[21] Fuelled by state and business fear of working-class unrest, the approach of peace in Europe was matched by an increase in repression under the War Measures Act. A series of federal orders-in-council resulted in the banning of organizations and publications, and in the prohibition of strikes. A meeting to protest the orders held by the Toronto District Labor Council five days after the Armistice demonstrated both the anger and the changing composition of the labour movement. The Council leadership expressed greater concern about the radicalism of those in attendance (including, it pointed out, large numbers of immigrants) than about the actions of the government. Meetings of the Council came to reflect deep divisions as conservatives and radicals fought for control of the central organization of Toronto workers;[22] subsequent developments delivered the Council into the hands of the latter.

The arrests of radicals and labour militants at the end of the war spurred protests led by socialists in the movement. The police raids of the night of 19–20 October 1918 in twenty Ontario towns and cities were followed by other arrests. The large machinists' and carpenters' unions organized mass meetings to demand the release of members of their respective unions. The machinists threatened a general strike over the arrests.[23] In Massey Hall, at a carpenters' meeting held to protest the arrests, TLC President Tom Moore was shouted down for asking workers to confine themselves to 'constitutional action.'[24] As in the West, growing working-class organization and self-confidence brought to the fore the possibility of general sympathetic strikes. In Stratford workers threatened a general strike to free a colleague charged with possessing banned literature. Workers in Windsor threatened the same action when the army arrived to defend strike-breakers who were running the city's streetcars. In London and Ottawa – cities not known as bastions of militancy – workers debated the general strike. The Guelph Trades and Labour Council urged the creation a National Council of Labour that would unite the Trades and Labor Congress with the national unions and various radical industrial unions in the West and have the power (which the TLC lacked) to declare sympathetic strikes.[25] Respected labour spokespersons such as James Simpson and former Knight of Labor Phillips Thompson added their voices, declaring that the general strike was a necessary weapon in the face of bosses who 'act[ed] collectively against striking workmen.'[26]

It was in Toronto that the long-simmering movement came to a boil. In 1917 the city's machinists threatened a general strike over conscription and, in 1918, the Toronto District Labor Council, with an eye to events in Winnipeg, discussed a general strike in support of Toronto's newly organized civic workers.[27] (The Imperial Munitions Board privately worried that a local street railway strike was about to ignite such a conflagration.)[28] In 1919 the Council debated calling a general strike, on one occasion to free political prisoners and, on another, as a protest against unemployment.[29] If union militants were looking for an opportunity to organize a general strike and demonstrate labour's newfound strength, the city's metal trades employers were obliging. There would be no breaches in the employers' front. Speaking through the secretary of the city's Employers' Association, the employers responded with a single 'no' to all the workers demands.[30] There seemed to be no alternative to a general strike, and so in April 1919 the local metal trades council, which represented four thousand workers in 232 factories, approached the Toronto District Labor Council with a request for just such support.

At this point the Council was an ideological battleground. Conservatives still held office, but they had ceased to represent the mood of the majority of the delegates. The character of the organized labour movement in Toronto had changed rapidly in the preceding two months, a period in which some ten thousand Toronto workers joined the ranks of organized labour. Unions that had grown quickly during the war (for example, the machinists' union) had a growing numerical weight on the Council and were increasingly represented by radicals whose ideas found new favour in their locals. The Council's organization committee, recently expanded from five members to twenty-one – almost all of them radicals committed to organizing the skilled and unskilled alike – played a key role in this growth. Predictably, delegates from new unions that did not share the craft privileges or ideology of their brothers in older unions tended to lend their often considerable weight to the radicals. The new butcher workers local, for instance, was eligible for seventy-nine delegates on the Council.[31]

Council leaders urged that action be delayed until the international officers could be consulted, a procedure increasingly ignored within international unions. There was, indeed, little reason to believe that patience would bring rewards, for the employers had made their position quite clear. An acrimonious debate led to an agreement that a delegated convention of all the city's unions would meet on 20 May 1919 to vote on a general strike. Ensuing events demonstrated clearly the differences between Winnipeg and Toronto. Winnipeg workers voted overwhelmingly in favour of a general strike. In Toronto the general strike convention demonstrated a solid core of support for such action as well as substantial opposition. Delegates representing 9985 workers voted in favour of the strike; those representing 5150 workers voted against. Given such deep divisions, a lack of confidence in the success of the strike, rather than strong opposition to general strike action per se was probably the source of the abstentions registered by delegates representing 15,550 unionists.[32]

With a mandate to strike, and employers' refusal to make even token concessions, events acquired their own dynamic. Given the weakness of the strike mandate, the 'Committee of Fifteen' that the convention had elected to conduct the strike could only attempt to make the best of a perilous situation. The committee agreed to a last-minute conference with employers and Prime Minister Borden. The meeting was unsuccessful, and when the committee attempted to address a meeting of the street railway employees in order to win their support for the strike, it was prevented from doing so by the street railway leaders. What followed, despite solid participation by several unions, was a debacle for proponents of sympathetic strikes. Two thousand carpenters and a similar number of garment workers joined the strike. On Monday, 2 June, some seventeen thousand workers were on strike. It was a strong show of support, demonstrating that those who had proposed the strike were not isolated within the city's labour movement. But as the *Toronto Star* suggested, it was a general strike 'in name only.'[33] That evening the strike was ended at the request of the Metal Trades Council, in whose support it had been called.

The defeat of the general strike, and the news that the Winnipeg General Strike had been physically smashed by the mounted police and the army, signalled no victory for trade union conservatives. In executive elections held in July 1919, the Toronto District Labor Council went 'Red.'[34] Socialists who had supported the general strike won every post. Throughout the region craft unionism and notions of class compromise seemed in disfavour. Indeed, outside of Toronto there were at least as many strikes – and striker days lost to production – in 1920 as in 1919.

The events of May and June 1919 did, however, force union radicals to rethink their strategy, and particularly their earlier attraction to the emerging One Big Union. Once again, the metal trades took the lead. The Toronto and Hamilton locals of the Amalgamated Society of Engineers, who were rhetorically (if not always in practice) less craft-oriented than the American Federation of Labor, were among the first to declare their sympathy with OBU aims and principles. The machinists were also interested; two large Toronto locals voted to endorse the One Big Union, and OBU representative R.J. Johns was assured that immediately following the general strike serious consideration would be given to affiliating the Toronto locals with the new movement. The Toronto Metal Trades Council used through its organ, *Ontario Labor News*, to publicly praise the OBU, which also gained an important voice in Hamilton when Fred Flatman offered the *New Democracy* as a lively and insightful vehicle for OBU organizing in central Canada. The carpenters, too, were interested and directed their officers to order fifteen thousand pieces of OBU literature for distribution.[35]

Despite such sponsors, the Toronto *Mail and Empire* was quite wrong in seeing the Toronto general strike as a stepping stone to the One Big Union.[36] Indeed, the opposite was true. With some significant exceptions, such as Flatman and Isaac Bainbridge, partisans of the OBU quickly recognized that recent events demonstrated that the course they had been following threatened to split and weaken the Ontario labour movement. Although individual OBU speakers such as Johns and Joe Knight often received positive responses, the fact was that most unions and trades councils expressed little interest in the One Big Union. While craft unionism could not match the élan of of the radical sentiments behind the general strike and, increasingly, the amalgamation movement, it was far from a spent force. As the proponents of industrial unions and sympathetic strikes were forced to recognize, trade union conservatives retained enough support and power to undermine the general strike movement in the radicals' stronghold of Toronto. It followed, then, that any secession along the lines of that taking place in the West could only lead to a fratricidal battle that would demoralize the labour movement, dissipate its recent membership gains, and marginalize the radicals.

The radicals' prognosis, however, was not so bleak since amalgamation, rather than secession, appeared to be a sure route to industrial unionism. Although many workers had been attracted to industrial unionism and the general strike, they were not as yet willing to abandon their existing unions, which had for the most part proven responsive to reform. Thousands of new workers had been brought into the fold of the union movement, and, even more significantly, the province's craft unions appeared willing and able to transform themselves into industrial unions through amalgamation.

It followed that James Simpson's initial response to the Calgary Conference and the creation of the One Big Union became, after the abortive

Toronto general strike, the accepted wisdom of the majority of Ontario's union radicals. Simpson observed that the 'constant improvement of machinery is reducing a skilled labourer to merely dexterous labor' ... [a] condition that lends itself to the one big union which [western unionists] have decided upon.' He added that 'the closer federation of [existing] organizations would be more in harmony with the evolution of industry.'[37] Developments seemed to bear him out. The Toronto Metals Trade Council took a unified stand against the precondition – established by the Employers' Association – that affiliated unions bargain separately. The source of such sentiment within the rank and file of the unions was revealed in the fact that no member of the Toronto Metal Trades strike committee had been a paid union official. In Hamilton representatives of the machinists and the Amalgamated Society of Engineers, who had fallen out over the outcome of the 1916 munitions strike, organized a Metal Trades Council with the avowed purpose of amalgamating the metal trades throughout North America. On the waterfronts there emerged an audacious Marine Trades Federation that was soon covering twenty shipbuilding yards from the Lakehead to the Atlantic. It declared its intention of organizing unskilled workers into an affiliated Federal Labor Union and signalled its opposition to the existing hierarchy of trades by demanding a common wage for all crafts. The Toronto Building Trades League moved to raise a $25,000 strike fund that would be under its own control – a declaration of autonomy from the international headquarters and a prerequisite for sympathetic strike action. Affiliated unions authorized the league to strike in support of the painters, and soon set their sights on a single agreement with the builders exchange, one that covered all workers in the industry. In 1920 building trades unions throughout the province fought long battles to establish and preserve industry-wide bargaining.[38]

The impetus to amalgamation was not confined to Toronto, or even to unions considered radical. Workers in the furniture industry, eleven thousand of whom were scattered throughout small towns of western Ontario, had streamed into the carpenters' and painters' unions at the end of the war. As one organizer commented (exaggerating somewhat the trends in the industry), '[It] would be silly to ask these men to organize upon craft or trade lines when there is no longer any need of the skill such workmen were able to sell before the machine did its work.' Relatively weak traditions of craft unionism and the existence of a well-organized Furniture Manufacturers' Association were two factors behind the formation of a furniture workers' council. On the Niagara

Peninsula four thousand workers on two huge construction projects – the new Welland Canal and a hydroelectric canal – formed the Niagara District Trades Federation, with the active participation of unskilled labourers. A Public Utilities Council of public-sector workers in Toronto was formed by, of all people, one of the central opponents of the Toronto general strike.[39] Craft unionism, as such, had few supporters. Even Tom Moore, the conservative president of the Trades and Labor Congress of Canada, predicted its gradual eclipse. Employers such as Colonel W.M. Gartshore of the McClary Manufacturing Company in London were among few proponents of a return to the values of craft unionism.[40] The decline of craft unionism was underscored when the traditionally anti-union *Financial Post* nostalgically declared that '[in] the present social crisis the way of safety is the way of the old-established Trades Unions.'[41]

Ontario Labor News, produced by revolutionary socialists, recognized the weakness of secessionist sentiment and the potential of the amalgamation movement, and retracted its earlier support for the OBU. The collapse of Fred Flatman's attempt in May 1919 to unify Ontario units of the OBU, Federal Labor Unions, the DeLeonite Workers International Industrial Union, and various other small left-wing unions demonstrated that no organizational alternative to international craft unionism existed.[42] The rejection of the OBU in Ontario, then, was in large part a strategic decision – based on a careful assessment of the relationship of forces – rather than a declaration of conservatism. Indeed, Winnipeg General Strike leader William Ivens was well received throughout the region in October 1919. Commenting on the tour, Gordon Cascaden, editor of the *Detroit Auto Workers' News*, still felt that Ontario was ready to explode, lacking for nothing but 'someone to break the ice.'[43]

By any measure of sheer militancy, Cascaden's assessment was correct. The year 1920 showed no decline in strike activity. There were, however, important differences. Following their major defeat in Toronto, the metal trades were relatively inactive, and strikes no longer seemed to threaten to widen into class battles as they had the previous year. Without major gains, working-class militancy would exhaust itself. But suddenly the terrain shifted and workers' hopes were rekindled. Such optimism had a new source: electoral success.

The Forces of Democracy

In the fall of 1919 working-class hopes turned from the unions to the ballot box. The barriers to working-class power seemed to collapse in the electoral arena just as employers were demonstrating their ability to withstand the challenge of the amalgamation movement. Workers still fought innumerable battles against individual employers, but broader social change, it seemed, would be heralded in the legislatures. Strikes in 1920 no longer seemed to have the broader potential they had had in 1919. The task of realizing workers' hopes was left to the Independent Labor Party of Ontario (ILP).

Developments in the electoral arena represented the culmination of a decades-long political project of a tenacious core of trade unionists who viewed the Liberal and Conservative parties as political machines beholden only to their capitalist benefactors. Although socialists often participated in movements to elect labour candidates, such campaigns often attracted many workers who rejected socialism as unworkable or unnecessary. The aim of such 'labourists' was simply to elect representative (generally skilled) workers to legislatures where, it was assumed, they would adequately represent labour instead of the 'special interests which have permitted the profiteering and exploitation of the people for their own benefit.'[44] Their attacks were aimed less at capitalism than at 'partyism' – a political system in which blind allegiance to established parties served to perpetuate the abuses of wealth in public office. They were anxious to right the imbalance. Representative of this current was labour member Allan Studholme, who had won a by-election for the Hamilton East seat in the Ontario legislature in the wake of a bitter street railway strike that had polarized Hamilton in 1906 and stimulated the unions to coalesce around their own candidate. In the legislature Studholme studiously guarded his independence from the other parties and spoke out in the interest of trade unionism, women's suffrage, and democratic reform.[45]

Although Studholme remained for over a decade a singular figure in the legislature, labourist ideals were evident in trades and labour councils across the province. While international trade union bodies were organized along craft lines, and federal and provincial organization was rudimentary at best, local trades councils effectively united organized workers with diverse skills and experiences. Municipal politics proved more tractable than politics at other levels of government because of the weakness of partisan ties and the concentration of workers in particular wards. As craft distinctions were increasingly overlooked during the war and as the active membership of unions soared, the role of trades councils grew. As they had before the war, such councils nominated candidates to run for municipal councils and school boards. They achieved notable success, electing candidates in Hamilton, St Catharines, Peterborough, and Welland, as well as in smaller centres. Although such efforts sometimes fell into the orbit of the old parties (in the case of Toronto and London, the Liberals), trades councils generally met fortnightly and kept a close eye on their representatives. Labour politicians fought for better wages for municipal employees, better education for working-class children, and the democratization of the municipal franchise, still restricted by property qualifications.[46]

Municipal success led many unionists to consider ways of breaking the hold of the old parties on provincial and federal governments. At the same time, forces from within and without were pushing the labour movement to act within a broader electoral arena. On the eve of the war Joe Marks had used the *Industrial Banner* to vigorously promote the campaign that won the passage of the Workmen's Compensation Act. In contrast to the largely unsuccessful lobbying efforts of the Trades and Labor Congress, Marks and his colleagues mobilized 750 local unions and trades councils across the province.[47] Not since the nine-hour movement of the 1870s had Ontario's workers transcended craft distinctions to organize so broad a movement, and never with such success. Marks and other proponents of labour electoral activity dedicated themselves to building upon the enthusiasm and confidence gained in the campaign.

The war provided a new impetus to their efforts. As an increasingly interventionist state became a major player in workplace relations, established practices of confronting individual employers became less effective: now the Imperial Munitions Board organized production; registration and eventual conscription served to reorganize the labour market; federal legislation regulating strikes and lockouts was extended to all munitions production; and the Department of Labour stepped up its efforts to prevent work stoppages. Industrial problems became provincial and national political problems, and the labour movement was pressed to respond at that level.

These developments took place in the highly charged atmosphere that accompanied the war. The barrage of appeals to service, to a broader spirit of sacrifice, to democracy, and to morality in international relations carried no deadline or geographical limit. Commentators of all kinds pondered the post-war 'reconstruction' created by a war fought ostensibly against the forces of autocracy and militarism. Reconstruction was increasingly perceived as a second crusade, following the fight to preserve 'civilization' in Europe. The Hamilton *Labor News* declared that '[i]n its broad sense the meaning and implication of the word "reconstruction" transcends mere schemes for orderly demobilization. It connotes the reorganization of society along lines hitherto unknown. It has come to mean the conscious application of science to the conduct of human affairs.'[48] Reconstruction thus signalled the dawn of a new age.

It was a notably vague goal. From the *Financial Post*, which declared that victory would be the 'victory of the masses,' to the *Industrial Banner*, which foresaw 'a better world and a nobler civilization,' an entire spectrum of opinion sought to redeem the sacrifices of the war with the promise of a new and vigorous 'democracy.'[49] Behind such declarations stood markedly different visions of the future. Notwithstanding a Kitchener shoeworker's comment before the post-war Royal Commission on Industrial Relations that Canadian workers 'were under the impression that something was promised them but they did not know what,' the labour movement had fashioned its own, albeit inchoate, plans for reconstruction. According to one long-time craft union leader, workers had determined that to be treated as mere commodities 'is not making the world safe for democracy ... and it is not liberty.' Others spoke of a 'new vision'[50] that included shorter work hours and a higher standard of living, but also a much broader democracy. Such a vision was evident, for instance, when the Toronto District Labor Council proposed as an appropriate war memorial the construction of a hall for large public gatherings and discussion; a similar proposal was made by London labour.[51] Perhaps most significant was the quasi-millenarian character assigned to the period of reconstruction. A glowing article written by Joseph Marks for the *Industrial Banner* in 1918 was typical in this regard:

> [I]n Canada, on every hand, may be seen manifestations of the coming resurrection, the throb of the new life, and the hope of future achievements, when the workers of the Dominion will take their rightful place and make their influence felt in shaping the destinies of the Dominion, in conjunction with the other progressive forces of the state, so that the sacrifices of those who have died to make the bounds of democracy greater yet shall not have been in vain, and Canada shall achieve her destiny as a nation that stands for the greatest good to the greatest number of its citizens, and a civilization in which service and character shall count for more than wealth or titles of nobility.[52]

In the midst of the war, however, it was apparent that 'service and character' counted for little. Canada was shaken by repeated profiteering scandals, the federal Conservative-cum-Unionist government ensured its power by means of extraordinary laws restricting the franchise, orders-in-council constrained democratic action, and the patronage machines remained unreformed. Reconstruction would not come from the 'big interests and special privileges that have made millions in profits as a result of war-time conditions.'[53] As John MacDonald told a crowd of three thousand at one of Toronto's 1919 May Day celebrations, 'if there [is] to be any reconstruction it ha[s] to be thru the workers themselves.'[54] As the major confrontations of 1919 developed, the Metal Trades Council voiced the alternatives confronting Canadians: 'Let them choose between slavery and service.'[55]

As such sentiments developed during the war, Marks and other supporters of independent labour political action determined the moment was ripe to launch a campaign on a province-wide level. On the basis of their experiences in municipal elections, and as a consequence of an incessant campaign in the pages of the *Industrial Banner*, sixteen local labour parties met in July 1917 to form the Independent Labor Party of Ontario. Despite its roots in diverse local experiences, the founding convention of the ILP was remarkable in its unanimity. Little political debate took place. Rather, as had occurred at the founding of the Greater Toronto Labor Party in 1916, a statement of general principle substituted for an elaborate programmatic statement. 'Performance is better than promise,' it declared, 'and [we] rest our claim for support of organized and unorganized labour in the general declaration that we stand for the industrial freedom of those who toil and the political liberation of those who for so long [have] been denied justice.'[56] In established labourist fashion it was assumed that direct working-class representation would inevitably unfetter democracy from the constraints of the profiteers and the patronage machines. Rather than challenging the rules and assumptions of liberal democracy, the ILP became its greatest defender. Released from the control of the 'big interests,' the liberal democratic state, it was implicitly assumed, could represent all citizens. To this end the ILP proposed the abolition of property qualifications for voting and holding office and proportional representation.

This project of cleansing the political system of opportunists and parasites was reminiscent of that of nineteenth-century producerism. Like their allies in the United Farmers of Ontario who also had no 'special interests' to protect, labourists considered themselves citizens par excellence. Unlike proponents of earlier producerist ideologies, however, manufacturers had long disqualified themselves from the alliance by their opposition to unionism and by their profiteering during the war. The crux of this new democracy was independence from the old and corrupt parties; the constitution of the ILP expressly forbade entertaining any discussion of fusion or cooperation with any party 'other than a bona fide Labor Party.'[57] Although not socialist, the new party was not explicitly anti-socialist. Significantly, its recognition of the Social Democratic Party as another 'labour party' opened new avenues for socialist–labour cooperation. At the same time, the ILP offered itself as a party 'that every democrat could support.'[58]

While the war continued, the new party faced clear disadvantages. The 1917 federal election, which offered clear alternatives among the established parties on the issue of conscription, threatened to marginalize the ILP. Nevertheless, the party did well enough to establish its credibility; its candidates averaged well over two thousand votes each. The ILP's failure to elect members to Parliament was attributed to inexperience, weak organization, and the Borden government's heavy-handed manipulation of the election.[59] The strength of labour's commitment to electoral victory was reflected both in the success of ILP financial appeals to local unions and in the widespread condemnation of American Federation of Labor President Samuel Gompers, who, on a visit to Ottawa in support of the war effort, denounced political action. The same Hamilton labour paper that decried socialism in its statement of policy printed the angry response of a local craft union leader to 'the most indiscreet and rottenest remark Sam Gompers has ever made.'[60]

That such sentiment went far beyond long-established circles of labourist activists was dramatically revealed in a by-election in early 1919 in the Tory stronghold of St Catharines. Although St Catharines was an important manufacturing centre, many leaders of its local trades councils were Liberals, and a branch of the ILP had not been organized in the city until December 1918. Despite such unpromising terrain, the support for the labour candidate, a returned soldier and unemployed machinist, exceeded all expectations: the ILP lost by a hair. A comment by a *Toronto Star* reporter caught the essence of the party's appeal:

> As in similar cases elsewhere it isn't the particular planks in the Labor platform, either good or bad, that create the issues, but something much more intangible, a feeling justified or unjustified that power hitherto has been exercised by a comparatively few men to their own advantage, and that the common people have been making a mistake not only in the class of representatives they have been sending, but in bowing the knee to inflexible idols of partisan party politics.[61]

The Independent Labor Party presented itself not as a mere party of reform, but as the party of a new, reconstructed social order. ILP stickers were printed to read 'Every Vote for Labor is a Vote for Democracy.'[62]

Events in the wake of the St Catharines by-election were demonstrating that democracy was attainable at the ballot box. A party membership drive to recruit ten thousand new members in three months was inaugurated.[63] Only three years old, the ILP had grown to seventy-eight branches. In combination with the growing strength of the unions, a political space opened in which new movements could emerge and new ideas could be debated by people who had never before had a voice. The ILP, which had exhibited a 'movement culture' from the outset through the promotion of 'entertainments, educational and literary evenings' held a series of 'monster picnics' including one attended by twenty-five hundred people in Hamilton.[64] In Toronto the party established a weekly forum series that for several years running averaged audiences of eight hundred. Appearances by such figures as the militant American labour leader William Z. Foster, Scottish Labour MP Neal MacLean, and French socialist Jean Longuet resulted in soaring attendance. Topics varied widely, reflecting a lively, if eclectic, working-class passion for self-education.[65]

The flowering of labour political action opened a new and public space for working-class women. While many male workers jealously guarded workplace privileges and sought access to a family wage that they hoped would make women's paid employment unnecessary, the electoral movement presented few such barriers to women's participation. With the enfranchisement of women, the ILP recognized that electoral success required the active recruitment of both sexes. From the outset two of the central male protagonists of electoral action made women's participation in the ILP a priority. Joe Marks gave hour-long speeches on the need to organize women politically, while Fred Flatman's call for 'absolute sex equality' in the first issue of *New Democracy* recognized the sources of women's subordination in the family, the workplace, and the electoral arena.[66] As a new mass movement, the ILP had few exclusionary traditions and its demand for 'equality of opportunity for men and women, politically, socially and industrially'[67] suggested that the political space opened by Ontario's labour revolt was about to challenge established gender barriers.

Women were quick to assert themselves within the ILP. When the men of the Hamilton branch of the ILP recommended that the women form an auxiliary along the lines of craft union auxiliaries, the women responded that the electoral field was not analogous to the unions and that women could play a more central role. As Annie Cassidy (herself a member of the women's auxiliary of the carpenters' union) explained to the provincial convention of the ILP, the Hamilton women 'decided as they had the vote they would run a party of their own.'[68] Thus was born the Hamilton Women's ILP.

The potential of such a working-class women's electoral organization became evident in the ground-breaking St Catharines by-election of February 1919, which definitively established the ILP's credentials. Journalists noted of the ILP campaign that '[w]ives of workingmen and soldiers' wives are throwing themselves into the contest with a determination quite new to St Catharines politics.' 'Carriages and go-carts' crammed the halls outside ILP meetings, as 'hundreds of women' listened to speakers inside. A local women's branch of the ILP soon boasted four hundred members, and seven branches of the Women's ILP were affiliated with the provincial party.[69]

Other initiatives followed. Reflecting the gains of the broader women's movement, a debate that began in the Hamilton branch was brought to the provincial ILP convention of 1919: should women in the ILP affiliate with the National Council of Women, a federation of middle-class women's organizations?[70] While Hamilton union organizer and former church activist Mary McNab argued that it was important to bring the interests of 'the working girl' into the existing women's movement, the majority were clearly more interested in focusing their efforts within the working-class. They formed the United Women's Educational Federation of Ontario. Described by the *Industrial Banner* as 'Labor's National Council of Women,' the federation united women unionists, women's auxiliaries, union label leagues, and women's ILP branches. In Toronto the Women's Labor League was formed with a somewhat larger socialist component, including leaders of the Women's Social Democratic League.[71]

All of this activity had the effect of increasing the scope of debate and action for working-class women. A new 'women's page' in the *Industrial Banner* written by Harriet Prenter rejected discussion of 'cooking, children, church and clothes,' and raised issues of socializing housework by questioning its status as unpaid labour.[72] The Women's Labor League was the driving force behind the organization of domestic servants in Toronto.[73] Alberta Jean Rowell used London's labour paper, *The Herald*, to promote women's 'social emancipation' and to attack the 'sentimental and false ideal of womanhood' that served to perpetuate separate moral codes for men and women.[74]

Although such ideas were gaining new currency, the political and social character of women's organizations was shaped by the 'distinctive culture and life-experience'[75] of the women who formed them. With few exceptions these were the wives of unionists who led the ILP and the craft unions. Notwithstanding their interest in improving the conditions and wages of women workers, their experiences in the paid labour force had been temporary, their organizational vision had largely been shaped in union auxiliaries, and their husbands' hopes of a wage sufficient to support their families had never been questioned as a social model. Not surprisingly, then, the activities of women and men in the ILP had a distinctly gendered quality. For men the ILP brought, along with public electoral activity, many of the familiar trappings of a fraternal order; for women it brought demands that they continue to fulfil a support role. The activities of the Hamilton Women's ILP were little different from those undertaken at other women's organizations. The Hamilton women organized at-homes and socials for themselves and for ILP men, raised money for a 'soldier bed' at the sanitarium, and knitted socks for the men still overseas.[76] It is true that such familiar forms provided a welcoming context in which innovative developments occurred, including talks on national and international events in the labour and women's movements.[77] Nevertheless, the tendency of men in the ILP to dismiss the women's ILPs as 'auxiliaries'[78] explains the decision of women in Toronto and London to eschew separate organizations and operate within a mixed party. Whatever form it took, the activism of these women testifies to both the possibilities and the limits of the social and political space opened by the Ontario labour revolt.

The Farmer-Labour Government

On the evening of 20 October 1919 Ontarians learned that the potential of labourism was to be tested in office. The Independent Labor Party of Ontario, just over two years in existence, had received 124,564 votes, and in both the industrial cities of southern Ontario and the resource centres of the north it won a series of convincing victories. In Hamilton the two ILP candidates won both of the city's ridings by huge majorities. In the industrial areas of Brantford, south Waterloo County, and the Welland peninsula, ILP candidates won handily. In London the Tory-populist champion of state development of the hydroelectric utility, Sir

Adam Beck, was soundly defeated by the Labor candidate. In Sault Ste Marie Conservative Premier Hearst lost his seat to an ILPer. There were some gaps: the ILP failed to gain a foothold in Windsor and Guelph, and although Toronto ILP candidates performed credibly, they were all defeated. The election of eleven ILP members to the provincial legislature, along with forty-five members of the United Farmers of Ontario, led to the formation of a coalition government headed by E.C. Drury. Hidebound partyism had been routed in Ontario.

The exuberant ILP revised its organizational goals to a hundred new branches and a hundred thousand new members. In the spring of 1920 an ILP by-election victory in Temiskaming gave the party a foothold in the federal Parliament. Candidate Angus McDonald swept both Catholic and 'Orange' polls, and attracted both English- and French-speaking constituents.[79] Labourism had effectively challenged past allegiances. The ILP's steady growth reinforced a sense of confidence and even predestination. For those frustrated by the results of the Winnipeg and Toronto general strikes, the party encouraged a narrower electoralism. While many saw the party as a corollary of militant unionism, to others who had questioned the militancy of the recent past, the party offered an alternative. As the *Labor News* suggested, 'Vote as you strike – it is more effective and it don't cost so much.' In the *International Molders' Journal*, a local officer of the moulders' union in Sault Ste Marie praised the ILP for *preventing* strikes.[80] Electoral success was not only fuelled by industrial militancy, but it could also serve as an escape valve by robbing the union movement of its sense of urgency. For the moment, as the ILP marched toward government, few could argue with its success; the obstacles to partyism had collapsed and the way ahead seemed clear.

Swept into the legislature by a 'rain of democratic ballots,'[81] the ILP caucus and the farmer-labour government seemed to be facing a future of unlimited promise. But the ILP had offered their representatives little direction. The absence of a political agenda and the lack of constraints on caucus members led to disagreements that quickly became personal animosities, often fuelled by individual ambitions. Indeed, from the outset the caucus and provincial party occupied much of their time attempting to quell the opportunism of Brantford's M.M. MacBride, dubbed 'Me-Me' MacBride following his public outburst when passed over for the labour portfolio in the new government.[82]

While MacBride's opportunism was disheartening to those who had assumed that such activity was confined to the old patronage-riddled parties, even greater problems lay ahead. As the junior partners in a coalition government, the ILP members had little room in which to manoeuvre; an uncertain mandate exacerbated their difficulties. In the election campaign the ILP and the United Farmers had both advocated a 'new democracy' freed from partyism and patronage. While the ILP branches in the larger centres of Toronto and Hamilton were far removed from the rural revolt, the differences between the workers and the farmers faded in smaller centres. In a large number of mixed urban-rural constituencies across the province, joint conventions or saw-offs were concluded with a minimum of conflict. A common idiom and a distaste for 'party platforms,' concealed deep class differences. As the slogan of the Guelph ILP stated, all could '[f]ight for the rights of the People.'[83] Once in office, of course, 'the People' vanished and the government faced the quite different demands of workers and farmers, as well as the imperatives of managing a capitalist state. The United Farmers proved to have neither a firm grasp of trade unionism nor sympathy for the eight-hour day, a demand which had galvanized the provincial labour movement at the end of the war.

Political differences could not remain submerged for long in the post-war economic depression that began in mid-1920. The biggest battle was waged over the tariff. While farmers almost uniformly supported free trade, the craft union movement had long favoured the protective tariff wall behind which much of the industrial structure of central Canada had been constructed. Support for protectionism was particularly firm in the ILP stronghold of Hamilton, where branch plants of such U.S. firms as Westinghouse, International Harvester, and Procter and Gamble had been built in an effort to jump the tariff barrier. As the tariff came, once again, to dominate federal political discourse – particularly in the context of disorganized international markets following the war and a anti-protectionist farmers' movement whose electoral potential was just becoming clear – it became apparent that the disavowal of the old parties was not necessarily extended to the abandonment of old ideologies. The debate in the ILP soon saw former Conservatives defending protectionism against socialists, single taxers, and liberals. Although not a provincial issue, the tariff controversy could not fail to revive buried animosities in the provincial party. The 1920 ILP convention, after reaffirming the alliance with the farmers, passed a tariff policy favouring the 'gradual elimination of import duties on all necessities of life.'[84] The Hamilton ILP dismissed the convention as 'none too representative' and successfully campaigned for a special convention to have the policy reversed before the 1921 federal election.[85] Not only was the bubble of unanimity burst, but on the tariff question some Hamilton ILPers experienced a greater sense of solidarity with their employers than with their comrades in the provincial party. Compounding an already bad situation, the caucus was soon torn apart by a rather poorly articulated debate rooted in the contradictions between a mass movement and the constraints of the parliamentary system. Hamilton member George Halcrow argued that ILP members who submitted to party discipline and uncritically supported a farmer-labour government that was deaf to working-class voices would be submitting, in essence, to the re-entry of partyism through the back door.[86]

While the image of the ILP in the legislature slowly tarnished, its fate was being decided elsewhere. In the summer of 1920 the two thousand workers on the hydroelectric power canal project at Chippewa on the Niagara Peninsula took on the provincial commission that ran the utility. Backed by the powerful Niagara District Trades Federation – a product of the movement towards more centralized union structures – the workers set their sights on the eight-hour day. On the eve of the strike M.M. MacBride and the region's two ILP members of the legislature pursuaded the workers to leave matters in their hands. The members soon discovered how little influence they had over both the farmer-dominated government and the officers of the provincially owned utility. They had to content themselves with a legislative commission established to investigate the workers' demands as well as conditions on the project. The commission's final report underscored the powerlessness of the caucus. Although the report recognized 'the basic principle' of the eight-hour day, it rejected the workers' demands and recommended that the ten-hour day be retained in order to keep the project on schedule. A dissenting statement by a member of the United Farmers attacking the eight-hour day as 'a vicious principle' added little to the ILP's credibility in its alliance with the farmers. The bitter and disastrous strike that followed shattered illusions in the government, the ILP caucus and, by extension, the party. For a large group of Ontario's unionized workers, labourism had failed them at a crucial juncture.

For the first time in its history, the ILP caucus attempted to set out a political agenda focusing on unemployment relief, old-age pensions, and improvements in the new Mothers' Allowance Act. At the same time, in a move that reflected both the growing Red Scare and the ILP's vulnerability to rising discontent within its ranks, a joint meeting of the provincial executive and legislative caucus resolved that 'extremists [i.e., revolutionary socialists] should decline nomination to executive positions within the party.'[87] Such actions on the part of the ILP leadership revealed that a socialist critique of the ILP was gaining support within and beyond the ranks of the party. Some legislative improvements were made to factory and health legislation, but they were far from sweeping, or even effective. As left-wing unions such as the Lumber Workers' Industrial Union rhetorically queried, 'What use is a labour government?,' claiming that 'Ontario has the best health laws and the worse Camps in Canada.'[88] More tangible was the protective legislation for women passed by the Drury government, particularly the Mothers' Allowance and Minimum Wage acts. Although such measures brought tangible relief to many women, they were not out of step with reforms being introduced by the old parties in other jurisdictions. Moreover, they fit well into the 'maternalist' tradition, a tradition that idealized, rather than challenged, women's position within the family.[89] (Such an outcome was to be expected from a movement that, as has been noted in the case of such organizations as the Women's Independent Labor Party, sought to defend the working-class family.) Beyond this limited list of reforms, the 'forces of democracy' had brought few tangible gains to Ontario's workers and working-class families.

Disenchantment with the government permitted some conservative trade unionists to voice their reservations about political action. For Tom Moore, in particular, the ILP's ineptitude in supporting the Hydro workers justified the rejection of the electoral movement. In the 1921 federal election the leaders of the Trades and Labor Congress announced their defection from the movement by producing a questionnaire for candidates, the American Federation of Labor's traditional means of identifying 'friends of labour' from among all the parties. They also attempted to dismiss their earlier support for the ILP.[90] Sensing the shifting political wind, a number of labour politicians shed their ILP colours and ran (mostly unsuccessfully) as independents.[91] Not surprisingly, in the 1923 provincial election the ILP was decimated; the ILP caucus was reduced to three, two of whom soon drifted to the Liberal and Conservative parties. Perhaps the best measure of what had happened can be seen in voter turnout. In twenty-two ridings contested by the ILP in 1919 352,342 voters had gone to the polls; in 1923 this number declined to 258,174. The vision of a new democracy no longer stirred working-class voters.

If labourism was the dominant ideology of the Ontario workers' movement in the years after the First World War, there was an important current of opinion that questioned many of its assumptions. Why had the socialists not been capable of posing their own alternative strategy, particularly in response to the crisis of labourism in 1920? Indeed, Ontario's socialists had always been wary of the ideological morass of labourism. The emergence of the Independent Labor Party sparked a fierce debate in the Social Democratic Party, southern Ontario's dominant socialist organization: did the ILP contribute to the struggle for socialism by providing a political focus for working-class demands, or were its vague politics and implicit acceptance of capitalist social relations a hindrance to the development of a socialist confidence? A major wing of the SDP, led by James Simpson, felt that there should be no 'hard and fast rule' regarding the ILP, since it was not yet clear where the movement was headed.[92] In cities like Toronto where socialist strength was concentrated in the unions, an electoral united front of the ILP and the unions was constructed, allowing socialists a somewhat greater voice. There seemed to be no pressing reason (at least before 1920) to question the ILP's electoral strategy or lack of programmatic clarity, particularly in light of its apparent success in gaining members and public attention.

The predominance of labourism in the region should not obscure the fact that many socialists, particularly those on the left of the SDP and in the revolutionary Socialist Party of North America, rejected participation in the ILP and instead focused their attention on promising developments in the unions. Only in 1921, with the emergence of the Workers' Party of Canada, would socialism regain an organized presence, and even then it would be shrouded for some time in the secrecy of a largely underground movement. Yet the new Worker's Party did attract many of the most well-known leaders of the 1919 revolt, particularly in Toronto where John MacDonald and a host of other respected union militants rallied to its banners. In 1920 the Toronto District Labor Council adopted a program of support for industrial unionism through amalgamation, a united front of all workers' organizations in the political field, and an explicit radical critique of the leadership of the Trades and Labor Congress.[93] The Workers' Party (subsequently renamed the Communist Party) was deeply rooted, both in personnel and program, in the union radicalism of 1919. By 1921 industrial defeat, political demoralization and unemployment would combine to deplete the soil in which labour radicalism might grow.

In 1921 an attempt was made to fashion a federated party using the British Labour Party as a model. The Ontario Section of the Canadian Labor Party – an alliance of the ILP (which maintained its own existence), reformist socialists, and the communists in the Workers' Party – was soon able to claim an affiliated membership of forty thousand.[94] Yet socialist organization in Ontario had already been checked – in 1919 by the popularity of the ILP, and in the early 1920s by its demise.

Most devastating was the string of wage cuts and union defeats that began in the summer of 1920. As the Hydro strike had demonstrated, workers would receive little support from their elected representatives. To a remarkable extent the union and the electoral movements had flowered in near isolation from each other. This separation of 'political' and 'economic' spheres, which is a central feature of the ideology of liberal democracy, was consistently maintained. Labourism's uncritical acceptance of parliamentary institutions was very much its hallmark. Indeed, the ILP considered its task to be the defence of these institutions against the profiteers and patronage machines. As a result, the party remained blind to the individualist premises of the political system. Labour's collective power in the workplace, a power that had given workers the confidence to stage an electoral challenge, was not considered a resource to be used by its elected representatives. Labourism conceived of no way to tap the power of a broader movement; instead, its fate rested in the hands of a few elected representatives.

Programs that focused on parliamentary activity as opposed to 'direct action' had their supporters across Canada, but particularly in Ontario. The principal reason for this is that the state appeared far more benign in Ontario. In the tumultuous class battles waged in British Columbia and Alberta, the federal state – and sometimes in defiance of its own laws – resorted to military or judicial force to defend employers and, increasingly, business unionism. The experience of Ontario workers was different. Even throughout the post-war crisis, direct state intervention in the province remained ad hoc and minimal.[95] Ontario workers had every reason to feel that they could reorganize society by simply getting elected and passing laws. There is surprisingly little discussion in ILP literature about the extent to which economic and social power lay beyond the reach of Parliament. The relative ease with which the barriers to working-class electoral representation seemed to fall provided a further boost to workers' confidence: they felt they had discovered the path of least resistance.

The contradiction between electoral politics and direct action ran deeply in the labour movement. Only after the war would various socialist currents attempt to overcome the dichotomy that had debilitated the movement. Within the Co-operative Commonwealth Federation (CCF) labourism and the reformist socialist current would eventually coalesce. The distinction between the two currents was effectively drawn by the paper of the Workers' Party when it contrasted the activities of James Woodsworth in the House of Commons with the activities of the provincial ILP caucus. Although critical of Woodsworth, *The Worker* praised his innovative and effective use of Parliament to 'focus attention on the issues of the mass struggles outside of parliament ... and so perhaps force whatever concessions possible from the capitalist class.'[96] While the Communists would later reverse this assessment of Woodsworth, it effectively highlights the character of the post–World War One labour revolt in Ontario. This period, which witnessed a workers' movement of extraordinary breadth throughout the province, gave birth to two autonomous labour movements with an overlapping composition and ideology. One sought to challenge power at the workplace, the other in the halls of the legislature. As apparent in the comments of Gideon Robertson and Joseph Marks that began this paper, the challenge of the industrial movement in Ontario was widely recognized. And the creation of an effective electoral force was itself no small accomplishment. As Arthur Mould, labour candidate for London in the 1921 federal election, noted in his memoirs, 'The remarkable fact is, the workers and farmers did overturn the Government, and did elect people of their own choice. No matter what one may think of the Farmer Labour Government, its failures and shortcomings, its very election was a demonstration of a people in revolt.'[97]

In the end, however, neither movement could direct the industrial militancy of 1919 and 1920 towards attainable political goals. The defeat and demoralization that ensued was to cloud historical memory and create a misleading image of quiescence in the 'East,' an image sharply opposed to the rebellion of the West against the inequities of industrial capitalism. A closer look reveals far greater complexity.

Notes

1 *Industrial Banner* (Toronto), 25 August 1916.

2 National Archives of Canada (NAC), MG 30, A16 (Sir Joseph Flavelle Papers), Vol. 38, File: 'Irish, Mark H., 1918–19, 1924,' Irish to Flavelle, 15 November 1918.

3 See, for instance, Morton with Copp, *Working People*; and Jamieson, *Times of Trouble*.

4 See, for example, an example, *Labor News* (Hamilton), 3 August 1917.

5 NAC, MG 30, A16, Vol. 18, File: 'Demobilization of Labor – Cable Correspondence, etc., 1918–1919,' 'Memo. Showing Geographical Location and Percentages of Workpeople Employed on Munitions'; *Industrial Banner*, 8 August 1919. On the IMB, see Rider, 'Imperial Munitions Board.' In Bliss, *Canadian Millionaire*, Flavelle is acquitted of profiteering, although Bliss uses a much narrower definition of the term than was in common parlance during the war.

6 On pre-war struggles struggles over workplace control, see Heron and Palmer, 'Through the Prism of the Strike'; and Heron, 'Crisis of the Craftsman.'

7 Siemiatycki, 'Munitions and Labour Militancy'; *Industrial Banner*, 16 June 1916. The failure of the strike was attributed in part to pressure from the ASE leadership in Britain on local leaders to return to work; see *Machinists' Monthly Journal*, September 1916, 899.

8 *Industrial Banner*, 22 February 1918.

9 NAC, MG 30, A16, Vol. 2, File 11, Gerald Brown to Flavelle, 7 June 1916.

10 Naylor, *New Democracy*, 255–6.

11 On the carpenters, see Labour Canada Library (Hull), Royal Commission on Industrial Relations (RCIR), Evidence, 2147; and *Industrial Banner*, 23 May, 18 July 1919. On garment workers, see *Advance* (New York), 18 January 1918; NAC, RG 27 (Department of Labour, Strikes and Lockouts Files), Vol. 316, Strike 19 (254); and *New Democracy*, (Hamilton), 25 December 1919.

12 On bank clerks see Canada, Dept. of Labour, *Labour Organization in Canada*, 1919, 107, and *Labor Leader* (Toronto), 19 December 1919; on firefighters, *Toronto Star*, 31 May 1919; on labourers, *Labour Leader*, 24 October 1919, 5, 12 March 1920; on rubber workers, *Toronto Star*, 9 April, 11 June 1919; on civic workers, *Industrial Banner*, 8 February 1918 and *Labor Leader*, 20 February 1920; on retail clerks, *Labor Leader*, 28 November 1919, 19 March 1920; on domestics, *Labour Organization in Canada*, 1919, 106; on teamsters, *Toronto Star*, 5 May 1919; on telephone operators, Sangster, '1907 Bell Telephone Strike' and *Industrial Banner*, 16 August, 20 Sepember 1918, on machinists, *Machinists' Monthly Journal*, April 1917, 367. Ontario lodges of the machinists' union voted heavily in favour of admitting women to membership, *Machinists' Monthly Journal*; April 1917, 371. On the machinists' strike, see NAC, RG 27, Vol. 308, Strikes 1918 (84) and 1918 (87).

13 *Labor Leader*, 3 October 1919.

14 Ibid., 2 July 1920. See also Brody, *Steelworkers in America*; and Heron, *Working in Steel*, chapter 4.

15 *Mail and Empire* (Toronto), 6 May 1919; *Toronto World*, 6, 9 May 1919; *Industrial Banner*, 9 May 1919.

16 Heron, *Working in Steel*, 85; *Toronto Star*, 3 August 1918.

17 In a 1917 conference of leaders of international unions in Canada in 1917 condemned employers for taking advantage of the war to unnecessarily dilute labour. Trades and Labor Congress of Canada (TLC), *Proceedings*, 1917, 32; NAC, MG 28, I 44 (Toronto District Labor Council, Minutebooks [TDLC]), 19 June 1917. The 1919 Royal Commission of Industrial Relations was told that deskilling was a major source of friction. RCIR, 1990.

18 NAC, RG 27, Vol. 319, Strike 1920 (10).

19 *Plumbers, Gas and Steam Fitters' Journal* (Chicago), May 1919, 14; *Industrial Banner*, 21 July 1916, 28 March 1919; *Labor Leader*, 18 July 1919.

20 *Toronto World*, 20 May 1919; *Montreal Star*, 28 May 1919.

21 University of Toronto Library, J. McA. Conner Papers, 'The Canadian Socialist Movement'; Roberts, 'Studies in the Toronto Labour Movement.'

22 See Naylor, 'Toronto 1919.'

23 Angus, *Canadian Bolsheviks*, 29; *Industrial Banner*, 27 December 1918, 3 January 1919; *Toronto Star*, 20 and 31 December 1918, 1 January 1919.

24 NAC, RG 6, E (Chief Press Censor Records), clipping, n.d., 'Extremists at Toronto Heckled Labor President.'

25 On Stratford, see *Toronto Star*, 26 December 1918; on Windsor, *Toronto Star*, 12 May 1919; on London, *Labor Leader*, 27 June 1919; on Ottawa, *Labor Leader*, 18 July 1919; on Guelph, *Labor Leader*, 27 June 1919, and *New Democracy*, 10 July 1919.

26 *Industrial Banner*, 6 June 1919, 23 January 1920.

27 TLC, *Proceedings*, 1917, 144; Canada, Dept. of Labour, *Labour Organizations in Canada*, 1917, 29; *Industrial Banner*, 14 June 1918.

28 NAC, MG 30, A16, Vol. 38, File: 'Irish, Mark H., 1918–19, 1923,' Irish to Edward FitzGerald, 28 June 1918.

29 *Toronto Star*, 31 December 1918, 6 February 1919; *Industrial Banner*, 14 February 1919.

30 *Toronto Telegram*, 28 April 1919; *Globe* (Toronto), 29 April 1919; *Toronto Star*, 27 May 1919.

31 Provincial Archives of Manitoba (PAM), MG 10, A14/1 (R.B. Russell Papers), Cassidy to Russell, 13 April 1919; *Globe*, 5, 6, 7 May 1919; *Toronto Star*, 2, 5, 19, 22 May 1919.

32 *Toronto Star*, 27, 30 May 1919.

33 Ibid., 30, 31 May, 2 June 1919; NAC, MG 28, H (Sir Robert Borden Papers), OC Series, Vol. 564, T. Church to Borden, 2 June 1919.

34 *Labor Leader*, 18 July 1919.

35 PAM, MG 10, A 3 (One Big Union Papers), Correspondence, D. Sime to F.W. Welsh, 3 April 1919, J. Ferguson to V. Midgley, 22 April 1919, F.J. Flatman to Midgley, 22 April 1919, R.B. Russell to Midgley, 24 April 1919, J.G. Robinson

to Midgley, 27 April 1919, John Cottam to Midgley, 2 May 1919, R.J. Johns to Midgley, 7 May 1919, and R.B. Russell Papers, Box 3, File 7, Johns to Russell; *Labor News*, 25 April 1919; *New Democracy*, 7 August 1919; *Ontario Labor News*, 1 May 1919. On the ASE's attitude to craft unionism, see Hinton, *First Shop Stewards' Movement*.

36 *Mail and Empire*, 3 June 1919.

37 *Toronto Star*, 15 March 1919.

38 On the metal trades, see *Industrial Banner*, 12 April 1918, and *Toronto Star*, 30 Apr. 1919; on the marine trades, see *Industrial Banner*, 7 June 1918, 17, 31 January, 7 March, 9 May 1919. See also *Plumbers, Gas and Steam Fitters' Journal* (Chicago), June 1918, 18; January 1919, 14; February 1919, 13; April 1919, 14; May 1919, 20; *Machinists' Monthly Journal*, February 1919, 133–4; April 1919, 330; June 1919, 552; *Ontario Labor News*, 15 May 1919; and United Brotherhood of Carpenters and Joiners, Provincial Council, *Proceedings* 1919, 410–11. On the building trades, see *Industrial Banner*, 14 March 1919.

39 On furniture workers, see *London Free Press*, 5 July 1920; and *Industrial Banner*, 1 October 1920. For an appraisal of the skills involved in the industry, see Parr, *Gender of Breadwinners*, 140–64. On Niagara district workers, see *Toronto Star*, 23 May 1919; Archives of Ontario (AO), RG 18, B-60, 'Inquiry into Wages and Living Conditions of the Men Employed by the Hydro-Electric Power Commission at the Queenston-Chippewa Development (1920),' 1.

40 RCIR, 2169.

41 *Financial Post*, 31 May 1919.

42 *Industrial Union News* (Detroit), 21 June 1919; *New Democracy*, 26 June 1919.

43 *New Democracy*, 23 October 1919. A similar report was made by Ivens himself in the *One Big Union Bulletin*, 18, 25 October 1919.

44 Private Maycock cited in NAC, MG 30, A31 (Tom Moore Papers), File: 'Speeches, Memoranda and Clippings, 1918–46,' 'Vote for MacBride ...'

45 On Studholme, see Heron, 'Working-Class Hamilton,' 606ff.

46 For a survey of municipal activity, see Naylor, 'Ontario Workers and the Decline of Labourism,' 282.

47 Roberts, 'Studies in the Toronto Labour Movement,' 403–8; *Industrial Banner*, 3 April, 29 May 1914.

48 *Labor News*, 29 November 1918.

49 *Financial Post*, 15 September 1917; *Industrial Banner*, 22 March 1918.

50 RCIR, 2602, 2392, 2424.

51 TDLC, 17 November 1921; *Industrial Banner*, 19 December 1919.

52 *Industrial Banner*, 22 February 1918.

53 Ibid., 8 November 1918.

54 *Toronto World*, 2 May 1919.

55 *Toronto Star*, 19 June 1919.

56 Canada, Dept. of Labour, *Labour Organization in Canada*, 1917, 40–1.

57 On labourism, see Heron, 'Labourism and the Canadian Working-Class'. On producerism, see Palmer, *Culture in Conflict*, 98, 101, 108–9; AO, Arthur Roebuck Papers, File: 'Elections, 1917: Federal – Temiskaming,' 'The Independent Labor Party – Declaration of Principles, Platform and Constitution.'

58 *Industrial Banner*, 6 July 1917, 19 December 1919.

59 The Wartime Elections Act disenfranchised many foreign-born workers and gave the vote to all members, and female relatives, of members of the Armed Forces. The Military Voters Act allowed for soldiers' votes to be distributed to ridings across the country at the discretion of the electoral officer. Brown and Cook, *Canada 1896–1921*, 271.

60 *Labor News*, 8 March, 3 May 1918.

61 *Toronto Star*, 13 February 1919.

62 *Industrial Banner*, 11 June, 30 July 1920.

63 *Labor News*, 15 August 1919.

64 *Industrial Banner*, 13 July 1917; *Labor News*, 8 August 1919. For a discussion of the concept of 'movement culture,' see Goodwyn, *Populist Moment*, Chapter 2 and 293–310.

65 Queen's University Archives, Andrew Glen Papers, Box 1, File 4, 'I.L.P. Forum, 1920–1921,' Box 2, File 7, 'Central Executive Report, Annual Convention of Ind. Labor Party of Toronto, Sat. 21st, Oct. 1922,' 'I.L.P. Forum Session 1921–1922' and 'Forum Meetings Session 1922–1923.'

66 *Industrial Banner*, 7 June 1918; *New Democracy*, 22 May 1919.

67 *Industrial Banner*, 24 October 1919.

68 Ibid., 6 July 1917.

69 Ibid., 17, 24 January, 14, 21 February, 14 March 1919; *Toronto Star*, 11 February 1919; *Machinists' Monthly Journal*, March 1919, 246.

70 *Labor News*, 18 April 1919.

71 *Industrial Banner*, 15 March 1918, 9 July 1920.

72 Ibid., 11 June 1920.

73 Ibid., 14 November 1919.

74 *Herald* (London), 24 March, 21 April, 19 May 1921.

75 Milkman, ed., *Women, Work, and Protest*, xiii.

76 *Labor News*, 15, 29 March, 12 April, 17 May 1918, 28 February 1919; *Industrial Banner*, 1 February, 3 May, 7 June 1918, 5 December 1919.

77 *Labor News*, 14 February, 14 March, 28 March 1919.

78 *Industrial Banner*, 2 August 1918, 7 February 1919.

79 Ibid., 9, 23 April 1920; *New Democracy*, 15 April 1920.

80 *Labor News*, 6 September 1919; *International Molders' Journal* (Cincinnati), November 1919, 926.

81 *Industrial Banner*, 24 October 1919. On the farmers' experience, see Badgley, 'Ringing Out the Narrowing Lust of Gold.' On the government, see Johnston, *E.C. Drury*.

82 *Industrial Banner*, 23 July 1920.

83 NAC, MG 28, H, RLB series, File 1690, Guelph ILP to Borden, 24 January 1918.

84 *Industrial Banner*, 9 April 1920.

85 *Labor News*, 9 April 1920, 28 October 29 November 1921; *Industrial Banner*, 25 November 1921.

86 *Brantford Expositor*, 7, 12 November 1919, 3 January 1920; *Labor Leader*, 23 January 1920; *New Democracy*, 28 January 1920.

87 *Labor News*, 25 November 1920; *Labor Leader*, 26 November, 17 December 1920; *New Democracy*, 16 December 1920.

88 Cited in Radforth, *Bushworkers and Bosses*, 118.

89 On 'maternal feminism,' see Linda Kealey, ed., *A Not Unreasonable Claim*. On similar reforms elsewhere, see Findlay, 'Protection of Workers in Industry.'

90 *Toronto Star*, 3 July 1920; *Labor Leader*, 24 September 1920; NAC, MG 28, I, 103 (Trades and Labor Congress of Canada, Executive Minutes), 11 January 1922; *Canadian Labor World* (Hamilton), 21 October 1924.

91 For examples see Naylor, 'Decline of Labourism,' 290–1.

92 On the debate in the SDP, see *Canadian Forward*, 28 October, 2 December 1916, 24 April 1917, 24 February, 10, 24 March 1918.

93 The texts of the resolutions, for distribution at the upcoming Trades and Labor Congress convention, are in TDLC, Minutebooks, 19 August 1920.

94 *Labor Leader*, 29 July, 19 August, 7 October 1921, 3 March 1922; TDLC, 6 October 1921; *Industrial Banner*, 22 February 1922.

95 See Naylor, *New Democracy*, chapter 7.

96 *Worker* (Toronto), 15 May 1922.

97 University of Western Ontario, Regional Collection, M-719, Arthur Mould Papers, 'Reminiscences of Arthur Mould' (typescript), 74.

The Prairies: In the Eye of the Storm

TOM MITCHELL and JAMES NAYLOR

It is, first and foremost, their resistance that makes visible the conditions and limits of bourgeois civilization, the particularity and fragility of its seemingly neutral and timeless social forms.[1]

In the spring of 1919 all eyes were on Winnipeg. This was the point at which the workers' revolt most visibly strained at the established limits of liberal capitalism. Understanding the events in the Prairie metropolis is to appreciate both the main dynamics of the pan-Canadian revolt and the central place of Winnipeg within it. At the same time, militancy and radicalism were widely diffused through the Prairie west. This chapter will assess how the crisis in class relations reached such proportions in Winnipeg and throughout the region.

Participants in the events of 1919 and commentators in its aftermath all debated whether a revolution was under way. Historians have tended to dismiss such considerations too off-handedly, arguing that workers in Winnipeg and beyond were merely seeking basic collective bargaining rights.[2] Such a conclusion closes the door too quickly on an understanding of the tensions and assumptions that lay behind the different meanings ascribed to the strike in 1919 and after.[3] We argue that the crisis on the Canadian prairies was a dynamic and complex process with multiple possible outcomes. Winnipeg was at the centre of a social maelstrom that was unique in Canadian – and perhaps North American – history. The strike triggered a historic reformation of both social relations and the Canadian state; in this process definitions given to the events that occurred in the West in 1919 were key to how class and state relations would be remade. We have tried, then, to avoid the 'strike or revolution' paradigm and instead probe the nature of the strike in accounts both 'from below' and 'from above.' Moreover, we have considered both the state and civil society as theatres of conflict integral to the strike.[4]

'We Are Going to Run This City':[5] Origins and Meanings

In early May 1919 Winnipeg's building and metal trades workers went out on strike. Having confronted employers unwilling to bargain with them, the unions had taken their cases to the Winnipeg Trades and Labor Council, which unanimously decided to conduct a vote of all affiliated unions on a general strike. A week later the tally was in: 11,112 organized workers had voted for the general strike, while 524 had opposed it.[6] At the appointed hour, 11:00 a.m., factories fell silent, telephones went dead, newspaper presses ground to a halt – the city stopped. From the moment it began on 15 May 1919, the general strike spread like a contagion. For six long weeks in the hot early summer of 1919, thirty thousand working-class Winnipeggers withstood physical deprivation from lost wages, threats of permanent dismissal, and an unprecedented ideological barrage from the strike's opponents.

The Winnipeg Trades and Labor Council was no doubt taken aback by the response to the strike. It had never called on non-union members to join the walkout, but thousands did. It had never claimed that the strike had some ultimate purpose beyond forcing specific employers to bargain with the chosen representatives of their workers over wages and hours of work, but from the outset their bourgeois opponents accused the strike leadership of 'revolutionary' intentions to overthrow capitalism and run the city, and perhaps the country, on the model of Soviet Russia. In part this construction was placed on the strike because of its apparent connection with the Western Labour Conference held in Calgary in March 1919. The Calgary Conference, at which delegates from across the West decided to secede from the Trades and Labor Congress of Canada (TLC) and join a proposed One Big Union (OBU), was marked by several tendencies that were already apparent in Winnipeg and beyond. These included the willingness to draw upon the general strike weapon,[7] an overt identification with revolutionary struggles in Russia and Germany (the conference sent greetings to the Bolsheviks and Spartakus), a rejection of craft forms of organization, and a willingness to accept socialists, particularly members of the Socialist Party of Canada (SPC), in positions of leadership.

While the Calgary Conference has been painted as a 'coup' by the SPC,[8] historians of the party are quick to reject this characterization. The sentiment behind a general strike extended far beyond the influence of any organized socialist current. Local after local in the West passed motions in favour of joining general strikes without having ever heard or seen an SPC speaker.[9] Yet throughout the region SPCers inherited the general strike movement because of their skills and radicalism. They were willing to abandon old forms of organization and action, to organize the unorganized, to articulate the excitement that workers felt about events in Russia and elsewhere, and to propose new ways of channelling workers' anger and hopes.

In fact, the OBU had no particular place in SPC ideology. The general strike movement was potentially at odds with the party's advocacy of a revolutionary working-class movement developed through a long process of education. Indeed, some SPCers saw the general strikes, if not the OBU itself, as interfering with this process.[10] Still, like other labour activists, SPCers were caught up in the general strike movement. They reflected the wider enthusiasms, and, given the vacuum created by the rejection of the national leadership of the Trades and Labor Congress, they largely inherited the leadership of the regional labour movement.

This was certainly true of the small group of SPC militants in Winnipeg. Delegates from Winnipeg had been particularly active at all stages of the reorganization of the western labour movement, beginning with the TLC meeting in Quebec in 1918. In March of that year, the Winnipeg Trades and Labor Council elected two prominent SPCers (R.B. Russell and R.J. Johns) to represent the council in Calgary. As Peter Campbell has observed, Russell and Johns played a key role in uniting the Calgary Conference behind the One Big Union project.[11] Their commitment to the OBU project had its roots in the radicalism that swept through Winnipeg in the last two years of the war.

This radicalism irradiated the proceedings of the famous Walker Theatre meeting of 22 December 1918. Over seventeen hundred Winnipeggers crowded the palatial Walker Theatre to hear the city's most prominent labour and socialist speakers denounce the Canadian state for its subversion of civil liberties during and after the war, and to express their solidarity with the Russian Revolution.[12] The crowd (which comprised 'Anglo-Saxon, Polish, Ukrainian, Hungarian, and others,' according to D.C. Masters) was made to feel part of an international movement. Echoing through the theatre were the 'deafening cries of "Long live the Russian Soviet Republic! Long live Karl Liebknecht!

Long live the working class!"' – cries that suggested a vision of the future that lay far beyond capitalism, and Winnipeg.[13]

The co-sponsorship of the Walker Theatre meeting by the Socialist Party of Canada and Winnipeg Trades and Labor Council symbolized a convergence between the growing militancy of the labour movement and the expanding currency of revolutionary socialist ideas. Such a convergence deeply troubled authorities.[14] Indeed, the meeting reflected substantial common ground among various currents of the workers' movement. The meeting was addressed by members of the SPC and Social Democratic Party (SDP), and Bob Russell, himself an SPCer, spoke under the auspices of the trades and labour council. This is not to say that there was no tension in this relationship. The same month, the left failed to attain the council presidency when James Winning defeated Russell to win the post.[15] In addition, the council pulled out of a planned follow-up meeting that the SPC held under its own auspices.[16]

The Walker Theatre meeting also illuminated the radical traditions of many of Winnipeg's large non-British immigrant communities, a fact that helps explain why the city became an SDP centre after 1911. The SDP's willingness to accept separate national or 'language' organizations had made it far more appealing to many central and eastern European immigrants than the older Socialist Party of Canada. Veteran Winnipeg socialist Jacob Penner recalled that the English-speaking branch was the smallest of its various 'language' branches in the city.[17] Between mid-1917 and its banning by the federal government a year later, the Ukrainian Social Democratic Party grew from six hundred to two thousand members, largely in Winnipeg, and published a lively newspaper, *Robochyi narod*.[18] Despite the pressures of the war (and the Ukrainians' designation as 'enemy aliens'), there was a tradition of working-class activity. The spring of 1915 saw a series of demonstrations of up to fifteen thousand largely non-unionized, non-British workers demanding 'bread and work.'[19] In 1917 Ukrainian socialists were active in a large strike of unskilled construction workers in Winnipeg – a strike that involved strike-breakers, state repression, and the arrests and internment of twenty-three strikers.[20]

Radicalism was even more deeply rooted, and more diverse, in the city's Jewish community. A 'Help the Strikers Conference' organized as Winnipeg's labour scene heated up in 1917 attracted delegates from ten organizations, including the Jewish branch of the Social Democratic Party, the Poale Zion (Labour Zionists), the Social Democratic women's organization, Bundists, and various branches of the Arbeiter Ring

(Workmen's Circle), that numbered revolutionary marxists and anarchists among their membership. The liveliness of the Jewish community is reflected in such meetings as the April 1918 'Debate about Poale Zion,' which attracted over eight hundred people.[21] In the autumn of 1918 the radicalism of the non-British left had provoked repression in the form of a government ban on a series of 'alien' newspapers and organizations, including the Social Democratic Party. Interestingly, the rising star on the left – the Socialist Party of Canada – was not banned, perhaps because of its almost completely Anglo-Celtic leadership.[22]

The turn towards the general strike strategy did not require a rejection of 'politics' as suggested by those who argue that the Socialist Party or the Winnipeg labour movement was engaged in a syndicalist crusade.[23] Across the country workers oscillated between electoral and extra-parliamentary tactics, depending on the opportunities that arose; Winnipeg was no different. The call for sympathetic strikes in the latter part of the war had a resonance far stronger than a call to the ballot box. Situations arose that required the immediate and massive responses that elections did not offer. Widespread anger and frustration fuelled mass mobilizations. By 1919 Winnipeg had seen a series of such events. The conscription crisis offered a case in point. In the spring of 1917 an election or referendum on the issue did not seem forthcoming, and so the Winnipeg Trades and Labor Council organized a general strike ballot among its affiliates. By a margin of well over two to one, they voted to participate in a general strike against compulsory service if other cities followed suit.[24]

By 1918 such hesitancy had dissipated and the city moved towards a general strike on four separate occasions. In the summer of 1918 between fourteen and seventeen thousand Winnipeggers joined in an escalating strike movement in support of the newly organized civic workers. The issue was collective bargaining rights. In the context of a war being fought ostensibly for democracy, the refusal of the state to allow a group of workers the right to participate in determining their own future reeked of autocratic rule. By passing the 'Fowler Amendment,' which prohibited civic workers' strikes, city council demonstrated that it had no interest in abandoning a monopoly of power and triggered a response that was 'immediate and electrifying.'[25] Confrontation was in the air. Martial law and arrests were threatened from the outset.[26] Working-class solidarity with the civic workers was palpable and explosive. Locals of international unions immediately offered financial support, and the machinists called for a general strike.[27] Even moderate union leaders took up the call. Trades council secretary Ernest Robinson urged workers, '[T]hrow down your tools and stand together in the battle for organized labor ... We want fighters, men who are class conscious.'[28]

Working-class cohesion was met by militancy and solidarity on the part of the city's capitalist class. The Fowler Amendment received the vocal support of the Rotary Club, the Board of Trade, and the Real Estate Board. Such were the forces behind formation of the Citizens' Committee of 100, which pulled together the 'greatest assembly of those prominent in business and industrial life in the history of Winnipeg' to determine how to break the strike.[29] They were unsuccessful in 1918, in part because of the solidarity of the city's unions, and in part because they were not able to mobilize the forces of the state, which was still primarily concerned with winning the war in Europe. Federal cabinet minister Gideon Robertson persuaded the city council to back down.[30] The 1918 strike ended in victory for the unions, reinforcing the efficacy of the general strike as a tactic as well as the radical conclusions reached by some of its supporters. According to SPCer Samuel Blumenberg, '[If] the capitalist class were not afraid that the strike in Winnipeg would spread throughout the country and grow into a social revolution, they would not have settled the strike as easily as they did.'[31]

Whatever the political consequences, more general strikes threatened and there seemed little reason to suspect that they would be confined to Winnipeg. In July 1918 a national strike of letter carriers over wages almost ignited a regional general strike. When western Canadian letter carriers showed their resolve by staying out after their union leadership had led their counterparts back to work in the rest of the country, local labour councils rallied to their defence. Their cause was a popular one, combining complaints about low pay with a callous and inaccessible government. As the post office began hiring strike-breakers, labour councils in Vancouver, Regina, Victoria, Saskatoon, and Moose Jaw, as well as Winnipeg, announced that they would organize general strike votes. The outcome was the same as that of the Winnipeg civic strike: the federal cabinet intervened and offered the strikers important concessions. Not only had militancy succeeded again, but the potential for a regional uprising increased when the Calgary freight handlers went on strike in October 1918.[32] These workers maintained their strike in defiance of the Borden government's ban on strikes and lockouts. The arrest of five strike leaders brought Calgary to the edge of a general strike, and CPR shopworkers in several centres in Alberta and Saskatchewan walked out in support. In response, the Winnipeg Trades and Labor

Council authorized a general strike vote. Only after Gideon Robertson rushed to Calgary to mediate (and pressure the CPR to make concessions) was the crisis averted. Clearly, the region was clearly poised to explode; just as clearly, the government had little authority to enforce its prohibition of strikes.[33] Finally, in the summer of 1918 the Winnipeg trades council obtained an overwhelmingly positive vote of affiliates for a general strike in support of the metal trades, which had been engaged in an interminable struggle to negotiate with the city's three contract metal shops. However, the strike itself collapsed before the city's union movement had a chance to test its mettle. The metal trades struggle also secured SPCer and machinist R.B. Russell's place in the labour movement at the expense of less militant representatives such as former trades council president Fred Tipping.[34] Each of these strikes – the civic workers', postal workers', freight handlers', and machinists' – appeared to portend the larger explosion that came in May 1919.

Given the immediate historical context in which the Winnipeg General Strike developed, the existence of sharply distinct views about the meaning of the event is hardly surprising. As the strike briefly silenced the presses of the regular Winnipeg newspapers, two new dailies faced each other: the unions' *Special Strike Edition* of the *Western Labor News*, and the *Citizen*, the organ of the new Citizens' Committee of 1000 (the chief opponents of the strike).[35] The latter took aim at the claims of the strike committee, which had been formed to organize the strike. 'No thoughtful citizen,' declared the *Citizen*, 'can any longer doubt that the so-called general strike is in reality revolution – or a daring attempt to overthrow the present industrial and governmental system.'[36] The strikers presented a different story. As the *Special Strike Edition* patiently repeated, the strike had no ulterior motive beyond three unexceptional demands: the right of collective bargaining, a living wage, and reinstatement of all strikers.[37]

Yet no matter how carefully the strikers posed their actions in the language of industrial relations, their opponents could not fail to contemplate how readily thousands of workers had joined the struggle; how enemy aliens and British Canadians alike had hailed the Bolsheviks and derided the Canadian government; how a revitalized labour movement had ceased to be the preserve of respectable craftsmen and now recruited among the more 'dangerous classes' of immigrants and labourers; and how self-declared revolutionaries stood at the head of the labour movement. Although the strike was never an overtly revolutionary challenge for state power, it was certainly (particularly in the context of the events of 1918) a militant and dramatic rejection of the hegemony of capital in, and potentially beyond, Winnipeg. It was far from clear where the crisis would end.

The unprecedented character of this 'class moment' can also be seen in the way class appeared to supersede other social identities such as ethnicity and gender.[38] In the context of nativist animosities driven to a fevered pitch by the war, this class solidarity was most dramatically apparent in terms of ethnicity. On the eve of the general strike, Winnipeg was embroiled in a series of violent attacks perpetrated by returned soldiers against 'enemy aliens.' In January 1919 a large crowd of returned soldiers targeted immigrants and radicals in a violent attack in which they wrecked the offices of the Austro-Hungarian society and the SPC, and forced the wife of prominent socialist Samuel Blumenburg to kiss the Union Jack. It was an event that did not bode well for the future of labour solidarity in the city. The veterans' initial plan was to prevent a socialist tribute to the recently murdered Karl Liebknecht and Rosa Luxemburg, underlining their equation of radicalism with 'enemy aliens'; they then proceeded to protest against the Swift's meatpacking company for retaining 'alien workers.' Given the pervasive fear of joblessness in the post-war depression, distinctions of ethnicity, politics, employment status, and war record threatened to drive deep faultlines through Winnipeg's working class. The leadership of the Great War Veterans' Association, the *Winnipeg Telegram*, and the mayor backed the veterans' actions. Authorities made no attempts to restrain the crowd, and those who had attacked immigrants and their property were not arrested or punished.[39] The lesson was clear: extra-legal violence had official sanction.

The Winnipeg working class was, of course, hierarchically structured by ethnicity. For the most part, the secure, skilled trades, and the craft unions that grew out of them, belonged to Anglo-Celtic men. But the traditional isolation of these craftsmen from the less skilled was giving way to a new unity. Unorganized workers were confronting new labour market conditions that made it easier to organize, and a changing labour movement was more committed to organizing the unorganized, including immigrants, women, and unskilled workers in general. A doctrine of inclusivity that saw unions as class organizations rather than as a series of exclusive craft bodies is perhaps best exemplified by the One Big Union. Indeed, the Calgary Conference explicitly rejected a body politic that determined its membership by ethnicity rather than class, declaring that 'no worker can be an alien so far as we are concerned. Our alien ... is the master class.'[40] Socialists took a principled stand against nativism in their unions and trades councils.[41] Indeed, the very idea of a 'general' strike was predicated on mobilizing the working class as a whole, a notion incompatible with older exclusivist attitudes.

During the general strike itself, working-class unity across ethnic lines held quite solidly, despite a venomous and ceaseless anti–immigrant campaign by the Citizens' Committee of 1000 and its newspaper.[42] Implicitly, the state contributed to these attacks by rewriting the Immigration Act and thereby adding official credence to the notion that a liberal immigration policy lay behind the troubles. Equating radicalism with non-British values and with immigrants themselves enabled the strike's opponents to define the strike as 'bolshevik' (and therefore alien) and at the same time to underscore participation by immigrants. The strikers, on the other hand, claimed that 'for the workers of Winnipeg, the barriers of color, race and creed had been torn down and are now beyond hope of being rebuilt. "*Which is how it should be*"'[43] (emphasis in original).

There were limits to class solidarity. Older attitudes and other considerations (particularly maintaining favour with returned soldiers) came into play. Thus the Winnipeg Trades and Labor Council participated in the Alien Investigation Board, which had been established by the Norris government in the wake of the January riots. Ostensibly aimed at defending 'loyal aliens' from discrimination, the board served to isolate and victimize those that did not fit this definition.[44] In addition, the leadership of the strike was almost exclusively Anglo-Celtic; the central and eastern Europeans who were responsible for much of the strike's effectiveness were barely represented. Moreover, concerns over the crucial issue of maintaining the support of most of the returned soldiers meant that the strikers were often defensive about the multi-ethnic character of their struggle. As Chad Reimer has carefully argued, this position did not mean overt anti-immigrant rhetoric, but rather a defence of the strike in a language of citizenship and 'British justice' that did not challenge the status of non-British immigrants as 'the other.'[45] Organizationally, the role of immigrants in the strike was downplayed, for example by reducing the number of 'foreign speakers' at the Labor Temple.[46] On the other hand, the *Western Labor News* insisted that British justice be available to all 'irrespective of birth.'[47] What is remarkable is that, despite six weeks of hardship, strikers stood shoulder to shoulder in defiance of long-standing animosities and incessant prodding by the strike's opponents.

Men waiting to enlist at a recruiting tent in Toronto in 1914.

Enlistment was heavy in many working-class communities, especially those where large numbers of British immigrants had settled before the war. One such community was Earlscourt, a workers' suburb on the northern edge of Toronto.

Many wage earners bought war bonds to support the war effort. Here CPR employees (including two women workers) in Toronto help to stir up interest.

These Toronto women were among the thousands who found jobs in Canadian munitions plants in the last two years of the war.

James Watters, president of the Trades and Labor Congress of Canada from 1911 to 1918, led the labour movement's largely unsuccessful lobbying efforts aimed at the federal government.

By the spring of 1916 large numbers of angry machinists like these men in Toronto had taken out union cards and were challenging the munitions manufacturers over the terms of their employment.

In many cities garment workers like these women in Edmonton walked out on strike.

These steelworkers in Trenton, Nova Scotia, were among the many previously unorganized workers swept up into new unions by the end of the war.

LEST WE FORGET–

That in 1913 Mr. Bowser had nothing better than bullets, chains and prison sentences for the miners: while in 1916 (when he needs their votes) he asks them to consider him their ever loving friend.

By the middle of the war, workers like the miners of Fernie, British Columbia, were having second thoughts about their traditional political allegiances.

Canadian Labor Will Crush Bolshevism

MANY OF OUR INDUSTRIAL LEADERS WERE ONCE WORKMEN. In Russia there is [illegible] for labor. All men there must work, and you cannot quit your job. The boss has authority to beat you and to even kill. You must obey orders rigidly. You receive paper money called rubles which was made by a printing press, but you cannot buy much with it. People go from the cities to the country to get food and the poor peasants have very little, because their surplus is taken from them by force. The factories in the cities cannot run if people are hungry. If nothing is produced, there is nothing to distribute. The agitator sits close to the money and the men who are clinging to power. You will be butchered without trial if you protest.

Bolshevism and Socialism are similar theories and are children of autocracy. They spring up in defeated countries where great hunger exists. They appeal best to those who have nothing to lose. In Canada we cannot understand the hatred for government that you see in immigrants from despotic countries.

Canadians Cannot Feel Bolshevism

THE SPIRIT OF CANADIANISM IS THE BEST ANTIDOTE, as we are all citizens of a great and free nation we do not want class distinctions. Employers and employees are getting closer together and the workers are participating in industrial affairs more and more every day.

Keep industry humming so that wages will not be reduced. Our returning soldiers must be given jobs. They are fighting men and will lend new energy to any industry. Now is the time to put your shoulder to the wheel and help adjust things so that we can get back to a peace basis as quickly as possible

In May and June 1919 a series of full-page ads placed by the 'Canada First Publicity Association and intended to whip up 'anti-red' hysteria appeared in newspapers across the country.

LABOR CHURCH

AS USUAL—SUNDAY, 7. P.M.
Victoria Park. Speakers:
J. S. Woodsworth, F. J. Dixon and Ald. Robinson.
Music.

MEETINGS FOR SATURDAY, JUNE 21.

Victoria Park . . . . 3.00 p.m.
St. James Park . . . . 7.30 p.m.
Lord Selkirk School . . . . 7.30 p.m.
Salisbury School E. K. . . . . 7.30 p.m.
St. James Park (Home St.) . . . . 7.30 p.m.
Central Park . . . . 7.30 p.m.
Lord Roberts School . . . . 7.30 p.m.
Principal Sparling School . . . . 7.30 p.m.
St. Mary's Road (Guay Ave.) . . . . 7.30 p.m.

During the Winnipeg General Strike, the Labor Church organized many meetings to promote the strikers' cause.

NO NEED TO HUNGER

The Women's Labor League is doing splendid work through their restaurant adjoining the Strathcona Hotel. Hundreds of free meals are suplied there daily. No one need want.

This institution is receiving fine financial support from individuals and organizations and is well able to carry on.

Strikers, get your meals at the Labor League Restaurant. If you can pay for them do so. If you can't you are welcome.

This is the biggest thing in town today.—Real Brotherhood.

Advertisement that ran in the *Western Labor News* during the Winnipeg General Strike.

During the general strike huge crowds gathered in Winnipeg's Victoria Park to listen to the passionate oratory of the strike leaders and their supporters. Here they listen to Roger E. Bray, a socialist, former Methodist lay preacher, and war veteran who would be arrested with other strike leaders on 17 June 1919.

The government's 'special' constables set out with wooden clubs to clear Winnipeg's streets of strike supporters on 10 June 1919.

On 'Bloody Saturday,' 21 June 1919, Mounted Police dispersed the crowd from Winnipeg's streets.

The Citizens' Committee of 1000 united Winnipeg's business community against the strikers. As this post-strike banquet indicates, the committee's efforts to undermine the workers' revolt continued.

Protests like this march in Winnipeg erupted across the country after the arrest and conviction of the Winnipeg strike leaders.

These unidentified Toronto workers were among the tens of thousands on strike in 1919.

Angry about their treatment at the end of the war, these Toronto veterans marched on Thanksgiving Day, 1920.

In Everything

HALIFAX HERALD

HALIFAX, CANADA, SATURDAY, MAY 1, 1920. 24 PAGES.

"OF ALL THE GLAD NEW YEAR, MOTHER, THE MADDEST, MERRIEST DAY—"

[illegible] INDUSTRY

GLACE BAY, April 30.—There has been no change in the May Day situation here and it is practically certain that all the Dominion Coal company's collieries will be idle to-morrow. All the U. M. W. locals have voted in favor of the one day lay off.

MONTREAL, April 30.—May First will be observed [illegible]

PARIS, April 30.—Miners through France will continue the May Day demonstration into a general strike in accordance with the decision of railroad workers and the result of the general labor federation, according announcement made today by the secretary of the miners' union. Other unions are awaiting orders from the federation.

The assault on the workers' revolt included this cartoon impugning the masculinity of the Nova Scotia miners' leader, J.B. McLachlan.

In the same vein, there are several ways of looking at the role of women in the strike. The five hundred women telephone operators who were the first workers to go out in sympathy symbolized the new union members in 1919,[48] as did the seven hundred bakery and confectionery workers who walked out. Over the previous months many women in the garment industry, retail trades, and a handful of other sectors had been organized, largely through the efforts of the Women's Labor League and its leading light, SPCer Helen Armstrong.[49] However, most women workers were not union members; rather, they were among the thousands of unorganized who joined the walkout.[50] Some female job sectors such as retail shops and restaurants represented the most public face of the strike. The almost exclusively male strike committee, unsure of the commitment of 'the girls' to the strike, worried about a back-to-work movement among them.[51] But the women's resolve held.

Although most working-class women were not in the paid labour force, they were still very much part of the strike. The response to the strike suggests that the events in Winnipeg were in some ways similar to the 'communal' revolts in Europe that Temma Kaplan has analysed.[52] It was clearly not just solidarity at the point of production that drew Winnipeg workers out: the workforce that struck was simply too diverse. No doubt debates about the appropriate response to the crisis raged in working-class neighbourhoods. Here lived women who had shared the pains of war – absent loved ones, maintaining families in the midst of rising prices, and an unsure future. And it would be they who would bear the brunt of responsibility for supporting their families on non-existent wages until the strike was solved, drawing not only on their own resources but on those of neighbours and kin.[53] Women were active participants in neighbourhood strike activities. In the working-class area of Weston, near the CPR shops, women pulled scab firemen from the firehall and wrecked department-store delivery trucks. Others intimidated strike-breakers who lived in their neighbourhoods. All of this is reminiscent of crowd activities in Europe and North America where women were drawn into battle over the price and accessibility of the necessities of consumption. (Here the politics of production is not distinct from the politics of consumption, and the willingness to engage in street confrontations is clear.)[54] Another important institution was the food kitchen (established by the Women's Labor League), which served upwards of fifteen hundred meals a day. Although the kitchen was open to all strikers, Mary Horodyski points out that it was primarily intended for use by women whose low wages made survival during the strike particularly precarious.[55]

Social hierarchies of ethnicity and gender were challenged in action as the excluded came to play crucial roles in the struggle. There was little acknowledgment of the oppression of immigrants or women. In the struggle for 'working-class rights' such factors were glossed over in the interests of the broader unity deemed necessary for the strike's success. Yet by allowing the normally passive to become active agents in their own collective future, the general strike raised possibilities about the reshaping of all kinds of social relations.

Another potential wedge that hung over the strike concerned those who had served in the trenches. Veterans returned to their homes with deep feelings of alienation from those whose lives had proceeded with relative normalcy while they had faced mud and death and vermin.[56] Strong ties of comradeship had been built in the trenches of France. It is testament to the strength of working-class solidarity in Winnipeg that labour remained united while the veterans' organizations fractured along class and political lines.[57] Attempts to turn the mass of veterans against labour by associating the general strike movement with enemy aliens, shirkers, and Bolsheviks demonstrably failed. Nevertheless, as we shall see, the veterans were an organized and volatile force who would maintain their own identity throughout the strike.

That unity was forged in the face of so many dissonant social forces bespeaks the prevalence of class identities in 1919, and the willingness of Winnipeg workers to follow the lead of the trades council and the strike committee into the unknown. Even divisions among political currents in the labour movement seemed to dissolve.[58] What, then, was the political character of the strike? Its 'radicalism' has to be measured not just in terms of the workers' demands but also in terms of the depths of their counter-hegemonic challenge. In practice they had rejected old loyalties and old values.[59] Capital could hardly ignore the fact that workers were expressing themselves as a class as they had never done before. In so doing they were implicitly challenging the basis for a liberal democracy predicated on a presumed legal equality of 'citizens.' In this context even the demand for 'collective bargaining' could be construed as revolutionary, for employers were being asked to deal with an organization that presented itself not as a discrete group of skilled workers, but as a *class*. The Metal Trades Council was but a way station on the road to the One Big Union, a class organization dismissive of the need for employers at all.

On 15 May workers were essentially running the city, determining the division of resources within Winnipeg on the basis of a more egalitarian concept of need and the demands of the strike. While the strike committee and its various subcommittees (which dealt with everything from food distribution to propaganda) organized the city, local unions were left to make decisions about services in their own areas.[60] The 'soldiers' parliament' that met every morning in Victoria Park provided a starkly democratic contrast to the military hierarchy. Michael Butt has calculated that a total of 171 mass meetings took place over the course of the strike.[61] Whatever its limitations, the strike was an exercise in mass participation that represented a dramatic departure from workers' marginal role in liberal democracy.

All of this suggests that we should not draw too sharp a line between radicalism (as exemplified by Winnipeg's various socialist groups) and militancy.[62] The two operated in tandem. The self-confidence that came from mass strikes made radical change seem more achievable; perhaps the working class really could run society![63] If radical ideas about 'run[ning] the city' and defeating capitalism were not loudly articulated – the general strike period was remarkable for workers' rhetorical restraint – was it because they were no longer thought? Or was it because the deepening of the crisis meant that they were closer to fruition and thus more dangerous to voice? Most narratives of the general strike miss or downplay its explosiveness, a quality privately conceded by its opponents.[64]

Moreover, Winnipeg's strikers believed that the transformation of an unjust social order was both justified and achievable. The Labor Church movement showed how pervasive this sentiment was becoming. Its founder was William Ivens, a featured speaker at the Walker Theatre meeting in December 1918 and a former Methodist minister who had lost his charge due to his anti-war sentiments. In the summer of 1918, Ivens accepted the editorship of the trade council's new and very successful paper, the *Western Labor News*, which had just been established in response to the failure of Arthur Puttee's *Voice* to reflect the new militancy of the local labour movement. (The issue that had defeated Puttee was his denunciation of the general strike as 'I.W.W. methods' anathema to the international trade union movement.)[65] Around the same time, Ivens established the Labor Church as a radical forum for discussion of 'live issues' of war and peace, the roots of social problems, and whether or not 'civilization ... [was] tottering to its fall.'[66] From its original home in the Labor Temple, the Labor Church moved into progressively larger theatres to accommodate the growing audiences. In the winter of 1918–19 the church 'offered a mixture of politics, philosophy and religion, informed largely by a Marxian analysis of class relations.'[67] The Labor Church also became an organizing centre when its resources were turned over to the Dominion Labor Party for the civic elections of November 1918. During the strike the Labor Church played a fundamental role in shaping working-class cohesion and promoting solidarity.

The Central Strike Committee, consisting of 200 representatives from all the city's locals, had been formed to direct the strike. When this arrangement proved too cumbersome, the General Strike Committee of 15 took charge.[68] The committee's mandate in part was to maintain discipline, to avoid violent confrontations that would give authorities an excuse to impose martial law, to win support for the strikers, and to determine how to maintain essential services in the city. In all of this the committee was remarkably successful. Indeed, once the strikers played their trump card – the withdrawal of services – they were notably restrained. How could this be read as a revolution?

Beyond Winnipeg

Part of the answer lies in the breadth of the challenge. Throughout the region workers strained at the limits imposed by craft unionism, contemplated and experimented with the tactic of the general strike, and questioned the morality and efficacy of 'production for profit.' This restlessness was most dramatically displayed at the Western Labour Conference in March 1919. Attended by 237 delegates representing 178 local unions and trade councils from forty-six centres, the Calgary Conference was the most representative meeting of the western Canadian labour movement ever held, representing both a broad radicalization and the confluence of various streams of local labour politics and action.[69] For the moment, labour activists throughout the region could seriously ponder the eruption of general strikes over any number of issues, and look forward to a dramatic shift of social forces in favour of the labour movement.

This astounding challenge has played little role in historians' understanding of the region. There are several reasons for this. First, Winnipeg dominated the Prairies. With a population of 180,000 (without its suburbs), Winnipeg equalled the combined total of Regina, Saskatoon, Calgary, and Edmonton. These smaller, less industrially diversified cities were relatively isolated within a burgeoning agrarian economy. Many of the international actors of the 1919 revolt – the shipbuilders of Seattle or the Clyde, the butcherworkers of Chicago or Toronto, and the steelworkers of the American Midwest or the Ruhr – were simply not there. Yet the local labour movements of the Prairies were dominated by two groups of workers that reflected the growth and character of the region: building trades workers and workers in the railway shops. The fact that these were sectors with deep craft traditions, but where workers worked closely together, inexorably raised the issue of industry-wide bargaining through councils, or even of the One Big Union. The fate of these issues in small towns and cities clearly hung on the dramatic developments in Winnipeg, as well as on the ability of workers to form a movement, such as the OBU, that transcended locality.

Second, the tendency of Canadian historians to isolate regionalism as a variable has led them to overlook these immediate post-war developments and instead concentrate on discerning a broader 'western' identity. Even the most coherent study of the prairies during the war, John H. Thompson's *Harvests of War,* leaves the immediate post-war events largely an enigma. Thompson describes a Prairie West that was united behind the war effort until late in the war when it recoiled, as a region, against the Union government and its management of both the war effort and the national economy. While the war certainly had a popular resonance, there is little in Thompson's account to explain the fissures along class lines that developed in all of the region's main urban centres at the end of the war. The large numbers of votes received by some labour candidates in the 1917 federal elections (William Irvine got 32 per cent of the vote in Calgary East, while R.A. Rigg and James Somerville received over 20 per cent each in Winnipeg North and Moose Jaw) is dismissed by Thompson as a 'poor' showing.[70] Yet Calgary East and Winnipeg North would emerge as labour electoral bastions in the aftermath of the events of 1919. However 'overwhelming' support for the Union government appeared in 1917, the alternative was based on ethnicity and, increasingly, class.

Finally, local historians have attempted to measure the degree of militancy or radicalism by using the events in Winnipeg as a gauge. Not surprisingly, other conflicts pale by comparison. Where else did thirty thousand workers strike for six weeks? Worse, there is a clear tendency to assume that if events did not follow the pattern set in Winnipeg, no 'labour revolt' occurred.[71] In fact, local configurations shaped conflicts in any number of ways. The deep crisis of social relations that sparked the Winnipeg dispute found parallels in other cities, but other avenues of expression were also available.

Everywhere the events of the war challenged the pre-war character of citizenship by recasting relationships of power and authority. This was particularly true of the debates over registration and conscription in 1917. Local trades councils quickly emerged as the appropriate venue for such discussion, even if responses varied. Some centres, such as Moose Jaw, appeared to respond with determination and unanimity to wartime challenges, beginning with their solid rejection of national registration and their support for industrial unionism and the idea of the general strike.[72] Other cities were more hesitant in their response. Edmonton unionists avoided dealing with the vexing questions of registration and conscription by referring them to the Trades and Labor Congress or to individual affiliates who were unlikely to speak with a single voice.[73] The mood of Regina unionists was notably volatile. Historian W.J.C. Cherwinski notes the uncertain and rapid changes within that city's trades council that led it to denounce the 'double burden of war and the profit takers.'[74] An invasion of the council by returned soldiers forced it to recant its opposition to conscription, but at the same time it reiterated its denunciation of profiteering. Despite the sharp tension apparent at this moment, the basis of a post-war convergence on domestic issues was already apparent. Such a rapid transformation occurred in Brandon. At the start of 1917 the city's labour movement appeared moribund, unable to maintain a local trades council.[75] Within a few months the local trades council was functioning as the executive committee of a deeply political and militant labour movement. The hot labour market made possible the rapid organization of semi-skilled and unskilled workers for whom craft skills meant little. The newly radicalized trades council could conceive of an organization of retail clerks, sanatorium workers, and federal government employees that was integral to their vision of social reconstruction.[76]

Calgary reflected trends that existed across the country. The war years saw a shift within the city's labour movement as the metal trades, and particularly the machinists, displaced the building trades as the dominant force in the local trades council. The radical new leadership, which included machinists Robert J. Tallon and Andrew Broatch from the CPR's Ogden shops (both of whom were elected to city council in this period),[77] were unable to challenge Alex Ross's presidency of the trades council until he resigned upon his election as Alberta's first labour MLA in 1917.[78] Although the transition to a new and more radical leadership in Calgary did not have the features of an ideological battle that it might have had in 1918 or 1919, two important points are worth noting: radicals did come to lead the trades council without serious opposition, and labour did make an important electoral breakthrough that compensated somewhat for the disappointing federal foray of the same year. Electoral activity, which was to mushroom in 1919, was an important element in the multifarious labour revolt.

This was a real transformation. The Tallon-led council conducted whirlwind drives to organize the unorganized. Teamsters, retail clerks, street railway workers, postal workers, civic employees, laundry workers not only organized, but struck in 1918 to win recognition and improved conditions. Women workers, including telephone operators, stenographers, and even some domestic workers, joined unions. As in other cities throughout the region, a Women's Labor League soon emerged.[79] A new Federal Workers' Union sought to organize workers of all nationalities, including the Chinese. As elsewhere, the police and firefighters were caught up in the movement and succeeded in winning recognition. The trades council played a crucial coordinating role, particularly during the ultimately victorious six-week strike of hotel and restaurant employees in March and April 1918. Not only did the council spend $700 in support of the employees – a large sum for a group of workers with tenuous craft credentials – but it also threatened to organize a general strike on their behalf. It was virtually a new trades council with a new definition of the organizable working class.[80] There was not, of course, unanimity, and craft ideals persisted often in uncomfortable tension with the ideas of a broader unionism. As the Building Trades Council moved towards an industrial union form, some trades (including the stonecutters and operating engineers) baulked.[81] Nevertheless, craft unionism was on the defensive.

As the forums through which the labour movement determined its actions and directions, trades councils sprang to life. Moreover, they became the prize to be won in the battle of ideas that accompanies any moment of social crisis. In some cases, as in Brandon or Moose Jaw, the preponderance of the current that would soon coalesce into the One Big Union seemed to preclude debate.[82] Elsewhere, as in Regina, the balance would prove more precarious. Yet, before the Winnipeg strike, the Regina Trades and Labor Council seemed committed to a radical program. When the local Builders' Exchange attempted to freeze the carpenters out of a settlement won by other workers in the industry by locking them out, the trades council rallied quickly to their side. A referendum on a general strike received 'overwhelming support' from all unions except for a couple of railway locals.[83] Interestingly, when the carpenters settled (no doubt feeling the wind of solidarity in their sails), the Regina trades council decided to continue its preparations. As a council report noted, '[I]n the event of the necessity of a general strike we shall have certain well defined plans that will allow of us being assured of success.'[84] This was not a new stance. In 1918 the Regina council, like many others, had considered a general strike in support of the postal workers.[85] Radicals Ralph Heseltine and Joseph Sambrook had assumed the leadership of the council and brought back to Regina the program of the Calgary Conference. Sambrook, a bricklayer who officially represented the Regina and Labor Trades Council before the Royal Commission on Industrial Relations (the Mathers Commission), was unequivocal: 'If you ask me what my personal opinion is, I would adopt the form of the Russian Soviet platform.'[86]

Testimony before the Mathers Commission has been unfairly derided as a source.[87] That such testimony is 'self-selected' is obvious; witnesses were not subpoenaed. But those who appeared often brought with them the imprimatur of their organizations. More important, one cannot but be struck by the common observations and language that seemed to transcend political distinctions among labour and reform witnesses. Sambrook is a case in point. While he publicly identified with the Bolsheviks, the explanation he gave for his political conclusion was rooted in the much broader discourse of profiteering, political misrepresentation, and anxiety about new efficiency methods – methods, he testified, '[that] instead of bettering the condition of the workers, releases more of them from employment, defeats demands for higher wages and generally lowers the standard of the whole working class.'[88]

In addition, testimony was generally consistent with the events that were developing beyond the halls in which Justice Mathers convened his hearings. Railway machinist Daniel MacDonald clearly articulated the transformation of the labour movement. Following a description of the travails of the male breadwinner, he concluded that the worker

> looks ahead and sees no hope of escape from this condition except through the cemetery gates and the knowledge embitters him ... He reads all the literature he can get dealing with his condition and at last comes to the conclusion that the system of production for profit under which the capitalists pile up their millions while workers one generation after another are starved, body and soul, is the

true cause of his misery, and he takes an oath with himself to work day in and day out for the abolition of the system to which he ascribes his miserable conditions in life. That is the cause of unrest.[89]

MacDonald's call for a 'change from production for profit to production for use' appealed to the entire spectrum of reform and socialist witnesses, eliding programmatic differences in the spring of working-class unity in 1919.[90]

Evidence from the Mathers Commission also underlines the danger of interpreting struggles within the labour movement as a fight between moderates defending a status quo and radicals hoping to precipitate a revolutionary crisis. Take, for instance, the important character of James Somerville, an officer of the International Association of Machinists (IAM) who is generally portrayed as a bulwark of conservatism in the western Canadian labour movement. Within the IAM he led the opposition to amalgamation of railway crafts at the December 1918 meeting of District 4 in Winnipeg. At a meeting in Calgary he spoke against secession from the TLC,[91] acknowledging that he spoke as 'one of those individuals who have been getting a meal ticket in the organization.'[92] His sort was on the defensive.

Yet the strategic questions raised by Somerville cannot be dismissed as irrelevant to other political tendencies in the labour movement. He claimed that a general consensus existed for industrial unionism but objected to the proposed OBU because, he argued, it demanded that 'we must destroy what we have before we start to proceed building.'[93] While Somerville's high regard for existing union structures was clearly not shared by his audience, the fate of labour unity was a real concern. As the later Communist critique of the OBU would demonstrate, trepidation about splitting the union movement was not necessarily solely a 'moderate' trait. What is more notable was the confidence of the secessionists in western Canada in 1919. The sense of solidarity that had developed in 1918 (as a result of the Winnipeg civic workers' strike, regional disputes involving the postal workers and the freight handlers, and the Calgary Conference) encouraged a sense of complacency about the possibilities and consequences of secession.

Nor was Somerville merely the 'labor fakir' his opponents accused him of being.[94] He too was in revolt against pre-war business as usual and won the nomination as the Independent Labor Party candidate in the 1917 federal election. Before the Mathers Commission he spoke of 'transferring the natural resources and the means of wealth production from private ownership to collective ownership.' The program Somerville proposed was a gradualist one that included negotiations with (and compensation of) capitalists, and that was reflected in his commission testimony that if American southerners had been willing to compromise with the slaves, there would have been no civil war.[95] For the benefit of the commissioners, Somerville explored the roots of the class-based social crisis. He pointed to the deep unrest and 'the want of confidence in constituted authority arising out of what has transpired during the past four or five years.' And he pointed to the dramatic self-education of workers and their interest in books on 'Sociology and Education.' As a trade union leader, Somerville clearly represented before the Mathers Commission some combination of his own views and the sentiment of his membership with whom he had to maintain legitimacy. He noted too that testimony before the commission was not representative: as in Winnipeg, 'quite a number' of workers who harboured 'radical extreme' views boycotted the hearings.[96]

Somerville's excursion into electoral politics in 1917, along with other, increasingly successful labour campaigns over the next few years, should not be dismissed; labour's revolt at the polls cannot be easily separated from the other events of the period. Martin Robin's attempt to establish a clear schism between advocates of direct action and supporters of political action obscures the fact that few workers found the two strategies mutually exclusive.[97] Each represented a class-based rejection of the political and social status quo. This was apparent in one of the few divisions that arose at the Calgary Conference. The two Calgary trades council delegates, A.G. Broatch and J.S. Hooley, argued strongly that the proposed OBU should have both industrial and political strategies, and that it should support labour electoral action. The Broatch Amendment, was dismissed by SPCer Jack Kavanagh who spoke disparagingly of parliamentary 'hot air houses.' On the face of it, the response of Kavanagh and the Socialist Party of Canada members who played such a large role at the conference is inexplicable: the SPC was a political party and regularly participated in elections. The Broatch amendment was defeated not because Kavanagh et al. rejected political action, but rather because they did not want to see the industrial movement hijacked by a handful of labour politicians who were more interested in winning parliamentary sinecures than in mobilizing and educating the working masses. More than a few socialists could agree with Kavanagh without qualifying as anti-political syndicalists. No other explanation would be consistent with the fact that OBUers subsequently undertook electoral campaigns with no indication they felt they were acting inconsistently with OBU principles.

Broatch, it is worth noting, stayed with the OBU. Far from an attack on the new movement, his amendment was a contribution to a debate on how best to realize workers' power. There were those present, such as Somerville and Alfred Farmilo, who objected to secession and to the general strike, but they mostly kept their mouths shut rather than stand against the tide. The deeply anti-radical Farmilo had defeated Sarah Johnston-Knight to become the Edmonton trades council delegate to Calgary. But even within what the *Western Labor News* described as 'the most reactionary of all Labor Councils in Western Canada,'[98] Farmilo avoided a direct confrontation with the proponents of industrial unionism. Rather, he campaigned for amalgamation – the so-called Seattle Plan – as an alternative to secession.[99] Few workers were inclined to make such distinctions: the plan had associations with the massive Seattle general strike, and when its author, James A. Duncan, visited Winnipeg in the midst of its general strike, he received a tumultuous welcome.[100]

Whatever the value of electoral action, the problems that confronted Prairie workers would not wait until the next trip to the polls. Sympathetic strikes would ensure that problems would be dealt with before workers' power was drained by post-war unemployment. Workers responded enthusiastically to the addition of strikes to the agenda. In October 1918 Calgary was at the centre of what Myer Siemiatycki has described as 'the most extraordinary sympathetic strike of the year.'[101] The day after strikes were banned by order-in-council, twelve hundred workers at the Ogden shops struck to support striking freight handlers. Within a week civic employees, street railway workers, and teamsters struck in support, and the trades council started to mobilize others to join what the *Calgary Herald* feared would be 'a volcano of class reign.'[102] Working unions assessed a levy on their members to support the strikers. The strike spread to CPR shops in Saskatchewan (Moose Jaw was a centre of this activity), and a general strike was proposed in Winnipeg. On 17 October five union leaders from the Ogden shops were arrested for defying the strike ban; on the first day of their trial, a crowd of four hundred demonstrated at the Calgary court house. Gideon Robertson rushed to the city and attempted to get the freight handlers back to work. The sympathetic strike ended only after the CPR was persuaded to take back almost all the strikers (the fate of a small group would be decided by arbitration) and the charges against the five strikers were dropped.[103] According to historian David Bright, the avoidance of a general strike bespeaks a failure of radicalism in Calgary. '[A]lthough twenty-two unions supported the [Calgary Trades and Labor Council] campaign for a general strike in support of the freight handlers,' he notes, 'it is more significant that not one chose to risk prosecution by realising this threat.'[104] However, the fact that the process was cut short when the government and the railway acquiesced to the threat of a general strike suggests that, as was so often the case in 1918, militancy won; such was the conclusion that would be taken into 1919.

By the spring of 1919 there was plentiful evidence of a class-based social crisis throughout the region, including the massive growth of the labour movement, the growing success of labour electoral campaigns, the organization of previously unorganizable workers, the leadership of trades council offices by self-declared revolutionaries, the attacks on capitalist social relations by a wide range of witnesses who appeared before the Mathers Commission, the frequent threats of general strikes, and the wholesale rejection of the established craft union movement at the Calgary Conference. Despite this evidence, historians have generally offered only a single test of radicalism: did workers in other centres strike in sympathy with Winnipeg in May and June 1919? This is a high standard. Expressed differently, the question becomes, were workers willing to forego wages and in many cases risk the permanent loss of their jobs to support workers in a distant struggle whose goals were unclear and whose outcome was far from certain?

Astonishingly, the answer is yes in several cases. In Brandon there was unabashed solidarity with the struggle under way in the provincial capital. In April civic workers there had won a strike with the help of the trades council, which had initiated preparations for a general strike. A month later they placed their gains on the line by joining the strike in sympathy with Winnipeg. The events and language of the Brandon strike mirrored those of the Winnipeg strike: the strike committee issued a regular *Strike Bulletin*, the city council issued ultimatums and debated the loyalty of the police force, and essential services were maintained 'by authority of the Strike Committee.' The confidence of Brandon workers survived the end of the Winnipeg strike. To force the rehiring of all civic employees, the strike committee called a new general strike starting 26 June and wired centres across the prairies to follow suit. Not surprisingly, the effort fizzled. How radical was the Brandon strike? Like their counterparts in Winnipeg, Brandon strike leaders denied any revolutionary intent. However, their language belied such a benign conclusion. The

Strike Bulletin cautioned workers to do 'nothing that will give the master class the occasion they so much seek: of covering the labour movement with stigma by accusing us of breaking their sacred law.'[105] There is little sign here of consent or deference to 'their' law, and every indication that the strikers were making an appropriate decision not to provoke a military confrontation for which they were in no way prepared.

Saskatoon is a particularly noteworthy case given, as several witnesses at the Mathers Commission noted, the relative lack of local conflicts (or even animosity) and the growing willingness to strike in sympathy with workers elsewhere.[106] As the City Commissioner commented, there was 'no unrest as to conditions,' but there was 'labor unrest over the general well being of the worker.'[107] The only local precursor of substance was a large and successful petition campaign to free a local railway clerk jailed under an order-in-council for three years for possessing banned literature. Saskatoon workers were mobilized by their identification with the concerns and hopes, however vague, of a wider class movement. The decision in July 1918 to participate in a general strike in support of the postal workers was virtually automatic and unanimous.[108] In response to the Winnipeg General Strike, the Saskatoon Trades and Labor Council unanimously endorsed a general strike vote that was passed by thirteen of the seventeen unions that took part. The strike began the next day and remained solid until it was called off on 26 June. Local historians Don Kerr and Stan Hanson suggest that, with an average of twelve hundred people on strike throughout the month, Saskatoon was the scene of perhaps the country's strongest strike in sympathy with Winnipeg.[109]

In Regina and Calgary the response was more complex. In Regina the vote on striking in sympathy with Winnipeg was mixed: eleven unions voted in favour, five voted against, and nine were undecided.[110] The apparent unity over supporting the local carpenters by calling a general strike fractured over the issue of similar action in favour of a more distant struggle and with more vague ends. It is important to note that the Winnipeg strike was almost two weeks old at this point. The notion that the ruling class could be immediately brought to terms by a general strike was fading. Not surprisingly, there was some trepidation and those wary of general strike action were more willing to speak their minds. While the trades council abandoned the general strike, those who supported the action formed a provisional strike committee and led some two hundred workers, 'primarily electricians, CNR shopmen, and building labourers,' out on strike.[111] That the workers soon drifted back to work should not obscure the fact that a substantial group of workers had risked their livelihoods to support a distant and perhaps futile struggle.

The failure of the general strike deepened fissures in the Regina labour movement. After the Calgary Conference the trades council (the typographers were the only dissenters) had voted its support for the One Big Union. But the defeat of the general strike, the events of 'Bloody Saturday' in Winnipeg, and the subsequent RNWMP raids on the homes of Ralph Heseltine and Joseph Sambrook undermined the confidence of workers and reminded them of the risks of resistance. By late August, 'with two ranking officials of the TLC and AFL in attendance,' the trades council voted overwhelmingly to stay with the Congress; the radical leadership resigned.[112] While the exciting prospects that had appeared on the horizon in early 1919 had faded, it is easy to exaggerate the transition. Many Regina unionists maintained dual membership in their craft union and the OBU, no doubt wanting to maintain the security of the former without losing the utopian vision of the latter.[113] And despite the 'purge' of the left in 1919, one-time OBU stalwarts Ralph Heseltine and Fred Kinsella were acclaimed to the two top positions in the trades council in 1923.[114]

Events in Calgary suggest the importance of looking closely at the concatenation of events. There the referendum on the OBU preceded the issue of a sympathy strike with Winnipeg. Of the thirty-four unions that voted (the failure of two dozen unions to do so might be explained by membership apathy or by a refusal on the part of local executives to take the question to the membership),[115] fourteen were unanimously opposed; among the others the OBU lost by a vote of 728 to 951. The OBU's strength was in the railway shopcrafts; the union fared most poorly among the building trades. Certainly the experience of different sorts of workers was far from homogeneous. To a great extent, the OBU referendum served as a poll on workers' experiences with their own international unions; many workers, whatever their broader social attitudes, felt no need to make that break.

Even for workers who had rejected craft unionism, there were other compelling reasons to be wary of secession and the general strike movement. The debate on the OBU was fractious. Alex Ross led the charge against the OBU, associating it with 'dual' movements such as the Industrial Workers of the World (IWW) and claiming that it would dangerously divide the continental labour movement. The language of the OBU response, exemplified by trades council president J. Hooley's denunciation of his own international boilermakers' union as 'racist, untrustworthy and undemocratic,' while no doubt representative of the thinking of many, could add credence to Ross' argument.[116] Divisiveness was also apparent at a meeting, organized by some craft union leaders, in which TLC president and Mathers' Commissioner Tom Moore criticized local Metal Trades Council president (and SPCer) George Sangster for his characterization of the local labour situation before the commission. Such events demonstrated that there was not likely to be a unitary One Big Union in Alberta. Rather, voting in favour was a vote for division.

The same equation was doubly applicable to the general strike; without an overwhelming display of unity, it was doomed. On 21 May the trades council endorsed the principle of a general strike in sympathy with Winnipeg, and set about organizing a strike vote of its affiliates. As with the OBU vote, several unions did not comply, but of those that did, eighteen favoured the strike and seven opposed it. A similar situation existed in Toronto, where a majority of the unions that voted supported the general strike; however, opposition in that city was strong enough to prevent its success.[117] On 26 May fifteen hundred Calgary workers struck. Two-thirds of the strikers were from the Ogden shops. Most dramatic was the participation of the metalworkers who had just ended a five-week-long strike that had won them the eight-hour day and substantial wage increases. To risk these concessions, and their livelihoods in Calgary, was a sign of their determination and solidarity. Although fifteen hundred might seem a disappointing showing, that such a number would maintain their isolated struggle in sympathy with workers two provinces away is a striking testimony to the ethos of the period. Other workers were less inclined to assume the risk.[118] The civic workers, who had organized themselves into the strong and effective Calgary Federation of Civic Employees, and who allegedly held the city 'in the palm of their hands,' opted not to wager their newly achieved collective agreement.[119]

This was not, however, the end of the story. When the federal government fired postal workers involved in the Calgary sympathetic strike, a louder chord was struck. Here was an issue that was more immediate and concrete. The alleged conservative core of anti-OBU sentiment joined the struggle as the building trades walked out in sympathy. Although David Bright suggests that the general strike 'gained momentum only when it became confused with a separate dispute involving city postal workers,'[120] it is difficult to see what is 'separate' about a dispute that appears to have reflected the spread of the general strike idea.

At the same time, victory in Winnipeg appeared increasingly elusive as the strike dragged on for six long weeks. The Calgary strike ended in disarray. The class-based anger and hopes that had been expressed during the strike would find a new release in 1921 with the election of Calgary labour MP William Irvine, who, like J.S. Woodsworth in North End Winnipeg, was an unquestionable heir of the labour revolt.[121]

On the face of it, Edmonton appears a more uncertain case. In part, this can be explained by the tactics of trade union conservatives in the city, particularly Alfred Farmilo, who moved quickly to outflank such radicals as Carl Berg, Joe Knight, and Sarah Johnston-Knight. Immediately after the Calgary Conference, conservatives organized a careful and selective purge of OBU proponents from the trades council. In many other cities, more conservative unionists held trades council office, often to be voted out in the process or the aftermath of the 1919 revolt. Only in Edmonton did they strike first and secure their positions. On 21 April council president R. McCreath (from the typographers) expelled 'secessionist' delegates from Joe Knight's carpenters union, the United Mine Workers, and the Federal Labor Union, itself largely a creation of radicals who had no craft affinity. The expulsions were just enough to maintain the relationship of forces in the conservatives' favour; the purge was endorsed at the next council meeting by a vote of twenty to nineteen.[122] That the purge was undertaken *before* the Winnipeg strike meant that response to events in Winnipeg would be decided by a labour movement that had just isolated its left wing.

Still, the response was significant. The council agreed to a union-by-union poll on a sympathy strike with Winnipeg. Thirty-four locals supported the strike; four (garment workers, musicians, sheet metal workers and postal workers) were opposed. Eleven unions, including those of McCreath and Farmilo, did not vote. The final tally was 1676 to 506, with the strongest support coming from the machinists and mineworkers.[123] Guided by a one-hundred-member strike committee, with large rallies nightly, the strike started on 26 May. As in Regina and Calgary, the Edmonton strike was not general, and many workers soon abandoned it as a lost cause. Those who stayed out, such as the railway craft workers, were often involved in broader disputes. The return of the more visible workers, such as the civic employees and the street railway workers, created the impression that the dispute had died away. Nonetheless, the Central Strike Committee continued to meet through the month of June.[124]

The fate of the Edmonton strike was also affected by the intervention of the city's mayor, Joe Clarke. On the eve of the Edmonton 'general strike,' he sent telegrams to local Members of Parliament and to the mayors of other cities in Alberta and Saskatchewan in which he lamented the 'great hardship and loss [that] will be caused disinterested cities and people unaffected by matters at Winnipeg if Federal government does not take steps to prevent unduly flouting labor unions and stop such actions as refusing to recognize unions in negotiations with employers.'[125] Subsequently, he protested the arrests in Winnipeg.[126] Almost everywhere else, and most dramatically Winnipeg, the strike movement had coalesced with local antagonisms; in Edmonton it confronted an ostensibly pro-labour mayor.

A few years earlier such a scenario would have seemed unlikely. In 1916 the city council locked out the street railway workers and used strike-breakers despite a series of conciliatory moves on the union's part.[127] A conflict in 1918, however, divided the city along quite different lines. In February of that year the firefighters struck when the city ignored seniority from within the department and hired an outsider, from Chicago, as fire chief. The *Edmonton Journal*, owned by Liberal Frank Oliver and supportive of Laurier's attempt to build a cross-class alliance in opposition to the Tories, took up the firefighters' cause. In contrast, the Southam paper, the *Journal*, helped to recruit strike-breakers.[128] The city council responded to pressure by organizing a plebiscite on the issue: they lost 6539 to 2250, and the imported fire chief was dismissed. Voter turnout for the plebiscite had exceeded that of the previous civic election by a thousand. It was on this wave that Joe Clarke, endorsed by the *Journal* and the trades council, was elected mayor. At the same time, the local Dominion Labor Party (DLP) increased its representation on city council to two. By the end of 1919 Clarke had lost the *Journal*'s endorsement but retained the mayor's chair, along with a third DLPer on council. An editorial entitled 'The Reds Win' appeared in the *Bulletin*.[129]

However far-fetched, the characterization of Clarke and the DLP as 'reds' stemmed from an impressive accumulation of working-class resources. Edmonton labour had become a force to be reckoned with. It had mustered enough electoral support to re-elect a mayor whose career had come to rely on an explicit identification with working-class interests. This may seem an unusual 'labour revolt,' particularly if the term is limited to apply only to a specific and radical set of strategies. But workers in Edmonton did come into their own, electing representatives in their own name. Farmilo and the DLP were interested in augmenting working-class power as they understood it, and their successes gave them a strong credibility. There was little reason, in the minds of many, to risk this progress, or their jobs, in a general strike. (That supporters of the OBU gained the ear of as many workers as they did suggests that there was a sizeable contingent in Edmonton who felt that labour gains made to date were insufficient.) Edmonton is a prime case of all the cards being stacked against the OBU and the SPC by an astute opposition within the labour movement whose strategy, it seems, was working. Still, for many workers, this strategy seemed insufficient compared to the hopes embodied in the OBU and the general strike movement. Whereas in Winnipeg the general strike was a tactic developed by the labour movement as a whole (including the trades council and craft union leaders), in Edmonton it had the unmistakable imprimatur of secession upon it before it was subjected to serious consideration. Committed craft unionists interpreted the strike in terms of their own organizational interests; Edmonton union leaders saw it primarily as an abandonment of their organizations and their positions within them.

The example of Edmonton underlines the salient feature of the 1919 labour revolt. Despite being characterized by a myriad of different ideas and programs (few of them well defined), this was a real social movement and one in which authority was challenged in the name of class. A wide variety of witnesses testifying at the Mathers Commission expressed the 'common-sense' view that, in the future, social 'use,' not 'profit,' would govern social decisions. There was clearly no consensus on what this meant (not even within the OBU), but it marked the ethos of the labour revolt. To dismiss the labour revolt because of its diversity – a characteristic of any mass movement – is to minimize the achievement of a working class that had struggled to the centre of the historical stage. Certainly, the opposition took the labour revolt seriously. Only in the rare instance of Edmonton did authorities feel they might be able to constrain the movement by cooperating with it. Elsewhere, the example of the Citizens' Committee of 1000 in Winnipeg spawned the Law and Order League (Brandon), the Committee of 350 (Regina), and the Citizens' Committee (Calgary) as instruments to uphold 'constituted authority.'[130] Local employers and professions were hardly confident of the loyalty of their local working classes. (No doubt federal authorities felt similarly as they considered their next move in Winnipeg.) The ability of business and the state to respond to events in Winnipeg was severely constrained by developments throughout the region.[131] Isolating the general strike in Winnipeg was crucial to the preservation of the existing order.

'The Perfection of Bolshevism': Combating the Strike in Winnipeg

The federal government was acutely aware of the geographical breadth of the labour challenge. Arthur Meighen told the House of Commons that the Winnipeg strike was a challenge to the state and that if it were to succeed the result would be a mushrooming of labour organizations across the country and 'the perfection of Bolshevism.'[132] Bourgeois Winnipeg needed no convincing that a revolution was in the making. As a result, as Kenneth McNaught has observed, 'the structural and ideological unity [of the Winnipeg General Strike's opponents] was even more startling than the original cohesion of the working class.'[133] From its creation on 19 May 1919 the Citizens' Committee of 1000 had blunted the impact of the strike by organizing volunteers to provide services withdrawn by strikers. Committed to the strike's unconditional defeat, the committee (publicly and privately) discouraged efforts to find a negotiated solution to the conflict. Drawn principally from the Board of Trade and the Winnipeg branch of the Canadian Manufacturers' Association, the committee also included several prominent members of the Winnipeg legal community, among them A.J. Andrews, Isaac Pitblado, Travers Sweatman, and J.C. Coyne.[134] Andrews, a founding member, became the principal architect of the suppression of the strike following his appointment by Arthur Meighen to advise Ottawa on how to defeat the strike.[135]

While the federal, provincial, and municipal levels of government were inextricably involved in the strike, only the federal state had the resources to definitively smash it. From the outset the Citizens' Committee was determined to marshal the authority and power of the federal state against the strike. The response of the federal state to the committee – and, for that matter, to the strikers and other fractions of organized labour during the strike – illuminates the real, yet limited, autonomy of the state in relation to civil society. Ralph Miliband has noted that while the state 'may appear to be the "historical subject," [it] is in fact the object of processes and forces at work in society.'[136] On 15 May Winnipeg's labour movement had played its hand. Thereafter the principle subject shaping events was a truculent regional business elite intent on reasserting its authority and crushing its adversaries.

The Citizens' Committee set about mobilizing the state by winning the cooperation of federal authorities. As we saw, in the unusual wartime circumstances of the 1918, the federal state had intervened on behalf of Winnipeg civic workers, western postal workers, and Calgary freight handlers in an effort to prevent threatened general strikes. The arrival of peace had dramatically weakened the strikers' leverage over the federal state. In 1919 they challenged the boundaries imposed by the liberal state on class relations, driving the state into an active alliance with the Citizens' Committee. In late May 1919 Arthur Meighen, acting minister of justice, and Senator Gideon Robertson, minister of labour, travelled to Winnipeg for a first-hand view of the paralysed city. They were met at Fort William by A.J. Andrews and A.T. Sweatman, emissaries of the Citizens' Committee, who advised them that the strike was an incipient revolution and that only resolute and decisive action could prevent disaster.[137] Both ministers readily accepted this perspective on the strike. Meighen concluded that the strike was motivated not by any principal of industrial relations, but rather by a drive for 'Soviet control.'[138]

Meighen's assessment of the strike had three fundamental implications for the state's role in the crisis. First, it was only the state that could legitimate the Citizens' Committee's portrayal of the strike as revolution and transform post-war labour radicalism into a criminal venture. Second, Meighen and Robertson's reading of the strike meant that from an early stage the resources of the state were publicly and unconditionally committed to the defeat of the strike. Third, the involvement of the state dramatically raised the stakes for proponents of the strike. The Citizens' Committee seemed to recognize that the strike's defeat could 'open the sluice gates of reactionary politics,'[139] isolating organized labour and discrediting it as an instrument of deeper social change.

On 26 May 1919 the federal govenment issued an ultimatum directing federal postal employees to quit the strike immediately or face dismissal.[140] On the same day, A.J. Andrews was appointed representative of the federal Justice Department in Winnipeg. His assignment was to determine whether the activities of the strike leaders were of a 'seditious or treasonable character' and to 'advise as to what should be done.'[141] In practical terms, Andrews had been appointed the principal strategist in Winnipeg of state efforts to contain and defeat the strike. He emerged as a tactician of state repression and contributed to a legacy of legislative weapons to be used by the state against agents of disorder. In January 1919 C.H. Cahan, who had coordinated the Union government's suppression of radicalism, had resigned from his post as Director of Public Safety. To all intents and purposes, Andrews was his replacement on the front lines.[142]

The vehemence of denunciations of the strike by Meighen and the Citizens' Committee may suggest that the state had been prepared from the outset to resort to violence in order to end it, but those in charge of the state's handling of the confrontation were mindful of how their actions might provoke a deeper crisis. Now burdened with state authority, the hitherto bellicose Andrews was determined to move cautiously. On 27 May, after examining RNWMP files, he concluded that precipitous arrests would be explosive and that 'the publicity and stir resulting from a trial would do more harm than good.'[143] Any state action against the strike would have to be legitimized by the exigencies of the moment as well as timed for maximum effect. Ill-considered action could have the unintended effect of rallying the strikers in Winnipeg and throughout the region, and undermining the authority of government. Only after it became clear that the strike would not collapse under its own weight did those in charge of the state's machinery of repression give in to the logic of the Citizens' Committee. Until at least 10 June 1919 Andrews and the state played a waiting game, marshalling the legal authority and physical force that might be required to suppress the strike.

Andrews looked to Ottawa for the legal weapons with which to destroy the strike. Since 1918 the federal government had been increasingly preoccupied with its ability to suppress social disorder. Reflecting what Gregory Kealey has termed the 'surveillance state,'[144] federal authorities in the spring of 1919 considered amendments to the Immigration Act and the Criminal Code that would exclude from the country, or imprison, persons who believed in or advocated either the violent overthrow of constituted government or the unlawful destruction of property.[145] Andrews was eager to have these and other changes approved. Appropriately framed and directed, the law provided a measure of force that could be employed to good effect with limited political cost. In early June Andrews exhorted Meighen to give him the legal weapons needed 'to reach the leaders of this revolutionary movement.'[146]

Optimism that the strike would fail soon vanished. The strikers remained wedded to their cause, rejecting ultimatums to return to work. In early June the stakes were raised even higher when contending groups of returned soldiers numbering in the thousands – the majority of them strike sympathizers – paraded repeatedly in the streets of Winnipeg. At the same time, mediation efforts initiated late in May by a committee of the Railway Brotherhoods were undermined by the Citizens' Committee, which demanded the arrest of the strike leadership and the total defeat of the strike.[147] On 3 June, in an attempt to pressure the provincial government to intervene on behalf of the strikers, the strike committee discontinued the delivery of bread and milk under its auspices. As the strike spiralled deeper into crisis, palpable alarm spread through the ranks of its opponents.

Historians have tended to belittle this apparent panic, labelling it as 'hysteria' or associating it with the Red Scare and 'foreign conspirators and bomb plots' in the United States.[148] Images of Winnipeg's middle-class residents guarding their homes with rifles and seeking refuge in church basements would seem to support such a view.[149] But these fears in ruling circles were not entirely unjustified. That the struggle was over 'wages and hours and collective bargaining'[150] does not mean that it would necessarily stop there, particularly given the intransigence of the employers and the high level of mobilization. Rapid transformations of working-class consciousness and aspirations were taking place around the world. Just two years earlier in Russia, the failure of the Tsar to supply the 'moderate' demands of 'Bread, Peace and Land' had brought down the monarchy, capitalism, and – in the minds of those under seige from their own workers in Europe and North America – civilization itself. Hungary and parts of Germany were following suit. Mass strikes from Glasgow to Turin to Seattle seemed to portend similar developments. As one historian has commented, '[I]f Lenin and Trotsky, Luxemburg, Liebknecht, and Gramsci were wrong in their optimism, they were no more misguided than their panic-stricken opponents, such as Churchill, Lloyd George, the diplomats at Versailles, and the various generals and police commanders charged with controlling and suppressing the volatile crowds of urban workers and discontented soldiers.'[151] The world was a dangerous place for capital at the end of the First World War.

It was in this context that Andrews pleaded with Meighen to hurry through amendments to the Immigration Act. Once the amendments were in place, the RNWMP Commissioner was prepared to deport 'one hundred dangerous aliens.' Andrews was also considering direct action that could be taken against the strike leadership under existing provisions of the Criminal Code. As in late May, however, arrests were rejected on the grounds that they would fuel sympathetic strikes across the West and allow the strikers to 'claim that they would have won but for the intervention of the Government controlled by the master class.' Perhaps even more critical, arrests would galvanize support for the strike such that, Andrews feared, 'we will not only have to fight the present strikers but all organized labour including the Great International Craft Unions.'[152]

While arrests were an impractical way to suppress the strike, Andrews believed that the approval of legislation allowing for the deportation of radicals would 'stem the tide of revolution.'[153] The Immigration Act was amended on 5 June and given royal assent the following day. Andrews angrily dismissed the amendment as useless. The fact that it did not cover 'the dangerous class not born in Canada' meant that the British radicals who dominated the leadership of the strike committee were unaffected by changes in the act.[154] Meighen took the objections of Andrew seriously.[155] On 6 June the Immigration Act was again amended by Parliament and immediately given royal assent.[156] The state now had the legal authority to detain and deport the British leadership of the strike.[157] Changes to the Criminal Code that had been prompted by the post-war wave of radicalism were not passed until late in June and thus were not available for the prosecution of the strikers.[158]

Although federal authorities had hoped that overt coercion would not be required to convince the strikers to abandon their cause, they opposed any mediated settlement that would grant the strikers even a vestige of victory. Ironically, the collapse of the conciliation efforts initiated by the railway running trades unions raised fears that the running trades would be provoked into joining the walkout, thereby shutting down railway transportation across the country and reigniting the smouldering general strikes in the West. With the stakes so high, Gideon Robertson was summoned to Winnipeg.

More than a widening strike loomed. It seemed there would be chaos on the streets of Winnipeg following the dismissal, on 9 June, of 240 members of the regular police force who had refused to sign a loyalty oath. In late May Andrews had rejected on both tactical and political grounds Winnipeg Mayor Gray's suggestion that the RNWMP take over the policing of the city. '[I]t would never do to have the Mounted Police take the place of striking Policemen,' Andrews advised Meighen. '[I]t would prejudicially affect our situation throughout Canada.'[159] In short, the use of the RNWMP as strike-breakers would both undermine an important aspect of the state's legal apparatus in the West and galvanize support for the strike as a political event. Accordingly, there was no middle ground between continuing with the present force and imposing 'martial law.'[160] On 30 May Andrews and General H.D.B. Ketchen of the Canadian Armed Forces in Winnipeg advised Mayor Gray that the RNWMP would not act as policemen for the City of Winnipeg if the city's force walked out. Faced with a choice between securing a new force or placing Winnipeg under martial law, Gray initiated the appointment of special police alongside the regular force.

On 10 June 1919 the force of 'specials' appeared on the streets. That afternoon a riot ensued following efforts of the 'specials' to direct traffic at Portage and Main. Mounted specials failed to disperse an angry crowd of some fifteen thousand people. Twelve hundred specials arrived to battle the crowd. Andrews, who watched the scene from the Industrial Bureau, reported to Meighen that the specials proved 'wholly inadequate and the net result [was] that they [were] chased off the streets, a number of them hurt, some badly wounded and the crowd [took] possession of a number of their clubs.'[161] This spreading disorder triggered a renewed interest in the militia by opponents of the strike. After the dismal showing of the specials, volunteers flocked to the barracks to join the military force being assembled by federal authorities.[162] On a more sinister note, Andrews explained to Meighen that while 'the loyal returned soldiers [would] not join the militia, they say they will form themselves into a body in support of the General.'[163] In creating a private armed organization of young men, the state could resort to illegal methods under the guise of legality. In their potential for violence, their susceptibility to anti-socialist and xenophobic appeals and, presumably in their social composition, the specials were analogous to the nascent fascist organizations that were being spawned by the inability of European states to stem the working-class challenge at the end of the war. Remarkably, neither Andrews nor Meighen acknowledged the illegality of such a force or counselled action against its creation.[164] On 11 June Major Lyall, who had been charged with supervising the organization of the special police, was replaced at the insistence of the Citizens' Committee and the work of getting the special force street ready proceeded anew. Events had reached a critical crossroads: Andrews advised Meighen, '[T]he time has arrived to act.'[165]

On the day of Lyall's replacement, Gideon Robertson arrived in Winnipeg. Confronting him was a report prepared by the Running Trades Conciliation Committee that was acceptable to the strike leadership. Some pressure by Robertson on the metal trades proprietors could well have settled the dispute – and the general strike – but at the price of encouraging the strikers. Only two days earlier Meighen had wired Andrews that a 'settlement now under pressure by [Robertson] will be generally accepted as a triumph for [the] general strike leaders.'[166] The challenge for Robertson, then, was to defeat the strike without drawing the increasingly restive running trades, and perhaps workers throughout the region, into the strike.

On 13 June Robertson advised Prime Minister Borden that conditions had deteriorated so badly that immediate steps were required 'to remove the cause of the whole trouble.'[167] In the wake of this wire immigration officers and the RNWMP were directed to follow the orders of A.J. Andrews. On 14 June Andrews informed Meighen that he had ordered the special police off the streets because such activity, he noted, 'would embarrass us in what we intend to do.'[168] Yet one further initiative was required to set the stage for a successful assault on the strike leadership. On the same day, in an attempt to diminish the prospects of a general walkout of the railway running trades across the West in reaction to the arrest of the strike leadership, Robertson convinced the metal trades proprietors to accept a collective bargaining system similar to that of the railway running trades in the West.[169] A declaration establishing bargaining with specific trades but not with a council representing all trades endorsed by the running trades was prepared for publication on 16 June. Consistent with its demand for recognition of the Metal Trades Council, the strike committee rejected the deal. Rejection notwithstanding, by keeping the running trades out of the strike, Robertson gained the vital strategic advantage he had sought.[170]

These developments marked a decisive turning point in the strike. While its defeat was the central goal of authorities from the outset, clearly success without the direct intervention of the state would have been preferred. However, the continued solidarity of the strikers, the prospect of the running trades joining the walkout, fear that the strike would spread, and the refusal of any settlement that could be viewed as a triumph for the advocates of the general strike weapon left no apparent option but the use of force to defeat the strike. The plan prepared by Andrews, C. Starnes of the RNWMP, and General Ketchen for the arrest of the 'revolutionary leaders' followed logically from the policy pursued by the federal government from the beginning of the strike.[171] Federal authorities were ready to end the crisis on their terms.[172]

With the running trades deal in place, authorities could feel relatively confident that repression would not provoke a regional general strike. During the night of 16–17 June ten individuals, including strike leaders R.B. Russell, William Ivens, R.E. Bray, John Queen, A.A. Heaps, and George Armstrong, were arrested and taken to Stony Mountain Penitentiary. In addition, R.J. Johns was picked up in Montreal and William Pritchard was arrested in Calgary. All eight men were charged with seditious conspiracy. In an effort to secure evidence that could be used against them, raids were made on the Labor Temple, Liberty Hall, and other sites. Also arrested were five 'aliens': Mike Verenchuck, a victim of mistaken identity; Michael Charitinoff, former editor of *Robochyi narod;* Moses Almavoff, a militant Jewish activist; Oscar Schoppelrei, a returned soldier who had been organizing veterans in support of the strike; and Samuel Blumenberg.[173]

In a letter to Meighen dated 18 June 1919, Andrews explained that it was his intention to deport those among the accused who could be deported and try the remainder on criminal charges.[174] As a precaution against the accused being allowed out on bail, an order for their detention under the Immigration Act was used. Andrews had an additional warrant for arrest prepared and placed an RNWMP officer, arrest warrant in hand, at Stony Mountain. He also arranged for the medical officer at the prison to ascertain the birthplace of each of the arrested men. Andrews was opposed to granting bail to any prisoner he could not deport, informing Meighen that to do so would be 'a fatal error and would be interpreted as weakness.'[175] Within twenty-four hours of the arrests, however, Andrews changed his mind on the matter of bail and deportation and concluded that the 'fairest course' towards all the English-speaking prisoners was to try them on criminal charges (although eventual deportation was not ruled out). Andrews was concerned not only that deportations of British-born subjects prove difficult to secure but also that flaunting British 'fair play' and legal traditions could well add fuel to the ongoing conflagration.[176] Most ominously, pro-strike veterans, whose volatility rightly concerned Andrews, met in Victoria Park on 17 June and cheered the imprisoned men during a meeting that was 'electrified by the arrests' and 'vibrant with emotion.'[177]

No less important in Andrews' calculations was the prospect that the strike would be called off in the event that the arrested strike leaders were released on bail. A deputation from the strike committee seeking the release of the arrested men had assured Andrews that 'the offer of the Metal Trades Employers was satisfactory to them and that they were prepared to recommend the calling off of the sympathetic strike.'[178] Andrews' release of the prisoners on bail (on condition they take no further part in the strike) did not meet with unanimous approval from his allies. General Ketchen condemned that action as a betrayal of the volunteer militia and special constables.[179] Enraged members of the Citizens' Committee claimed that Andrews 'had shattered the confidence of the Citizens that the strike would end soon as with the arrests the strike leadership had sought a way to end the strike.' That his action had backfired was evidenced by the fact that the strike leaders 'openly boast[ed] of the waywardness of the Government and [were] making plans to create further trouble.'[180]

'Trouble,' when it came, arrived in the form of a brutal armed attack by the RNWMP and specials on a returned soldiers' parade on North Main on Saturday afternoon, 21 June. To many in the anti-strike camp, 'Bloody Saturday' was a logical sequel to Andrews' release of the strike leaders. Andrews was stung by the criticism. Perhaps to regain the initiative and to show a renewed toughness in his dealings with the strikers, on June 23 he forbade publication of the *Western Labor News* and had warrants issued for the arrests of J.S. Woodsworth and Fred Dixon, who had taken over as editors following the arrest of William Ivens.[181] These actions were sufficient to crush the strike, which formally ended on 26 June with the agreement of the provincial government to establish an inquiry into its origins and nature.

Contested Identities and the Renegotiation of Hegemony

In 1919 contested juridical and idiomatic constructions of Canadian citizenship were advanced by labour and capital as the ideological core of the new epoch.[182] The Citizens' Committee sought to further a Canadian citizenship whose central structures included Anglo-conformity, capitalist relations of production, and cultural assimilation based on two assumptions: the superiority of British institutions and customs, and the undesirability of 'alien' notions of citizenship. Chad Reimer has argued convincingly that by asserting traditions of British law and justice in support of their demands, the strikers 'presented an historically distinct, working-class definition of citizenship and nation.'[183] Victories in this struggle were registered in a material way in the outcome of the strike and in various legislative enactments, institutional creations, and judicial decisions. They were also woven into the fabric of daily life through the constitutive power of language and culture.

In the end the contest for power at the core of the Winnipeg General Strike would be resolved by the state. As the *Toronto Star* explained, personalizing the conflict, '[R.B.] 'Russell was not worsted until Andrews was given the opportunity to use the powers of the State to put Russell in custody and eliminate him as a factor in the strike.'[184] But even the strike's defeat and the passage of draconian amendments to the Immigration and Naturalization acts and the Criminal Code were not enough to convince Andrews and his associates in the Citizens' Committee of 1000 that the threat of radicalism had been eliminated. Radicalism, they believed, was at the root of a persistent, deepening crisis that was eroding the stability of the social order.[185] Following the suppression of the strike, Andrews and the Citizens' Committee sought to mobilize the resources of the federal Department of Justice in a legal and ideological assault on labour radicalism. While this campaign represented the denouement of the May–June struggle in Winnipeg, it had a national focus and was designed to discredit and disperse proponents of labour radicalism in Winnipeg and elsewhere.

Yet, ironically, support for such a campaign of repression was not initially forthcoming from either Winnipeg or Ottawa. In July 1919 the province of Manitoba refused to proceed with the prosecution of the strike leaders who had been arrested on 16 June. Arthur Meighen, the acting federal Minister of Justice, rejected Andrews' demands that the federal government sponsor these prosecutions and take action against radicals using orders-in-council approved under the War Measures Act. Meighen also dismissed calls (advanced by leaders of the Citizens' Committee) for a national commission of inquiry into labour radicalism. The prosecutions of Russell and the others, he insisted, was a provincial responsibility. In response, Andrews argued that a persistent and effective campaign was being waged to promote Bolshevism; prosecutions and vigorous action on the part of government would cause 'fear and confusion in the ranks of the revolutionists.' While the government appeared to believe that 'repression and suppression tend[ed] to flame rather than destroy revolutionary tendencies,' Andrews and what he termed his 'associate council' were convinced that 'the only way to deal with Bolshevism is to hit it and to hit it hard, every time it lifts its ugly head.'[186]

While Andrews and the Citizens' Committee lobbied federal authorities for action, there was continued agitation against any criminal prosecution or summary deportation of the Winnipeg strike leaders. Across the country individuals, labour councils, Women's Labor Leagues, and informally organized groups of workers petitioned for 'British justice' for the arrested men.[187] Defence committees sprang up, organized to raise funds in support of the strike leaders and to campaign for their release. On 9 July 1919 F.J. Dixon warned an assembly in Winnipeg's Market Square that the Canadian people were in the process of having their 'rights and liberties stolen from them by the shabbiest pack of political jackals that ever harassed a civilized country.'[188]

In late July, following the return of Justice Minister C.J. Doherty to Ottawa, Andrews secured federal sponsorship of the prosecution of the

Winnipeg strike leaders. The historic Winnipeg strike trials were thus brought about by a combination of tenacious lobbying on the part of the Citizens' Committee and willingness on the part of Doherty to engage the resources of the Canadian state in an extraordinary assault on labour radicalism. Although the defendants in these trials had been arrested and charged for their roles in the Winnipeg General Strike, the twenty-seven-page indictment covered events dating back to the Walker Theatre meeting. It defined the terrain on which the Crown intended to mount its ideological assault on labour radicalism as sedition. Through the indictment the view of the 1919 labour revolt advanced by the Citizens' Committee was formally embraced by the state as a basis for the criminal prosecution and punishment of the strike leadership. The workers' revolt was transformed into a criminal venture. In short, the trials of Russell and the other strike leaders were not about bringing criminals to justice; rather they were ideological events designed to mobilize consent for the established order while constructing strict limitations on the legality of any criticism of the state and demands for fundamental change in relations of production.[189] Although convictions were secured, the trials generated only working-class antagonism as opposed to mass adhesion to the established order. Andrews had recognized the possibility of such an outcome when he tried to have the trial venue moved to the rural community of Morden on the grounds that 'a jury of farmers would be more likely to give a fair trial to these men than a jury from Winnipeg upon which there may be some strikers.[190] Across the country workers dismissed the prosecution as state repression under the guise of justice.

At another level, the struggle over citizenship was also being waged on the terrain of culture. The National Conference on Character Education held in Winnipeg in October 1919 represented an attempt by the city's business elite to promote a moral regulation of society that was rooted in their own version of Canadian citizenship. As Philip Corrigan and Derek Sayer have argued, the moral discipline achieved through such an initiative 'was not neutrally about "integrating society." It was about enforcing rule.' Moreover, the solidarity or compliance generated was rooted in an adherence to a particular kind of social order legitimated in terms of a particular vision of social reality.[191] The principal instrument for the creation of the polity envisioned by the Citizens' Committee was the public school. As a central instrument of state formation, the public school would be responsible, in the words of J.A.M. Aikins, '[for the] manufacture of souls of good quality.'[192]

Flowing from such basic purposes, it is evident that the National Conference on Character Education was a profoundly partisan affair designed to legitimize particular idioms of citizenship as a basis for public policy and the construction of the post-war order. Held in the Winnipeg Industrial Bureau – the home of the Citizens' Committee and its successor, the Citizens' League – the conference was one of the initiatives of the Winnipeg branch of the Canadian Reconstruction Association.[193] The convening committee was dominated by leading members of the Winnipeg business and professional community, including W.R. Bulman, Ed Anderson, A.L. Crossin, Issac Pitblado, H.M. Agnew, H.M. Tucker, and many executive committee members of the Citizens' Committee and its successor, the Winnipeg Citizens' League.[194] Funds for the conference were generated through an appeal to Rotary Clubs of Canada (the Winnipeg branch contributed over $10,000). As described by the *Western School Journal*, 'the rotary clubs of Canada, consisting for the most part of hard-headed business men, are alive to the possibilities of education ... They find something lacking in our social and civic life, and they recognize that the school is the agency through which the needed reform may be affected.'[195] At the October 1919 conference citizenship was touted as a primary weapon in the cultural offensive against radicalism on the terrain of citizenship. Not surprisingly, the One Big Union denounced the conference as a 'sinister' exercise in 'doping the kids.' The conference organizers, maintained the OBU, were conspiring to subject the country's schoolchildren 'to a systematic propaganda of imperialistic patriotism and its corollary, suspicion and hatred of all foreigners.'[196] The cultural and ideological battles at the heart of the 1919 revolt were far from over.

The cultural offensive waged by the Citizens' Committee suggests a lack of confidence in its previous victories, whether on the streets or in the courts. In this regard the committee was in agreement with those socialists who considered the strike revolutionary because it had challenged the verities of capitalist rule, honed the organizational capacities of the proletariat, and educated workers about the true nature of class rule. In these terms, clear gains had been made. SPCers were not blind to the power of the state and the setback the union movement had suffered. But the strike had unleashed an unprecedented display of working-class power, and, from the evolutionist perspective of pre-Leninist Marxism, the growth of capitalism could only increase labour's power. Moreover, SPCers had never entirely abandoned their faith in education and had felt deeply that even the western Canadian working class had much to learn.[197] Finally, the Citizens' Committee was probably right to be concerned about capitalism's legitimacy. How many socialists had been made by the Mounties' bullets on Main Street?

The counter-hegemonic challenge had not been killed that day on 21 June 1919. Even the idea of the general strike was resurrected the following September when the strike leaders were denied bail.[198] The November 1919 municipal elections also demonstrated the failure of the Citizens' Committee to win legitimacy. The Dominion Labor Party, the Social Democratic Party, and the recently formed Ex-Soldiers' and Sailors' Labor Party united behind a single campaign endorsed by the Winnipeg Trades and Labor Council. Labour won seven of the fourteen aldermanic seats, and only a restricted municipal franchise saved the mayor's chair for the Citizens' League. (C.F. Gray's narrow victory over S.J. Farmer was too close for comfort;[199] in 1920 ward boundaries were redrawn 'in one of the most blatant cases of gerrymandering in Canadian history.')[200] Ten branches of the Labor Church in Winnipeg, as well as the People's Church in Brandon,[201] provided the structure necessary to nourish a pluralistic labourism. In addition, the Defence Committee united all of the labour electoral parties, the Socialist Party of Canada, and the One Big Union. The 1920 provincial elections saw the election of eleven labour MLAs, including George Armstrong, Fred Dixon, William Ivens, and John Queen from Winnipeg and A.E. Smith from Brandon.[202] The following year would see the elections of Winnipeg labour candidates J.S. Woodsworth and A.A. Heaps. The echoes of 1919 were, perhaps, correspondingly weaker in other prairie centres, and the quiescence of the 1920s left little evidence of the fate of working-class hopes that mobilized so many. Association with the general strike was no liability in the labour movement. Although Woodsworth was only tangentially involved, his widespread political reputation rested upon his role in the strike's final days.

To be sure, the labour movement after the strike lacked clear perspectives, but it did share a common class identity and a vision that had been articulated in the *Western Labor News* during the strike: 'We have a historical mission to perform. We have no choice but to go forward. Our basis of organization must broaden still further, and develop until it embraces all who perform a useful function in society; until it eliminates the wages system with all its resultant evils of wealth and poverty, and establishes in its stead a system where usefulness and not profit will be the basis of production.'[203] None of this is to argue that labour 'won' the general strike.[204] Through the post-war depression and political reaction of the 1920s, as employers, the state, and the Trades and Labor Congress leadership attempted to rebuild the old world, the vision of a future that was labour's would wear thin. But in the fall of 1919 and on into 1920, it was still possible to dream.[205] In 1919 it had been a deep social crisis that had made that dream possible, that had made the older order open to contestation, and that had made working people feel that they would have a say about their own futures. Sam Blumenberg's 1918 declaration 'We are going to run this city'[206] had a variety of meanings for strikers and their opponents. But for both it promised (or threatened) a new social order. It is not to romanticize the strike to suggest that it sustained a generation of socialists and trade union militants through the reaction of the 1920s and the desperation of the 1930s.[207] It had shaped their world.

Notes

1 Corrigan and Sayer, *The Great Arch*, 3.

2 A contemporary example was O.D. Skelton's considered response to the question 'Was the Winnipeg strike in reality an attempted revolution?' in 'Western Strikes,' 125; see also the chapter entitled 'Strike or Revolution?' in Masters, *Winnipeg General Strike*. For a thoughtful consideration of the debate, see J.M. Bumsted's 'Was the Winnipeg General Strike of 1919 Revolutionary?' In '1919: The Winnipeg General Strike Reconsidered' and *The Winnipeg General Strike of 1919*, Bumsted fails to explore the implications of his observation that the word 'revolution' had different meanings for workers in 1919 and subsequent generations.

3 As H.C. Pentland has noted, 'A startling feature of the Winnipeg General Strike is the totally different conception held by the contending parties of what was happening.' Pentland, 'Fifty Years After,' 14.

4 We would agree with Perry Anderson's admonition that a history 'from above' is a necessary corollary to a history 'from below,' and that understanding the role of the state in this relationship is crucial because 'the secular struggle between classes is ultimately resolved at the *political* – not at the economic or cultural – level of society.' Anderson, *Lineages of the Absolutist State*, 11.

5 Samuel Blumenberg, speech at Columbia Theatre on 19 May 1918 (during the civic workers' strike), quoted in *Manitoba Free Press*, 27 May 1918.

6 *Western Labor News*, 16 May 1919.

7 At the conference the decision was made to organize a general strike in opposition to allied intervention in Russia and in support of the six-hour day. One Big Union, *Origin of the One Big Union*, 31, 33.

8 Robin, *Radical Politics and Canadian Labour,* 171; Bercuson, *Fools and Wise Men,* 84–6.
9 This apparent spontaneity, a feature of unrest throughout Europe and North America, was due in large part to the collapse of older working-class political formations following their rejection by workers who demanded more radical solutions than they were able to offer. See Peterson, 'One Big Union' and various contributions to Wrigley, ed., *Challenges of Labour.*
10 Two leading SPCers who shared this view were Vancouver Trades and Labor Council President Ernest Winch and R.B. Russell. Russell, an OBU supporter, opposed the Winnipeg General Strike because he believed it deflected attention from the immediate task of building the OBU. Campbell, '"Stalwarts of the Struggle,"' 45–6, 345. Gerald Friesen argues that the general strikes were a sign of the SPC's failure to control events in the West. Friesen, '"Yours in Revolt."' For a general discussion of the OBU, see Bercuson, *Fools and Wise Men;* and Warrian, 'Challenge of the One Big Union Movement.'
11 Campbell, '"Stalwarts of the Struggle,"' 343. See also Friesen, 'Bob Russell's Political Thought.'
12 Winnipeg SPC secretary W. Breeze commented that among working-class audiences 'anything on the Russian situation is in the greatest demand.' Quoted in Siemiatycki, 'Labour Contained,' 287.
13 Bercuson, *Confrontation at Winnipeg,* 86; Masters, *Winnipeg General Strike,* 3; Penner, ed., *Winnipeg 1919,* 16.
14 David Bercuson alludes to some dispute about whether the WTLC had actually co-sponsored the event (Bercuson, *Confrontation at Winnipeg,* 82). As Campbell points out, however, there is no evidence or reason to believe that the SPC was alone in calling the meeting. Campbell, '"Stalwarts of the Struggle,"' 340 n. 56.
15 Winning is discussed in Bercuson, *Confrontation at Winnipeg,* 85.
16 Penner, ed., *Winnipeg 1919,* 17n.
17 Jacob Penner, 'Recollections,' 377.
18 Martynowych, 'Ukrainian Socialist Movement,' 30. For examples of the paper's radicalism, see Thompson, 'Enemy Alien,' 40. See also Kazymyra, 'Ukrainian Opinion in Manitoba'; and Avery, 'Divided Loyalties.'
19 Melnycky, 'Political History of the Ukrainian Community,' 202–3.
20 Avery, *'Dangerous Foreigners,'* 72.
21 See Usiskin, 'Toward a Theoretical Reformulation,' 131 and 133, for a clear explanation of the various tendencies on the Jewish left. See also Usiskin, 'Winnipeg Jewish Radical Community'; and Trachtenberg, 'Winnipeg General Strike.' For an incisive biography of an individual raised in this milieu, see Smith, *Joe Zuken,* chap. 1. For discussion of other communities, see

Grenke, 'German Community of Winnipeg'; Entz, 'Suppression of German Language Press'; and Leckow, 'Canadians in the Making.' English ethnicity in Winnipeg is discussed in McCormack, 'Cloth Caps and Jobs' and 'Networks among British Immigrants.' See also Molnar, 'Winnipeg General Strike.'

22 Campbell has noted a drift out of the SDP and into the SPC in several centres at the end of the war, largely because of the SPC's 'hard-line stand' against the war and against parliamentary palliatives. See '"Stalwarts of the Struggle,"' 41.

23 See Robin, *Radical Politics and Canadian Labour*; Bercuson, *Confrontation at Winnipeg*, 98; and Morton with Copp, *Working People*, 116. In a recent reappraisal, Bercuson recognizes that the OBU's ideology was too 'fuzzy' to be so easily categorized. See Bercuson, 'Syndicalism Sidetracked,' 233. As McCormack has pointed out in *Reformers, Rebels, and Revolutionaries*, 'labourism' was particularly strong in Winnipeg even before the war. The war cemented the electoral movement: from 1913 on there was regular labour representation on city council and, from 1915 on, in the legislature. The general strike movement did not undermine this situation, although the radicalization of the labour movement may have pressed at the boundaries of any meaningful definition of 'labourism,' which is usually equated with a vague Lib-Labism. See also Mills, 'Single Tax, Socialism and the Independent Labour Party of Manitoba'; and Heron, 'Labourism and the Canadian Working Class.'

24 Canada, Dept. of Labour, *Labour Organization in Canada*, 1917, 32, cited in Robin, 'Registration, Conscription, and Independent Labour Politics,' 107.

25 Bercuson, *Confrontation at Winnipeg*, 61.

26 The *Winnipeg Telegram* of 2 May 1918 carried the headline 'Police May Arrest Civic Strikers.' Johnson, 'Strikes in Winnipeg,' 138, cites the *Telegram* of 16 May 1918, which noted that martial law had been discussed.

27 *Manitoba Free Press*, 16 May 1918. According to Eric Hobsbawm, 'militant labour movements [throughout Europe] could largely be written in terms of the metal workers,' particularly at the end of the First World War. Hobsbawn, *Labouring Men*, 360. See also Michell Perrot, 'Introduction: From the Mechanic to the Metallo,' in Haimson and Tilly, eds., *Strikes, Wars, and Revolutions*; and Haydu, *Between Craft and Class*, for some interesting parallels.

28 *Manitoba Free Press*, 17 May 1918, cited in Johnson, 'Strikes in Winnipeg,' 139–40. See also Bercuson, *Confrontation at Winnipeg*, 65–6.

29 *Winnipeg Telegram*, 16 May 1918, quoted in Johnson, 'Strikes in Winnipeg,' 138.

30 Bercuson, *Confrontation at Winnipeg*, 64–5.

31 *Manitoba Free Press*, 27 May 1918.

32 Siemiatycki, 'Labour Contained,' 207–9.
33 Ibid., 225–7; Taraska, 'Calgary Craft Union Movement.'
34 Bercuson, *Confrontation at Winnipeg*, 74.
35 The *Special Strike Edition* was launched on 17 May and the *Citizen* two days later.
36 *Winnipeg Citizen*, 27 May 1919. Another example of *Citizen* language is reprinted in Penner, *Winnipeg 1919*, 55–6: 'For nearly a month the citizens of Winnipeg have been fighting whole-heartedly, and with a very generous measure of success, against a determined attempt to establish Bolshevism and the rule of the Soviet here and then to expand it all over this Dominion.'
37 *Western Labor News*, 30 May 1919.
38 Lyle Dick, in 'Politics and Discourse,' contends that the 'binary structure' pervading the literature on the Winnipeg General Strike is little more than a discursive creation of historians of the strike. The fact remains, however, that those who participated in the strike did explicitly prioritize class differences over other social relationships.
39 Mott, 'Foreign Peril,' 23–4; Avery, 'Radical Alien,' 218–19.
40 One Big Union, *Origin of the One Big Union*, 31–2.
41 This was particularly true of R.B. Russell. Campbell rightly dismisses Bercuson's outrageous claim that the strike leaders 'were determined' to maintain the social exclusivity of the labour movement, hoping to 'keep their unions as lily white as they could.' Such a claim flies in the face of the whole trajectory of the post-war labour movement, and socialists in particular, explicitly attacked racism. Bercuson's attempt to equate the attitudes of the pre-war labour movement with 1919 makes the entire episode inexplicable. Campbell, '"Stalwarts of the Struggle,"' 338–9; and Bercuson, *Confrontation at Winnipeg*, 204.
42 One strategy employed by the Citizens' Committee was to take out large advertisements in the city's dailies on the theme of 'Canada for Canadians.'
43 Penner, ed., *Winnipeg 1919*, 78.
44 Avery, 'Radical Alien,' 219; Mott, 'Foreign Peril,' 25.
45 Reimer, 'War, Nationhood, and Working-Class Entitlement,' especially 231–2.
46 Provincial Archives of Manitoba (PAM), MG 10, A14–2, (R.B. Russell Papers), Box 11, Central Strike Committee Minutes, 20 May 1919.
47 Cited in Reimer, 'War, Nationhood, and Working-Class Entitlement,' 233.
48 Horodyski, 'Women and the Winnipeg General Strike,' 28–9; Linda Kealey, '"No Special Protection,"' 137. For a general discussion of women during the war period, see Linda Kealey, 'Prairie Socialist Women.'
49 Linda Kealey, 'Women and Labour during World War I.'
50 Tranfield, 'Girl Strikers,' 30.

51 There are several such references in the Central Strike Committee Minutes in PAM, MG 10 A14–2, Box 11.
52 Kaplan, 'Women and Communal Strikes.'
53 James Gray's reminiscences of family life during the 1918 strikes reflect the importance of women to the success, or collapse, of strike action. See Gray, *Boy from Winnipeg*, 128–30.
54 The examples of crowd activity are from Linda Kealey, '"No Special Protection,"' 140. Eric Angel explores the extent and consequences of crowd activity in 'Workers, Picketing and the Winnipeg General Strike.' It is interesting to compare the Winnipeg strike with neighbourhood risings that had been seen in previous decades. See Palmer, '"Give Us the Road and We Will Run It"'; Palmer, *Culture in Conflict*, 209–16; and Gregory Kealey, *Toronto Workers*, 199–212. For a discussion of the politics of consumption in this period, see Dana Frank, *Purchasing Power*.
55 Horodyski, 'Women and the Winnipeg General Strike,' 31.
56 See Graves, *Goodbye to All That*; and Fussell, *Great War and Modern Memory*.
57 Shaun Sephton incisively identifies the returned soldiers' corporate identity but, strikingly, this was not matched by a distinct social vision on the part of the veterans. Sephton, 'Soldier Problem.' The most complete study of the veterans, Morton and Wright, *Winning the Second Battle*, is unfortunately superficial in its treatment of class and political differences in the veterans organizations.
58 The careful typology that Ross McCormack constructed to distinguish different groups of 'reformers, rebels, and revolutionaries' does not seem to explain very much in Winnipeg in 1919. After describing a history of 'sharp struggle' between radicals and trade union 'conservatives,' D.C. Masters notes that '[w]hen the general strike came in May 1919 it was precipitated by a union of radicals and moderates.' Masters, *Winnipeg General Strike*, 17, 21.
59 See Reimer, 'War, Nationhood, and Working-Class Entitlement.'
60 This is apparent from the items referred to subcommittees and unions by the Central Strike Committee. See PAM, MG 10, A14-2, Box 11, Central Strike Committee Minutes.
61 Sephton, 'Soldier Problem'; Butt, '"To Each According to His Need,"' 113.
62 A sharp distinction is posed by Bercuson and David Bright. Although conceptually distinct, they are less so in practice, particularly in the context of a social crisis such as that of 1919. It is a dubious assignment to attempt to disentangle the 'militant' tactic of the general strike from the 'radical' desire to restructure the social order. See Bright, 'Bonds of Brotherhood?' 89; and Bercuson, 'Labour Radicalism,' 155.
63 According to Leopold Haimson, even 'ostensibly economic strikes ... came to

focus explicitly over issues of power and authority.' Haimson, 'Conclusion,' in Haimson and Tilly, eds., *Strikes, Wars, and Revolutions*. See also P.K. Edwards, 'Strikes and Politics in the United States, 1900–1919,' in the same volume. Similarly, in their study of France, Edward Shorter and Charles Tilly found that such a dichotomy failed to explain strike behaviour either in its timing or its character. Rather, they see the strike 'as an instrument of working-class political action.' *Strikes in France*, 348.

64 This tendency is apparent in the correspondence between A.J. Andrews and Arthur Meighen. See National Archives of Canada (NAC), RG 13, Access 87–88/103, Box 36, File A-1688, pocket #1.

65 The defeat of Puttee and the *Voice* is attributed to the SPC in McCormack, *Reformers, Rebels, and Revolutionaries*, 146. The circulation of the *Western Labor News* went from twelve hundred copies to eleven thousand copies in less than half a year. Butt, '"To Each According to His Need,"' 98.

66 *Western Labor News*, 6 September 1918, quoted in Butt, '"To Each According to His Need,"' 85. On the Labor Church movement, see ibid.; Allen, *Social Passion*; and Fast, 'Labour Church in Winnipeg.'

67 Butt, '"To Each According to His Need,"' 69, 86–7. For a fictionalized account of a Labor Church meeting with Ivens, see Sweatman, *Fox*, 94–7.

68 For a discussion of the transition between the two committees, see Campbell, '"Stalwarts of the Struggle,"' 347–8.

69 One Big Union, *Origin of the One Big Union*.

70 Thompson, *Harvests of War*, 140. Gerald Friesen's survey, *The Canadian Prairies*, is more conscious of the construction of class in the cities of the region.

71 This is precisely the argument David Bright applies to Calgary in 'Bonds of Brotherhood?' 100.

72 Cherwinski, 'Organized Labour in Saskatchewan,' 47.

73 Askin, 'Labor Unrest in Edmonton and District,' 33–5.

74 Cherwinski, 'Organized Labour in Saskatchewan,' 48; Siemiatycki, 'Labour Contained,' 150.

75 Black and Black, 'Labour in Brandon Civic Politics,' 3.

76 Mitchell, 'Brandon 1919,' 4. For a discussion of the electoral impact of these developments, see Mitchell, '"A Square Deal for All and No Railroading"'; and Black and Black, 'Labour in Brandon Civic Politics.'

77 Elizabeth Ann Taraska notes that 'labour radicals dominated organized labour on the surface' at this time. Taraska, 'Calgary Craft Union Movement,' 56. See also Bright, 'Bonds of Brotherhood?' 117.

78 Finkel, 'Rise and Fall of the Labour Party in Alberta,' 65.

79 Damji, 'Militancy to Passivism,' 87. In Regina, for instance, the Women's

Labor League soon won the right to send delegates to the local trades council. See Cherwinski, 'Organized Labour in Saskatchewan,' 323.

80 Taraska, 'Calgary Craft Union Movement,' 63–4; Damji, 'Militancy to Passivism,' 55–6; Bright, 'Bonds of Brotherhood?' 114.

81 Taraska, 'Calgary Craft Union Movement,' 64.

82 For a discussion of the Brandon trades council, see Mitchell, 'Brandon 1919.' Immediately following the Calgary Conference, the Moose Jaw trades council declared for industrial unionism but waffled on the question of affiliation with the OBU. By the end of May, W.J.C. Cherwinski notes, 'a general strike in sympathy with Winnipeg seemed inevitable.' Cherwinski, 'Organized Labour in Saskatchewan,' 69, 86.

83 Ibid., 67.

84 Regina TLC files, Executive Report, 26 May 1919, cited in ibid. Astonishingly, the dramatic development of a local labour revolt is ignored in Regina's main local history, Brennan's *Regina: An Illustrated History.*

85 Siemiatycki, 'Labour Contained,' 207.

86 Labour Canada Library, Royal Commission on Industrial Relations (RCIR), Evidence, 1133.

87 By, for example, Bercuson, *Confrontation at Winnipeg,* 202; and Bright, '"We Are All Kin,"' 63.

88 RCIR, Evidence, 1123.

89 Ibid., 1174.

90 The phrase was also pervasive in the United States. See Montgomery, *Fall of the House of Labor,* 399, 427.

91 Siemiatycki, 'Labour Contained,' 307; Cherwinski, 'Organized Labour in Saskatchewan,' 64; Friesen, 'Bob Russell's Political Thought,' 133.

92 One Big Union, *Origin of the One Big Union,* 77.

93 Ibid.

94 Ibid.

95 RCIR, Evidence, Somerville, 1334, 1335.

96 Ibid., 1331, 1333, 1341–2.

97 See the chapter entitled 'Direct versus Political Action' in Robin, *Radical Politics and Canadian Labour.*

98 *Western Labor News,* 3 May 1919.

99 Askin, 'Labour Unrest in Edmonton and District,' 65–6.

100 Bercuson, *Confrontation at Winnipeg,* 145.

101 Siemiatycki, 'Labour Contained,' 225.

102 *Calgary Herald,* 23 October 1918, cited in Caragata, 'Labour Movement,' 118.

103 Siemiatycki, 'Labour Contained,' 225–7; Taraska, 'Calgary Craft Union Movement,' 69–70.

104 Bright, 'Bonds of Brotherhood?' 104.

105 *Strike Bulletin*, No. 3, 23 May 1919. See also Mitchell, 'Brandon 1919,' 4–6.

106 At the Mathers Commission, among those who agreed with this assessment of conditions in Saskatoon were F.M. Beatty, employer at the Sash and Door factory; J.O. MacCallum, owner of the Saskatoon Cartage Company; and Walt Mills, president of the Saskatoon trades council. RCIR, Evidence, 1044, 1075, 1049.

107 RCIR, Evidence, C.J. Yorvath, 1096.

108 Makahonuk, 'Labor in a Prairie City' and 'Class Conflict in a Prairie City.'

109 Kerr and Hanson, *Saskatoon*, 199.

110 *Morning Leader*, 30 May 1919, cited in Cherwinski, 'Organized Labour in Saskatchewan,' 68. See also Makahonuk, 'Painters, Decorators, and Paper-hangers,' 201–2.

111 NAC, MG 26, H1(a) (Sir Robert Borden Papers), File 564, cited in Cherwinski, 'Organized Labour in Saskatchewan,' 68–9.

112 Ibid., 89.

113 Ibid., 90.

114 Brennan, *Regina*, 117.

115 It is an assumption, on Bright's part, to say that these unions 'did not even bother to register a vote.' '"We Are All Kin,"' 75.

116 Damji, 'Militancy to Passivism,' 66–9.

117 Naylor, 'Toronto, 1919.'

118 For a discussion of the various responses of workers to the crisis of 1919, see Naylor, 'Toronto 1919'; and Conley, 'Frontier Labourers.'

119 Damji, 'Militancy to Passivism,' 78–9.

120 Bright, '"We Are All Kin,"' 75.

121 Bright dismisses this achievement, citing Irvine as an example of cross-class collaboration. The point is that it was Irvine who abandoned his class, not Calgary labour. Bright, 'Bonds of Brotherhood?' 110–13. On Irvine, see Mardiros, *William Irvine*; and Palmer, 'William Irvine and the Emergence of Political Radicalism in Calgary.'

122 Askin, 'Labour Unrest in Edmonton and District,' 67.

123 Ibid., 85–7,

124 Ibid., 100.

125 *Edmonton Bulletin*, 23 May 1919, cited in Askin, 'Labour Unrest in Edmonton and District,' 102.

126 Askin, 'Labour Unrest in Edmonton and District,' 103; Caragata, *Alberta Labour*, 76.

127 Caragata, *Alberta Labour*, 64.

128 Askin, 'Labour Unrest in Edmonton and District,' 109–11, 123. For an analysis of the attempts of the Laurier Liberals to address working-class concerns in Ontario, see Naylor, *New Democracy,* 99. The Liberal strategy to build a cross-class alliance seems to have succeeded best in cities such as Edmonton and London, Ontario, where local working-class Liberals were able to take up the cause.

129 *Edmonton Bulletin,* 9 December 1919, cited in Askin, 'Labour Unrest in Edmonton and District,' 223 (the account of these events is based on chapter 6 of this thesis). Clarke testified before the Mathers Commission (RCIR, Evidence, 965–76) that the federal government was to blame for the current unrest, and particularly for protecting profiteers and limiting civil liberties.

130 Mitchell, 'Brandon 1919,' 6; Cherwinski, 'Organized Labour in Saskatchewan,' 74; Damji, 'Militancy to Passivism,' 83–4.

131 For a discussion of the small-town and rural response to the Winnipeg General Strike, see Yeo, 'Rural Manitoba.'

132 House of Commons, *Debates,* 1919, First Session, III, 2 June 1919, 3037–41.

133 McNaught, 'Political Trials,' 147–8.

134 On the origin and membership of the Citizens' Committee, see Bercuson, *Confrontation at Winnipeg,* 121. For a profile of Andrews, see the A.J. Andrews biographical file, Western Legal Archives, Faculty of Law, University of Manitoba. For a discussion of how the legal profession in early twentieth-century western Canada became preoccupied with containment of discontent and maintenance of order, see Pue, 'A Profession in Defence of Capital?'

135 A contemporary described Andrews as 'preeminently a trial lawyer, a strategist and tactician to be respected and feared but never hated by his opponents.' Stubbs, *Prairie Portraits,* 54. For a description of the role Andrews played in suppressing the strike, see Mitchell, 'To Reach the Leadership.' For a general discussion of the role of lawyers in the West at this time, see Pue, 'Lawyers and the Constitution of Political Society.'

136 Miliband, 'State Power and Class Interests,' 59.

137 Penner, *Canadian Left,* 28–9; Rea, 'Politics of Class.'

138 NAC, MG 26, H1(a), microfilm c-4341, telegram, Robertson to F.A. Acland, Deputy Minister of Labour, 27 May 1919. For Meighen's impressions of Winnipeg in May 1919, see NAC, RG 13, Department of Justice, Access 87–88/103, Box 36, File A-1688, Pocket #1. Additional evidence that Meighen accepted the committee's view of the strike can be found in Graham, *Arthur Meighen,* 236–7. The Meighen quote is from NAC, RG 13, Access 87–88/135, Box 36, File A-1688, Meighen to N.W. Rowell, 27 May 1919.

139 David Montgomery, review of Melvyn Dubofsky, *The State and Labor in*

Modern America, <http://h-net2.msu.edu/~books/H-Labor/0001.html>, 16 April 1996.

140 On the same day, similar ultimatums were issued to federal postal workers, provincial telephone workers, and Winnipeg civic employees, indicating a coordinated assault on the strike by the three levels of government.

141 NAC, RG 13, Access 87–88/103, Box 36, File A-1688, Pocket #1, Meighen to Andrews, 26 May 1919. In the days that followed, Andrews communicated regularly with Meighen through telegrams and letters. These letters and telegrams, secured from Department of Justice files in the National Archives under the Access to Information Act, constitute an important new source on the federal government's response to the strike. More varied and extensive than the disclosures of Peter Heenan in 1926 (see House of Commons, *Debates*, 1926, IV, 4004–9), the documents illuminate both Andrews' role in the conflict and Meighen's thinking on the central issues surrounding the strike. For a sample of the Andrews–Meighen correspondence, see 'A.J. Andrews to Arthur Meighen: Winnipeg General Strike Correspondence,' in *Manitoba History*, 24 (Autumn 1992). An introduction and index to the entire collection can be found in Kehler and Esau, *Famous Manitoba Trials*.

142 Andrews was recognized as 'the principle human factor opposing the strike movement' by the *Toronto Daily Star*, 27 June 1919.

143 NAC, RG 18, Vol. 3314, RNWMP, File HV-1, Superintendent C. Starnes Commanding Manitoba District, to Commissioner A.B. Perry, 30 May 1919.

144 Gregory Kealey, 'State Repression' and 'Surveillance State.'

145 Katz, 'Some Legal Consequences,' 47.

146 NAC, RG 13, Access 87–88/103, Box 36, File A-1688, Pocket #2, Andrews to Meighen, 3 June 1919.

147 Ibid. Andrews met with the executive of the Citizens' Committee and urged a more conciliatory position, but the committee remained committed to the total defeat of the strike. See also NAC, RG 13, Access 87–88/103, Box 36, File A-1688, Pocket #2, Andrews to Meighen, 2 June 1919 and 4 June 1919. A telegram from Andrews to Meighen, 5 June 1919, indicates that Andrews had asked the provincial attorney general to arrest the strike leaders.

148 Masters, *Winnipeg General Strike*, 62–4.

149 Bercuson, *Confrontation at Winnipeg*, 122; Penner, *Winnipeg 1919*, 68. Alderman W.T. Cox reportedly declared that he was 'learning to drill and shoot at Minto Barracks.' Ibid., 60. See also McNaught, *Prophet in Politics*, 105.

150 Masters, *Winnipeg General Strike* (1973 ed.), xv.

151 Cronin, 'Labor Insurgency and Class Formation,' 20–1.

152 All quotes from NAC, RG 13, Access 87–88/135, Box 36, File A-1688, Pocket #2, Andrews to Meighen, 4 June 1919.

153 Ibid.

154 NAC, RG 13, Access 87–88/103, Box 36, File A-1688, Pocket #2, telegram, Andrews to Meighen, 6 June 1919.

155 NAC, RG 13, Access 87–88/103, Box 36, File A-1688, Pocket #2, telegram, Meighen to Andrews, 6 June 1919.

156 The Immigration Act of 1910 and the first Amending Act of 5 June 1919 had provided for the deportation of any person, 'other than a Canadian citizen,' engaged in prohibited activities. In the second Amending Act, which was rushed through on 6 June, the definition of Canadian citizen was followed by the words 'either by reason of birth in Canada, or by reason of naturalization in Canada.' Given that British subjects remained ineligible for naturalization until the adoption of the Canadian Citizenship Act in 1946, the effect of the 6 June amendment was to leave British-born immigrants in Canada exposed to deportation under Section 41 of the new Immigration Act.

157 See Katz, 'Some Legal Consequences,' 47–8, for more detail on the legislative changes. See also Roberts, *Whence They Came*, 71–97.

158 Legislation introduced late in June and given force on 1 October 1919 made illegal any association or organization that proposed to implement governmental, industrial, or economic change within Canada by the use of force, or that advocated or defended the use of force, violence, or terrorism. The sentence for seditious conspiracy was raised from two to twenty years. Amendments to the Naturalization Act that provided for the denaturalization of immigrants to Canada were under consideration and approved in September 1919.

159 Mitchell, '"To Reach the Leadership,"' 241. A more general discussion of the RNWMP can be found in Horrall, 'Royal North-West Mounted Police and Labour Unrest.'

160 Mitchell, '"To Reach the Leadership,"' 241.

161 The riot is described in the *Toronto Daily Star*, 11 June 1919, and Masters, *Winnipeg General Strike*, 97. See also NA, RG 13, Access 87–88/103, Box 36, File A-1688, Pocket #2, Andrews to Meighen, 10 June 1919.

162 NAC, MG 26, H 1(a), C-4341, Andrews to Meighen, 11 June 1919. See also NAC, RG 13, Access 87–88/103, Box 36, File A-1688, Pocket #2, Andrews to Meighen, 13 June 1919. Ketchen's efforts to muster a military force to counter the strike are described in Bercuson, *Confrontation at Winnipeg*, 167–9.

163 NAC, MG 26, H 1(a), C-4341, Andrews to Meighen, 11 June 1919.

164 Gramsci makes the argument that as the state structure weakens, 'the commandos – i.e. the private armed organizations – enter the field, and they have two tasks: to make use of illegal means, while the State appears to

remain within legality, and thus to reorganize the State itself.' Gramsci, *Prison Notebooks*, 232.

165 NAC, MG 26, H 1(a), C-4341, Andrews to Meighen, 11 June 1919.

166 NAC, RG 13, Access 87–88, Box 36, File A-1688, Pocket #2, Meighen to Andrews, 9 June 1919.

167 NAC, MG 26, H 1(a), C-4341, Robertson to Prime Minister Borden, 13 June 1919.

168 NAC, RG 13, Access 87–88/103, Box 36, File A-1688, Pocket #2, Andrews to Meighen, 14 June 1919. For correspondence dealing with the arrangements that were being made for the arrests, see ibid., Andrews to Meighen, 13 June 1919; and MG 26, H 1(a), C-4341, Calder to Col. Starnes, 13 June 1919, Meighen to Andrews, 13 June 1919, and Borden to Sen. Robertson, 13 June 1919.

169 NAC, RG 13, Access 87–88/103, Box 36, File A-1688, Pocket #2, Robertson to Borden, 17 June 1919.

170 As expressed in the *Toronto Daily Star*, 27 June 1919, '[The] master stroke during the strike was the persuading of the ironmasters to suddenly concede collective bargaining and getting the railway brotherhoods and other railway managers to endorse it as being safe in effect and principle. This prevented the running trades from going out in sympathy and tying up transportation throughout Canada.'

171 NAC, RG 13, Access 87–88/103, Box 36, File A-1688, Pocket #2, Robertson to Borden, 17 June 1919, and Andrews to Meighen, 18 June 1919.

172 McNaught and Bercuson, *Winnipeg General Strike*, 79.

173 See Angel, 'Restoring Order,' 20. According to D.C. Masters, 'the timing of the arrests was decided by Andrews,' Masters, *Winnipeg General Strike*, 104. In fact, the decision to proceed with the arrests and raids was taken by Andrews and Robertson only after it became clear that the Central Strike Committee of 200, the body representing all unionized workers out on strike, had failed to reach an agreement to end the strike during a meeting held 16 June 1919 to consider the declaration of the metal trades' proprietors. For Andrews' detailed explanation of developments leading to the arrests, see NAC, RG 13, Access 87–88/103, Box 36, File A-1688, Pocket #2, Andrews to Meighen, 18 June 1919. The arrests, which were illegal under the amended Immigration Act, are discussed further in the following series of telegrams: J.A. Calder to Senator Robertson, 16 June 1919, Meighen to Andrews, 17 June 1919 (2 telegrams), Andrews to Meighen, 17 June 1919 (2 telegrams), Meighen to Andrews, 18 June 1919.

174 McNaught and Bercuson argue that Andrews, in the period immediately following the arrests, 'was a restraining influence both on Robertson and

upon extremists, like Meighen, in the cabinet,' and that he 'had no intention of permitting arbitrary deportation of British subjects.' McNaught and Bercuson, *Winnipeg General Strike*, 81.

175 NAC, RG 13, Access 87–88/103, Box 36, File A-1688, Pocket #2, Andrews to Meighen, 18 June 1919. As a first step in the prosecution of the cases, Andrews had begun to assemble a prosecution team comprising the best legal talent in Winnipeg: Isaac Pitblado, Ed Anderson, J.C. Coyne, Travers Sweatman, and E.K. Williams. Masters reports that, with the possible exception of Henderson, all were 'extremely active' on the Citizens' Committee. Masters, *Winnipeg General Strike*, 64.

176 Andrews reported to Meighen, 'I felt it was the fair thing to give these people a trial by jury if they so desired and bail followed as a matter of course as the situation then stood.' Surely Andrews' main concern was not the flaunting of 'fair play' per se but rather the explosive response that could result. NAC, RG 13, Access 87–88/103, Box 36, File A-1688, Pocket #2, Andrews to Meighen, 25 June 1919.

177 NAC, MG 26, H 1(a), C-4341, Andrews to Meighen, 19 June 1919. An account of the veterans' meeting is provided in Masters, *Winnipeg General Strike*, 105.

178 NAC, RG 13, Access 87–88/103, Box 36, File A-1688, Pocket #2, Andrews to Meighen, 25 June 1919.

179 NAC, MG 26, H 1(a), C-4341, Brigadier-General H.D.B. Ketchen, General Officer Commanding Military District No. 10, to Secretary, Militia Headquarters, Ottawa, 20 June 1919.

180 NAC, RG 13, Access 87–88/103, Box 36, File 36, Pocket #2, Dick Randolph to G. Wallin, M.P., 20 June 1919.

181 Ibid.

182 Brubaker, *Citizenship and Nationhood*, 13. See also Brubaker, *Immigration and the Politics of Citizenship*; Marshall and Bottomore, *Citizenship and Social Class*; and Roche, 'Citizenship, Social Theory, and Social Change.' For a discussion of Canadian citizenship, see Kaplan, ed., *Belonging*. Canadian citizenship as a central theme of reconstruction discourse is addressed in Owram, *Government Generation*, 80–117; and Ferguson, *Remaking Liberalism*.

183 Reimer, 'War, Nationhood and Working-Class Entitlement,' 220.

184 *Toronto Star*, 27 June 1919.

185 For a list of the committee executive, which included Pitblado, Sweatman, and Coyne, see NAC, RG 13, Access 87–88/103, Box 36, File A-1688, Pocket #2. The origin and membership of the Citizens' Committee is described in Masters, *Winnipeg General Strike*, 63–8. The interest taken by British intelligence in the counter-revolutionary potential of the Citizens' Committee is

addressed in Gregory Kealey, 'The RCMP, the Special Branch, and the Early Days of the Communist Party in Canada,' 170.

186 NAC, Access, 'Winnipeg' Justice, Pocket #2, A.J. Andrews to Arthur Meighen, 10 July 1919. See Mitchell, '"Repressive Measures."'

187 For a discussion of the workers' protest, see Muir, 'Demand for British Justice.' A list of letters and petitions, both for and against the detention and trial of the strike leaders, appears in Kehler and Esau, *Famous Manitoba Trials*.

188 *Winnipeg Free Press*, 10 July 1919.

189 The legal adventures associated with the Winnipeg General Strike illustrate Richard F. Devlin's comment that 'the manipulation of legality is one of the most important techniques employed by the capitalist state in its strategy of absorbing incipient conflict and eradicating dissent in such a way as to preserve the status quo.' Devlin, 'Law's Centaurs,' 247.

190 NAC, RG 13, Access 87–88/103, Box 36, File A-1688, Pocket #2, Andrews to Doherty, 2 August 1919.

191 Corrigan and Sayer, *The Great Arch*, 6.

192 National Conference on Character, *Report*, Inaugural Address. Aikins quoted in Mitchell, '"Manufacture of Souls of Good Quality."'

193 Clark, *Canadian Manufacturers' Association*, 87. The Citizens' League was inaugurated on 20 August 1919. Its first president was Isaac Pitblado, soon to be a prosecutor in the strike trials. See McKillop, 'Citizen and Socialist,' 61.

194 See NAC, RG 13, Access 87–88/103, Box 36, File A-1688, Pocket #1, for executive committee messages congratulating Sir Robert Borden on the arrest of the Winnipeg General Strike leaders. Information on the convening committee is provided in National Conference on Character Education, *Report*, Appendix A.

195 *Western School Journal*, 14, no. 10 (October 1919).

196 *One Big Union Bulletin*, 25 October 1919.

197 Campbell elaborates on SPC notions of education and politics in '"Stalwarts of the Struggle."'

198 This idea was raised by the OBU and supported by individuals such as Fred Dixon. See Wormsbecker, 'Rise and Fall of the Labour Political Movement,' 34.

199 McKillop, 'Citizen and Socialist,' 60.

200 Hiebert, 'Class, Ethnicity, and Residential Structure,' 84 n. 55; Peterson, 'Ethnic and Class Politics,' 77.

201 See Mitchell, 'From the Social Gospel to "The Plain Bread of Leninism"'; and Campbell, 'Beatrice Brigden.'

202 Wormsbecker, 'Rise and Fall of the Labour Political Movement,' 65; Hall, 'Times of Trouble,' 33–83.

203 *Western Labor News*, 24 May 1919.

204 Bercuson ascribes to Marxist historians the notion that labour 'won' the general strike. Such a view exists only in Bercuson's imagination. He does battle with it in Shilliday, ed., *Manitoba 125: A History*, 143; and Bercuson, *Confrontation at Winnipeg*. For a review of *Confrontation at Winnipeg*, see Norman Penner, 'Who Won at Winnipeg,' *This Magazine* 9, no. 2 (May–June 1975).

205 What, if not the labour dream, inspired seven thousand people to greet the recently released strike leader Bill Pritchard at the Vancouver train station? Campbell, '"Stalwarts of the Struggle,"' 191. The response of the established order to the labour dream is the subject of Mitchell, '"Repressive Measures."'

206 *Manitoba Free Press*, 27 May 1918.

207 Cf. Bercuson, *Confrontation at Winnipeg* , 203–4. J.E. Rea has demonstrated the continuing impact of the strike on Winnipeg municipal politics in 'Politics of Conscience' and 'The Politics of Class.' P.H. Wichern's attempts to characterize post-strike sentiment in Winnipeg in terms of an undifferentiated 'civic boosterism' fail to explain how the Communist Party maintained continuous representation on city council through to the 1980s. See Wichern, 'Historical Influences on Contemporary Local Politics.'

British Columbia and the Mining West: A Ghost of a Chance

ALLEN SEAGER and DAVID ROTH

Western Canada obviously did not stand in isolation from other regions during the period of the workers' revolt. That upsurge of organization and conflict, specifically in the narrow realm of industrial relations and the broader political setting of '1919,' unfolded across the nation. The debate over 'western exceptionalism,' however, has to some extent obscured the significance of the geography of labour protest. The fact that labour's revolt was part of a national and international experience does not, of course, negate the necessity of regional perspectives. Regional textures of capitalist development and class relations, as well as the broader experience of workers, shaped the character of class struggle and helped to determine its outcomes. If there existed a vaguely regional consciousness, typically couched in the language of appeals to the pride that many western workers felt in being part of a vanguard element of the international working class (whether in Butte, Seattle, or Vancouver, British Columbia, the rhetoric of the 'western clarion' was essentially the same), behind a legendary western radicalism lay a more tangled skein of contradictory structures and responses. Anna Louise Strong, an American West Coast activist who collaborated in the bold endeavour of mass-producing the first 'authentic' pro-Soviet propaganda on the continent (forty thousand copies of Lenin's April 1918 address to the Congress of Soviets, equal numbers of which were circulated out of Seattle and Vancouver) put her finger on relevant problems of political economy in 1935, when she recalled: 'We were marching to victory, ever on! We were a light to the workers (in the East) ... So we were – until the shipyards closed.'[1]

In 1919, buoyed by local, national, and international events in the war years and increasing organization and agitation in 1917 and 1918, labour militancy in British Columbia and the mining west rose to an unprecedented level as workers, regardless of sector, skill, sex, or race, battled the bosses in the region's factories, mines, mills, and municipalities. This new collectivity failed to sustain itself. In the 1920s a truncated British Columbia labour movement, like its counterpart in other provinces, returned to the fold of an essentially conventional craft unionism, while the historic militancy of such strategic industrial groups as the miners, whose movement extended across the provincial border into the Alberta coalfields, was marginalized to the point of near irrelevance. Nevertheless, the collective memory of the movements, events, and personalities of the First World War era remained an important legacy for labour in the far west. It is vital, then, that their record be clarified and contextualized. As we argue in this essay, the workers' revolt was not simply an isolated 'moment' in labour history; it was the product both of massive change and tension in the pre-war and immediate post-war period, and of an ongoing conflict between workers and industrial capitalism.

Immigrants and Workers

Since the 1880s Canada's far west had witnessed a surge of secular growth culminating in the last of the pre-war cycles of 'boom and bust' in 1909–13. Between 1891 and 1921 the number of people reporting gainful occupations in British Columbia rose from 47,000 to 220,000. Three-quarters of this increase occurred in 1901–11, a decade in which the province's population more than doubled. The population of the premier subregion, the lower Fraser Valley, registered an even steeper increase, from 36,000 to 142,000; by the census of 1921, 42 per cent of the provincial population was hived into this corner of a region that was, in a typical paradox of its political economy, highly urbanized and unevenly developed.[2]

Unique patterns of immigration and labour migration had shaped a culturally distinctive working class that possessed extremes of ethnic cohesion and fragmentation.[3] Significantly, one of the first tasks undertaken by the recently formed British Columbia Department of Labour was a systematic survey of 'countries of origin' of the industrial workforce. Reporting in July 1919, the survey canvassed 1207 enterprises in fifty industry groups, netting no fewer than forty-seven thousand employees. Close to one-fifth (18 per cent) were identified as having originated in China, Japan, or 'Hindustan,' countries that supplied a mere 2 per cent of total Canadian immigration at its 1913 peak, and whose emigrants accounted for fewer than 7.5 per cent of the British Columbia population as a whole in 1921.[4]

Native-born Americans constituted a surprisingly small minority (4.5 per cent) of industrial employees, given long-standing and frequently cited connections between British Columbia and the United States in the overlapping spheres of trade, business ownership, migration, and labour organization.[5] The numbers of workers who had actually crossed a porous international boundary would have been much larger, and must have included a substantial fraction of British Columbia's continental European immigrant workers.[6] In the Vancouver Island, Crow's Nest Pass, and Alberta coalfields, Slavs, Italians, and Western Europeans joined colliers from Great Britain and Nova Scotia; metalliferous mining also attracted a heterogeneous workforce to BC boom towns like Rossland and Sandon. The coal-mining industry of the western interior, however, was the only significant industrial locale where non-English-speaking European workers clearly predominated in 1919.[7] Indeed, it was a measure of the failure of the more grandiose expectations of heavy industrialization in the western hinterland that continental Europeans constituted only 14.5 per cent of the 1919 survey of industrial employees. Fully 63 per cent of workers in the labour department survey were apparently native sons and daughters of the British Empire, not including Punjab![8]

The largest group were probably working-class immigrants of a relatively homogeneous type: English, lowland Scots, and northern Irish.[9] Between 1891 and 1921 British Columbia received some 175,000 British newcomers, of whom an estimated 131,000 were working-class immigrants. (In 1911 a little over 30 per cent of the Caucasian population in the Pacific province were British-born, compared with about 20 per cent the Prairie provinces and less than 15 per cent in Ontario.)[10] Those who stayed, together with a substantial number of middle- and upper-class immigrants (a horde of 'English chappie clerks,' in the bitter phrase of one contemporary) would do much to shape the language and politics of class in British Columbia.[11]

English-speaking immigrants who found something like regular or skilled employment, and who established themselves and their families at opportune moments before the war, did comparatively well, perhaps acquiring a 'California bungalow' with a garden plot.[12] This particular class, not the proverbial 'blanketstiff,' would form the core of support for both trades unionism and labourist politics in British Columbia. Their expectations of 'fair wages,' protection for 'home industries,' and preservation of the essential rights of respectable labour – against the upper millstone of business monopolies and the nether millstone of competition in the labour market – formed, in turn, a clearly defined working-class agenda, regardless of rhetoric, circumstance, or leadership.[13]

The class consciousness of the invisible immigrant suffused this society for many decades. 'The temper of the Western Canadian people is entirely different from that in the United States,' commented American radical Scott Nearing. 'They are more English: they have a decided sense of self-respect. There are a number of dogged people who stand up and fight. The tone of the movement is not bourgeois like ours – the ordinary mechanic dominates the labour movement.' The One Big Union, which, as David Montgomery emphasizes, 'so neatly captured the spirit and the essential common beliefs' of working-class militants across North America, would be conceived in precisely this environment.[14] The 'ordinary mechanic' dominated a labour movement that was, however, structurally fragmented to an uncommon degree.

In 1920, according to the best available contemporary measurements, sixty-five cents of every dollar circulating in the goods-producing sector of the British Columbia economy was generated by the familiar trilogy of resource-based industries – forestry, mining, and the fishery. In contrast to central and eastern Canada, petty production was comparatively marginal in the resource economy of twentieth-century British Columbia. Nevertheless, not one of these core sectors could or would be fully organized until World War II.[15] Except for a brief period after World War I, the unions that existed in the extractive industries formed only a small minority of union members in the region. Economic dependence on extractive industries, of course, is not to be confused with occupational homogeneity. As census figures show, the residuum of the economy, including transportation, non-resource manufacturing, and the broad tertiary sector, provided the bulk of all employment. Nor did dependence on resource extraction preclude the existence of significant classes of agriculturists, as well as professional, upper-white-collar and self-employed people whom few unions could hope to enrol.[16]

Capitalist Structure

In the period before the First World War, workers in the hinterland, like their counterparts in the heartland, were employed by companies with increasingly sophisticated capital structures. Corporate mergers, scientific management, and streamlined production affected all of the key sectors in the early twentieth century. For example, in 1902 the salmon canning industry on the Pacific coast – a leading export sector accounting for about two-thirds of the total value of a superficially diverse fishery – responded to self-destructive competition over both natural and human resources by forming the BC Packers' Association. The 'Association' was, in fact, a single enterprise, engineered by eastern bankers. Together with a handful of other firms, BC Packers monopolized the industry's productive capacity until the 1930s and 1940s, when some West Coast fishers followed the lead of their Atlantic cousins and formed significant local cooperatives.[17]

In its early years, BC Packers successfully pitted coastal regions, and coastal workers – employed and self-employed – against each other in its drive for an acceptable level of profits. As fishers (whose licenses and gear were often owned by the company) fought a losing battle against falling prices, shore workers – primarily structurally marginalized women, Chinese and native Indian workers – found themselves at the mercy of plant owners. Skilled workers like the hand butchers would be substantially displaced with the introduction of the famous Smith Butchering Machine between 1902 and 1906. According to advertisers' claims, the ingenious device – popularly known as the 'Iron Chink' – replaced thirty craft workers with three semi-skilled operatives. In 1913 the solderless 'sanitary can' was introduced, further reducing the workforce and speeding up the work process. As BC Packers founder Henry Doyle observed, the same innovations set the pace for the rest of the workforce. 'The operators of the various machines,' Doyle assured his colleagues, 'can stand up to the press of work no matter if they even worked six or seven hours overtime.'[18]

Other resource-based enterprises underwent equally profound changes. Metalliferous mining had been a hive of petty commodity production and highly speculative industrial-capitalist endeavour. By 1906, however, the industry had spawned a significant Canadian 'trust,' Consolidated Mining and Smelting. A subsidiary of Canadian Pacific, the company would come to dominate prospecting, development, metal mining and refining, as well as transportation and hydroelectric power generation, in the Kootenays.[19] An article in *Blackwoods Edinburgh Magazine* in April 1903 described the key facility, the Trail smelter works acquired by the CPR in 1898:

On one bank of the river is a wilderness of trestlework; of huge wooden sheds, and pythonic iron pipes; of chimneys 200 feet high and 12 feet square; of great 'roasters' and ovens built of brick; and blast-furnaces; and baths of molten metal. Grimy-faced stokers, with the strange glassy stare of men who gaze into volcanoes of white heat, were pushing barrows carrying big pots full of 'matte': in the office buildings were glass cupboards containing specimens of ore ... mineral sea anemones of yellow, and heliotrope, and orange-red. Just outside the laboratory was a spectacled, clean-shaven professor in his shirt sleeves, superintending the unloading of lead bullion, and through the windows you could see studious looking youths examining test tubes.

The image of Dante's inferno, professionally managed by middle-class graduates of the mining schools, was apt.

Underground, the 'independent miner,' a 'jack-of-all-trades' who enjoyed autonomy at the workplace and commanded the respect of his community, was being steadily pushed aside by the managerial imperatives of so-called modern mining.[20] Thanks to carefully engineered extraction of low-grade ores, the gross productivity of the British Columbia hardrock miner would increase 500 per cent between 1900 and 1930. Miners' organizations called for the recognition of the underground proletarian as 'a human being, a modern man able to read, think, and appreciate the good things in life as other people do.' Their desires were of decidedly secondary importance to shareholders and investment-seeking governments. A strong section of the regional labour movement at the turn of the century, with eleven locals of the Western Federation of Miners representing three thousand workers, metalliferous miners would be reduced to one of the weakest components of western labour in both Canada and the United States by the mid-1920s.[21]

The burgeoning forest industries of the 'North West Woods' were far too extensive to be monopolized by any single group of enterprises. However, comparative titans like the Canada Western Lumber Company on the lower mainland and Foley, Welsh and Stewart on Vancouver Island dominated increasingly well-organized provincial industry associations. Representing sectoral trade and regulatory interests, they also had – potentially or actually – significant roles to play in an industrial relations system based on the principle of the open shop. Among hundreds of individual employers were a plethora of small capitalist players, including a legislatively protected class of hand-loggers, whose licenses prohibited the use of steam-operated machinery and other 'modern' techniques of twentieth-century logging.[22] Yet by 1918, argues

Gordon Hak, 'the logging industry's myth of the independent axeman had no basis in reality. Instead, for loggers in the coastal camps [accounting for 80 per cent of the provincial 'scale'] more classic forms of capital–labour relations were exhibited, as foremen, managers, and accountants separated employees from employers. Loggers were industrial workers, subject to the regimen of corporations engaged in large-scale accumulation.'[23]

Technical advances in lumber manufacturing affected other West Coast workers in a unique fashion. Members of the pivotal building trades found their crafts undercut by prefabrication of components such as doors, windows, and trim. By 1911 entire prefabricated homes were being mass-produced by integrated firms like BC Mills, Timber and Trading Company, the Prudential Investment Company, and the Bungalow Building and Finance Company.[24] Craft workers who found employment in these new industries faced equally new challenges of skill dilution and piece work negotiation. Other craft workers found themselves adapting here, as elsewhere in North America, to the 'revolution' in concrete and steel construction. The relationship between members of the Iron Workers local and the Ferro-Concrete Construction Company of Cincinnati, Ohio, as they worked on Vancouver's famous Hotel Europe 'skyscraper' project in 1908 bore little resemblance to traditional patterns of conflict and accommodation among skilled workers and small masters.

Not the least of the changes in the building and construction sector, Douglas Cruikshank notes, was the 'invasion of the professional engineer.'[25] Contractors on large-scale public works and railway building projects responded with alacrity to the gospel of F.W. Taylor, who is often – and wrongly – associated with deskilling only the manufacturing artisan. A labour newspaper in the United States noted the example of scientific management applied to outdoor labourers in New Westminster, who were being ordered to 'swing their shovels in a certain way, with a specified amount of sand therein, and fill the wagons in a set time.'[26] This, then, was not a region of unsophisticated frontier capitalism. Indeed, as Ross McCormack argues, advanced technology 'more than any other advantage' ensured rapid industrial development in the West.[27]

Solidarity and Fragmentation

Drawing on a regional tradition of labour organization and worker activism that reached back to the days of the 'Gold Colony,' workers in the far west were far from passive in the face of the challenges of the new century. According to the most recently published statistics, British Columbia recorded 237 strikes or lockouts between 1900 and 1913.[28] In 1911 the federal Department of Labour's first annual *Report on Labour Organization in Canada* noted the existence of 231 different unions in the province with a combined membership of 22,600 – equivalent to 15 per cent of all workers enumerated in manufacturing, service, construction, extractive-industry, transportation, and labouring occupations that census year.[29] In 1910 a majority of trades unions in British Columbia gathered in what was the first central provincial federation in the Dominion. The years 1909–14 would witness a regional echo of 'the great unrest' felt throughout Europe and North America, setting much of the stage for the post-war turbulence.

Significantly prominent in the pre-war events were the Industrial Workers of the World (IWW). John Riordan, a hardrock miner from the Kootenays, was a founding member of the IWW executive.[30] The heavy factionalism of the IWW in the United States unfortunately resulted in the severing of its ties with the Western Federation of Miners; henceforth, it lay outside the pale of the 'house of labour' in Canada and the United States. Nevertheless, the IWW took its call for 'the emancipation of labour from the slave bondage of capitalism' to a receptive audience among the unorganized. Between 1909 and 1912 there were unprecedented strikes involving as many as ten thousand railway 'navvies' on the BC sections of the Grand Trunk and Canadian Northern roads.[31] The IWW's presence was also felt in the course of a mass strike that briefly mobilized five thousand fishers and twelve hundred shore workers in the Fraser river and northern Rivers Inlet district in 1913.[32] Finally, in 1909 and 1912 IWW organizers using the tactic of the 'Free Speech Fight' for the right to organize in public drew a good deal of attention to their cause in major confrontations with the authorities in Vancouver.[33]

The IWW thus became a byword for militancy. However, the ginger of revolutionary industrial unionism should not obscure an equally significant features of the pre-war unrest, namely, the ways in which more conventional craft and industrial unions were being drawn (usually against their will) into mass confrontations. One of the largest was a strike of four thousand members of twenty-six different building unions, including predominantly Italian members of the AFL-chartered labourers' local, in Vancouver in 1911.[34] The leaders of the Master Builders' Association would have shared the analysis of J.R. Wilkinson of the

Carpenters' Union, who described the dispute as being 'a broad principle of closed shop versus open shop, capital against labor.' At the height of the dispute, the far from revolutionary Vancouver Trades and Labor Council apparently seriously threatened a general strike in sympathy with the building trades in the western metropolis. 'The plan,' said typographer Parm Pettipiece, 'is to tie up the town.' The plans of the building employers, however, would prevail in a contest with waning craft union strength.[35]

The building trades at least survived – perhaps to fight again. The longest of the mass strikes of the pre-war period, led by District 28 of the United Mine Workers of America (UMW) on Vancouver Island between 1912 and 1914, saw a violent reaffirmation of management rights in Vancouver Island's non-union collieries.[36] While the legacy of the nineteenth-century Scots-Canadian robber barons, the Dunsmuirs, lay heavy on this coalfield, the miners now fought against a combination of eastern and U.S.-based corporations, competition from California fuel oil, and the displacement of the skilled labour underground. One of the victorious companies, Western Fuel, was mining over half of its Nanaimo coal by machine in 1915.[37] The Island strike elicited even more passionate calls for a general strike, which again failed to materialize. Together with smaller disputes in metalliferous mining, navigation, fruit packing, and a host of other trades, the circumstances of the pre-war period illustrate the fact that the militancy of 1919 was not an isolated episode; its foundations lay in pre-war strikes whose outcomes suggested the need for new strategy and tactics. The region's workers were not unschooled in the militancy of their brothers and sisters elsewhere; as James Conley notes of the growing sympathy for syndicalism on the eve of World War I, workers were increasingly aware of the 'challenges faced by other workers, and their responses to those challenges.'[38]

A large minority of workers within the region, however, remained distant from the labour organizations and traditions of the dominant European sector of the working class. Aboriginal people in British Columbia were perhaps more successful than their counterparts in other provinces in maintaining a foothold in the industrial-capitalist order, – especially in the fishery and in maritime-related activities like longshoring. Local or band-based organizations of Indian fishers and dockers cooperated with non-native organizations, on their own terms, when the occasion warranted. 'It is beyond the ability of my mental apparatus to understand why those who boast of having a higher degree of intelligence and civilization than that of an Indian will be so base as to scab on their fellow workers when the Indian will not do so,' commented an observer during one maritime dispute. 'Were scabs able to understand the Indian language they would receive an education on an Indian's opinion of a scab.'[39] The colonial situation under which all aboriginal people laboured was not debated on the political left but was beginning to be challenged by British Columbia Indian organizations in the larger political arena by 1919.[40]

The salient ethnic or racial cleavages in the region were those that separated newcomers from Asia from all other groups, including aboriginal people, who resisted Japanese competition, for example, in the coastal fishery. Chinese and Japanese immigrants or citizens were victims of popular violence on at least two occasions in the pre-war period: an anti-Japanese riot that took place in downtown Vancouver in 1907, and the Vancouver Island strike riots of 1913, which were partly aimed at Chinese strike-breakers. In the summer of 1914, when Dominion authorities barred a party of Sikh immigrants aboard the *Komagata Maru* from entering the country, they were in some measure trying to avoid a repetition of these violent events in a context of already widespread unemployment.[41] What Gillian Creese calls the 'explicitly racist ideas' of the (white) labour movement have been well catalogued. Despite numerous examples of Asian workers' self-activity in job-centred protests or strikes, and, on rarer occasions, cross-ethnic alliances in specific circumstances, there is apparently no example of a union with a stable membership base that organized Asian and Caucasian workers together before the 1930s.[42]

In the 1890s it was axiomatic that 'capital ha[d] found in the Chinese a new ally ... [a] 'weapon' that [hung] like Damocles' sword, over the head of white labour.'[43] Ceaseless efforts by capitalists to wield that 'weapon' created a legacy of racial bitterness that, paradoxically, heightened the class consciousness' and political awareness of significant sections of the white working class.[44] In the period before the First World War, however, the rise of a small but significant class of Asian entrepreneurs drew the trades unions into a comparatively new set of alliances with white businesses. In a typical meeting of the Vancouver Trades and Labor Council in 1908, the Tailors' Union, the Cooks and Waiters' Union, and the Typographical Union all complained that declining standards were chiefly due to Asian business competition, and called on the attorney general to 'clean up [the] disease breeding Chinese sweat shops' in their trades.[45] Weakly if at all integrated into the dominant network of credit and exchange, Asian-Canadian businesses had a reputation for being 'panicky' and 'will[ing] to undercut practically any market for cash.'[46] Deputy labour minister Mackenzie King claimed that the steep rise of the anti-Chinese Head Tax (from $50 in 1885 to $100 in 1900 and $500 in 1904) 'administered a death blow to the work of the labour agencies and contractors,' who had hitherto advanced the entry fees to the immigrants they preyed upon.[47] On the other hand, the tax, which was supported by organized labour as a modest step towards total exclusion, naturally created a lively traffic in illegal immigrants, who were even more dependent on the 'Boss Chinaman' – or just the boss. An illegal immigrant might be a Chinese girl who would be sold into prostitution for a specified period of time before making her way into the wider labour market. 'Slave prices' in a gruesome flesh trade went as high as $2000 before the war, while oral histories of Chinese women suggest that well into the 1920s they continued to earn about a dollar a day on farms, in Chinese-owned stores, and in garment factories.[48]

If the Gordian knot of racialism defied solution in this period, much the same could be said of sexual inequality. Just as prevalent social attitudes towards race were replicated among a majority of working people, so too were the structural and cultural constraints of traditional gender roles. Despite the fact that working women were involved in numerous pre-war strikes, fighting laundry owners, telephone companies, meat processors, and restaurant owners, male unionists generally believed that the presence of women in any industrial situation either undercut the standard of wages or diluted militancy. The resulting lack of serious or genuinely sympathetic attention to working women's particular problems was a fairly universal phenomenon, but the unique background of the western situation deserves mention.

'As a rule,' notes Carlos Schwantes, 'men on the wage workers' frontier never labored alongside women.'[49] The peculiar demographic characteristics of a region of recent settlement are seen in the fact that in British Columbia at the turn of the century males outnumbered females by a ratio of close to two to one. As a corollary, the province had a consistently lower per centage of women's paid employment than the national average. Nevertheless, between 1891 and 1921 the numbers of women and girls enumerated in the census of occupations jumped from 3000 to 25,500, and increased as a share of the census workforce from 6.75 to 11 per cent. By 1921 working women netted by census takers were also typically distributed across the economy, with clusters of employment in clerical jobs, trade and finance, and the 'women's professions' of teaching and nursing. A disproportionate number were employed in the metropolis of Vancouver, where limited opportunities for manufacturing and service occupations were found.

Unmeasured by the census were a wider range of women's activities in the domestic and rural economies, together with various forms of penny capitalism, including prostitution. D.S. Cameron, vice-president of the New Westminster Trades and Labor Council, claimed to have personally interviewed prostitutes 'in the restricted area.' 'On several occasions,' he testified before a royal commission on labour conditions, 'I asked them what caused them to descend to that life, and almost without exception the answer has been that they could not make enough money in the stores where they were employed to live respectably.'[50] Others were unapologetic about defending men's monopolies in the more 'respectable' trades. The barbers' union explained its policy: 'The general objection is that when women come to slopping around some of these dirty old bums the way [we] sometimes have to do we don't consider that they ought to be in that kind of business. I don't think you would choose a lady barber for a wife.'[51] In 1913 Sir Richard McBride's faltering Conservative government, in an effort to win working-class support, established the Provincial Labour Commission, which focused some attention on the scandalous conditions affecting a growing number of women workers. The incoming Liberal government would legislate on behalf of women in the lowest-paid occupations, though not in the general interest of women seeking paid employment or job mobility. In 1918 British Columbia's newly formed Female Minimum Wage Board was attempting to enforce a floor salary of $12.75 per week. Early investigation found that up to 73 per cent of the client groups (a sample of 2043 wage earners in 'the mercantile industry') were below this meagre norm. Despite a sustained effort by chairperson Helen Gregory McGill, the BC Board would be notoriously ineffective in achieving uniform standards in, for example, small ethnic businesses.[52]

Although led by middle-class women like McGill, British Columbia's feminist movement was a potential ally of the labour left. 'Working women need the ballot to regulate conditions under which they work' declared the pro-suffrage *Victoria Champion* in 1914.[53] The province's leading left-wing journal, the *Western Clarion*, was at best lukewarm towards the suffragists, and groused in 1908 that 'women are socialists generally because some man is.' This editorial comment drew a critical response from an apparently large number of female readers who called for a new column devoted to the concerns of working-class women. The *Clarion* answered as follows: 'That the *Clarion* is a "man's paper" is largely the fault of women, and if women are given a column we expect they will prove this by petering out.'[54] (Ironically, the one regional newspaper devoted to a socialist feminism, *Toveritar: Organ of the Finnish Working Women of America*, published at Astoria between 1911 and 1929, was one of the more successful of alternative media in this period.)[55] The 'Woman Question' was debated with an increasing measure of seriousness after 1908, partly owing to the influence of British-immigrant suffragists like Helena Gutteridge, secretary of the Vancouver Trades and Labor Council.[56]

Working-class women were unusually prominent in the miners' strike of 1912–14, engaging in support and relief activities. Two socialists who represented the Island mining area, J.H. Hawthornthwaite and Parker Williams, pressed the parliamentary demands of the suffragists (demands that would be met by the Liberal government in wartime). But it is also fair to say that the suffrage issue was placed on the back burner as men and women scrambled to keep their lives together as the boom economy of the West crumbled in 1912–15.

The Economy, 1913–1918

The crash of the western economy on the eve of World War I was every bit as spectacular as its post-1896 expansion. Heavy speculation in mining, timber limits, pulp and paper, and land and real estate came to an abrupt halt. Foreign investment dried up; important regional financial institutions quickly collapsed. The distress of the middle classes was mirrored in a widely read pamphlet entitled *The Crisis in British Columbia.* Published by the Protestant Ministerial Union of the Lower Mainland in May 1915, the pamphlet began: 'Present conditions in British Columbia as regards financial stringency, business stagnation and unemployment are such as need no comment.' Sections entitled 'How the Speculator Bleeds the Settler,' 'Fabulous Wealth Alienated to Syndicates,' 'How the Coal-grabbers Rob the Public,' 'Colossal Burdens Imposed by Railroads,' and 'Amazing Capitalization Sanctioned by Government' all testified to the sudden disrepute into which British Columbia's boosters, promoters, and politicians had apparently fallen.[57] The fragility of the major commodity markets was an underlying cause of regional economic woes. Between 1913 and 1915 the timber industry lost 600 million board feet worth of business. Coal and coke production in the Crow's Nest Pass, untouched by strikes or lockouts between 1912 and 1916, fell by a stunning 50 per cent in two years. Large numbers of jobless from the interior and coastal areas gravitated to Vancouver, regional 'Mecca of the Unemployed.'[58] As escalating relief expenditures and continuing tensions centring on the unemployment issue indicate, Canada's entry into the war was not an instant cure-all for British Columbia's economic ills. The construction industry remained moribund throughout the war.[59] Timber and metals remained soft until 1915, when prices and production began to increase,[60] and employment in the metal shops was less than might be expected in the first two years of the war.[61]

Mining was one of the first sectors to heat up due to war conditions. Even the metal producers were amazed at the demand. 'Apparently no one,' wrote the Minister of Mines in 1915, 'foresaw or appreciated the trend of modern warfare, with its unprecedented use of artillery, nor the tremendous amounts of metal that would be consumed thereby.' In a four-day period along a twenty-mile front the French Army had used 4.5 million shells. This represented about 18 million pounds of lead, 30 million pounds of copper, and 8 million pounds of zinc. The Minister of Mines calculated that British Columbia's 1915 output of these minerals, representing the greatest proportion of its metallic minerals production, would have lasted twelve days at most.[62] In 1916 metallic minerals production increased 54 per cent over the previous year and 76 per cent over the pre-war record year of 1912.[63] The need for coal, for both transportation and industry, also increased substantially during the war years. The war years saw new development as well as the resurrection of old mines as prices rose with demand in the coal industry.[64]

The forest industry also began to awaken by 1915. Production increased steadily from one billion board feet in 1915 to nearly two billion in 1920. Lumber prices also doubled, from $14.00 per thousand board feet in 1914 to $30.00 per thousand in 1920. The same figures translated into huge profits for the forest companies and high revenues for the Crown, while loggers and mill men remained near the bottom of the region's industrial hierarchy.

By 1917 shipbuilding, once a minor industrial player, had moved into the big leagues. In 1916–17 the Canadian government's superagency, the Imperial Munitions Board, lent its unlimited financial and political resources to the existing effort of the provincial administration to gear up the province's shipyards to meet war demands for wood, and later, steel-hulled vessels.[65] Prior to the European conflict British Columbia's shipbuilders built only wooden schooners, sternwheelers, tugs, and small ferries. Others focused on repairing and refitting, but on a very small scale. Under the auspices of the wartime state, 118 vessels, mostly freighters of medium tonnage, were produced in three short years. Thousands of trades people and labourers worked in the shipyards of Vancouver and Victoria, mopping up surplus labour from weak sectors like the building trades. As the economy expanded, unemployment among trade unionists declined substantially, from 15 per cent in December 1915 to 3 per cent in December 1917.[66]

Many workers entered the industrial and service establishments happy to find full-time employment. Others, caught up in the patriotic spirit or a sense of adventure, joined in the war effort more directly, fighting in the trenches of France. 'In British Columbia,' wrote the Minister of Mines in 1916, 'the recruiting sergeant has found such a ready response ... that prospecting is at a standstill.' In 1917 he lamented, 'Owing to the fact so many men in the province have enlisted the problem of getting sufficient labour has often been serious, and there is no doubt that with ample labour a still larger production would have been made.' But this apparently overwhelming patriotism was not the only salient factor. For all their support of bond drives and the Canadian Patriotic Fund, British Columbia workers did not embrace a corporatist vision of capital–labour relations.[67]

Labour Unrest

Under war capitalism workers sought to consolidate their position, to organize when the opportunity was greatest, and to protect their income against wartime inflation.[68] In 1915 and 1916 suit and cloak makers joined shoe and boot workers in taking to the streets and demanding increased wages and union recognition; the summer of 1917 saw both Chinese and white shingle weavers striking against mill owners. Waitresses, laundry workers, and butchers also clashed with employers over a variety of issues, but particularly wages and union recognition. In March 1917 women laundry workers won their fight against a wage cut; in September 1918, however, only two of seven laundry owners caved in to union demands. Twelve striking waitresses were fired in October 1917, but in August 1918 fifty Hotel Vancouver employees won shorter hours and a wage increase.[69] Shipyard workers' organizations surged in 1917. Their organizations dominated the new Metal Trades Council in Victoria and resurrected a previously moribund council in Vancouver. In 1917 they successfully struck for a closed shop and standardized rates. In a second showdown between shipyard workers and the Imperial

Munitions Board, the shipyard workers' unions shut down nearly all production for two weeks in the spring of 1918, an action that won them wage parity with Seattle shipyard workers.[70]

District 18 of the United Mine Workers of America, representing coal miners in south-eastern British Columbia and Alberta, took full advantage of the situation by expanding its representation in the Crow's Nest Pass district and east of the Rockies. Membership nearly doubled from thirty-five hundred in 1914 to over sixty-seven hundred in 1919. The district rank and file, well aware of its newfound power, refused to be tamed by the UMW's 1915 district agreement, aimed at suppressing pithead strikes 'for the duration.' Between November 1916 and April 1917 District 18 miners carried out a series of unauthorized strikes that severely limited both coal and coke production. These actions resulted in the partial closure of both copper smelters and mines and threatened domestic coal supply, especially to railroads.

The miners' threat to the war effort and industrial profits led to the de facto nationalization of the interior coal mines in July 1917. Wages, prices, and supplies were placed under the dual authority of the Director of Coal Operations in District 18, a coal owner named W.H. Armstrong, and the Dominion Fuel Controller, an old CPR hand named C.A. McGrath. The new regulatory structure served both labour and capital well, increasing production, profits, and pay scales appreciably. Miners saw minimum pay per shift rise from $3.50 to $5.00 between 1915 and 1918. National control served to foster an uncharacteristic armistice between coal operators and labour in the militant Crow's Nest district. (In October 1918 this armistice would be broken by a strike against double shifts in some of the mines.) To many miners, wartime government stewardship was but a precursor to full nationalization of the coal mines – a development long called for by miners throughout North America and Europe.[71]

The success of strikes, however, was closely tied to the economic strength of the workers involved. For example, the gold mines of Rossland were closed for several months in 1918. As described in the Minister of Mines *Report*, '[T]here was some disagreement between the miners and the operating company, and a strike seemed imminent, the properties were closed before such actually took place.' The Rossland miners were locked out by owners who, faced with a soft gold market, could well afford to 'soften up' the miners with a long, cold, jobless winter.[72]

Smelter workers in Trail encountered a similar tactic. Unhappy with a contract signed by the International Union of Mine, Mill and Smelter

Workers, local workers stuck for pay rate increases and the eight-hour day. They were met with the extreme intransigence of their employer (the Consolidated Mining and Smelting Company), the misfortune of weak lead and zinc prices, and the refusal of their international union to break a legal contract. As a result, both the smelter workers and their union were crushed and militant workers were blacklisted.[73] For these workers, militancy alone did not guarantee success. Economic clout remained the key to successful labour action, a truism that evoked the lesson of strength in solidarity but also raised the spectre of defeat for militant unions when the inevitable economic downturn arrived with the end of the war. Remarkably, as shown in the following table, the momentum of industrial conflict continued into the post-war period and affected an increasing variety of workers.

Number of Strikes by Economic Sector, British Columbia, 1914–1920

	1914–16	1917–20
Transportation	14	47
Manufacturing	14	76
Mining	11	33
Fishing	3	–
Logging	–	99
Building	5	17
Trades and services	2	22
Other	1	26
Total	50	320

Source: Douglas Cruikshank, unpublished research.

Labour and the Left

In addition to economic grievances, the traditions and influence of left-wing unionism played a part in the labour revolt. The dominant type of labour organization in British Columbia, as elsewhere, were the AFL-TLC unions, which banded together in 1910 to form the British Columbia Federation of Labor (BCFL). Despite the dominance of so-called bread-and-butter unions, socialism had a powerful voice in the Federation. The Socialist Party of Canada (SPC), dominated by West Coast figures such as G. Weston Wrigley, an expatriate Ontarian, and E.T. Kingsley, a Californian, was the main political expression of the pre-war labour movement. The radical Marxism of the party co-existed with the task of securing parliamentary representation for the party's working-class supporters. In provincial elections held between 1903 and 1912, the socialists positioned themselves electorally in about a dozen industrial constituencies and formed a small but relatively effective 'labour' caucus in the legislature at Victoria after 1902.

In Nanaimo City, the socialists captured as much as 62 per cent of the popular vote, while in the neighbouring coal-mining constituency of Newcastle their share of the vote was upwards of 52 per cent. The elected SPC members from these two seats normally constituted the party caucus. Large minorities of voters were persuaded to vote the Socialist Party ticket in the ridings of Grand Forks (43 per cent), Fernie (42 per cent), Greenwood (35 per cent), Ymir (34 per cent), Comox (34 per cent), Slocan (30 per cent), Revelstoke (22 per cent), Cranbrook (20 per cent), and New Westminster (11 per cent). Considering that the eligible voters were a fairly narrow pool – male British subjects resident in British Columbia for at least six months, and in their constituency for at least one month before election day– these numbers seem impressive. However, workers in the major cities (whose multi-member constituencies make it impossible to gauge the political temperature by citing any percentages) tended to reject Socialist Party candidates while supporting municipal labourism. One would be hard pressed to describe the skilled workers and trade union officials who were active in local politics in Vancouver as 'impossibilists,' as many radical Marxists were then known. At the other end of the spectrum were the syndicalists of the IWW who viewed political enthusiasm as sadly misplaced in the context of a system that had disenfranchised the majority of its constituency. It was an article of faith among conservative elites that too many people had the vote in British Columbia, but neither the hopes nor the fears that the Pacific province would see a major breakthrough for North American socialism came close to materializing in this period.[74]

Divided among 'reformers, rebels, and revolutionaries,' the labour left was obviously factionalized, and the imported schism between the Socialist Party and the Social Democratic Party (SDP) contributed to labour's declining influence at the outbreak of the Great War. All of the socialist organizations opposed the military mobilization on pacifistic grounds, and paid for their 'lack of patriotism' when their electoral bases were eroded in wartime. In 1916 only four SPCers and one SDPer were nominated in the provincial elections, polling fewer than two thousand votes among them, compared to twelve thousand votes cast for the SPC in 1909. Fuelled by both national and international developments, British Columbia labour politics shifted left once again in 1917 and 1918, as radicals regained the political initiative.

The shift began as early as 1916 when Prime Minister Borden ordered a nationwide manpower inventory through the National Service Board. Trades councils in both Victoria and Vancouver 'urged members to defy registration and accused Trades [and Labor] Congress leaders of knuckling under to the government.' In May 1917 Borden validated the claims of radicals by announcing his government's intention to introduce conscription. The calls of militant unionists throughout the nation for strikes in opposition to the conscription proposal were defeated in the Trades and Labor Congress; electoral action was pursued instead. The subsequent fiasco of the Laurier-Labour alliance in the 1917 federal election saw the defeat of every TLC-endorsed candidate.[75] Thus the conscription crisis served to undermine conservative labourist politics in British Columbia.

In 1918 the British Columbia Federation of Labor broke its loose ties with the Socialist Party of Canada to create an autonomous political instrument, the Federated Labor Party (FLP). The formation of the FLP reflected both the new hopes born of recent events and the erosion of socialist support in the early part of the war. The Socialist Party, argued BCFL President James McVety, was 'no longer a factor in the political life of the province, despite the correctness of its platform.' The new party's platform – which included the nationalization of mines, forestry, and fisheries, along with other mainstays of the economy – reflected the socialist vision of its authors, among them the founding philosopher of West Coast impossibilism, E.T. Kingsley. A core of Socialist Party loyalists and revolutionary socialists refused to follow Kingsley into the FLP, but they shared a common political view and a hope for political change. FLP and Socialist Party candidates agreed not to split the socialist vote by contesting the same single-member ridings.[76]

International developments directly affected labour politics in British Columbia as workers increasingly echoed the sentiments of their European and British brothers and sisters. Federated Labor Party MLA J.H. Hawthornthwaite (returned in the Newcastle by-election of January 1918) described the Bolsheviks as the 'hope of the world today.' The BCFL's newspaper, the *BC Federationist*, railed against the Union government, declaring that 'from the time these emissaries of the parasitic class stole the seats in Ottawa they have gradually tightened the screws until today the workers have no rights but are weighed down with everything but iron shackles.'[77]

Labour's battles in this period encompassed the pragmatic concerns of labour, such as increased wages and union recognition, and more explicit political action. For example, on 2 August 1918 Vancouver workers staged a one-day general strike to protest the fatal shooting of labour activist and anti-conscriptionist Albert ('Ginger') Goodwin by a Dominion Police constable. The strike was met by virulent opposition on the part of a large contingent of returning soldiers. The soldiers rioted, broke into the Labor Temple, and – after attempting to throw him out of a second-storey window – forced labour leader Victor Midgley to kiss the Union Jack.[78] The soldiers' response indicated the acceptable limits of worker protest in the war years; it also indicated that a significant portion of Vancouver's workers were willing to parade their political convictions, popular or not, on the streets of the city. Those who claimed the Vancouver Trades and Labor Council had acted without membership support were incorrect. Council delegates supported the strike call by a vote of 117 to 1. After the strike they resigned to prove their point, and nearly all were re-elected. The council members were clearly supportive of both direct political action and job-related activism. Similarly, in July 1918 the Victoria Trades and Labor Council voiced support for a general strike in sympathy with striking postal workers.[79]

The increasing militancy of British Columbia labour took on a concrete, organizational form at the March 1919 convention of the BC Federation of Labor. This extraordinary conclave convened in Calgary, Alberta, so that delegates could attend the Western Labour Conference of Trades and Labor Congress delegates from the four western provinces. The BC federation convention posed a resolution that 'called for the building up of organizations of workers on industrial lines for the purpose of enforcing, by virtue of their industrial strength ... laws and conditions deemed necessary.'[80] The resolution passed with no dissent. Another resolution called for a referendum on whether to withdraw from the international unions and form an organization to be called the One Big Union (OBU). Despite some opposition, the motion received unanimous support. At the Western Labour Conference that followed, the federation's resolutions were essentially repeated and passed with minimal discussion. It was here that OBU sentiments crystallized and provisional organizing committees were struck.

To employers and people in high places, the One Big Union represented bloodthirsty Bolshevism; to many others it represented a practical means of bringing about socialist principles of 'production for use' and 'thorough and democratic organization and management of industry by the workers.' J.S. Woodsworth described its development as 'natural.'[81] The OBU attempted to legitimize itself through referendum votes among all organized workers. The potential stakes were high. Although the statistics are far from clear, British Columbia's unions enrolled between twenty thousand and forty thousand members in 1919–20. The American Federation of Labor and the Trades and Labor Congress of Canada rejected both the OBU and its referendums as the products of dangerous fallacies; as a result of their counter-agitation within the ranks of the so-called labour aristocracy, a majority of locals in British Columbia never participated in the referendums. Of the eighty-seven that did, all but sixteen voted 'yes' on the double-barrelled question of support both for the OBU and for a national strike in support of the six-hour workday. The most significant support for the OBU came from workers in shipbuilding, mining and smelting, and forestry, the three largest industrial payrolls in the province.

The OBU referendum received substantial support from the mining locals (eleven in favour, none opposed); from the City of Victoria, where thirteen locals were in favour and fourteen were opposed (in the largest unit, Shipyard Laborers 38A, 2230 of the 2290 voting members were in favour) and from the Vancouver Trades and Labor Council, whose jurisdiction included every lumber camp in the province. Vancouver returned thirty-two locals in favour and fourteen opposed. Among members of the largest unit, the BC Loggers' Union, 89 per cent voted for class-conscious industrial solidarity and a general strike; among members of the second-largest unit, the boilermakers, 86.5 per cent were in favour. The membership-in-good-standing of unions voting 'yes' in the Vancouver Trades and Labor Council alone numbered 15,744. Taking into condideration the miners and other supporters, the OBU was theoretically capable of mobilizing a majority of British Columbia unionists.

The Temperature Rises

The 'one big union from below' was being forged not only in the traditional meeting halls and labour temples but also on numerous picket lines in varied locations and work sectors. Striking workers in the early months of 1919 included truckers, cereal workers, Powell River paper workers, Vancouver teamsters, Crow's Nest coal miners, Anyox smelter workers, and women telephone operators in Chilliwack.[82] As the participation of telephone operators in the spring strike wave indicates, workers traditionally considered on the periphery of labour activism were beginning to flex their collective muscle. In subsequent months women workers intensified their battle for fair wages and working conditions as they struck in the laundries, butcher shops, and hotels of Vancouver. Another sign of the times was the successful strike by Victoria schoolteachers in February 1919 (127 of the 163 strikers were women).[83] Despite the increasing prominence of working women in western labour's ranks, the *BC Federationist* continued to view the woman question with a jaded eye. Application of the principle of equal pay for equal work, the newspaper stated, 'would prevent *our* own wages and conditions from being drawn down to a lower-standard by any successful attempts of employers to use female labour at a lower price'[84] (emphasis added).

The labour activism of Asian workers similarly increased in this period.[85] This was especially true for Chinese workers in the shingle mills of coastal British Columbia. In 1917 the Chinese Canadian Labour Union and the Shingle Weavers' Union, a craft-type union of white workers, joined forces in the first industry-wide strike of shingle mills in British Columbia. Their solidarity was fragile, and the strike collapsed when Chinese workers returned to work before the members of the Shingle Weavers' Union. In March 1919, however, Chinese workers resumed the struggle against the shingle-mill operators. Over one thousand workers, under the new banner of the Chinese Shingle Workers' Union, mounted an industry-wide strike against a 10 per cent wage reduction. The strikers successfully retained the old rate and in May their union gained an additional increase without having to resort to job action.[86]

The response of white unionists remained ambiguous. Despite occasional calls for solidarity by some socialist politicians and progressive unionists, the discourse of the left remained racially dichotomized. For example, in May 1919 F.W. Welsh of the Metal Trades Council of Vancouver publicly called for comprehensive minimum-wage legislation in order to eliminate Asian competition.[87] Thus the rising temperature of the labour climate is not to be measured by an abstract solidarity of workers across the divisions of race and sex, for the acceptance of women and Asian workers by traditional unionists remained limited. The fact that women and Asian workers, despite their marginal status, were ready and willing to take job action to defend their rights is a much more accurate measure of working-class militancy.

The formation of the One Big Union and continuing actions on the shop floor were augmented by vocal critiques of capitalism in various public forums. The response of workers to the Mathers Commission is perhaps the best example of that critique. In Victoria, the first stop on the commission's route, the local trades and labour council refused to officially participate in the hearings, claiming that the commission was a 'waste of time ... simply an "employers' proposition" and in the interest of Capital.'[88] The Vancouver council viewed the commission with even greater distaste. Nevertheless, the two councils allowed their members to testify on an individual basis, and few council leaders could resist the opportunity to school the general public and the commissioners on theories of economic and social change.[89] M.S. Woodward, president of the Victoria council, gave his personal views on labour and capital, declaring that 'if he were a dictator, he would start by expropriating the Canadian Pacific Railway' and go on to cancel all land titles. 'Mr. Woodward,' reported the *Vancouver Daily Province*, 'told the Commissioners he had little faith in the government that appointed them, little faith in themselves and none whatever in their mission. He declared that the collapse of the present economic system was due sooner or later, and he only favoured the present commission because it might "ease the sore place ... during the transition of one system to the next."'[90] In view of F.W. Welsh of the Metal Trades Council, 'workers had reached the conclusion that the present system of production for profit was wrong.' Speaking on behalf of the painters' union, Albert Patterson asserted that there could be no co-operation 'as long as the employers are out after every ounce that is in a man.'[91]

At the same time the Mathers Commission and its witnesses were engaging in participatory theatre, the state was gathering its own intelligence on what Montreal financier and government adviser Herbert Holt called 'a tincture of Bolshevism' in the West. A security memorandum on 'Revolutionary Tendencies in Western Canada,' circulated among top military and Royal North-West Mounted Police (RNWMP) officers in April 1919, argued that 'a revolution by force of arms [is] conceivable under existing conditions.' A closer inspection of available security dossiers inspires little confidence in this interpretation. The 'principal centers of plotting' identified in the far west – 'Vancouver, the Crow's Nest Pass, and subsidiary coal fields of Alberta' – were those locales into whose workplaces, labour unions, and ethnic associations low-level agents had insinuated themselves. Their collective 'bad temper' was the main topic of the informers' reports. The RNWMP's overall political analysis, however, was not unsophisticated.[92] 'Organized socialism,' the April memo concluded, 'has been swallowed up [by a more] pernicious agitation.' In urban centres the additional threat of radical agitation among large numbers of demobilized soldiers was 'exceedingly dangerous.' Finance Minister Thomas White supported a request for British warships from the China station: '[The] situation [in Vancouver and Victoria] is undoubtedly getting out of hand by reason of propagandaism [*sic*] from Seattle and workers and soldiers.'[93] The February 1919 general strike in Seattle, Washington, sparked by the industrial demands of several tens of thousands of militant shipyard workers,[94] served to fuel the fires of local unrest. When thousands of Winnipeg workers took to the streets in May, a significant portion of British Columbia's labour force was ready to follow suit.

General Strike

The response of British Columbia unionists to the events of May and June 1919 would illustrate both the depth of working class feeling and the dearth of working-class effectiveness at this critical juncture. Although the statistics of strike participation are impressive, many unions were reluctant to support the protest movement; others were unable to sustain it. More representative than unique in this context, British Columbia labour was beset by rising unemployment and besieged by effective countermeasures on the part of employers and government. Most important, the marriage between industrial and political issues in British Columbia was incomplete. Throughout the strike the leadership of the BC Federation of Labor and the local trades and labour councils assumed a defensive posture of solidarity with strikers in Winnipeg that marginalized their own activity.

At the beginning of the strike, the Vancouver Trades and Labor Council cabled Winnipeg '[to congratulate] the workers for their "cohesion."' When striking postal workers were fired, the executive called a vote on the question of a sympathetic strike in support of Winnipeg workers. On 30 May, with the vote complete, the council published the following demands:

Realizing that while there are many problems that face the workers that cannot be solved under capitalism, and that the end of the system is not yet; also realizing the present situation is a political one, due to the actions of the Dominion Government in the Winnipeg strike ... therefore be it resolved that the following be the policy of the workers in Canada now on strike, or about to come on strike in support of the Winnipeg workers:

1. The reinstatement of the postal workers ...
2. The immediate settlement of the postal workers' grievances.
3. The right of collective bargaining through any organization that workers deem most suited to their needs.
4. Pensions for soldiers and their dependents.
5. A $2000 gratuity for all those who served overseas.
6. Nationalization of all cold storage plants, abbatoirs [*sic*], elevators ...
7. A six hour day.

The list ended with a call for continuing strike action until the demands were met or the government resigned and called new elections. As the council's demands indicate, the general strike was no revolution in the making; rather, it was a political pressure tactic intended to support the workers in Winnipeg and to defend the right to organize. Collective bargaining, not Bolshevism, was the issue at hand. The hopes that labour reformers and many rank-and-file workers had invested in the One Big Union were mirrored in newspaper speculation that a second OBU gathering in Calgary in early June would become the site for a wide-ranging parley between the representatives of western labour and federal officials.[95]

The council's call for a broad solidarity across regions and various groups of workers achieved mixed results. Prince Rupert workers, drawing on long-standing IWW sympathies, did not wait for a Vancouver strike vote to make their decision; some three hundred people, most of them railroad workers, walked off the job on 30 May. The Vancouver vote indicated more limited support; the city's strike referendum passed by a vote of 3305 to 2499, with only 40 per cent of eligible members participating. The more conservative New Westminster Trades and Labor Council did not allow a referendum and did not call for a vote among affiliates on the issue until 11 June, at which time it failed with a count of five unions for and six against. On 12 June two thousand Victoria workers declared their support for a sympathy strike but took no immediate action. Individual unions such as the International Brotherhood of Electrical Workers and the Amalgamated Association of Street and Electric Railway Employees initially rejected the strike call but later reversed their stance. At one meeting William Yates of the New Westminster local of the transit workers declared, '[T]he realization is growing that there is a class war – a war in which there is no discharge.' Still other workers joined in only 'after much discussion on different job sites and at union meetings.' The typographical union withdrew from the protest because its constitution required two-thirds member support in order to take sympathetic strike action. Postal workers in British Columbia, cowed by the brutal dismissal of Winnipeg postal employees, did not support the general strike, prompting Jack Kavanagh – then secretary of the Vancouver longshoremen's union – to comment, '[A]ny man that thought more of his job than his class is making a wrong guess.'[96]

If this discussion of reluctant unionists paints an excessively bleak portrait, one must also remember that forty-five unions and (according to daily newspapers) eleven thousand workers struck in Vancouver alone. By late June a number of reluctant trade unions and labour centrals took part in job action. On 18 June, in response to the arrest of Winnipeg strike leaders, the New Westminster council released its members from the earlier vote, allowing each union to respond individually to the recent events. As a result, over five hundred members of the OBU-affiliated shop labourers' and operating engineers' locals, as well as Canadian Northern Railway car men and BC Electric transit workers, walked off the job. The events of 'Bloody Saturday' in Winnipeg on 21 June prompted walkouts by five thousand Victoria workers on 23 June. Typographers, despite their refusal to join in the general strike, sought 'to ensure the publication of strikers' views' and to prevent 'deliberate misrepresentation ... under penalty of cessation of work.' In the course of the strike, typographers successfully shut down both Vancouver dailies; the *Vancouver Daily Sun* was closed for five days in reprisal for anti-strike editorials and one issue of the *Daily Province* failed to appear when union members refused to set Citizen's League advertisements.[97] It is ironic that strike action took on its most unequivocal political tint among the more reluctant groups of unionists. The actions taken by New Westminster and Victoria workers were clearly acts of political protest that were generally unrelated to either broader trade union agendas or local demands. Other organizations such as the BC Fishermen's Protective Association and the Working Women's Association were sympathetic but unable to participate in a concrete way. As was the case in other Canadian centres, the aloofness of the powerful railway running trades brotherhoods assured that the disease of 'Winnipegitis' did not result in economic paralysis.

Among the general strikers on the West Coast was a core group of militant shipyard and dock workers who tied up the Vancouver waterfront beginning 3 June, the first day of the strike. However, the clout of shipyard workers was severely limited by the realities of the post-war economy. The downturn in the Canadian shipyards was a major factor in the rapid decline of reported trade union membership in British Columbia's 'manufacturing and mechanical industries,' from 6352 (4 per cent unemployed) in February 1919 to 2865 (22.5 per cent unemployed) in December 1920. Thus a strike of the 'few shipwrights still employed at the Pacific Construction Company's yards' was indeed a courageous statement of solidarity but could have no impact on the outcome in mid-1919. Loggers, a similarly militant group of workers, had little direct involvement given traditional lay-offs among coastal loggers in early summer. But the state of the economy was only one of several factors limiting working-class effectiveness.

Both employers and the government devised effective countermeasures in response to workers' initiatives. The City of Vancouver sought to undermine street railway strikers by rescinding the 'anti-jitney' by-law, thereby allowing private vehicles to carry passengers. City council also threatened striking city employees with dismissal if job action continued. Although a large number of civic workers did not immediately end their strike, they began returning to work by mid-June. CPR shopworkers abandoned the strike when warned by their international union leaders that strikers would return to work as 'brand new men' – if they returned at all. The Citizen's League also sought to limit the effectiveness of Vancouver's general strike. The city's mayor, R.H. Gale, accepted the offer of aid from this group of 'concerned citizens' the same day he delivered an ultimatum of work or termination to city employees. The Citizen's League published its own anti-strike broadsheet (*The Vancouver Citizen*), recruited strike-breakers for public transportation, and supplied British Columbia Telephone with seventy-six 'volunteer' telephone operators.[98]

Despite the anti-strike countermeasures, numerous strikers remained, leading Socialist Party stalwart Wallis Lefeaux to observe that, for once, 'the psychology of the mass ha[s] gotten outside the control of the upper class.' But the 'upper class' was prepared to exercise coercion. According to a report in the *Daily Province,* there was a machine-gun placement about '500 feet in front of the [Vancouver] Labor Temple.' Mayor Gale expressed regrets, but only about any assumption on the part of working-class voters 'that the city council had any connection with the placing of machine guns in prominent parts of the city.' The visible armament,' he declared, 'was none of the council's doing.'[99] The presence of troops and guns helps explain the absence of mass meetings and parades during the Vancouver general strike. Such demonstrations of solidarity and support would have bolstered morale among wavering union members and spread enthusiasm in unorganized sectors of the city's economy.

By early July the above factors, combined with the defeat of Winnipeg strikers, brought an end to the general strikes in Vancouver, Victoria, New Westminster, and Prince Rupert. The Vancouver strike committee ended 'the longest general strike in Canadian history,' and the remaining strikers returned to work and potential employer retaliation. Telephone operators stayed off the job for another two weeks in a moderately successful bid to protect themselves from employer retribution. But to all intents and purposes the British Columbia strikes were over by the first week in July. Given the situation in late May and early June 1919, it is remarkable that the militant elements in the coastal labour movement were able to stave off surrender as long as they did.

Aftermath

The most obvious casualty of the general strike was left-wing control of the trade union machinery in the major city centrals. By the end of 1919, the AFL forces had recaptured or reconstructed these bodies in British Columbia, forcing the OBU to the sidelines and steering its shrinking memberships back to the well-worn path of craft exclusiveness. The OBU sustained a parallel labour council in Vancouver for a time, but the net result was costly factionalism; Vancouver unionists lost their Labor Temple, proudly erected at the height of the pre-war boom, to financial receivers. The BC Federation of Labor disbanded, not to be reborn until 1944. The *BC Federationist* temporarily escaped a similar fate (owing to successful manouevres by editor A.S. Wells) but ceased publication in 1925. In September 1921 Wells was arrested for sedition after the paper serialized Lenin's *Left Wing Communism;* subsequent vindication for freedom of the press was typical of the 'moral victories' won by the more prominent victims of the post-Winnipeg repression.[100]

In the hinterland, as David Bercuson has shown, the currents behind the OBU and the general strike ran in several different eddies, but tenuously connected with each other. Hardrock miners rallied to the One Big Union in a last-ditch battle against the open shop. Economics conspired against them amid a wave of mine and smelter shutdowns in the Kootenays. The 1920s saw a substantial relocation of metalliferous mining activity to more isolated enclaves on the coast. In the coalfields of Vancouver Island, miners avoided confrontation with the now entrenched open-shop conditions. In the Crow's Nest and District 18, by contrast, almost the whole of the union rallied behind the OBU, only to be broken by the 'triple alliance' of the federal coal administrator, the operators' association, and the international officers of the United Mine Workers of America. A closed-shop contract for the UMW signed in Calgary by Gideon Robertson in the summer of 1919 only delayed the day of economic reckoning. When federal administration of the interior coalfields lapsed amid a falling market at the end of 1921, class struggle erupted afresh in strikes and lockouts over wage reductions. Eventually, the premier consuming interests – the railways – dictated the terms of surrender to 'home locals' like the BC Miners' Association at Fernie after the UMW's failed attempt at compromise in 1924. In 1927 Scott Nearing observed in the Crow's Nest Pass 'a sullen, helpless, inert mass of workers being slowly worn down and crushed by the 'system' ... an economic system that cannot pay them a living because there is too much coal (and too much of the other necessaries of life) being produced by the means of the modern machine industry.'[101]

By 1920 the defeat or isolation of the miners had left the BC Loggers' Union as the only significant base of support for left-wing unionism in the region. Established as an affiliate of the Vancouver trades council in 1918, the organization represented, in part, an effort by members of the Socialist Party (notably future CCF leader Ernest Winch) to pre-empt a regional organizing drive by the Industrial Workers of the World in the Pacific north-west states.[102] After transforming itself into the Lumber Workers' Industrial Union (LWIU), the loggers' union enjoyed the most spectacular growth of any significant Canadian union during the era of unrest, enrolling in 1920 as many as thirteen thousand members, including 'Chinese, Japanese, and Hindoo' sawmill workers.[103] At the grassroots, camp-committee level, the LWIU was dominated by IWW members or sympathizers who resisted any form of central control. In the autumn of 1919 and the spring of 1920, the locals of the LWIU struck hard against the operators in nearly a hundred uncoordinated strikes. When the timber market slackened in the autumn of 1920 and slumped badly in 1921, it was the operators' turn to organize in the form of a coast-wide employment agency. Dedicated to weeding out rebellious 'timber beasts,' the agency soon cast a pall over all union activities. A correspondent for the Toronto *Worker*, the weekly organ of the newly founded Communist Party, explained the dilemma: 'There is not enough room in this country to hold both the Lumber Workers' Industrial Union and the blacklist of the lumber barons at the same time. One or other must go.' It was the LWIU, not the blacklist, that disappeared into the

Pacific rain forest in 1922–23. *Worker* editor Maurice Spector, playing on U.S. President Warren G. Harding's successful campaign theme, observed that the demise of the loggers' union had finally brought about a condition of normalcy to the BC woods. In less than two years, wages for Vancouver Island fallers dropped from $7.00 to $4.75, with proportionately lower rates for other classes of labour.[104] The revolt in the woods did have an impact on the daily lives of forest workers; henceforth, according to one such worker, 'the camps weren't too bad; there was all kinds of food. The main problems were safety, wages, and individual rights.[105] Legislatively, British Columbia loggers in the 1920s won a statutory eight-hour day and inclusion under the workers' compensation board established in 1918. Syndicalism was not quite dead and buried; by 1925 the IWW was sufficiently strong to lead a major strike in Cranbrook, one of the interior districts where wages and conditions remained below the coastal standards.[106]

The political impact of the workers' revolt was profoundly ambiguous in British Columbia and the mining west. In stark contrast to the Ontario elections of 1919, provincial contests in British Columbia in December 1920 returned only three 'Labour' legislators in an assembly of forty-seven. Liberal Premier John Oliver had taken a strong stand against 'Bolshevism' in 1919, asking, 'which is better: government as we have it now, democratic and capable, or dictatorship by a handful of irresponsible and headlong agitators?'; he was returned with twenty-five seats. Tories captured fifteen seats and independents four.[107] The election tested the new coalition that had built up around the Federated Labor Party, and found it wanting. In outlying single-member constituencies, FLP standard-bearers polled popular votes in the 14–28 per cent range. Coal miners predictably elected two of their 'own class,' Sam Guthrie from Newcastle and Tom Uphill from Fernie, in the Crow's Nest Pass. In the six-member Vancouver constituency, the FLP and the SPC each fielded a separate slate of three candidates, alongside a plethora of independents, including Soldier's and Women's Freedom candidates. Analysis of the slate votes in the metropolis shows the FLP to have been a more attractive alternative than the other third parties but scarcely competitive with the powerful Conservative and Liberal machines. The mean number of votes cast for the SPC candidates was 1671, compared with 7336 for the FLP, 10,213 for the Conservatives, and 12,117 for the five men on the Liberal ticket. No candidate came close to matching the vote-getting appeal of the Liberals' feminist standard-bearer, Mary Ellen Smith, widow of Ralph Smith, former Trades and Labor Congress of

Canada president and miner MP. Almost certainly drawing support from FLP voters, among others, she topped the Vancouver poll with 17,510 ballots cast. The daughter of a Tyneside collier, Smith was a staunch and effective advocate for such Liberal reforms as the Female Minimum Wage Act of 1918 and the Mother's Pension Act of 1920. The Smith dynasty speaks to certain peculiarities of the English working class that eluded capture by the socialist left in British Columbia.[108]

The national elections of December 1921 would prove to be the swan song of the old-time socialist leadership in British Columbia and the mining west. Labour's public unity masked both a looming crisis over affiliation with the Third International and the demands of moderates who rejected its Marxist legacy. In virtually every federal district 'Labour' contested, a past or present member of the SPC took the local nomination: W.A. Pritchard polled 4000 votes in Nanaimo, R.P. Pettipiece took 3700 votes in New Westminster, and John Harrington received 2700 votes in Vancouver-Burrard. Jack Kavanagh, who had tried, unsuccessfully, to lead the remnants of the OBU into the Communist movement, polled 810 votes in the federal riding of South Vancouver. As if to underline the ideological divide, South Vancouver's artisans and small-property owners had delivered 3555 provincial votes to moderate typographer Harry Neelands, the one FLP candidate to win an urban seat in 1920. Alberta's Crow's Nest Pass delivered 1400 votes to a blacklisted miner named James Fairhurst. An equal number of votes did secure the election of P.M. Christophers, ex-president of District 18, to the Alberta legislature that year. Labour returned but one British Columbia MP in 1921, Nelson locomotive engineer Levi Humphrey in Kootenay West. Together with fellow railroaders Peter Heenan and James Murdoch from Ontario, Humphrey joined Mackenzie King's caucus in Ottawa, leaving the Prairie social democrats under the leadership of J.S. Woodsworth and William Irvine. In 1930 Woodsworth and Irvine were joined by Angus McInnis, ex-business agent for the street railway employees; the MP for Vancouver South was an exemplar of hard-headed reform politics whose motto was, 'Theory bakes no scones.'[109]

By the mid-1920s normalcy had returned to regional politics as well as industrial relations. Local battles in the woods and collieries, industrial and service establishments, and towns and cities of the West still occurred with some regularity. Socialist politicians and revolutionaries still met to discuss and plan for a new order and socialist ballots were still cast. But the promise – or threat – of worker revolt had faded. In the final issue of the Socialist Party's *Western Clarion*, J.D. Harrington made the despairing observation that '[f]rom the prophetic preaching of capital's collapse ... we have passed, through and beyond, back to a period void and empty of any revolutionary outlook.' In 1922 Kavanagh, the hopeful Communist, denounced his own party for the 'morass of opportunism into which they have sunk with the cloak of a United Front.'[110] Although communism and social democracy had a brighter future in the West than these statements would imply, the trauma of 1919 would in the years to come contribute both to the construction of the Communists' tragically sectarian identity and to the tendency of the right wing of the Co-operative Commonwealth Federation towards classless coalition politics.

Conclusion

The history of the labour revolt in British Columbia and the mining west is perhaps most significant for the ways in which local movements and conditions accentuated the characteristic strengths and weaknesses of Canadian labour in the First World War era. Fired by protest against both capitalism and the abuses of capitalists, a potentially powerful section of the region's working class had been moved to challenge the status quo. But labour in the far west had only pockets of industrial strength and, despite the promise of the One Big Union, had not grasped the nettle of organizing the unorganized, including growing numbers of working women and racial minorities. Defeats suffered by miners and loggers, who belonged to the classic paradigm of 'western radicalism,' reveal the bedrock of capitalist structures that remained impervious to labour militancy alone. The ebbing of the tide revealed quite well the difference between subjective evaluations and objective determinants of working-class effectiveness.

Notes

1 See Strong, *I Change Worlds*, 68, 78. Montgomery, *Fall of the House of Labor*, 429–30, contains a succinct account of the key institutional connections among 'western' progressives in Canada and the United States in 1919.

2 See Barman, *West beyond the West*, chapter 7. See also Roy, *Vancouver*, chapter 2. For the most recent survey of British Columbia capitalism in the period, see Allen Seager, 'The Resource Economy, 1871–1921,' in Johnston, ed., *The Pacific Province*, 205–52.

3 Phillips, *No Power Greater*, 14. In 1887, at the height of their power in British Columbia, the Knights of Labor launched a campaign in support of Asian exclusion.

4 British Columbia, Department of Labour (hereafter BCDL), *Report* (Victoria), 1919, K20. For Immigration statistics, see *Canada Yearbook*, 1914, 86. For statistics on the ethnic composition of the province as a whole, see Barman, *West beyond the West*, 363.

5 BCDL, *Report*, 1919. For a survey of Canadian–American relations in the far west, see Schwantes, *Radical Heritage*.

6 See, for example, the first-hand account of the migration of coal and metal miners in the Canadian mining west in Sisu, *'Even through a Stone Wall.'*

7 Seager, 'Class, Ethnicity, and Politics.'

8 BCDL, *Report*, 1919. It is noteworthy that Department of Labour statistics do not differentiate between British immigrants and Canadian-born individuals of British background.

9 On British immigrants to the West, see McCormack, 'Cloth Caps and Jobs.' For an early analysis of the impact of British immigrants on labour and politics in British Columbia, see Saywell, 'Labour and Socialism.'

10 Barman, 'A Tradition Emerges,' 202–3 n. 82.

11 'American Mining – Mining Englishmen,' *Lardeau Eagle*, 19 April 1901; Ward, 'Class and Race.'

12 Holdsworth, 'House and Home in Vancouver.'

13 McDonald, 'Working-Class Vancouver.'

14 Nearing quoted in *Worker*, 11 April 1925; Montgomery, *Fall of the House of Labor*, 427.

15 Gray, 'Woodworkers and Legitimacy'; Roth, 'Union on the Hill'; Clement, *Struggle to Organize*, 99–107.

16 Seager, 'Workers, Class, and Industrial Conflict,' 117–40, 220–39.

17 Shrum, 'Among Canada's West Coast Fishermen' (reference courtesy of Ron McGivern); Reid, 'Company Mergers in the Fraser River Salmon Canning Industry.'

18 Stacey, *Sockeye and Tinplate*, 20.

19 Roth, 'Union on the Hill,' chapter 1.

20 Hovis, 'Origins of Modern Mining.'

21 Quotation from British Columbia Archives and Records Service (BCARS), Premiers' Papers, Vol. 14, File 18, 'Resolution Passed by District 6, Western Federation of Miners' (n.d. 1899); Jensen, *Nonferrous Metals Industry Unionism*, 2–4.

22 Rajala, 'Managerial Crisis.'

23 Hak, 'British Columbia Loggers,' 70–1.
24 Conley, 'Class Consciousness and Collective Action,' 577; Taylor, *Timber,* 90–2.
25 Cruikshank, 'Young Masters and Old Journeymen.'
26 Leier, *Where the Fraser River Flows*, 21–2; Taylor, *Railway Contractors.*
27 McCormack, 'Western Working-Class Experience,' 118.
28 See Cruikshank and Kealey, 'Canadian Strike Statistics,' table E.
29 Phillips, *No Power Greater,* appendix A; Dominion Bureau of Statistics, 'Occupational Trends in Canada 1891–1931.' For a list of locals, see Canada, Dept. of Labour, *Labour Organizations in Canada*, 1911, 80–7.
30 Industrial Workers of the World, *Founding Convention*, 297.
31 For a discussion of IWW railway strikes, see *Labour History* (Vancouver), vol. 3, no. 1 (1981), special issue on railroads in British Columbia.
32 Leier, *Where the Fraser River Flows*, 37–40. See also Vancouver Province, 5 August 1913.
33 Leier, 'Solidarity on Occasion.'
34 National Archives of Canada (NAC), RG 27 (Strikes and Lockouts Files), Vol. 298, Strike 3378.
35 Ibid. Pettipiece quoted in *Montreal Gazette*, 26 May 1913.
36 Norris, 'Vancouver Island Coal Mines.'
37 Seager, 'Miners' Struggles in Western Canada.'
38 Conley, 'Employers' Strategies and Workers' Responses.'
39 'B.C. Indians Refuse to Scab,' in *Worker*, 29 December 1923.
40 Tennant, *Aboriginal Peoples and Politics*, 97–113.
41 Johnston, *Voyage of the Komagata Maru.*
42 Creese, 'Exclusion or Solidarity?' 44–7.
43 Cowan, 'Canadian Industry and the Chinese Question.'
44 Roy, *White Man's Province*, 166–73.
45 Creese, 'Exclusion or Solidarity?' 31.
46 MacPherson, 'Creating Stability,' 328.
47 Canada, Royal Commission, 70.
48 The relationship between prostitution and illegal immigration is addressed in Van Dieren, 'Response of the WMS to the Immigration of Asian Women.'
49 Schwantes, *Pacific Northwest*, 255.
50 BCARS, GR 684, 50 (Royal Commission on Labour Conditions in British Columbia, 1913), Proceedings and Testimony, Vol. I, 197–203.
51 Creese, 'Working-Class Politics, Racism, and Sexism,' 216.
52 Ibid. See also Crossley, 'B.C. Liberal Party and Women's Reforms.'
53 Quoted in Cramer, 'Public and Political,' 87.

54 *Clarion* quotations from Creese, 'Working-Class Politics, Racism, and Sexism,' 226.

55 Lindstrom-Best, *Defiant Sisters*, 156–7.

56 Wade, 'Helena Gutteridge.'

57 Ministerial Union of the Lower Mainland of B.C., The *Crisis in British Columbia: An Appeal for Investigation* (Vancouver 1915).

58 Roy, 'Vancouver: "Mecca of the Unemployed."'

59 Conley, 'Employers' Strategies and Workers' Responses,' 15.

60 British Columbia, Minister of Mines (hereafter BCMM), *Report*, 1917, K16.

61 Ibid., (1915), K16; Conley, 'Class Conflict and Collective Action,' 124.

62 BCMM, *Report*, 1916, K15.

63 Ibid., 1917, K15.

64 BCDL, *Report*, 1919, K13.

65 Lees, 'Business Not as Usual.'

66 *Labour Gazette*, 1921, 1399.

67 BCMM, *Report*, 1916, K15; 1917, K15. Western mining communities were among the most generous contributors to the Canadian Patriotic Fund, owing to the commonplace procedure of donating one day's pay per month through the check-off. See Morris, ed., *Canadian Patriotic Fund*, 91–2: 'By this method of systematic giving some wonderful results were obtained and their publication in Eastern Canada had a decidedly beneficial effect upon industrial subscriptions in that part of the Dominion.'

68 For data on inflation, see Urquhart and Buckley, eds. *Historical Statistics*, K1–7.

69 Creese, 'Working-Class Politics, Racism and Sexism,' Appendix B; and 'Exclusion, or Solidarity?' 39.

70 Lees, 'Business Not as Usual,' 11–16; NAC, RG 27, Vol. 309, Strike 122.

71 National control of coal mines in District 18 was finally precipitated by the general district strike of 1 April – 3 July 1917. A useful summary of events is found in the *Labour Gazette*, August 1917, 613–16. The wider issue of nationalization and the UMW, is addressed in Montgomery, *Fall of the House of Labor*, 385–99.

72 BCMM, *Report*, 1918, F15.

73 Scott, 'Profusion of Issues.'

74 Seager, 'Socialists and Workers'; McDonald, Working-Class Vancouver'; John D. Belshaw, 'Provincial Politics, 1917–1916,' in Johnston, ed., *The Pacific Province*, 134–64.

75 Bercuson, *Fools and Wise Men*, 62–3.

76 McVety quoted is from Robin, *Rush for Spoils*, 177.

77 Quoted in McCormack, *Reformers, Rebels, and Revolutionaries*, 138.

78 Bercuson, *Fools and Wise Men*, 81.
79 McCormack, *Reformers, Rebels, and Revolutionaries*, 138.
80 Phillips, *No Power Greater*, 78.
81 BCDL, *Report* ,1919; Woodsworth quotation from Penner, *Canadian Left*, 185.
82 BCDL, *Report*, 1920, K71–3.
83 On the teachers' strike, see Johnson, *History of Public Education in British Columbia*, 241–2.
84 Creese, 'Working-Class Politics, Racism, and Sexism,' 235.
85 Ibid., appendix B.
86 BCDL, *Report*, 1919, K71–9; Conley, 'Employers' Strategies and Workers' Responses,' 26–39.
87 Testimony before Mathers Commission, *Daily Province*, 2 May 1919.
88 *Nanaimo Free Press*, 26 April 1919.
89 Gregory Kealey, '1919,' 11–15.
90 *Daily Province*, 29 April 1919.
91 Ibid., 2 May 1919.
92 NAC, RG 24, Records of the Naval Service of Canada (Intelligence), Vol. 3985, 105–2–21: 'Secret: Memorandum on Revolutionary Tendencies in Western Canada, Prepared by Assistant Comptroller, Royal North West Mounted Police.' See also RNWMP documents in Gregory Kealey, 'Royal Canadian Mounted Police,' 216–7.
93 Ibid. White quoted in Brown and Cook, *Canada, 1896–1921*, 311.
94 O'Connor, *Revolution in Seattle*.
95 Gregory Kealey, '1919,' 32; *Daily Province*, 27 May 1919.
96 Gregory Kealey, '1919'; Bernard, *Long Distance Feeling*, 50–71. Yates quoted in the *New Westminster British Columbian*, 21 June 1919. Kavanagh quoted in the *Daily Province*, 11 June 1919.
97 Bernard, *Long Distance Feeling*, 110; *Daily Province*, 18 June 1919.
98 Bernard, *Long Distance Feeling*, 112–14.
99 *Daily Province*, 9 June 1919.
100 Avakumovic, *Communist Party*, 24–5.
101 Bercuson, *Fools and Wise Men*; Scott Nearing, 'Crow's Nest Pass,' *Labour Monthly*, February 1927, 120–3.
102 Hak, 'British Columbia Loggers.'
103 Steeves, *Compassionate Rebel*, 53.
104 *Worker*, 15 June 1922.
105 Hjalmer Bergren, quoted in Hak, 'British Columbia Loggers,' 86.
106 On the IWW's resurgence in the 1920s, see Leier, *Where the Fraser River Flows*, 40–1.
107 Elections BC, *Electoral History of British Columbia*, credits the Liberal Party

with 38 per cent of the vote and the Conservatives with 31 per cent. Oliver quoted in Steeves, *Compassionate Rebel*, 51.

108 Norcross, 'Mary Ellen Smith.'

109 McInnis motto quoted in Young, 'Ideology, Personality, and the Origin of the CCF,' 556: The 1921 elections are discussed in Canada, House of Commons, Sessional Paper No. 13 (Ottawa 1922), 520–8; Thompson and Seager, *Canada, 1922–1939*, 17; 'Dictatorship of the Proletariat' from NAC, MG 28, F104 (Canadian Labour Congress Papers), 'Proceedings of the Convention of the B.C. Federation of Labor, 1919,' 21.

110 Harrington quoted in McEwan, *He Wrote for Us*, 42; Kavanagh quoted in Akers, 'Rebel or Revolutionary?' 36.

National Contours: Solidarity and Fragmentation

CRAIG HERON

The great appear great to us because we are on our knees. Let us rise!

W.A. Pritchard[1]

Rarely in the history of capitalist society do workers stand poised to overthrow the social system in which they live and work. More limited hopes and horizons generally frame their lives. Workers may harbour an intense sense of injustice but feel powerless to achieve redress. They may grumble fatalistically. They may have come to believe that as workers they have no right to expect more from their society. Or they may channel their anger and aspirations into daily trench warfare over terrain marked by more immediate, and more modest, objectives. It takes a major rupture in the material underpinnings of their daily experience and in their understanding of the way the world works – their 'common sense' – to fashion a new and shared conviction that their subordinate status within capitalist society must and can change. Then masses of workers may suddenly rise boldly to assert a new place for themselves within transformed relations of production, politics, and social life generally. Capitalists, politicians, and others in positions of authority cannot ignore them. It then takes a grinding destruction of the bases of working-class strength in everyday life and an erosion of that heady new ideological openness to force workers back into compliance and resignation to their subordinate fate.

In the four years after 1916, workers in Canada developed a remarkably assertive sense of purpose and power – their society could be different and their actions could transform it. The war launched Canadian workers on a trajectory of escalating demands and expectations. By the mid-1920s, however, labour's upsurge had been snuffed out across the country. The rise and fall of the workers' revolt followed a distinctive rhythm in each region, but there were key features that emerged in all major industrial centres. We have already seen the common conditions of wartime society that were confronting most Canadian workers. The purpose of this essay is to examine country-wide patterns in the revolt and its defeat.

The Workers' Challenge, 1917–1920

The most visible manifestation of the emerging workers' revolt was the wave of strikes that began after 1916 – a clear indication that the more individualistic drifting and shifting of the preceding two years was moving towards more collective responses and longer-range concerns about post-war society. As the research of Douglas Cruikshank and Gregory Kealey indicates,[2] the 218 strikes recorded for 1917 involved more than fifty thousand workers, twice the previous year's total and far more than in any single year since the turn of the century. Moreover, militancy paid off. Aside from those in the coalfields, most of the few big confrontations of 1916 had resulted in failure, but the following year strikers were successful in an unprecedented 40 per cent of their strikes and settled for compromises in another 20 per cent; employers got clear victories in only 19 per cent of strikes.[3] Strikers were also more regularly jumping the gun on the slow procedures of the Industrial Disputes Investigation Act by engaging in illegal strikes.[4] The annual total of strikers had doubled by 1919, when nearly 150,000 workers marched out in 427 strikes. In 1920 the number of strikes peaked at 457, though the number of strikers dropped by half. Over the four-year period 350,000 wage earners participated in strikes in Canada, distributed remarkably evenly across the country: 17 per cent in the Maritimes; a fifth in each of Quebec, the Prairies, and British Columbia; and a quarter in Ontario. More than a third of strikes were in manufacturing and a quarter in mining; three out of five strikers in this period were in these two sectors. Within manufacturing, the metal trades, shipbuilding, and clothing and textiles were flashpoints; together they constituted 44 per cent of strikes and more than half the strikers in that sector. In all parts of the country but the Maritimes, the peak of this strike wave was in mid-1919; however, the rate of militancy's decline varied across regions. In particular, after the crushing of the Winnipeg General Strike, workers on the Prairies retreated from the picket lines much more quickly than elsewhere in the country.

Workers were not simply striking; they were also rapidly banding together into unions. There can be no doubt that the various workers' organizations that appeared across the country between 1917 and 1925 constituted a mass popular movement of wage earners throughout most of urban Canada. At the end of 1915 union membership reported to the federal Department of Labour bottomed out at just over 140,000, and during the next year rose to only 160,000, still below the totals for 1913 and 1914. By the end of 1917, however, it was just shy of 205,000 and then leaped to almost 250,000 in 1918. Yet the most spectacular increase was recorded in 1919, when total reported union membership in Canada reached 378,000, the highest to that point in Canadian history. That high-water mark held through 1920, when only five thousand members were lost from the total union rolls.[5] These official figures for 1919–20 amount to just under 18 per cent of the non-agricultural workforce counted in the 1921 census, a historic peak in union membership up to that point. Yet, as the labour department admitted, these totals are undoubtedly low since many unions did not submit membership statistics and the reporting was at the end of the year, well after the great defeats in the spring and summer of 1919. A reasonable estimate is that at least one worker in five took out a union card. Probably well more than one in four passed through a union in these years, a level comparable to that of the mid-1940s. The dramatic increase in membership after 1918 and the many demands for union recognition in the industrial battles of this period point to the change in working-class consciousness that had set in by the end of the war. Workers were not simply trying to win immediate demands; they were turning to unions to solidify wartime gains and to prevent a return to the insecurity and indignity of the pre-war era. 'If we don't do something we will get our heads taken off after this great war is over,' a Gananoque unionist warned.[6]

Initially, the growth in union membership primarily revived pre-war patterns of organization. The first to put their unions back on their feet were craft unionists, especially the metalworkers in the munitions plants and shipbuilding yards, and coal miners in the East and West.[7] Union locals then began to appear among the less skilled workers who also had a record of organizing – street railwaymen, teamsters, longshoremen, and the like. By 1918, however, workers who had never before shown much interest in unions were signing up. Among the new union members were factory workers in resource processing plants in

British Columbia and mass-production plants in southern Ontario, Quebec, and Nova Scotia; loggers in the West and northern Ontario; unskilled workers of various kinds; clerical workers in several cities; and public-sector workers at all three levels of government, including municipal labourers, policemen (in ten cities), firemen, teachers, and letter carriers.[8] In fact, public-sector strikes were often the most controversial and menacing to dominant social relations.[9] Wage earners in all parts of the country, in large cities and small towns, were entering the house of labour. Women were found in growing numbers among the unionized and even on union executives, although in a role subordinate to that of men.[10] There was also more ethnic diversity in many of these unions, especially those in the mass-production and resource industries, from Sydney steel mills to Thetford asbestos mines to Toronto meatpacking factories to Trail smelters. A number of unions were organized primarily along ethnic or racial lines – for example, the Chinese Shingle Weavers' Union and Japanese Camp and Mill Workers' Union in British Columbia, the Finnish loggers in northern Ontario, the Jewish clothing workers in Montreal and Toronto, the black sleeping-car porters on the CPR, and the Italian construction labourers in several cities.[11] Some of these workers were inspired by the Russian Revolution; many more rode a wave of ethnic self-consciousness and assertiveness as political change convulsed their homelands.[12] Whatever their inspirations, all these workers were eager to confront the oppression and exploitation they experienced as wage earners in Canada.

Joining a union in this period was no passive process under the manipulative control of union bureaucrats. The established labour leaders were overwhelmed by the flood of new members who eagerly signed their union cards with little prompting and by the restlessness and combativeness of rank-and-file unionists in all parts of the country. Labour officials tried frantically to cool this ardour as it reached the boiling point in many workplaces. Often the workers ignored their leaders completely and pressed on with bold demands and direct action. 'At the foundation of all this agitation is the general restlessness and dissatisfaction,' the national government's security chief warned. 'The greater number of labour men, and probably the community as a whole, are in an uncertain, apprehensive, nervous and irritable temper. Perhaps these agitators are but the foam on the wave.'[13] Montreal machinist J.O. Houston captured both the spirit and trajectory of working-class mobilization: 'More and more each worker is doing his own thinking, is becoming his own intellectual, and to the extent that this is so he is placing less and less trust in labour leaders. He is looking for neither a Moses nor a Saviour. All the Sammy Gompers are doomed. His new representative will be an instrument to perform a specific act decided upon by the rank and file of an industrial organization.'[14]

Rank-and-file activism and solidarity soon forged a qualitatively different labour movement. More than ever before, divisions between workers seemed to be giving way to a remarkable spirit of working-class unity and class consciousness. As we have seen, organizational structures became more flexible in devising imaginative experiments readily adapted to immediate needs and conditions. In addition to less exclusivist craft unionism and more widespread industrial unionism, there was an innovative, all–inclusive 'community unionism' that touched many centres with weak or non-existent union traditions, and in some cases, a small, diverse local workforce close to primary production. Across the country the objective was the same: to mobilize greater numbers in common cause. Before the middle of 1919, the great majority of these new unions were affiliated with international organizations headquartered in the United States. At the same time, Canadian branches everywhere found new ways to work together with other union locals while maintaining considerable independence from their American parents. District councils linked up locals of some of the larger unions, and many locals federated across occupational lines into more cooperative local, district, and provincial bodies. For the most part, it was the local trades and labour council or district miners' organization that played the active coordinating role of drawing together and speaking for the local wage-earning population. In many cities trades councils sponsored, directly or indirectly, local labour newspapers that were produced independently of the international union publications, and that grew in number from four in 1914 to seventeen by 1919 and became important forums of information on local issues, international labour news, and debate about evolving strategies.[15] Some radicals even began to envisage the trades councils as the new base of the labour movement.[16] Whatever their political cast, the councils reflected the decentralized, community-based focus of most of the workers' movements in these years.

The new spirit of solidarity and working-class consciousness was evident in action as well as organization. The best-known example, the general sympathy strike, was widely discussed and began to appear in many parts of the country in 1918. It had mass popular support when it got its first major tests in Winnipeg and Amherst, Nova Scotia, in May

1919. As sympathy strikes spread across the West in response to the repression of the Winnipeg strikers, the radical leadership could do no more than place itself at the head of a burst of solidarity and militancy that was largely beyond its control.[17]

In this context of militancy and confrontation, the thousands of new unionists quickly grew impatient with some of their more cautious leaders.[18] Although most of the existing labour leaders held on to their old power bases, they had to face an emergent cadre of feistier, more radical leaders in the new union locals: Pictou County's Clifford Dane, Cape Breton's J.B. McLachlan, Montreal's Tom Cassidy, Gananoque's Gordon Bishop, Toronto's Jack MacDonald, Hamilton's Fred Flatman, Winnipeg's R.B. Russell, Regina's Joseph Sambrook, Calgary's R.J. Tallon, Edmonton's Joe Knight, the Crows Nest Pass's Phillip Christophers, and Vancouver's Jack Kavanagh.[19] Among the best-known female militants were Helena Gutteridge in Vancouver, Amelia Turner in Calgary, Sarah Johnston-Knight in Edmonton, Helen Armstrong in Winnipeg, Mary McNab in Hamilton, and Rose Henderson in Montreal.[20] These were the men and women who chaired meetings, helped organize new unions, led strikes, edited labour newspapers, and generally tried to awaken workers to wider visions of a reconstructed society after the war. Many were local socialists who after years of conflict with the existing labour leadership had found a receptive ear among the increasingly militant workers. They were more popular partly because, as socialists, they had reassessed their long-standing reservations about industrial action and were undertaking, among themselves, an ideological renewal that reflected lessons learned from the massive militancy of Canadian workers in the period.[21] Ironically, the socialist parties to which they belonged made fewer adjustments in their formal programs and continued their narrow emphasis on socialist education and propaganda.

The workers' movements that took shape in the 1917–20 period were rooted first and foremost in industrial action. They followed in the long Anglo-American tradition of struggling for their goals primarily (though not exclusively) in the workplace, as opposed to the European tradition of forging a broader assault on an illiberal, authoritarian state through some kind of socialist party. It was powerful unions and tough bargaining with employers that held out the most promise for shoring up the male breadwinner's family wage and guaranteeing his dignity and relative independence in the workplace. Many radicals in this period put special emphasis on organizing the working class for confrontations at the point of production. Yet, apart from some voices in the

West Coast logging camps,[22] few were espousing genuine 'syndicalism' – that European brand of radicalism that rejected radical social change through electoral politics in favour of the revolutionary potential of direct action on the picket line. Canadian historians have too often applied the label loosely to cover various forms of radical rhetoric in favour of tough-minded industrial unionism.[23] Even in western Canada, the One Big Union was led by socialists who saw the value of solid industrial organization in mobilizing the working class but never imagined a general strike as anything more than the most militant form of exerting working-class power for immediate goals, whether in workplace negotiations or in confronting the government over specific grievances.[24] Despite the hysterical claims at the time, the general strikes in eastern and western Canada never involved any attempted seizure of state power. And there was no 'return to politics' after some kind of sydicalist interlude. In fact, as we have seen, the class solidarity of the picket line and the union hall started overflowing into Canadian politics in industrial centres across the country as early as 1917. Immediate issues had become so politicized in any case that the distinction between the two spheres of activity must have seemed increasingly obscure.

In a period of great experimentation and fluidity of working-class organization, the precise form of independent working-class politics could have been an open question. In 1917 James Simpson, the socialist vice-president of the Trades and Labor Congress, proposed that the labour movement respond to the introduction of conscription by organizing workers' and soldiers' councils similar to Russian soviets (and to some new organizations in Britain at that time, as Simpson must have learned during his three-month visit that year).[25] But before the middle of 1919, outside some limited socialist circles (especially the eastern European radicals who were inspired by the Russian Revolution),[26] that idea generally fell on deaf ears. Anglophone and francophone labour leaders of all stripes were thoroughly constitutionalist in their political orientation, and the vehicle chosen in working-class communities across the country was the independent labour party. Well before the Trades and Labor Congress of Canada put out its call for a Canadian Labor Party in the fall of 1917, many union leaders had taken the initiative in organizing such a party in their own communities. These local labour parties, which always remained completely separate from their union structures, soon began to federate into loosely structured provincial political organizations, though never into an official national labour party. By organizing speakers' bureaus, distributing literature, and generally acting as a clearing house for debate and strategizing, the provincial parties provided important coordination of political organizing and education. The political wing of the workers' movements in this period nonetheless remained highly decentralized, with the local city-based parties retaining the power to nominate their own candidates and run their own campaigns.[27]

The 1917 federal election marked the first major foray of independent labourism, but, under the heavy torrents of Unionist jingoistic hysteria, most of the thirty-five labour candidates lost their deposits (even though the Laurier Liberals stepped aside for thirteen of them).[28] More successful were efforts at the municipal level in several industrial centres. Handfuls of labour representatives were also elected to provincial legislatures in 1919–20 – two each in New Brunswick and Quebec, three in British Columbia, four in Nova Scotia, eleven in Manitoba, and the same number in Ontario, where they entered the country's first Farmer-Labour government.[29] That coalition was only the most visible of its kind. In an electoral system in which wage earners were outnumbered by independent commodity producers, the independent labour parties were motivated to look for political allies among the organized farmers. In some constituencies containing smaller urban centres, fusion candidates had the support of both groups, but generally the workers and farmers kept their own distinct organizations.[30] The other group that labour parties had to learn to work with were the returned soldiers, who were being pulled in different political directions as they pursued a better deal for themselves and their families. While officers tried to direct their men's anger against the new radicalism of the period, in some parts of the country a more proletarian, left-of-centre faction responded favourably to labourist proposals of electoral cooperation, one example of which was the Canadian Union of Ex-Servicemen, known as CNUX.[31] The labour parties themselves also began to attract disaffected middle-class citizens, including the famous 'social gospellers' J.S. Woodsworth, William Ivens, William Irvine, and A.E. Smith.[32] Yet, unlike the situation in the British Labour Party in this period and the Co-operative Commonwealth Federation in the 1930s, no radicalized middle-class intelligentsia moved into key roles in the parties.[33] On the whole, the leadership and membership of the various independent labour parties across Canada remained predominantly working-class.

The local labour parties became remarkably lively, relatively non-sectarian forums for discussion and debate about pressing concerns in working-class life and the most appropriate strategies for organizing.

Until the middle of 1919 a rare ideological openness, fluidity, and tolerance prevailed among the labourists, single-taxers, socialists, and sundry freethinkers who joined the parties. Each local branch tended to have a slightly different ideological emphasis that fell somewhere between the old pre-war working-class liberalism known as 'labourism' and unadulterated Marxist socialism.[34] Generally, these organizations had shifted considerably further to the left than their pre-war counterparts – a shift owing largely to the presence of committed socialists or a regular dialogue with members of the main socialist parties (especially the Social Democrats, who had now carved out a primarily educational role for themselves within the political wing of the workers' movements). Across the country the labourist–socialist alliance expressed itself through more visionary rhetoric and more ambitious programs aimed at, in the words of the Cape Breton ILP, 'the working class ownership and democratic management of all the social means of wealth distri-bution at the earliest possible date,' or, at least, in the words of the Ontario and Quebec labour parties, 'the industrial freedom of those who toil and the political liberation of those who for so long have been denied justice.'[35]

As the federal government's Royal Commission on Industrial Relations (the Mathers Commission) discovered on its cross-country trek in the spring of 1919, many workers shared in the search for a new vision.[36] In the words of Calgary postal worker Clifford Nichols, 'the worker has gotten enormous ideals and he is determined to work them out.'[37] The 'common sense' that had guided most workers' lives for so long had been shattered in the wartime crucible. As they looked to a future in which things would be different, workers across the country were receptive to a variety of voices that called for more working-class dignity, independence, and material well-being, and that proposed more power for them to influence decisions that affected their lives on the job, as citizens, and in society more generally. For some, these demands were part of a revolutionary project that would sweep away capitalist society and replace it with a democratically managed workers' republic; for others, they were the harbingers of social reforms that would democratize government and soften the impact of market forces. But the distinction between reform and revolution was frequently blurred in the millennial rhetoric of the period (how many hopes and dreams were hung on, for example, the oft-repeated slogans 'production for use' and 'New Democracy'?). Political distinctions were also blurred by the commitment of virtually all political factions to orderly social change through some combination of mass industrial action and parliamentarism.

At all points along the political continuum, the new vision was about workers' power. It was a revolt against the kind of subordination that workers had hitherto known in Canadian capitalist society, against the elitist, authoritarian, and paternalistic ways in which business and the state had grown accustomed to ruling in Canada. It was an affirmation of working-class pride in their role as producers and a deep sense of natural justice captured in the constitutional preamble of Toronto's Domestic Workers' Association (chartered as Local 599 of the Hotel and Restaurant Employees International Alliance), which proclaimed its belief in 'the natural right of those who toil to enjoy to the fullest extent the wealth created by their labor, realizing that under the changing conditions of our times it is impossible for us to obtain the full reward of our labor except by united action.'[38] If the whole social system was not to be replaced, it would have to be drastically democratized. 'Democracy' meant reforms to guarantee that political institutions were not in the tight, exclusive grasp of other classes. Political platforms bristled with long-sought-after reforms: the abolition of property qualifications and election deposits for candidates; the scrapping of the Senate and its provincial equivalents; proportional representation in legislatures; and popular democracy through referendums, initiative, and recall. Privilege should be removed from the economy by placing railways, public utilities, banks, and natural resources under public ownership and democratic management. The state should also intervene to soften the effects of an unrestrained market on workers, in the form of mothers' allowances, old-age and veterans pensions, and health and unemployment insurance. In contrast to later versions of social democracy, there was no call for state bureaucracies and rule by experts. Working-class redress was not to be achieved by proxy. Fundamentally, the workers' revolt was a movement rooted in notions of rank-and-file mobilization, autonomy, and democracy. In place of the traditional authority of bosses, politicians, and even union officials, working-class organization and action would be the surest safeguard of Canadian labour's interests.

In large part what was at stake was the contested meaning of democratic citizenship as workers strove to articulate their own sense of citizenship and nationhood within the British political and cultural heritage. As they invoked the traditions of British rights and justice, for which they believed the war had been fought and the peace treaty signed, they could more easily make common cause with returned soldiers and challenge both the undemocratic examples of 'Kaiserism' and the post-war capitalist efforts to define citizenship more narrowly as a matter of 'loyalism.' 'We, brought up under British laws, thought that the fight for political freedom had been fought and won ... [but] the fight is on!' the *Western Labor News* announced in the midst of the Winnipeg General Strike. For these workers, democratic citizenship brought broad entitlements within the body politic. The Union Jack itself became a contested symbol. For Peterborough's Labour Day parade in 1919, the moulders decorated their float with 'a bull dog in a setting of Union Jacks' and a sign announcing, 'What We Have We'll Hold.'[39]

At the same time, the 'industrial democracy' so often demanded would mean much more working-class power on the job. Organized wage earners used their unions to confront their employers with demands not only for immediate changes in the terms of their employment (especially higher wages) but also for a formalization of the union-management relationship that would give them greater decision-making authority in the workplace.[40] A huge proportion of the strikes in the period that did not formally include the demand for union recognition resulted from employers' refusal to deal with union leaders and the demands they carried from their members. By the end of the war many union leaders, confident of workers' labour-market leverage, were turning to the state for support and demanding that the once-despised Industrial Disputes Investigation Act (which now covered all munitions work) be used to compel their bosses to pay attention to their concerns. Union requests for boards of conciliation poured into the federal Department of Labour, as did demands for royal commissions to investigate various industries.[41] The department's Fair Wages Officers became roving conciliators sent into scenes of simmering industrial conflict. This state involvement, along with the urgent labour shortages and the unflinching determination of unionized workers, convinced reluctant employers in several sectors and all regions to agree to some kind of regular collective bargaining arrangement. In steel, meat packing, rubber, textiles, and pulp and paper, the agreements were generally informal and tenuous.[42] Workers and their employers on the railways, in urban construction and printing, in Nova Scotia and Alberta coal mining, and in the Toronto and Montreal clothing industries devised more elaborate agreements, with signed contracts and grievance and arbitration structures.[43] 'Industrial legality' became one concrete mechanism sought by many local union leaders in their campaign for 'industrial democracy.'

Determining the most appropriate negotiating structures provoked considerable debate and ideological disagreement. Many union leaders, including the Trades and Labor Congress executive, supported the single-enterprise industrial councils proposed by the British government's Whitley Committee – a model involving equal numbers of management and union representatives. This notion of collective bargaining was challenged on two fronts. Employers preferred the so-called Colorado Plan (developed for the Rockefellers by William Lyon Mackenzie King) because it involved no unions from outside the enterprise.[44] Radicals, for their part advocated a soviet-style council, described by a Victoria printer as an agreement in which 'the employer does not appear, he is pitched overboard, and the people themselves take control of the industry.'[45] Cape Breton's workers had some of the country's most elaborate plans for workers' self-management presented to them in their local labour paper in the early 1920s.[46] Visions of some kind of workers' control of production began to assume a mass resonance.

The strike weapon, and especially the sympathy strike, could also be used to advance political goals. Radical propaganda promoted the general strike as an effective response to both the challenge of post-war reconstruction and for such political outrages as the repressive orders-in-council of 1918, the brutal crushing of the Winnipeg General Strike the following spring, the arrogance of Montreal's unelected city administration in 1920, and the heavy-handed use of troops against Sydney steelworkers in 1923.[47] The mass general strike and the increasing interest in strikes as political weapons set this working-class upsurge dramatically apart from most of its predecessors in Canada.

The single demand that probably rolled up most of the aspirations of the workers' movements in this period was for a shorter workday. In 1919 a quarter of strikes incorporated this issue, far more than ever before or since.[48] The One Big Union was prepared to launch a general strike across the West over the issue.[49] Labour leaders raised it in every forum of discussion – especially the Mathers Commission and the National Industrial Conference in September 1919 – and labour representatives carried it into the provincial legislatures.[50] Most often the demand was for an eight-hour day, though the western labour movement and radicals elsewhere in the country wanted only six hours. The demand for a shorter workday served many functions: it encapsulated the desire for greater independence from the rigours of intensified work in mines and mills of Canadian industry; it held out the promise of minimizing unemployment by spreading around available work; it raised the possibility of a fuller social, recreational, and political life for wage earners, a prospect first introduced in the shorter-hours campaigns of the 1870s and 1880s; and it could touch a responsive chord among middle-class sympathizers. By 1919 several groups of workers had convinced their employers to shorten their hours of work, though no legislature would yet touch the issue.[51]

Overall, then, workers were united in the search for greater economic security, on-the-job independence and power, political influence, and overall dignity for the working class. In that sense, the vision of a different kind of society at the heart of the workers' revolt was greater than the sum of its individual parts. The democratizing vision behind all these demands nonetheless incorporated important distinctions within the working class itself. This imaginative vision was conceived primarily by white, English-speaking men (especially married men) whose manhood was deeply enmeshed in their status as breadwinners for their families. Throughout the language of the workers' revolt their notion of entitlement assumed male dominance of public life and the dependence of women and children on their men. Most working-class leaders continued to believe that the best place for women was tending the home fires while their menfolk earned the family's wages. Yet these same leaders gave more help to women who wanted to unionize than had ever been extended before, allowed a few into leadership roles, and welcomed small bands of committed working-class housewives into a special supportive relationship within the workers' movements with their own Women's Labor Leagues and Women's Independent Labor Parties. Female activists used this separate space provided for them, along with the greater public receptiveness to gender equality that had flowed from the granting of voting rights to women during the war, to push for a wider social and political role – one that recognized their participation in both the men's world of production and the domestic realm of reproduction. The main thrust of their activities nonetheless remained a working-class variant of what has become known as 'maternal feminism,' in this case a central concern with family and community needs.[52] Similarly, labour leaders carried an image of the typical worker as not only male but also white and English-speaking. Yet while they still suspected the European newcomers as a potential threat to their 'skilled' status in the workplace and to their expectations of a 'British' standard of living, they willingly gave them union membership cards.[53] Distinctions and prejudices did not disappear during the workers' revolt, but they were certainly eroded.

By 1919 most Canadians of any class would have been aware that something profoundly different was afoot in working-class Canada. They could even see it from their windows. The new assertive class-consciousness brought a new use of urban space. The 'constitutionalism' of the revolt included the rights to free speech and association and to open assembly. Instead of keeping to the confined paths of their individual daily lives, workers used the public spaces of their towns and cities for parades, mass picnics and sporting events, huge educational forums featuring guest speakers, and spontaneous gatherings for particular protests. Since their towns and cities had few facilities built to hold large numbers, they took control of streets, parks, theatres, and churches. In reasonably compact urban centres where most workers still got around by foot or on streetcars, the working-class crowd was an aggressive force to be reckoned with. Strikes would become massive community events as working-class families extended their long-standing patterns of mutual support out of their neighbourhoods and into picket-line support, collective action against strike-breakers, or sympathy strikes. Workers thus became a much more publicly visible force in Canada's urban centres.[54]

The Workers' Defeat, 1919–1925

The workers' revolt had emerged in full form by the spring of 1919, and maintained much of its momentum across the country for at least another year. (In the eastern and western coalfields, the buoyancy lasted through 1922.) Yet, as early as the spring of 1919, the severe limitations on the workers' movements were becoming evident. From that point onward, workers were on the defensive. By 1922 most of their gains had been lost almost everywhere outside the coalfields. Strikes were defeated, union locals lost members and often disintegrated, provincial federations collapsed, independent labour parties expired, and the spirit of hope and determination drained away. The decline and fall of such a major social force was a complex process. In part, as so many Canadian historians have argued, the momentum of the revolt was sapped by ideological disagreements between a right and a left that had serious consequences for the strategic direction of the movements. To a much greater extent, however, the workers' revolt foundered on the hard, inhospitable rocks of the Canadian economy, class formation, and state.

Workers never get to choose the terrain on which they confront capital or the state. By 1919 a variety of capitalists had already made some decisions about the location and structure of their enterprises and the kind of workforce they would need. At the same time, the larger market forces continued to set constaints on what kind of working-class resistance would be possible. In Canada the industrial capitalist economy was fragmented into a myriad of widely separated projects in capital accumulation that followed quite different rhythms of development and crisis. The many isolated parts of the resource economy struggled to secure a space in highly competitive markets, the manufacturers cowered behind their tariff walls, and the transportation industries tried to survive on the success of the others. After the war each of these sectors, and their many subsectors, faced its own agonizing readjustment. Every capitalist economy contains this diversity, but Canada seemed to be an exaggerated version, not least because of the vast distances that separated industrial activity but even more because of the various sectors' disarticulated links to the larger international economy that were unconnected to each other. Here was a good part of the explanation for the regionalism that ran through the workers' movements, as it did through the rest of Canadian society. Yet none of the regions itself had a single industrial pattern. So, despite their efforts at solidarity, wage earners found themselves divided by the fragmented, uneven structure of the Canadian economy and drawn into the ideological framework of regional politicians and businessmen who had their own agendas for coping.

Reinforcing those divisions was the unevenness of working-class power within the production processes of the various industries. While this different leverage was partly a matter of the skill content of jobs and workplace independence of wage earners, skilled workers usually had the additional advantage of ethnic and sexual homogeneity. Once again, these were for the most part structural characteristics of particular occupations that emerged from that process of capitalist planning and organizing. But, by World War I, occupational identities of skilled, white, English-speaking (and many French-speaking) male wage earners bore the stamp of long-standing fights to preserve their shop-floor power, independence, and self-esteem. The occupational groups at the forefront of the workers' revolt – coal miners, metal trades workers, and 'frontier labourers' – had each fashioned a version of the distinctive muscular, masculine working-class culture that was idealized in the visual arts of the period, whether art nouveau or socialist realism.[55] This reservoir of resistance was not available to wage earners made vulnerable by their limited skills or by their gender or ethnic identity. The weaker participation of factory workers in the workers' revolt is not surprising given that skills had been drastically reduced or eliminated in many factories, while the skills that survived were industry-specific and tied closely to occupational mobility inside individual firms. This was also where female and non-Anglo-Celtic labour had often been integrated into the least skilled jobs and lacked the social sanctions enjoyed by the skilled male breadwinners. These were also workers with little accumulated history of mobilization in their own defence. What is remarkable about the working-class revolt in this period is the extent to which these vulnerable workers participated aggressively, and to which the better-placed workers often reached out to offer them support. However, occupational and ethnic differences, in combination with the industrial fragmentation of the country, made holding together a broad-based revolt a formidable task.

However much workers in all parts of the country shared common aspirations and similar patterns of organizing in the 1917–25 period, the various working-class movements that emerged faced very different opportunities and obstacles. The consciously decentralized nature of the movement made coordination of these distinct struggles extremely problematic. Canada had an archipelago of isolated industrial centres between which it was difficult to maintain regular, informed communication among the various workers' movements. The failure of western radicals to make common cause with their comrades east of the Lakehead was one of the best indicators. National labour institutions in Canada were weak, and national debate and the bonds of national solidarity were never fully developed.

Differences based on gender and ethnicity further divided Candian workers. The white, anglophone and francophone male wage earners who marched in the front ranks of the workers' revolt remained ambivalent about the role of women in the workforce and labour movement. 'There is no doubt that the women are being exploited by the manufacturers,' wrote a machinists' union official in 1917, 'and their use in the munitions factories has been the cause of reducing the wages of men shell operators.'[56] Despite women's enhanced role in working-class organizing, the patriarchal mould of the working-class family had certainly not been broken. On the contrary, a central goal of the workers' revolt of 1917–25 was to defend the household economy that had been the bedrock of working-class life in Canada for more than half a century and of the husband-father's role as chief breadwinner.[57] Working men took their families on labour picnics and welcomed them onto mass picket lines, yet the vast sea of men's faces that fill up photographs of labour meetings taken during the Winnipeg General Strike suggest how thoroughly male the public life of the workers' movements still was.[58] Even the radical left had a heavily male-centred, productionist focus that left little room on its agenda for the female half of the working class.[59]

Not all men were welcome, however. Anglo-Canadian wage earners had often been highly suspicious of capitalists' use of non-Anglo-Celtic and non-white immigrants as cheap labour in many industries and feared a direct threat to their status and earnings within the rapidly changing capitalist labour process. As a result, Anglo-Canadian and other workers eyed each other cautiously and often resentfully in ways that suggested that the elements that employers had drawn together into a workforce had not yet congealed into a full community of working-class solidarity, especially considering the continuing transiency of so many of the non-Anglo-Celtic 'sojourners.' Three vigorous counterpoints to the workers' revolt stood out in the 1917–20 period: the French Canadians' blistering anger over their forced participation in the 'English' war; rising Anglo-Canadian hysteria about European 'enemy aliens,' accompanied by demands (spearheaded by the veterans) for their expulsion from industry;[60] and the revival of anti-Asian agitation in British Columbia. The two exclusionary campaigns, which led to the immigration restrictions of 1920, must have sown deep bitterness in immigrant urban enclaves. Many labour leaders refused to be associated with such nativist activities and appealed for tolerance and working-class brotherhood. But the ethnic fissures did not disappear. The French kept their distance from the Jewish and English-Canadian radicals in Montreal.[61] Rarely were European immigrants as well integrated into the rising workers' movements as they would be in the CIO period. They were virtually never found within the ranks of the labour parties in this period (although left-wing elements in some eastern European communities maintained contact with radical socialists). The Asians, who were so numerous in West Coast industries, were completely shut out.[62] Not until the 1930s and 1940s, when the endless waves of sojourners and newcomers stopped and the working-class communities stabilized somewhat, would the ethnic divides start to close. In the meantime, the wage-earning members of many ethnic groups were drawn into rising cross-class nationalism within their own communities in Canada, especially in Quebec and in many European immigrant ghettoes in central and western Canada. These ethnic divisions had different dimensions in each region, and, aside from the West Coast anti-Asian animus, they may not have amounted to the same wall of hostility that rose up in the United States as hundreds of thousands of blacks moved north in this period.[63] But they did deflect some of the energy of the workers' revolt along paths that weakened class-conscious solidarity.

In addition to overcoming internal fragmentation and division, working classes in industrial capitalist societies sought to situate themselves within a larger configuration of classes. In most industrialized countries outside Britain, they found themselves in a minority, and the Canadian class structure was essentially no different. Unless the workers' movements opted for the Bolshevik model of seizing power and imposing the dictatorship of the proletariat, as few Canadian labour leaders suggested before 1920, they had to find political allies. In Canada labour leaders attracted, or maintained a friendly dialogue with, disaffected elements of the urban middle class whose influence could be great but whose numbers were not large. In fact, aside from such celebrated exceptions as J.S. Woodsworth, most of the middle class either stood uncomfortably aloof from the workers' revolt or participated in attempts to contain or repress it. The white-collar workers who organized their own unions, especially teachers and civil servants, generally kept their distance from the rest of the labour movement.[64] Even the country's most celebrated suffragist, Nellie McClung, nervously opposed the Winnipeg General Strike.[65] Most social gospellers began looking for some mechanisms for reconciling the warring camps of capital and labour.[66]

In most industrialized countries in the period, the largest other class was usually some version of independent commodity producers, whether peasants or commercial farmers. At the end of the war, farmers were still by far the largest and electorally most powerful element in Canada, at least east of the Rockies. They posed the same 'agrarian question' that perplexed working-class movements throughout the world. As we have seen, in their relationship with workers, farmers were, at best, ambivalent allies and, at worst, strong hindrances. They occasionally sniped at the militancy, showed limited concern about the mass working-class unemployment of the early 1920s, and refused to support labour's most prized legislative measures, most notably the eight-hour day.[67] But this rural population posed an even thornier problem. People in the rural world of early-twentieth-century Canada often shaded over from independent primary producer to wage earner, bringing far more uncertainty about their quasi-proletarian status and far less commitment to urban-based movements.[68] Much of the logging, fishing, and construction industries rested on their labour. Some undertook remarkable organizational campaigns on an unprecedented scale – the Fishermen's Protective Union of Newfoundland under William Coaker and the Lumber Workers' Industrial Union in British Columbia, in particular.[69] But most rural workers remained outside the workers' revolt or were only tangentially connected. The same point could be made about native peoples, especially on the West Coast.[70] Canadian capitalism would not be seriously challenged on this front.

Beyond calling for unity and solidarity, the leaders of Canadian workers' movements rarely reflected on the structural constraints of economic, regional, sexual, and ethnic fragmentation and isolation of Canadian workers. Probably pondering such dilemmas was a luxury the immediate organizational exigencies did not allow them. Whatever theorizing they did drew not from the specifics of the Canadian social formation but rather from the thinking of labourists or Marxists elsewhere. In this sense they were clearly disadvantaged in the face of corporate capital and the state in Canada, whose existence rested on their ability to overcome that kind of fragmentation and to integrate diverse parts of the social formation. By the end of World War I, workers confronted highly centralized corporations with national or continental networks of organization and a national state with a remarkably strong executive branch (much more aggressive as a result of its interventionist wartime experience). The workers' movements were thus overwhelmed by powerful forces that were better able to manoeuvre in the difficult Canadian setting. Whatever the structural constraints, the real crisis facing wage earners came from the aggressive resistance of employers who dug in their heels against workers' demands, and the state, which set out to undercut the radical potential of the workers' movements. Both employers and the state followed a course of crushing the militants and radicals and then appealing to 'safe and sane' wage earners and, if necessary, their leaders.

The surest indication of unprecedented class conflict in post-war Canada was the extent to which both capital and labour mobilized to assert their interests. The economic dislocations and instability rampant across Canada in the immediate aftermath of hostilities drove both to new extremes in attitude and organization. In 1919–20 the prospect of a renewed rivalry with both European and American industry (the return of 'competitive competition again,' in the telling redundancy of one BC manufacturer)[71] convinced many Canadian employers that the viability of their operations was now at stake. Capitalists across the country worried that markets for the products of their vastly expanded productive apparatus were disappearing, that price inflation had made them uncompetitive (especially in terms of labour costs), that the creation of many new unions limited their ability to alter wages and labour processes (perish the thought of an eight-hour day!), and that the free-trade sentiments of the powerful new farmers' movements would threaten their tariff protection. At a more general level, they sensed that a large mass of the population had come out of the war with a cynical, if not openly hostile, view of corporate dominance over Canadian social and economic life. Capitalists had not only to secure the subordination of the working class but also to restore the legitimacy of their hegemony more generally.

After the Armistice employers launched a concerted offensive of union-busting and wage-cutting in an effort to reclaim ground conceded to labour under extraordinary wartime circumstances. Workers in virtually all the twenty-eight cities visited by the Royal Commission on Industrial Relations in the spring of 1919 complained of extensive firing and blacklisting of union supporters since the end of the war.[72] Many of the protracted (and ultimately defeated) strikes of the post-war era were marked as much by capitalist intransigence as by labour's militancy. In 1920 workers won less than one strike in five, and employers were clear winners in a third – a dramatic reversal of the strike outcomes in 1917–18. From 1921 to 1924 close to half these confrontations ended on employers' terms, to which could be added many of those strikes whose outcomes were classified as 'Indefinite' (27 per cent in 1920, 24 per cent in 1921, and 20 per cent in 1922).[73] The decisive defeats came at different points in each industry and region. The collapse of the Winnipeg General Strike and the various sympathy strikes marked the beginning of the end in urban centres across the West. The defeat of the prolonged metal trades strikes in several Canadian cities in 1919 was devastating, but for most manufacturing industries in Ontario, Quebec, and Nova Scotia the major symbolic defeats did not arrive until mid-1920. The shipyards strikes of that year were catastrophes for organized labour in several parts of central and eastern Canada. Even the solidly entrenched printers' unions were dealt a crippling blow in their unsuccessful struggle for the forty-four-hour week.[74] Sydney steelworkers did not meet their Waterloo until 1923, and coal miners in Cape Breton and Alberta held on for two more years.[75] The final confrontation of Cape Breton's miners and corporate bosses in 1925 was as bitter, brutal, and devastating as any in the whole period under study.

As the many studies of strikes in the period have revealed, a common pattern emerged almost everywhere. Companies forced a strike by refusing to negotiate and then frequently hired strike-breakers, often from professional strike-breaking operations such as the Pinkerton or Thiel detective agencies. As defeated workers drifted back, employers blacklisted local union militants to drive them out of town; some even installed spies on the shop floor to watch for potential troublemakers. Little of this activity was carried out under the defiant 'open shop' banner that American capitalists were unfurling at this time,[76] but the outcome was the same. Anti-union tactics became much easier to implement in the context of a rapidly declining economy. The 16.5 per cent unemployment rate among unionized workers in the spring of 1921 was destroying their leverage in the labour market.[77] Nearly universal wage cuts of 10–20 per cent in the early months of that year met with little resistance. By the end of 1922 the Department of Labour's statistics showed over 100,000 fewer union members than at the 1919 peak – a loss of 27 per cent.[78]

As workers were taught the lesson that militancy and unionism would not be tolerated, many corporations tried to sweeten the medicine with a package of welfare reforms for their employees to promote loyalty and dedication to the individual firm rather than to the working class. Out of corporate boardrooms cascaded safety plans, lunch rooms, company magazines, recreation programs, and pension and insurance plans. To workers who were once again facing economic insecurity, the pension and insurance plans were far more attractive than patronizing programs aimed at constructing a 'corporate family.' In a few large plants, corporations also responded to the call for 'industrial democracy' with industrial councils (made up of equal numbers of management and employee representatives) in which issues arising in the workplace could be addressed. Company executives quickly found they had to deflect their employees' attempts to discuss wages and hours, and the councils rapidly dissolved into toothless forums for debate on safety and recreation issues.[79] Probably only a small minority of Canadian wage earners ever enjoyed any crumbs from the table of welfare capitalism in any case.

At the same time, capitalists launched a campaign to relegitimize their dominant role in Canadian society. In addition to publicizing their corporate welfarism,[80] they sought a common enemy against which workers and the broader population could be rallied. Industrialists contributed heavily to propaganda that tried to terrorize Canadians into believing that the democracy they had just fought for was endangered by blood-thirsty Bolshevists. Lurid, full-page advertisements informed newspaper readers of the 'alien' quality of the workers' revolt. A Canadian-made, employer-funded movie called *The Great Shadow* depicted Bolshevik subversion of labour struggles in a shipyard (several companies supplied free tickets for their employees).[81] Some capitalists even bought the support of conservative labour leaders by funnelling money to them secretly and by supporting such red-baiting newspapers as the Ottawa-based *Canadian Labor Press*.[82]

The various (mostly rural) forces threatening the tariff structure could be constructed as another common enemy. The most powerful corporate capitalists threw their support behind Sir John Willison's Canadian Reconstruction Association, the statesmanlike public face of capital that highlighted the benefits of corporate welfarism and built broader support for the tariff.[83] Eventually, the Tories held onto most of industrialized Ontario in the 1921 federal election, as they had in 1911, by exploiting working-class fears of job loss in a free-trade economy.[84] In Quebec the Catholic Church provided another successful alternative in the form of Catholic unionism, which preached worker–employer harmony (within a framework of Catholic values) and began to mushroom in size and influence in 1919. Quebec's employers were pleased.[85] Finally, in the East, local employers placed themselves at the head of a new Maritime Rights movement in the early 1920s.[86] In each case workers' anger and insecurity were deflected into class-collaborationist channels, though only once their industrial militancy had been crushed.

The Canadian state made no effort to curb the attacks on workers and their organizations. On the contrary, as we saw in the essay by Heron and Siemiatycki in this volume, politicians and state officials had moved decisively to repress and undermine working-class militancy and radicalism. They turned loose against radical leaders their secret-service spies, federal troops, and new criminal-law and immigration legislation, as well as their blandishments of more moderate leaders with a royal commission and a National Industrial Conference. The federal government offered no solid inducements or protection for working-class organization.

At this point the structure of Canadian federalism played its complicated role in mediating class relations. Workers' movements across the country had directed much of their political energy into provincial politics wherein resided many of the constitutional responsibilities for such worker concerns as the eight-hour day. That meant battling on nine different fronts. Provincial governments had been the first to respond to the general unrest in the population after 1916, and several administrations (especially those run by reform-minded Liberals) had used such measures as minimum-wage legislation and mothers' allowances to try to buy back some legitimacy for the social and political system.[87] Some provincial politicians, such as Ontario's Henry Cody, looked to longer-term means of restoring the legitimacy of the social order with increased schooling for adolescents to inculcate appropriate notions of 'citizenship,' as did the National Conference on 'Character Education' held in Winnipeg in October 1919.[88] Each of these moves by the provincial branches of the Canadian state reinforced the regional particularities in the timing and rhythms of the workers' revolt. Since no federal election was called until 1921, workers' movements were not able to confront the national Borden government directly on the hustings until after the revolt had lost most of its momentum.

It is against this agonizingly difficult backdrop of structural constraint and repressive counter-attack that we must assess the splits that had opened up within the labour leadership by the spring of 1919. Once again, they hit each region at different moments. Yet this was fundamentally a divergence between left and right, not East and West. In every region of the country labour leaders were engaging in heated debate about the appropriate industrial and political working-class response to the new resistance that the revolt was facing. While the left urged escalation, the right called for a retreat. The major points of disagreement concerned the most appropriate form of union organization, the link with the international unions centred in the American Federation of Labor, and the willingness of the workers' movements to show more aggressiveness in pursuit of their goals. Since the middle of the war, labour leaders had argued over these issues, and, as we saw, those who constituted the movements' national voice in the Trades and Labor Congress of Canada had always counselled and practised restraint. The confrontation came to a head at the 1918 Congress convention, where a minority report denouncing the executive's cozy relations with the government sparked a furious debate about the directions of the labour movement. A set of militant tactical resolutions was defeated and a more conservative slate, headed by carpenters' union organizer Tom Moore, was elected to the Congress executive. Moore had been a solid supporter of conscription and a central figure in the rapprochement with the Borden government in 1918. The defeat for the left at the 1918 convention was not simply a matter of the East overpowering the West (fifty-one easterners joined twenty-nine westerners on the losing side, against a majority of three from the West and eighty-one from the East). It was quite significant, however, that the Western delegates constructed the defeat in regional terms. They chose to minimize the evidence of support for their position East of the Lakehead and to use a Western Labour Conference as a springboard for reconstruction of the whole labour movement. Then, in the early spring of 1919, they moved decisively towards secession with the creation of the One Big Union.[89]

That spring well-established craft union leaders in most major cities began to consider the risks associated with the widening solidarity and political radicalism. In the Western conferences leading up to the formation of the One Big Union, there were dissenting voices. J.H. McVety in Vancouver, David Rees in Fernie, Alfred Farmilo in Edmonton, Alex Ross in Calgary, and Ernie Robinson in Winnipeg all opposed withdrawing from the international unions to form the One Big Union. The Calgary labour movement was lukewarm about this new experiment, while the Edmonton trades council stayed out altogether.[90] In southern Ontario and Montreal the more entrenched craft union leaders were not prepared to see their organizations disrupted by surging notions of industrial unionism.[91] All these men were still looking to the state and capital for the legitimacy and recognition they believed caution and moderation would bring. Their strategy was to raise the threat of labour unrest and to present themselves as the restraining force that would curb militancy and radicalism. In an address to the Canadian Manufacturers' Association in February 1919, Tom Moore was reported to have advised his audience that 'the responsible, intelligent trades unionist was the capitalist's strongest bulwark, if only a friendly co-operation were extended to him, since the trade unionist, and indeed, the worker fully realized that the downfall of the capitalist, and the cessation of the work in the factory spelled his own idleness and possible starvation.'[92] (Moore later insisted that he had referred to unions as *'civilization's* strongest bulkwark'; misquote or not, his message was clear.) The same concern with cementing an accord with the state and capital explains the enthusiastic participation of the craft union leadership in the National Industrial Conference.[93]

By the end of 1919, the fluidity of the previous two years had evaporated, and positions on the right and left were hardening. In the wake of the OBU breakaway, the Canadian branches of the international unions threw themselves into a campaign to win back the West and to prevent any further secessions. The more conservative craft union leaders steadily withdrew their support for the more experimental organizational forms and practices that had blossomed alongside the normal channels of international union procedure. They insisted on the honouring of contracts negotiated with individual employers. (This abiding faith in 'industrial legality' discouraged various groups of wage earners from joining larger struggles.)[94] They used the disciplinary power of their organizations to curb unauthorized sympathy or general strikes. In many cases they seriously undermined local struggles by curtailing solidarity actions by their members. By rejecting cooperation and amalgamation of crafts and rigourously defending individual craft jurisdiction and rights, these union officials undoubtedly robbed less skilled workers of leadership, resources, and negotiating strength. Over the next two years the leading figures in the craft union movement distanced themselves from the main currents of the workers' revolt. They also opened a rhetorical barrage against the left in general, using some of the existing labour newspapers as well as the new *Canadian Labor News*, the *Edmonton Free Press*, and, from the end of 1919, *New Democracy*. By 1921 the leaders of the Trades and Labor Congress even refused to endorse the independent labour candidates who were running in that year's federal election. These craft unionists settled solidly into the cautious, complacent, apolitical mould that had been developed in the Gompersite American Federation of Labor and would not wander far from those moorings until World War II.[95]

Facing these men across the increasingly bitter political battlefield were a variety of militants and radicals who, as we have seen, were spread across the country. Region does not help explain their location as much as industry, occupation, ethnicity, and the recent history of industrial relations in their respective communities. Some were based in the older male occupations with long traditions of workplace pride and independence and recent success in confronting their employers, especially the coal miners and the highly skilled railway shopcraft workers.[96] Others had a solid following in the newly organized unions of semi-skilled and unskilled workers, notably in mass production, resource processing, and water transport.[97] Also providing some ginger were clusters of European-born socialists who were found in logging, mining, and clothing production.[98] The radicals' success depended on the strength of the local unions in their respective industries and on the established power of the international craft union leadership in the local labour movement. AFL-style craft unions were much weaker in the Maritimes and the West, where they had never put down as deep roots and had always had to coexist with bumptious industrial unions, usually most solidly based in mining.[99] They were also somewhat weaker in Quebec, where their insensitivity to francophones had limited their impact (the AFL finally appointed a bilingual organizer for the province in 1918).[100] Southern Ontario was the heartland of this cautious brand of unionism and the headquarters of a solid cadre of full-time labour officials – business agents, organizers, Canadian vice-presidents, and the leading officials of the Trades and Labor Congress of Canada – who were committed to the link with the AFL and industrial legality in collective bargaining. Their caution was more than a slavish mimicking of an American model; it was also the product of experience in a harshly anti-union climate that had kept unions out of Ontario's major industries since the turn of the century. The craft unionists' prominence and strength in the region's labour movement rested in large part on the lack of a substantial industrial union movement based in the province's many factories until the end of the war. Those industrial unions that eventually did emerge in cities like Toronto and Hamilton were latecomers and remained extremely fragile. The craft unionists greeted them with coolness and some apprehension.[101]

The divisions in the labour leadership went beyond the right–left tensions. The radicals themselves were divided on the issue of staying with the international unions. The great majority of westerners voted to leave and form the One Big Union. In central and eastern Canada, this strategy had its supporters.[102] (Because unions in these regions generally refused to hold referendums on secession, it is impossible to gauge the precise amount of support for the OBU.) However, most militant leaders in central and eastern Canada opted to remain within the international union movement. The left within the workers' movement was therefore divided at a crucial moment. By the end of 1919 the radicals' secessionist project in the West had foundered. East of the Lakehead those who remained in the mainstream labour movement became increasingly isolated. Only in the Maritimes did they maintain a leadership role, which persisted until 1923.

Beset by failures and a heavily repressive environment, many socialist militants began to gravitate towards the emerging Communist movement. The old Social Democratic Party had disintegrated soon after the state's iron heel came down on it late in 1918. Socialists from the party's right wing (notably James Simpson in Toronto) settled into independent labour party work. At the same time, feistier members of its left wing joined forces with a handful of revolutionary socialists and radical members of some Eastern European immigrant groups, some of whom had already begun clandestine propaganda early in 1919. In the heat of state repression and the general Red Scare, this new pro-Bolshevik left had both an underground life for theorizing and strategizing and a public forum for revolutionary education and unbridled attacks on the dominant labour leadership. Many of the militant sparkplugs from the workers' revolt – including Jack MacDonald in Toronto, Fred Flatman in Hamilton, Annie Buller in Montreal, and J.B. McLachlan in Cape Breton – were drawn to this emerging movement, as were many European-born socialists. In May 1921, at a secret meeting in a barn outside Guelph, the underground Communist Party of Canada was founded, uniting all these revolutionary socialists east of Manitoba. Its public face, the Workers' Party of Canada, emerged in February 1922. In the West the aging Socialist Party of Canada eventually disintegrated as branches left to join the Workers' Party. Branches of a few local labour parties in such places as Halifax and Fernie followed suit. Ironically, shortly after its founding the Communist Party, in line with the new direction of the Third International in Moscow, began to favour the politics of coalition over sectarian attacks on the established labour institutions and their leaders. The Workers' Party affiliated with the Canadian Labor Party, and individual Communists directed their energies back into locals of international unions, the trades councils, and the Trades and Labor Congress. However, the craft union leadership was unwelcoming, and by the late 1920s most Communists had been expelled from unions for their agitation.[103] The left, then, had also been unable to meet the challenge of the crisis facing workers after 1919. At that critical moment, the radicals' flamboyant sectarianism may have sometimes been unrealistic, but it was the divisive issue of secession from the mainstream international labour movement, combined with the ideological hardening that had taken place in the context of the well-orchestrated Red Scare, that deprived the radicals of the credibility and effectiveness that would have allowed them to take a larger role.

A substantial number of activists from the workers' revolt chose to embrace neither narrow craft unionism nor Communism. The minority of non-Communist socialists left behind after the splits in the old socialist parties continued to find common cause with the handfuls of still-committed labourists. Most of their political energy was devoted to maintaining the local labour parties. But the 1921 federal election, called in the depths of the post-war depression when most of the momentum of the workers' revolt had already been destroyed, was the final death knell for these socialists. They struggled on, but, with only two representatives in the House of Commons, without a majority in any provincial legislature, and thoroughly compromised in the Ontario Farmer-Labour government,[104] they had little to show for their efforts. Their constituency rapidly vanished. For several years in the mid-1920s they worked with the Communists in a revived Canadian Labor Party, but with no significant success. A handful of labour representatives would hang on in city councils, provincial legislatures, and Parliament, partly on the basis of personal popularity and probity, and a decade later would help to launch a new social democratic party, the Co-operative Commonwealth Federation.[105]

By the mid-1920s labour leaders from all these politial camps must have looked back in sober dismay at the opportunities that had been lost. In the years between 1917 and 1920 a massive number of Canadian workers had become part of a great collective groping for a new kind of society. With the limited resources available in working class neighbourhoods across the country, they had united in countless ways to show their determination to change the lot of workers in Canada. They had pursued their goals in a constitutionalist fashion through the existing institutions of society, especially unions and political parties, rather than armed insurrection, but their open-ended vision of working-class power had nonetheless carried radical dimensions and potential that did not escape the notice of bourgeois leaders. The workers had never been given the opportunity to carry their planning and dreaming far forward into the post-war era because Canadian capitalists would not consider the shift in power that even the mildest reforms implied, and because those in control of the state had shared this apprehension about a more powerful working class. When the crunch had come, the workers' revolt had failed to transcend the great diversity and structural weaknesses of the Canadian working class. Workers in every part of the country, in almost every occupational group, had participated in the revolt, but they had failed to coalesce (sometimes even at the local level) into an effective, coherent force able to withstand the crippling attacks of capital and the state and the enervating impact of unemployment. In this moment of crisis the leadership of the workers' movements had fragmented into three distinct currents according to their divergent readings of how to respond – cautious craft unionism, revolutionary Communism, and social democratic parliamentarism – none of which managed to capture the dynamism, mass mobilization, and ideological and strategic diversity of the early stages of the revolt.

Meanwhile, thousands of workers on the defensive by 1920 had begun to lose their optimism that working class movements could deliver the 'New Democracy.' The spirit of class solidarity had quietly faded away. Workers accepted what they could get from employers willing to hire them, abandoned their unions lest membership get them fired, and stopped voting for labour candidates (if they voted at all). Fearful caution and cynicism, if not fatalism, had settled in.

The long-term impact was devastating for the Canadian working class. For the next twenty years, despite some determined efforts in the 1930s, workers did not come close to regaining the collective power they had summoned up in 1917–20. Although unions did not disappear (total union membership by the mid-1920s had not, in fact, tumbled to the pre-war lows), they were for the most part marginal to Canadian industrial life. Most industrial corporations could confidently expect to operate in a 'union-free' environment. Canadian political life would take some time to recover from the various post-war crises, but in working-class communities voter absenteeism or traditional Liberalism and resurgent Toryism were predominant by 1925. The moment when the Canadian capitalist system faced one of its most serious challenges in the country's history had clearly passed.[106]

The legacy of the workers' revolt would nonetheless endure. The most negative part of this legacy concerned working-class organization. The lessons of the period had left labour activists of all political stripes sceptical about the ideological and organizational fluidity of the revolt. Craft unionists, social democrats, and Communists hardened permanently into their own increasingly rigid views of the most appropriate forms of working-class mobilization. The survivors of the revolt also shaped the options for the future. Rather than the imaginative organizational flexibility for uniting workers in 1917–20 period, the feeble torch that was passed on to the next generation of militants in the 1930s was two variants of cautious, rigid, bureaucratic organization – namely, the AFL's craft unionism and the narrower industrial unionism promoted by the United Mine Workers and the clothing unions. Both regarded challenges to capitalist property rights or its attendant industrial legality as anathema. Labour leaders would use their control of trade unionism to ensure that working-class aspirations were confined to issues of 'reconcilable class differences,' leaving industry controlled by capital and unions controlled by their officers.[107]

On a more positive note, the working class had undoubtedly carved out a somewhat larger place in Canadian public life. Canadian politicians could never again ignore the concerns of workers to the extent they had in the past. A small residue of social legislation remained on the statute books,[108] and a handful of labour parliamentarians at all three levels of the state would continue to voice workers' concerns. J.S. Woodsworth's success in extracting an old-age pension plan from Mackenzie King in 1926 was the most impressive example.[109] Moreover, in some parts of the country where the revolt was not buried beneath the suffocating blankets of Maritime Rights, francophone nationalism, or industrial protectionism, the struggles of 1917–20 were not forgotten and would be used to rally workers in future battles. It seems that the mass strikes (such as those in Winnipeg and Cape Breton) that had drawn workers into direct confrontation with the armed might of the state, rather than simply mobilization through the ballot box, had etched the deepest memories.

The working class in Canada would indeed rise up again a quarter-century later. The form of the new workers' movements would be as different as this one had been from its predecessors in the 1880s, but workers' renewed aspirations for economic security, independence, and dignity would make clear that they were not prepared to remain on their knees forever.

Notes

1 Quoted in Smith, *Let Us Rise!*, 1.

2 Cruikshank and Kealey, 'Canadian Strike Statistics'; and Gregory Kealey, 'Parameters of Class Conflict.' Their statistics provide the basis for the following discussion.

3 Bob Russell's analysis of wartime strikes assumes that a compromise was a loss for strikers, but in this period it was more likely that gaining any ground, even if less than they wanted, was a major accomplishment for workers. Russell, *Back to Work?*, 140–52.

4 Bob Russell calculates that nearly three-quarters of strikes in 1917–18 and two-thirds in 1920 were illegal. Russell, *Back to Work?*, 161–3.

5 Canada, Dept. of Labour, *Labour Organization in Canada*, 1914–20. A careful reading of these Labour Dept. reports makes clear that the totals were rough estimates and undoubtedly underestimated union membership. Tables that broke the statistics down by province reveal that generally about a third of the locals failed to report their membership. The dept. then filled in the holes 'from dept. records and other sources' (ibid., 1919, 243).

6 Quoted in Heron and De Zwaan, 'Industrial Unionism,' 167.

7 Siemiatycki, 'Munitions and Labour Militancy'; Marine Workers and Boilermakers Industrial Union, *History of Shipbuilding*, 10–20; Frank, 'Cape Breton Coal Miners'; Seager, 'Proletariat in Wild Rose Country'; Canada, Dept. of Labour, *Organization in Canada*, 1916–20.

8 Siemiatycki, 'Labour Contained'; Kealey, '1919'; Heron, *Working in Steel;* Naylor, *New Democracy;* Montague, 'Trade Unionism in the Canadian Meatpacking Industry'; Schonning, 'Union–Management Relations in the Pulp and Paper Industry'; Scott, 'Profusion of Issues'; Hak, 'British Columbia Loggers'; Radforth, *Bushworkers and Bosses;* Thomson, '"The Large and Generous View"'; McLean, *'Union amongst Government Employees'*; Marquis, 'Police Unionism' and 'History of Policing in the Maritimes,' 94; Doherty, *Slaves of the Lamp;* and the regional essays in this volume.

9 Gregory Kealey, 'Parameters of Class Conflict,' 225–6.

10 Linda Kealey, '"No Special Protection"' and 'Women's Labour Militancy'; Roome, 'Amelia Turner and Calgary Labour Women'; Bernard, 'Last Back' and *Long Distance Feeling*, 50–71; Horodyski, 'Women and the Winnipeg General Strike'; Campbell, 'Sexism in British Columbia Trade Unions; Smillie, 'Invisible Workforce'; Frager, 'No Proper Deal.'

11 Avery, *'Dangerous Foreigners'*; Creese, 'Class, Ethnicity, and Conflict'; Radforth, *Bushworkers and Bosses*, 110–19; Martynowych and Kazymyra, 'Political Activity in Western Canada'; Wickberg, ed., *From China to Canada*, 130; Rouillard, 'Les travailleurs juifs'; Frager, *Sweatshoop Strife*, 35–54; Calliste, 'Sleeping Car Porters.'

12 Burnet, *'Coming Canadians'*; Harney, *Italians*, 20–2; Zucchi, *Italians in Toronto;* Radeki, *Member of a Distinguished Family;* Montgomery, 'Immigrants, Industrial Unions, and Social Reconstruction.'

13 Quoted in Gregory Kealey, '1919,' 39.

14 International Association of Machinists, *Bulletin* (Winnipeg), August 1918.

15 In 1914 there were four labour papers: Vancouver's *BC Federationist*, Winnipeg's *Voice*, Hamilton's *Labor News*, and Toronto's *Industrial Banner.* By mid-1919 all but the *Voice* were flourishing and had been joined by the *Citizen* (Halifax), the *Eastern Federationist* (New Glasgow), *Workers' Weekly* (Stellarton), the *Union Worker* (Saint John), *Le Monde ouvrier* (Montreal), *l'Unioniste* (Quebec City), the *Canadian Labor Press* (Ottawa), the *Labor Leader* (Toronto), *New Democracy* (Hamilton), the *Herald* (London), the *Western Labor News* (Winnipeg), the *Confederate* (Brandon), the *Searchlight* (Calgary), and the *Edmonton Free Press*. Canada, Dept. of Labour, *Labour Organization in Canada*, 1919, 295.

16 At the famous 1918 convention of the Trades and Labor Congress of Canada, radicals failed to win majority support for their proposal that the officials at this level should be consulted by the government, not the officers of interna-

tional unions. The One Big Union later made these bodies the centre of its organizational structure. Robin, *Radical Politics and Canadian Labour*, 161; Bercuson, *Fools and Wise Men*, 149.

17 Siemiatycki, 'Labour Contained,' 279–325; McCormack, *Reformers, Rebels, and Revolutionaries*, 145–6; Bercuson, *Confrontation at Winnipeg*; Reilly, 'General Strike in Amherst'; Friesen, '"Yours in Revolt."'

18 Among the discredited or ignored were Nova Scotian miners' leader John Moffatt, the aging Quebec Lib-Lab MP Alphonse Verville, prominent Hamilton labour journalist Sam Landers, Winnipeg's venerable Arthur Puttee, Alberta miners' leader David Rees, and Vancouver's J.H. McVety and W.R. Trotter. MacEwan, *Miners and Steelworkers*, 46; Ewen in this volume; Heron, 'Working-Class Hamilton'; McCormack, *Reformers, Rebels, and Revolutionaries*, 137–64; Bercuson, *Fools and Wise Men*, 65–7.

19 Heron, 'Great War and Nova Scotia Steelworkers'; Frank, 'Cape Breton Coal Miners'; Heron and De Zwaan, 'Industrial Unionism,' 170–1; Angus, *Canadian Bolsheviks*, 66–9; Heron, 'Working-Class Hamilton,' 251–9; Bercuson, *Fools and Wise Men*, 65–8; Akers, 'Rebel or Revolutionary?'

20 Wade, 'Helena Gutteridge'; Linda Kealey, '"No Special Protection"'; Roome, 'Amelia Turner and Calgary Labour Women'; Horodyski, 'Women and the Winnipeg General Strike'; Heron, 'Working-Class Hamilton,' 380–489.

21 Peterson, 'Revolutionary Socialism and Industrial Unrest'; Angus, *Canadian Bolsheviks*, 3–62; Friesen, '"Yours in Revolt."'

22 Hak, 'British Columbia Loggers.'

23 Robin, *Radical Politics and Canadian Labour*, 170–7; McCormack, *Reformers, Rebels, and Revolutionaries*, 143–5; Bercuson, *Fools and Wise Men*, 83 (but see also his rethinking of this subject in 'Syndicalism Sidetracked').

24 On this point the interpretations of the Western revolt by Gerald Friesen and Larry Peterson are more convincing; see Friesen, '"Yours in Revolt,"' 145–7; Peterson, 'One Big Union in International Perspective,' 53–8. See also Akers, 'Rebel or Revolutionary?' 19–20.

25 Robin, *Radical Politics and Canadian Labour*, 130; Coates, ed., *British Labour and the Russian Revolution*.

26 McCormack, *Reformers, Rebels, and Revolutionaries*, 142; Angus, *Canadian Bolsheviks*, 27–48; Krawchuk, *Ukrainian Socialist Movement*; Usiskin, 'Winnipeg Jewish Radical Community.'

27 Heron, 'Labourism and the Canadian Working Class,' 48–9.

28 Scarrow, *Canada Votes*, 28–9.

29 Canada, Dept. of Labour, *Labour Organization in Canada*, 1917–20.

30 MacKenzie, 'Farmer-Labour Party in Nova Scotia'; Watson, 'United Farmers of Ontario'; Naylor, 'Ontario Workers and the Decline of Labourism'; Mardiros, *William Irvine*.

31 Akers, 'Rebel or Revolutionary?' 24.

32 McNaught, *Prophet in Politics;* Allen, *Social Passion;* Mardiros, *William Irvine;* Petryshyn, 'From Clergyman to Communist'; Mitchell, 'From the Social Gospel to "The Plain Bread of Leninism."'

33 Horn, *League for Social Reconstruction.*

34 Labourism was a brand of working-class liberalism that challenged political privilege, undemocratic practices, economic monopoly, and the exclusion of workers from social and political power, but stopped short of a full-scale assault on the capitalist system. Heron, 'Labourism and the Canadian Working Class.'

35 Quoted in Frank, 'Cape Breton Coal Miners,' 304–5; and Canada, Dept. of Labour, *Labour Organization in Canada,* 1919, 57.

36 Gregory Kealey, '1919,' 11–15; Siemiatycki, 'Labour Contained,' 279–325.

37 Labour Canada Library, Royal Commission on Industrial Relations, Evidence, Calgary, 3 May 1919.

38 *Globe* (Toronto), 20 March 1919.

39 Reimer, 'War, Nationhood and Working-Class Entitlement' (quotation on 231); *Examiner* (Peterborough), 2 September 1919; Naylor, *New Democracy;* McKay and Morton, and Mitchell and Naylor in this volume.

40 Wages were an issue in 46 per cent of the strikes in 1917, 44 per cent in 1918, 39 per cent in 1919, and 45 per cent in 1920. Gregory Kealey, 'Parameters of Class Conflict,' 240.

41 Selekman, *Postponing Strikes,* 168–78. The device of the royal commission was used, for example, in the Toronto and Hamilton munitions industry and Cobalt silver mining in 1916, and the Nova Scotia coal and steel industries several times after 1916. Siemiatycki, 'Munitions and Labour Militancy'; Hogan, *Cobalt;* MacEwan, *Miners and Steelworkers;* Heron, 'Great War and Nova Scotia Steelworkers.'

42 Heron, *Working in Steel,* 141–2; Schonning, 'Union–Management Relations in the Pulp and Paper Industry'; Montague, 'Trade Unionism in the Canadian Meatpacking Industry'; Naylor, *New Democracy,* 51–3, 209–10.

43 Peitchinis, *Labour–Management Relations in the Railway Industry,* 104–12; Naylor, *New Democracy* ,185–8; Zerker, *Rise and Fall of the Toronto Typographical Union,* 178–204; McKay, *Craft Transformed,* 68–73, and 'Industry, Work, and Community'; Seager, 'Proletariat in Wild Rose Country'; Brecher, 'Patterns of Accommodation in the Men's Garment Industry.'

44 Scott, '"A Place in the Sun"'; Naylor, *New Democracy,* 159–88; Levant, *Capital and Labour: Partners?,* 9–36; McGregor, *Fall and Rise of Mackenzie King.*

45 Royal Commission on Industrial Relations, Evidence, Victoria, Phil Smith, 26 April 1919.

46 Frank, 'Contested Terrain,' 114–18.

47 McCormack, *Reformers, Rebels, and Revolutionaries*, 146, 165–6; essays by Ewen and Naylor in this volume; Macgillivray, 'Military Aid to the Civil Power.'

48 Gregory Kealey, 'Parameters of Class Conflict,' 40.

49 Bercuson, *Fools and Wise Men*, 85.

50 MacEwan, *Miners and Steelworkers*, 71–2; Naylor, *New Democracy*, 193–4.

51 See Palmer, *Culture in Conflict*; Gregory Kealey and Palmer, *Dreaming of What Might Be*. The issue of shorter hours within workers' movements has been the subject of much fascinating recent research. See Roediger and Foner, *Our Own Time*; Cross, *Quest for Time*; Cross, ed., *Worktime and Industrialization*; and Hunnicutt, *Work without End*.

52 Parr, *Gender of Breadwinners*, 149–52; Linda Kealey, '"No Special Protection"'; Roome, 'Amelia Turner and Calgary Labour Women'; Naylor, *New Democracy*, 129–55; Campbell, 'Sexism in British Columbia Trade Unions'; Lindstrom-Best, *Defiant Sisters*, 147–55; 'Finnish Socialist Women in Canada'; Lindstrom-Best and Seager, '*Toveritar* and Finnish Canadian Women'; Penfold, '"Have You No Manhood in You?"'

53 Scott, 'A Profusion of Issues'; Seager, 'Class, Ethnicity, and Politics'; Heron, *Working in Steel*, 135.

54 Bercuson, *Confrontation at Winnipeg*; Penner, ed., *Winnipeg 1919*; Horodyski, 'Women and the Winnipeg General Strike'; Morton, 'Labourism and Economic Action'; Naylor, *New Democracy*; Heron and De Zwaan, 'Industrial Unionism in Eastern Ontario'; Ewen in this volume.

55 See Donegan, 'Iconography of Labour.'

56 Quoted in Heron, 'Working-Class Hamilton,' 388–9.

57 Joy Parr has appropriately dubbed this collective defence of the family wage 'social fathering' and 'breadwinner unionism.' Parr, *Gender of Breadwinners*, 149–50.

58 See photos in Penner, ed., *Winnipeg 1919*, and Bumstead, *Winnipeg General Strike*. Even the large Central Strike Committee had only two female members.

59 McKay and Morton in this volume; Frager, 'Class and Ethnic Barriers' and *Sweatshop Strife*.

60 The 'Reconstruction Policy' of the Greater Toronto Labor Party called on the government to 'tax all Aliens and enemy aliens very heavily; immigration after the War to be of friendly Aliens only for a definite period.' *Canadian Annual Review* (Toronto), 1918, 343.

61 Ewen in this volume.

62 Seager and Roth in this volume.

63 See, for example, Tuttle, *Race Riot*.

64 The BC Provincial Service Association affiliated with the Trades and Labor Congress but refused to join the Victoria Trades and Labor Council. McLean, '*A Union amongst Government Employees*,' 5, 15. See also Thomson, '"The Large and Generous View"'; and Makahonuk, 'Masters and Servants.'

65 Savage, *Our Nell*, 142–3.

66 Allen, *Social Passion*, 104–96.

67 Naylor, 'Ontario Workers and the Decline of Labourism'; Yeo, 'Alliance Unrealized'; and 'Rural Manitoba'. On the general topic of rural workers, see Samson, ed., *Contested Countryside*.

68 This important feature of the Canadian social formation has had far too little attention from Canadian historians, especially in English Canada. For some discussion, see McKay and Morton and Ewen in this volume; Séguin, 'L'économie agro-forestière'; Hardy and Séguin, *Fôret et société*; Hughes, *French Canada in Transition*; Ramirez, *On the Move*; Igartua, 'Worker Persistence'; Radforth, *Bushworkers and Bosses*; Parr, 'Hired Men'; Thompson, 'Bringing in the Sheaves'; Avery, 'Canadian Immigration Policy'; Sandberg, 'Dependent Development'; Sacouman, 'Semi-Proletarianization and Rural Underdevelopment'; Johnson, 'Precapitalist Economic Formations'; Knight, *Stump Ranch Chronicles*.

69 McDonald, '*To Each His Own*'; Hak, 'British Columbia Loggers.'

70 Knight, *Indians at Work*; Ray, *Canadian Fur Trade*.

71 Royal Commission on Industrial Relations, Evidence, Vancouver, J.J. Coughlin, 29 April 1919.

72 Siemiatycki, 'Labour Contained,' 249.

73 Gregory Kealey, 'Parameters of Class Conflict,' 241.

74 Zerker, *Rise and Fall of the Toronto Typographical Union*, 178–204; Allen, *Social Passion*, 175–96.

75 Heron, 'Great War and Nova Scotia Steelworkers'; Seager, 'Proletariat in Wild Rose Country'; Frank, 'Cape Breton Coal Miners'; Macgillivray, 'Industrial Unrest'; MacEwan, *Miners and Steelworkers*; McKay and Morton in this volume.

76 Naylor, *New Democracy*, 188–214.

77 *Labour Gazette*, May 1921, 709; and June 1921, 817.

78 Two years later total reported union membership had fallen by a further 17,000 to 260,000. Canada, Dept. of Labour, *Labour Organization in Canada*, 1921, 257; and 1924, 10.

79 Scott, '"A Place in the Sun"'; Naylor, *New Democracy*, 188–214; Parr, *Gender of Breadwinners*, 39–49; Seager, 'New Era for Labour?'; Heron, *Working in Steel*, 98–111; McCallum, 'Corporate Welfarism.'

80 Heron, *Working in Steel*, 105.

81 Morris, *Embattled Shadows*, 67–9; Naylor, *New Democracy*, 199. The Red Scare

deserves fuller research; see Avery, *'Dangerous Foreigners'* and *Reluctant Host;* Baxter, 'Selected Aspects of Canadian Public Opinion'; Samuels, 'Red Scare in Ontario'; Boudreau, 'Enemy Alien Problem'; Askin, 'Labour Unrest in Edmonton and District.' On the same campaign in the United States, see Murray, *Red Scare.*

82 Naylor, *New Democracy,* 199–201.

83 Ibid.; Naylor, 'Workers and the State'; Traves, *State and Enterprise,* 15–28.

84 Naylor, *New Democracy;* Heron, 'Working-Class Hamilton,' 522–59.

85 Rouillard, *Les syndicats nationaux;* Ewen in this volume.

86 Forbes, 'Rise and Fall of the Conservative Party' and *Maritimes Rights Movement;* McKay and Morton in this volume.

87 McCallum, 'Keeping Women in Their Place'; Linda Kealey, 'Women and Labour'; Campbell, 'Balance Wheel of the Industrial System'; Oliver, 'Sir William Hearst.'

88 Heron, 'High School and the Household Economy'; Mitchell, '"Manufacture of Souls of Good Quality."'

89 Siemiatycki, 'Labour Contained'; Robin, *Radical Politics and Canadian Labour;* Bercuson, *Fools and Wise Men;* Friesen, '"Yours in Revolt,"' 141. Gregory Kealey presents slightly different figures for the 1918 vote (a minority of fifty-eight easterners and thirty-two westerners versus a majority of three westerners and ninety-seven easterners) but notes that the pattern remains the same. The West sent only 45 of the 440 delegates to the 1918 convention, which was held in Quebec City. Kealey, '1919,' 36.

90 Bercuson, *Fools and Wise Men;* Bright, 'Bonds of Brotherhood?'; and '"We Are All Kin."'

91 Naylor, *New Democracy;* Ewen in this volume.

92 *Canadian Labor Press,* 1 March 1919.

93 Siemiatycki, 'Labour Contained.'

94 See Ewen and Naylor in this volume.

95 Robin, *Radical Politics and Canadian Labour;* Siemiatycki, 'Labour Contained'; Naylor, *New Democracy.*

96 Frank, 'Cape Breton Coal Miners'; Seager, 'Proletariat in Wild Rose Country'; Bercuson, *Confrontation at Winnipeg* and *Fools and Wise Men;* and the regional essays in this volume.

97 Naylor, *New Democracy;* Ewen in this volume; Heron, *Working in Steel.*

98 Radforth, *Bushworkers and Bosses;* Seager, 'Finnish Canadians' and 'Class, Ethnicity, and Politics'; Hogan, *Cobalt;* Rouillard, 'Les travailleurs juifs'; Frager, *Sweatshop Strife.*

99 McKay, *Craft Transformed;* Frank, 'Cape Breton Coal Miners'; MacEwan, *Miners and Steelworkers;* Heron, 'Great War and Nova Scotia Steelworkers.'

100 Ewen in this volume; Rouillard, *Histoire du syndicalisme québécois*, 134.

101 Heron and Palmer, 'Prism of the Strike'; Heron, 'Working-Class Hamilton'; Naylor, *New Democracy.*

102 In Amherst, Nova Scotia, the local labour movement affiliated with the OBU, as did its counterpart in Carleton Place, Ontario, and several northern Ontario miners' and loggers' organizations. In Montreal, Toronto, Hamilton, and a few smaller towns in southern Ontario, small groups of socialist militants set up local OBU units and set out to compete with the established local leadership for working-class support. Fred Flatman expanded the circulation of his Hamilton paper *New Democracy*, which became the eastern mouthpiece for the OBU. Reilly, 'General Strike in Amherst'; Bercuson, *Fools and Wise Men*; Naylor, *New Democracy*, 64–71.

103 Angus, *Canadian Bolsheviks*, 63–80; Rodney, *Soldiers of the International*; Avakumovic, *Communist Party*, 1–53; Buck, *Yours in the Struggle*, 89–140; Watson, *She Was Never Afraid*, 1–20; Vance, *Not by Gods*, 1–45; Avery, *'Dangerous Foreigners'*, 116–23; Frank, 'Working-Class Politics'; Akers, 'Rebel or Revolutionary?'; Campbell, '"Making Socialists"'; Manley, 'Preaching the Red Stuff'; Heron, 'Frederick J. Flatman.'

104 Naylor, 'Ontario Workers and the Decline of Labourism.'

105 McNaught, *Prophet in Politics*; Heaps, *Rebel in the House*; Steeves, *Compassionate Rebel*, 70–92; Mardiros, *William Irvine*, 109–204; Young, *Anatomy of a Party*, 2–37; Caplan, *Dilemma of Canadian Socialism*, 7–18; Avakumovic, *Socialism in Canada*, 11–70.

106 Palmer, *Working-Class Experience*, 214–67.

107 Ian McKay has developed this argument more fully in 'Industry, Work, and Community,' 800–28; *Craft Transformed*, 55–144; and (with Michael Earle), 'Introduction: Industrial Legality in Nova Scotia,' in Earle, ed., *Workers and the State*, 9–23.

108 Findlay, 'Protection of Workers in Industry.'

109 McNaught, *Prophet in Politics*, 215–20.

Conclusion

CRAIG HERON

Hoda hadn't even known she was a natural revolutionary till that day. Sure she was all for the strike and the workers, but she didn't really know what she could do till the day of the great parade when she saw the way the mounties were treating the strikers, and especially the way that cop was pushing Mr. Polonick around.

Adele Wiseman, *Crackpot*

'Don't make any mistake about it, the reasons these fellows were branded as Reds and Bolsheviki was because of what they had in here' – he struck his breast as he spoke – 'not because of their wrong thinking. The guys on the other side of the business, the big fellows who called out the Mounties and had the streets cleared with bullets, don't worry any about how we think. It's how we feel that's got them worrying.'

Douglas Durkin, *The Magpie*

The people are sitting with their heads in their hands, their eyes on the floor or the woolcoat back of a friend, their chins on their palms, all ears, *Listening*. And the words stitch their brows, harrow thinkinglines from eye to eye. When a face is full of such listening, it lights up from inside like a piece of paper written by the sun through a lens.

Margaret Sweatman, *Fox*

Something quite fundamentally new and different was happening in working-class Canada between 1917 and 1925. The *Winnipeg Citizen* was convinced it saw 'a determined attempt to establish Bolshevism and the rule of the Soviet here and then to expand it all over this Dominion.'[1] From far across the Atlantic, the Italian socialist Antonio Gramsci was similarly convinced that the struggles of Canadian workers had taken on 'the overt character of a bid to install a soviet system.'[2] Claims of an impending Russian-style proletarian revolution in Canada were without question exaggerated. Yet this is not to say that Canadian workers had no interest in changing their world in fundamental ways. The essays in this volume suggest that the story is much more complex than most accounts to date. They have attempted to shed light on four major controversies in the writing on the Canadian workers' revolt of 1917–25, namely, its overall shape, its goals, the causes of its demise, and its regional dimensions.

First, we have tried to clarify the proportions and the contours of the revolt. We traced its origins to the pre-war concerns about household economies and workplace rights, and found them intensified and transformed in the crucible of the wartime economy and state regulation. The revolt was a grass-roots movement that developed in working-class communities across the country in which rank-and-file workers' anger, frustration, and confidence overflowed the bounds of their employers' established workplace regimes, the mainstream political parties, and the existing craft union structures. It was evident in the explosion of strikes, the huge growth in union membership, the challenge to exclusivist union structures, the blossoming of independent labour parties, the expansion of the labour press, and the aggressive acts of solidarity taking place in the public spaces of towns and cities – all on a scale never before seen simultaneously across the country. Coordinating all this activism were community-based labour organizations that operated with increasing independence within the international craft union movement, that were often led by militants and radicals from outside the entrenched labour officialdom, and that were loosely linked to provincial or regional workers' movements. Although they moved boldly in mass industrial action, these organizations remained solidly within what they understood to be constitutional procedures. However passionately some elements within the workers' movements hoped to eradicate Canadian capitalism, European-style armed insurrection against an authoritarian state was not on the agenda. Far more important – and threatening to bourgeois rule – was the creation of powerful, autonomous working-class organizations capable of mobilizing support and championing workers' interests. Together the new workers' movements shook up political, social, and economic spheres and forced capitalists, politicians, labour officials, and clergymen, among many others, to respond. The generalized common sense about where workers fit in Canadian society was temporarily opened up to new definitions.

Second, we considered the working-class aspirations that lay at the heart of the revolt. While a revolt is not necessarily a revolution, it is implicitly and overtly a challenge to the structures of bourgeois power and the forms of workers' subordination. In this regard, the workers' revolt might best be seen as a resistance movement that emerged in response to the major changes that swept through Canadian society in the early twentieth century – changes that were accelerated in the wartime economy and spearheaded by corporate capital. The most visible banner over all the working-class agitation and organization of the period was inscribed with the simple yet flexible word 'democracy,' which took on clearly anti-capitalist overtones when used by workers to challenge the dominant social, economic, and political institutions of Canadian society. In all its manifestations, democratizing Canadian society meant more power for workers (especially male, white, English- and French-Canadian wage earners) – power to exercise some control over their workplace environment, to guarantee security for their families, to influence political decision-making, and, in general, to live a life of independence, dignity, and relative freedom. How much more power this would involve remained fluid and flexible. The yearning for a different kind of world that ran through so much of the almost millenarial rhetoric, and even the testimony before the Mathers Commission, suggests a much more open-ended vision of the future than the simple lists of political reforms or collective bargaining demands might suggest. To attempt to measure the degree of 'radicalism' or 'conservatism' among Canadian workers at this time is to overlook the open-ended potential of workers' movements organized and mobilized on an unprecedented scale; it was this potential that sent shivers through corporate boardrooms and cabinet chambers.

Third, we considered why working-class hopes were never realized in the post-war period. As we saw, the structure of Canadian industrial capitalism was such that workers were divided by industry, occupation, region, gender, and ethnicity. Their ability to withstand the organized resistance of capital and the state was further undermined by severe post-war depression. In addition, the isolation and numerical weakness of wage earners within the Canadian class structure forced awkward political alliances with farmers (and occasionally middle-class Canadians) that too often frustrated and undercut working-class demands. Most important, businessmen and political officials took their own anxious reading of Canadian political economy and, in an effort to ensure maximum flexibility for capital accumulation, launched a vigorous campaign to crush the radicals and mollify, at least temporarily, the more moderate labour leaders. In this context the internal tensions and limitations of the revolt became severely debilitating. Ethnic strains pitted workers against each other. Working-class women were largely marginalized. Even more damaging was the retreat of craft union officials who controlled the material and organizational resources for mobilizing and sustaining the revolt into a cautious and opportunistic exclusivism. At the same time, their socialist opponents split over an appropriate alternative strategy and eventually veered off into less effective brands of radical politics, namely, communism and parliamentary socialism. In the end it was the old-fashioned discipline of an overstocked labour market in the post-1920 depression that must have drained the hope and determination from the workers' revolt and pressed working-class families back into their own desperate survival strategies. Many responded to the call of various bourgeois forces that reformulated their grievances and resentments within less class-conscious frameworks of regional protest, ethnic nationalism, or industrial protectionism, thereby restoring the old 'common sense' of capitalist hegemony in a rigidly hierarchical society.

Finally, and perhaps most important, we explored the different regional experiences within the workers' revolt. No part of urban, industrial Canada went untouched by this working-class ferment, but in each region of the country its timing, intensity, and outcome reflected a particular industrial, occupational, and ethnic mix; distinctive provincial political cultures and government responses; and the region's accumulated history of working-class mobilization. The factors that led, for example, Winnipeg workers to walk off the job in May 1919 both anticipated and departed from those that compelled Cape Breton steelworkers and coal miners to down their tools four years later.

In the Maritimes we saw the spirit of solidarity, spearheaded by the coal miners and inspired by various radical leaders, spread through the urban industrial workforce in numerous towns and cities. In 1919, at a time when many workers in the West were under seige, many of the new unions in the Maritimes won remarkable concessions from their employers, while independent labour parties made significant breakthroughs into provincial politics. Serious defeats began only in 1920 and stretched through 1923 and 1925 in the steel and coal towns. One major weakness of the urban workers' movement had been the failure to cement a solid alliance with the region's many widely dispersed 'quasi-proletarian' rural workers. In the early 1920s the surging Tory-led Maritime Rights movement was better able to draw on the region's paternalistic traditions and cast its mantle over all 'producers.' By shifting the battle lines to federal–provincial relations, these Tories touched a responsive chord in a region beset by economic crisis and helped to diffuse the class consciousness that still emanated from the last isolated bastions of the revolt in the coal towns.

The revolt in Quebec had the same militant character that distinguished labour upsurges in the rest of the country. Like its counterpart in the Maritimes, it carried into 1920 before the first crushing defeats were felt. And it too suffered from a lack of urban–rural solidarity. The divide between the dynamic centre of working-class activism in Montreal and the rural workforce in resource industries widened as Catholic unionism recruited its largest numbers outside Montreal. Perhaps most important, the workers' revolt in Quebec foundered on the rocks of ethnic tension. Mutual suspicion among francophone, anglophone, and European-born workers made the deepening right–left splits even more complicated. In a familiar pattern in Canadian history, the French in particular were isolated from other workers by their intense hostility to military conscription, the lingering strength of 'Lib-Labism' among francophone labour leaders, the new support for Catholic unionism, and male francophone indifference to the rights of working-class women. The obstacles to working-class unity in the province were thus almost insurmountable.

Southern Ontario's working class was similarly confronted with long-entrenched forces of containment. Yet the province's many new radical leaders, together with thousands of wage earners (including the all-important factory workers), challenged corporate power and small-town paternalism and managed to win some fragile concessions by the end of the war. Thousands more helped to propel the Independent Labor Party into a coalition government with the farmers in 1919. But the workers' challenge was restrained by the deep commitment of well-entrenched craft union officials to industrial legality and their equally strong suspicion of industrial unionism. In the post-war strike wave, the region's industrialists gave no ground in workplace struggles, and, when workers' political representatives also failed to implement an effective legislative program, soon managed to re-establish their concerns about tariff protection as the central dynamic of southern Ontario's Tory political culture.

In the Prairie provinces working-class movements generally took their lead from the small clusters of urban craftsmen and, even more so, from the highly skilled metalworkers in the region's important railway shops (Canada's closest equivalent to the famous British shops stewards). Their ranks contained a sprinkling of mostly British and European-born socialists whose impact on the local workers' movements was greater than that of their counterparts in central Canada, in part because craft union officialdom was more distant and much weaker in the Prairie provinces, and in part because wage earners there had a wartime history of successful mass mobilization. While the ideology of regional elites had little appeal to these workers, their antipathy to the power and behaviour of institutions in the 'East' did help to shape a regional consciousness that prompted a secession from the mainstream in the form of the One Big Union. This particular mix of industrial and occupational structure, politics, and accumulated experience of struggle helps to explain how this region witnessed the most celebrated expression of the workers' revolt – the Winnipeg General Strike – and the series of sympathy strikes that followed.

The workers' revolt in British Columbia and the mining west shared with its Prairies counterpart pockets of radicalism (in this case, in some of the major resource industries) that flourished far from craft union headquarters. As in the past, coal miners in the eastern Rockies (though not on Vancouver Island) and other resource-industry workers gave the region's working-class movements much of their dynamism and drew them into the One Big Union experiment. But the intractable division between whites and Asians, coupled with the fragility of many of the resource industries, left organized wage earners highly vulnerable to the counter-attacks of employers and the state.

Viewed in its entirety, the workers' revolt of 1917–25 created a moment of crisis in the evolution of Canadian industrial capitalism. Like the massive farmers' revolt in the same period, it raised questions about how much freedom Canadian industrialists should have in pursuing their capital accumulation strategies, and about how democratically the state would function. The defeat of both movements meant that for the next two decades Canada's corporate capitalists, like their American counterparts, would not be obliged to negotiate either their right to rule or their mechanisms of power, as their counterparts in Britain and several European countries did to some extent. The repressive policing power of the state had been permanently strengthened just in case. The beleaguered craftworkers who had played such an important, if ambivalent, role in the post-war upsurge had made their last stand on the principles of craft pride and democracy – principles that had guided labour organizing since the mid-nineteenth century. They sank beneath the waves of authoritarian discipline, scientific management, and mass production that swept over Canadian workplaces in the 1920s.[3] Indeed, the heyday of a working class dominated by male blue-collar wage-earners had begun its long-term decline, as the huge, centralized corporate administrations continued to expand their clerical and professional staffs.[4] Moreover, as Canadian workers were forced away from mass collective organizing and back to family and neighbourhood for survival strategies, they faced increasing pressures to reshape the family economies and community cultures that lay at the heart of working-class life – pressures resulting from prolonged unemployment (and underemployment) in the interwar decades, compulsory schooling and the rapid decline of child labour, interventions by social workers and public health professionals, the growth of commercialized entertainment (especially movies and radio), and the first glimmer of consumerism.[5] The working-class indentities of the next generation of activists would be informed by experience within smaller families, prolonged schooling, mass-market popular culture, and consumerist persuasions.

There remains much to be written on the subject of the post-war workers' revolt. We still know relatively little about the stirrings of both 'quasi-proletarian' rural wage earners and white-collar workers such as teachers or state employees. Our understanding of non-Anglo-Canadian working-class communities after the war is similarly limited. Labour historians need to follow wage earners into their tight-knit working-class neighbourhoods to see what role these small urban communities played in the wider class mobilization.[6] The role of veterans in post-war working-class Canada has also escaped scholarly attention for far too long.[7] The political impact of workers at the municipal level and their ability to influence the evolution of urban life in Canada deserve further research as well,[8] as do the various responses of provincial governments, which have for too long been overshadowed by the manoeevres of federal governments.[9] For a better understanding of working-class politics in general, we need to examine socialism not as a synonym for Bolshevism but as an evolving ideology within the larger revolt.[10] More work remains to be done, as well, on the organization and impact of the post-war Red Scare. Finally, we need a much more thorough study of the post-1920 slump in the Canadian economy, a depression that gave the lie to the expression 'roaring twenties.'

Like so many other unsuccessful social movements in Canadian history, the workers' revolt of 1917–25 has been forgotten, ignored, or marginalized in the historical record. Throughout this book we have presented the workers' revolt as a defining moment in Canadian working-class history. Thousands of Canadian workers tried to get the power to give 'progress' a different meaning. Their failure should never be seen as demeaning their commitment or their aspirations. At the close of the twentieth century, as capitalist nations celebrate the triumph of 'democracy' in the former Communist countries, we should remember that masses of Canadian workers once confronted capitalism as a denial of democracy and justice. They could well do it again.

Notes

1 Quoted in Penner, ed., *Winnipeg 1919*, 55.

2 J. Matthews and Quintin Hoare, eds., *Gramsci: Selections from the Prison Writings, 1910–1920* (New York 1977), 61 (thanks to Allen Seager).

3 Parr, *Gender of Breadwinners*; Manley, 'Communists and Canadian Autoworkers'; Heron, 'Working-Class Hamilton.'

4 Lowe, *Women in the Administrative Revolution*.

5 Thompson and Seager, *Canada, 1922–1939*, 76–103, 175–92; MacIntosh, 'Boys in the Nova Scotia Coal Mines'; Copp, *Anatomy of Poverty*; Coulter, 'Working Young of Edmonton'; Heron, 'High School and the Household Economy'; Canada, Dept. of Labour, *Employment of Children*; Sutherland, *Children in English-Canadian Society*; Pitsula, 'Emergence of Social Work'; Struthers, 'Profession in Crisis'; Morton, *Ideal Surroundings*; Rosenfeld, '"It Was a Hard Life"'; Parr, *Gender of Breadwinners*.

6 There are helpful insights in Harney, ed., *Gathering Place*; Working Lives-Collective, *Working Lives*; Morton, *Ideal Surroundings*; Harris, '"Canada's All Right"'; Harris and Sendbuehler, 'Hamilton's East End'; Hiebert, 'Class, Ethnicity, and Residential Structure.'

7 Morton and Wright provided a good starting point in *Winning the Second Battle*. See also Morton, *When Your Number's Up*; Lees, 'Problems of Pacification'; and Sephton, 'Soldier Problem.'

8 See, for example, Barman, 'Knowledge Is Essential'; Maciejko, 'Public

Schools and the Workers' Struggle'; Frank, 'Company Town/Labour Town'; Rea, 'Politics of Class'; Avery, 'Ethnic Loyalties and the Proletarian Revolution'; Nelles and Armstrong, 'Great Fight for Clean Government'; and Taylor, 'Sources of Political Conflict.'

9 See, for example, Irving, 'Development of a Provincial Welfare State,' 158–62; McCallum, 'Keeping Women in Their Place'; Crossley, 'B.C. Liberal Party and Women's Reforms'; Strong-Boag, 'Wages for Housework'; and Lorentsen and Woolner, 'Fifty Years of Labour Legislation,' 102–14.

10 An excellent start is made in Akers, 'Rebel or Revolutionary?'; Campbell, '"Making Socialists"' and '"Stalwarts of the Struggle"'; Friesen, 'Bob Russell's Political Thought'; and McKay, ed., *For a Working-Class Culture.*

Bibliography

Abella, Irving, and David Millar, eds. *The Canadian Worker in the Twentieth Century.* Toronto: Oxford University Press 1978.

Akers, David. 'Rebel or Revolutionary? Jack Kavanagh and the Early Years of the Communist Movement in Vancouver, 1920–1925.' *Labour/Le Travail* 30 (Fall 1992), 9–44.

Allen, Richard. 'Salem Bland and the Social Gospel in Canada.' MA thesis, University of Saskatchewan 1961.

– *The Social Passion: Religion and Social Reform in Canada, 1914–1928.* Toronto: University of Toronto Press 1973.

Anderson, Perry. 'The Antimonies of Antonio Gramsci.' *New Left Review* 100 (November 1976–January 1977), 5–78.

– *Lineages of the Absolutist State.* London: New Left Books 1974.

Andrae, C.G. 'The Swedish Labour Movement and the 1917–18 Revolution.' In Steven Koblik, ed., *Sweden's Development from Poverty to Affluence, 1750–1970,* 232–53. Minneapolis: University of Minnesota Press 1975.

Angel, Eric, 'Restoring Order: The RNWMP and the Winnipeg General Strike of 1919.' Unpublished paper, Queen's University 1992.

– 'Workers, Picketing, and the Winnipeg General Strike of 1919.' MA thesis, Queen's University 1995.

Angus, Ian. *Canadian Bolsheviks: The Early Years of the Communist Party of Canada.* Montreal: Vanguard Press 1981.

Armstrong, Elizabeth. *The Crisis of Quebec, 1914–1918.* Toronto: McClelland and Stewart 1974 [1937].

Armstrong, Robert. 'The Quebec Asbestos Industry: Technological Change, 1878–1929.' In Duncan Cameron, ed., *Explorations in Canadian Economic History: Essays in Honour of Irene M. Spry,* 189–210. Ottawa: University of Ottawa Press 1985.

Askin, W.R. 'Labour Unrest in Edmonton and District and Its Coverage by the Edmonton Press: 1918–19.' MA thesis, University of Alberta 1973.

Avakumovic, Ivan. *The Communist Party in Canada: A History.* Toronto: McClelland and Stewart 1975.

– *Socialism in Canada: A Study of the CCF-NDP in Federal and Provincial Politics.* Toronto: McClelland and Stewart 1978.

Avery, Donald. 'Canadian Immigration Policy and the "Foreign" Navvy, 1896–1914.' In Michael S. Cross and Gregory S. Kealey, eds., *The Consoldiation of Canadian Capitalism, 1896–1929,* 47–73. Toronto: McClelland and Stewart 1983.

– *'Dangerous Foreigners': European Immigrant Workers and Labour Radicalism in Canada, 1896–1932.* Toronto: McClelland and Stewart 1979.

– 'Divided Loyalties: The Ukrainian Left and the Canadian State.' In Lubomyr Luciuk and Stella Hryniuk, eds., *Canadian Ukrainians: Negotiating an Identity,* 271–87. Toronto: University of Toronto Press 1991.

– 'Ethnic and Class Tensions in Canada, 1918–1920: Anglo-Canadians and the Alien Worker.' In Frances Swyripa and John Herd Thompson, eds., *Loyalties in Conflict: Ukrainians in Canada During the Great War,* 79–98. Edmonton: Canadian Institute of Ukrainain Studies, University of Alberta 1983.

– 'Ethnic Loyalties and the Proletarian Revolution: A Case Study of Communist Political Activity in Winnipeg, 1923–1936.' In Jorgen Dahlie and Tissa Fernando, eds., *Ethnicity, Power, and Politics in Canada,* 68–93. Toronto: Methuen 1981.

– 'The Radical Alien and the Winnipeg General Strike of 1919.' In Carl Berger and Ramsay Cook, eds., *The West and the Nation: Essays in Honour of W.L. Morton,* 209–31. Toronto: McClelland and Stewart 1976.

– *Reluctant Host: Canada's Response to Immigrant Workers, 1896–1994.* Toronto: McClelland and Stewart 1995.

Babcock, Robert H. *Gompers in Canada: A Study in American Continentalism before the First World War.* Toronto: University of Toronto Press 1974.

– 'Saint John Longshoremen during the Rise of Canada's Winter Port, 1895–1922.' *Labour/Le Travail* 25 (Spring 1990), 15–46.

– 'Samuel Gompers and the Berlin Decisions of 1902.' In Richard A. Preston, ed., *The Influence of the United States on Canadian Development: Eleven Case Studies.* Durham, N.C.: Duke University Press 1972.

– 'Samuel Gompers and the French Canadian Worker.' *American Review of Canadian Studies* 3, no. 2 (Autumn 1973), 47–66.

Bacchi, Carol Lee. *Liberation Deferred? The Ideas of the English-Canadian Suffragists, 1877–1918.* Toronto: University of Toronto Press 1983.

Badgley, Kerry. 'Ringing out the Narrowing Lust of Gold, Ringing in the Common Love of Good: The United Farmers of Ontario in Lambton, Simcoe, and Lanark Counties, 1914–1926.' PhD diss., Carleton University 1996.

Baker, Angela. 'Drawn to Hegemony: The Maritime Rights Movement and the *Halifax Herald*, 1921–1926.' MA thesis, Queen's University 1995.

Barman, Jean, '"Knowledge Is Essential for Universal Progress but Fatal to Class Privilege": Working People and the Schools in Vancouver during the 1920s.' *Labour/Le Travail* 22 (Fall 1988), 9–66.

– *The West beyond the West: A History of British Columbia*. Toronto: University of Toronto Press 1991.

– 'A Tradition Emerges.' In Patricia E. Roy, ed., *A History of British Columbia: Selected Readings*. Toronto: Copp Clark Pitman 1989.

Barrett, Gene. 'Development and Underdevelopment and the Rise of Trade Unionism in the Fishing Industry of Nova Scotia, 1900–1950.' MA thesis, Dalhousie University 1976.

– 'Underdevelopment and Social Movements in the Nova Scotia Fishing Industry to 1938.' In Robert J. Brym and R. James Sacouman, eds., *Underdevelopment and Social Movements in Atlantic Canada*, 127–60. Toronto: New Hogtown Press 1979.

Bartlett, Eleanor A. 'Real Wages and the Standard of Living in Vancouver, 1901–1929.' *BC Studies* 51 (Autumn 1981), 3–62.

Bausenhart, Werner A. 'The Ontario German Language Press and Its Suppression by Order-in-Council in 1918.' *Canadian Ethnic Studies* 4, nos. 1–2 (1972), 35–48.

Baxter, Theresa Catherine. 'Selected Aspects of Canadian Public Opinion on the Russian Revolution and Its Impact in Canada, 1917–19.' MA thesis, University of Western Ontario 1973.

Bercuson, David J. *Confrontation at Winnipeg: Labour, Industrial Relations, and the General Strike*. Kingston and Montreal: McGill-Queen's University Press 1974; 2nd ed., 1990.

– *Fools and Wise Men: The Rise and Fall of the One Big Union*. Toronto: McGraw-Hill Ryerson 1978.

– 'Labour Radicalism and the Western Industrial Frontier.' *Canadian Historical Review* 58, no. 2 (June 1977), 154–77.

– 'Organized Labour and the Imperial Munitions Board' *Relations industrielles/ Industrial Relations* 28 (1973), 602–16.

– 'Syndicalism Sidetracked: Canada's One Big Union.' In Marcel van der Linden and Wayne Thorpe, eds., *Revolutionary Syndicalism: An International Perspective*, 221–36. Aldershot, Eng.: Scolar Press 1990.

– 'Western Labour Radicalism and the One Big Union: Myths and Realities.' In S.M. Trofimenkoff, ed., *The Twenties in Western Canada*, 32–49. Ottawa: National Museum of Man 1972.

Berkowski, Gerry. 'A Tradition in Jeopardy: Building Trades Workers' Responses to Industrial Capitalism in Winnipeg, 1880–1914.' MA thesis, University of Manitoba 1986.

Bernard, Elaine. 'Last Back: Folklore and the Telephone Operators in the 1919 Vancouver General Strike.' In Barbara K. Latham and Roberta J. Pazdro, eds., *Not Just Pin Money: Selected Essays on the History of Women's Work in British Columbia*, 279–86. Victoria: Camosun College 1984.

– *The Long Distance Feeling: A History of the Telecommunications Workers' Union.* Vancouver: New Star Books 1982.

Bertrand, Charles, ed. *Revolutionary Situations in Europe, 1917–1922: Germany, Italy, Austria-Hungary.* Montreal: Centre interuniversitaire d'études européennes 1971.

Black, Errol, and Tom Black. 'Labour in Brandon Civic Politics: A Long View.' *Manitoba History* 23 (Spring 1992), 2–16.

Bland, Salem. *The New Christianity, or the Religion of the New Age.* Toronto: University of Toronto Press 1973 [1920].

Bliss, Michael. *A Canadian Millionaire: The Life and Business Times of Sir Joseph Flavelle, Bart., 1858–1939.* Toronto: Macmillan 1978.

– 'The Methodist Church and World War I.' *Canadian Historical Review* 49, no. 3 (September 1968), 213–33.

Borden, Robert. *Memoirs.* Toronto: McClelland and Stewart 1969 [1938].

Boudreau, Joseph. 'The Enemy Alien Problem in Canada, 1914–1921.' PhD diss., University of California 1964.

– 'Western Canada's "Enemy Aliens" in World War One.' *Alberta Historical Review* 12, no. 1 (Winter 1964), 1–9.

Bradbury, Bettina. *Working Families: Age, Gender, and Daily Survival in Industrializing Montreal.* Toronto: McClelland and Stewart 1993.

Bradwin, Edmund. *The Bunkhouse Man: A Study of Work and Pay in the Camps of Canada, 1903–1914.* Toronto: University of Toronto Press 1972 [1928].

Bray, R. Matthew. 'The Canadian Patriotic Response to the Great War.' PhD diss., York University 1976.

– '"Fighting as an Ally": The English-Canadian Response to the Great War.' *Canadian Historical Review* 61, no. 2 (June 1980), 141–68.

Brecher, Michael. 'Patterns of Accommodation in the Men's Garment Industry in Quebec, 1914–1954.' In H.D. Woods, ed., *Patterns of Dispute Settlements in Five Canadian Industries*, 89–186. Montreal: Industrial Relations Centre, McGill University 1958.

Brennan, J. William. *Regina: An Illustrated History.* Toronto: James Lorimer 1989.

Bright, David. 'Bonds of Brotherhood? The Experiences of Labour in Calgary, 1903–1919.' MA thesis, University of Calgary 1990.

– '"We Are All Kin": Reconsidering Labour and Class in Calgary, 1919.' *Labour/Le Travail* 29 (Spring 1992), 59–80.

British Columbia, Department of Labour. *Reports*. Victoria: Queen's Printer.

Brody, David. *Steelworkers in America: The Nonunion Era*. Cambridge: Harvard University Press 1960.

Brown, Desmond H. 'The Craftsmanship of Bias: Sedition and the Winnipeg General Strike Trial, 1919.' *Manitoba Law Journal* 14, no. 1 (1984), 1–33.

– *The Genesis of the Canadian Criminal Code of 1892*. Toronto: University of Toronto Press 1989.

Brown, Robert Craig. *Robert Laird Borden: A Biography*. Vol. 2, *1914–1937*. Toronto: Macmillan 1980.

Brown, Robert Craig, and Ramsay Cook. *Canada, 1896–1921: A Nation Transformed*. Toronto: McClelland and Stewart 1974.

Brubaker, Rogers. *Citizenship and Nationhood in France and Germany*. Cambridge: Harvard University Press 1992.

Buck, Tim. *Canada and the Russian Revolution: The Impact of the World's First Socialist Revolution on Labor and Politics in Canada*. Toronto: Progress Books 1967.

– *Thirty Years: The Story of the Communist Movement in Canada, 1922–1952*. Toronto: Progress Books 1952.

– *Yours in the Struggle: Reminiscences of Tim Buck*. Edited by William Beeching and Phyllis Clarke. Toronto: NC Press 1977.

Bumsted, J.M. '1919: The Winnipeg General Strike Reconsidered.' *The Beaver* 74, no. 3 (May 1994), 27–44.

– 'Was the Winnipeg General Strike of 1919 Revolutionary?' Paper presented to the Manitoba History Conference, University of Manitoba 1994.

– *The Winnipeg General Strike of 1919: An Illustrated History*. Winnipeg: Watson Dwyer 1994.

Burnet, Jean, with Howard Palmer. *'Coming Canadians': An Introduction to a History of Canada's Peoples*. Toronto: McClelland and Stewart 1988.

Butt, Michael. '"To Each According to His Need, and From Each According to His Ability. Why Cannot the World See This?": The Politics of William Ivens, 1916–1936.' MA thesis, University of Winnipeg 1993.

Cahan, Jacqueline F. 'A Survey of the Political Activities of the Ontario Labour Movement, 1850–1935.' MA thesis, University of Toronto 1945.

Cahill, Barry. '"More Echoes from Labor's Wars" in Comparative Legal History: *Howe* (1835), *Russell* (1919) and *Dixon* (1920), and the Historiography of *R vs McLachlan*, 1923.' Paper presented to Atlantic Workshop on History and the Law, Dalhousie University 1995.

Calliste, Agnes. 'Sleeping Car Porters in Canada: An Ethnically Submerged Split Labour Market.' *Canadian Ethnic Studies* 19, no. 1 (1987), 1–20.

Cameron, James M. *Industrial History of New Glasgow District*. New Glasgow: n.p. 1960.

– *The Pictonian Colliers*. Halifax: Nova Scotia Museum 1974.

Campbell, Allison. 'Beatrice Brigden: The Formative Years of a Socialist Feminist, 1888–1912.' MA thesis, University of Winnipeg 1991.

Campbell, Elizabeth Jane. '"The Balance Wheel of the Industrial System": Maximum Hours, Minimum Wage and Workmen's Compensation Legislation in Ontario, 1900–1939.' PhD diss., McMaster University 1980.

Campbell, Marie. 'Sexism in British Columbia Trade Unions, 1900–1920.' In Barbara Latham and Cathy Kess, eds., *In Her Own Right: Selected Essays on Women's History in B.C.*, 167–86. Victoria: Camosun College 1980.

Campbell, Peter. '"Making Socialists": Bill Pritchard, the Socialist Party of Canada, and the Third International.' *Labour/Le Travail* 30 (Fall 1992), 45–63.

– '"Stalwarts of the Struggle": Canadian Marxists of the Third Way, 1879–1939.' PhD diss., Queen's University 1991.

Canada. Department of Labour. *The Employment of Children and Young Persons*. Ottawa: King's Printer 1930.

– *Labour Organization in Canada*. Ottawa: King's Printer 1911–25.

Canada. Dominion Bureau of Statistics. *Canada Yearbook*. Ottawa: King's Printer 1914–25.

Canada. National Industrial Conference of Dominion and Provincial Governments with Representative Employers and Labour Men, on the Subjects of Industrial Relations and Labour Laws, and for the Consideration of the Labour Features of the Treaty of Peace. *Official Report of Proceedings and Discussions Together with Various Memoranda Relating to the Conference and the Report of the Royal Commission on Industrial Relations*. Ottawa: King's Printer 1919.

Canada. Royal Commission to Inquire into the Methods by which Oriental Labourers Have Been Induced to Come to Canada. *Report*. Ottawa: King's Printer 1908.

Caplan, Gerald L. *The Dilemma of Canadian Socialism: The CCF in Ontario*. Toronto: McClelland and Stewart 1973.

Caragata, Warren. *Alberta Labour: A Heritage Untold*. Toronto: James Lorimer 1979.

– 'The Labour Movement in Alberta: An Untold Story.' In David Leadbeater, ed., *Essays in the Political Economy of Alberta*, 99–137. Toronto: New Hogtown Press 1984.

Carnegie, David. *The History of Munitions and Supply in Canada, 1914–1918*. London: Longmans, Green 1925.

Carr, E.H. *The Bolshevik Revolution, 1917–23*. London: Pelican 1966.

Chapman, J.K. 'Henry Harvey Stuart (1873–1952): New Brunswick Reformer.' *Acadiensis* 5, no. 2 (Spring 1976), 79–104.

Charpentier, Alfred. *Cinquante ans d'action ouvrière: Les mémoires d'Alfred Charpentier.* Quebec: Les Presses de l'Université Laval 1971.

– 'Le mouvement politique ouvrière de Montréal (1883–1929).' In Fernand Harvey, ed., *Aspects historiques du mouvement ouvrier au Québec*, 147–68. Montreal: Boréal Express 1973.

Chartrand, Rodolphe, *Une certaine alliance: 60 ans ... et après*. Montreal: Alliance des professeurs de Montréal (CEQ) 1980.

Cherwinski, W.J.C. 'Organized Labour in Saskatchewan: The T.L.C. Years, 1905–1945.' PhD diss., University of Alberta 1972.

Chisick, Ernest. 'The Development of Winnipeg's Socialist Movement, 1900–1915.' MA thesis, University of Manitoba 1972.

Clark, S.D. *The Canadian Manufacturers' Association: A Study in Collective Bargaining and Political Pressure*. Toronto: University of Toronto Press 1939.

Clement, Wallace. *The Struggle to Organize: Resistance in Canada's Fisheries*. Toronto: McClelland and Stewart 1986.

Cleverdon, Catherine. *The Woman Suffrage Movement in Canada*. Toronto: University of Toronto Press 1950.

Coates, Ken, ed. *British Labour and the Russian Revolution: The Leeds Conference, A Report from the Daily Herald*. Nottingham, Eng.: Russell Press n.d. [1917].

Cole, Curtis Johnson. 'The War Measures Act, 1914: Aspects of Emergency Limitation of Freedom of Speech and Personal Liberties in Canada, 1914–1919.' MA thesis, University of Western Ontario 1980.

Colpitt, Nancy. 'Alma, New Brunswick and the Twentieth-Century Crisis of Readjustment: Sawmilling Community to National Park.' MA thesis, Dalhousie University 1983.

Communist Party of Canada, *Canada's Party of Socialism: History of the Communist Party of Canada, 1921–1976*. Toronto: Progress Books 1986.

Conley, James R. 'Class Conflict and Collective Action in the Working Class of Vancouver, British Columbia, 1900–1919.' PhD diss., Carleton University 1986.

– 'Employers' Strategies and Workers' Responses in Five Vancouver Industries, 1900–1919.' Paper presented to the B.C. Studies Conference, November 1988.

– 'Frontier Labourers, Crafts in Crisis, and the Western Labour Revolt: The Case of Vancouver, 1900–1919.' *Labour/Le Travail* 23 (Spring 1989), 9–38.

Connor, Ralph. *To Him that Hath: A Novel of the West Today.* Toronto: McClelland and Stewart 1921.

Cook, D.G. 'Western Radicalism and the Winnipeg Strike.' MA thesis, McMaster University 1921.

Cook, Ramsay. *The Politics of John W. Dafoe and 'The Free Press'* Toronto: University of Toronto Press 1971.

Copp, Terry. *The Anatomy of Poverty: The Condition of the Working Class in Montreal, 1897–1929*. Toronto: McClelland and Stewart 1974.

Corrigan, Philip, and Derek Sayer. *The Great Arch: English State Formation as Cultural Revolution*. Oxford: Basil Blackwell 1991.

Corry, J.A. 'The Growth of Government Activities in Canada, 1914–1921.' Canadian Historical Association. *Annual Report*, 1940, 63–73.

Coulter, Rebecca. 'The Working Young of Edmonton, 1921–1931.' In Joy Parr, ed., *Childhood and Family in Canadian History*, 143–59. Toronto: McClelland and Stewart 1982.

Cowan, George. 'Canadian Industry and the Chinese Question.' In J. Castell Hopkins, ed., *Canada: An Encyclopedia*, 499–507. Toronto: Linscott Publishing 1898.

Cramer, Michael H. 'Public and Political: Documents of the Women's Suffrage Campaign.' In Barbara Latham and Cathy Kess, eds., *In Her Own Right: Selected Essays on Women's History in B.C.*, 229–54. Victoria: Camosun College 1980.

Craven, Paul, *'An Impartial Umpire': Industrial Relations and the Canadian State, 1900–1911*. Toronto: University of Toronto Press 1980.

Craven, Paul, and Tom Traves. 'The Class Politics of the National Policy, 1872–1933.' *Journal of Canadian Studies*. 14, no. 3 (Fall 1979), 14–38.

Creese, Gillian. 'Class, Ethnicity, and Conflict: The Case of Chinese and Japanese Immigrants, 1880–1923.' In Rennie Warburton and David Coburn, eds., *Workers, Capital and the State in British Columbia: Selected Papers*, 55–85. Vancouver: UBC Press 1988.

– 'Exclusion or Solidarity? Vancouver Workers Confront the "Oriental Problem."' *BC Studies* 80 (Winter 1988–89), 24–51.

– 'Organizing against Racism in the Workplace: Chinese Workers in Vancouver before the Second World War.' *Canadian Ethnic Studies* 19, no. 3 (1987), 35–46.

– 'The Politics of Dependence: Women, Work, and Unemployment in the Vancouver Labour Movement before World War II.' In Gregory S. Kealey, ed., *Class, Gender, and Region: Essays in Canadian Historical Sociology*, 121–42. St John's: Committee on Canadian Labour History 1988.

– 'Working-Class Politics, Racism, and Sexism: The Making of a Politically Divided Working Class in Vancouver, 1900–1939.' PhD diss., Carleton University 1986.

Cronin, James E. 'Labor Insurgency and Class Formation: Comparative Perspectives on the Crisis of 1917–1920 in Europe.' In James E. Cronin and Carmen Sirianni, eds., *Work, Community, and Power: The Experience of Labor in*

Europe and America, 1900–1925, 20–48. Philadelphia: Temple University Press 1983.

Cross, Gary. *A Quest for Time: The Reduction of Work in Britain and France*. Berkeley: University of California Press 1989.

– ed. *Worktime and Industrialization: An International History*. Philadelphia: Temple University Press 1988.

Crossley, Diane. 'The B.C. Liberal Party and Women's Reforms, 1916–1928.' In Barbara Latham and Cathy Kess, eds., *In Her Own Right: Selected Essays on Women's History in B.C.*, 229–54. Victoria: Camosun College 1980.

Cruikshank, Douglas. 'Young Masters and Old Journeymen.' Paper presented to the Vancouver History Group Workshop, November 1989.

Cruikshank, Douglas, and Gregory S. Kealey. 'Canadian Strike Statistics, 1891–1950.' *Labour/Le Travail* 20 (Fall 1987), 85–145.

Cuff, R.D. 'Organizing for War: Canada and the United States during World War I.' In R.D. Cuff and J.L. Granatstein, eds., *Ties That Bind: Canadian–American Relations in Wartime from the Great War to the Cold War*, 3–20. Toronto: Samuel Stevens Hakkert and Company 1977.

Dagenais, Michèle. 'Division sexuelle du travail en milieu bancaire: Montréal, 1900–1930.' MA thesis, Université du Québec à Montréal 1987.

Dales, John H. *Hydroelectricity and Industrial Development: Quebec, 1898–1940*. Cambridge: Harvard University Press 1957.

Damji, Alimohamed. 'Militancy to Passivism: The Calgary Labour Movement, 1919–1924.' MA thesis, University of Calgary 1987.

Dansereau, Bernard. 'Le mouvement ouvrier montréalais et la crise de la conscription, 1916–1918.' MA thesis, Université du Québec à Montréal 1994.

Deux grèves de l' 'Internationale': Aux chantiers Davie et à la Dominion Textile. Quebec: L'Action catholique 1919.

Devlin, Richard F. 'Law's Centaurs: An Inquiry into the Nature and Relations of Law, State, and Violence.' *Osgoode Hall Law Journal* 27, no. 2 (Summer 1989), 220–93.

De Zwaan, George. 'The Little Birmingham on the St. Lawrence: An Industrial and Labour History of Gananoque, Ontario, 1871–1921.' PhD diss., Queen's University 1987.

Dick, Lyle. 'Politics and Discourse. A Review of "1919: The Winnipeg General Strike: A Driving and Walking Tour."' *Manitoba History* 13 (Spring 1987).

Doherty, Bill. *Slaves of the Lamp: A History of the Federal Civil Service Organizations, 1865–1924*. Victoria: Orca Book Publishers 1991.

Donegan, Rosemary. 'The Iconography of Labour: An Overview of Canadian Materials.' *Archivaria* 27 (Winter 1988–89), 35–56.

Doré, Michel, et al. *The History of the Quebec Labour Movement*. Montreal: Black Rose Books 1988.

Dumont, Fernand. 'Histoire du syndicalisme dans l'industrie de l'amiante.' In Pierre Elliott Trudeau, ed., *La grève de l'amiante*, 125–34. Montreal: Editions du Jour 1970.

Durkin, Douglas. *The Magpie*. Toronto: Hodder and Stoughton 1923.

Earle, Michael, ed. *Workers and the State in Twentieth Century Nova Scotia*. Fredericton: Acadiensis Press 1989.

Eksteins, Modris. *Rites of Spring: The Great War and the Birth of the Modern Age*. Toronto: Lester and Orpen Dennys 1989.

Elections BC. *The Electoral History of British Columbia, 1871–1986*. Victoria 1988.

English, John. *The Decline of Politics: The Conservatives and the Party System, 1901–1920*. Toronto: University of Toronto Press 1977.

Entz, W. 'The Suppression of the German Language Press in September 1918.' *Canadian Ethnic Studies* 8, no. 2 (1976), 56–70.

Ewen, Geoffrey. 'La contestation à Montréal en 1919.' Regroupement des Chercheurs en Histoire des Travailleurs et Travailleuses Québécois, *Histoire des Travailleurs Québécois* 36 (Autumn 1986), 37–62.

– 'The Ideas of Gustave Francq as Expressed in *Le Monde Ouvrier/The Labor World*.' MA thesis, University of Ottawa 1981.

Fast, Vera. 'The Labour Church in Winnipeg.' In Dennis L. Butcher et al., eds., *Prairie Spirit: Perspectives on the Heritage of the United Church of Canada in the West*. Winnipeg: University of Manitoba Press 1985.

Ferguson, Barry. *Remaking Liberalism: The Intellectual Legacy of Adam Shortt, O.D. Skelton, W.C. Clark, and W.A. Mackintosh, 1890–1925*. Kingston and Montreal: McGill-Queen's University Press 1993.

Fillmore, Nicholas. *Maritime Radical: The Life and Times of Roscoe Fillmore*. Toronto: Between the Lines 1992.

Fillmore, Roscoe. 'Early Socialism in the Maritimes.' *Acadiensis* 11, no. 2 (Spring 1982), 84–94.

Findlay, Marion. 'Protection of Workers in Industry.' In W.P.M. Kennedy, ed., *Social and Economic Conditions in the Dominion of Canada*, 254–66. Philadelphia: American Academy of Political and Social Science 1923.

Finkel, Alvin. 'The Rise and Fall of the Labour Party in Alberta, 1917–1942.' *Labour/Le Travail* 16 (Fall 1985), 61–96.

Forbes, Ernest R. *The Maritime Rights Movement, 1919–1927: A Study in Canadian Regionalism*. Kingston and Montreal: McGill-Queen's University Press 1979.

– 'Prohibition and the Social Gospel in Nova Scotia.' In E.R. Forbes, *Challenging the Regional Stereotypes: Essays on the Twentieth-Century Maritimes*, 13–40. Fredericton: Acadiensis Press 1989.

– 'The Rise and Fall of the Conservative Party in the Provincial Politics of Nova Scotia, 1922–1933.' MA thesis, Dalhousie University 1967.

Foster, John Bellamy. 'On the Waterfront: Longshoring in Canada.' In Craig Heron and Robert Storey, eds., *On the Job: Confronting the Labour Process in Canada*, 181–308. Kingston and Montreal: McGill-Queen's University Press 1986.

Fournier, Marcel. *Communisme et anticommunisme au Québec 1920–1950*. Laval: Editions Albert Saint-Martin 1979.

Fox, Paul. 'Early Socialism in Canada.' In J.H. Aitchison, ed., *The Political Process in Canada*, 79–98. Toronto: University of Toronto Press 1963.

Foy, James. 'Gideon Robertson, Conservative Minister of Labor, 1917–1921.' MA thesis, University of Ottawa 1972.

Frager, Ruth. 'Class and Ethnic Barriers to Feminist Perspectives in Toronto's Jewish Labour Movement, 1919–1939.' *Studies in Political Economy* 30 (Autumn 1989), 143–66.

– 'No Proper Deal: Women Workers and the Canadian Labour Movement, 1870–1940.' In Linda Briskin and Lynda Yanz, eds., *Union Sisters: Women in the Labour Movement*, 44–64. Toronto: Women's Press 1983.

– 'Radical Portraits: The Roots of Socialism in Toronto's Immigrant Jewish Community, 1900–1939.' Unpublished paper, Department of History, McMaster University.

– *Sweatshop Strife: Class, Ethnicity, and Gender in the Jewish Labour Movement of Toronto, 1900–1939*. Toronto: University of Toronto Press 1992.

Francq, Gustave. *Bolchévisme ou syndicalisme, lequel?* Montreal: Monde ouvrier 1919.

Frank, Dana. *Purchasing Power: Consumer Organizing, Gender, and the Seattle Labor Movement, 1919–1929*. New York: Cambridge University Press 1994.

Frank, David. 'The Cape Breton Coal Industry and the Rise and Fall of the British Empire Steel Corporation.' *Acadiensis* 7, no. 1 (Autumn 1977), 3–34.

– 'The Cape Breton Coal Miners, 1917–1926.' PhD diss., Dalhousie University 1979.

– 'Class Conflict in the Coal Industry: Cape Breton 1922.' In Gregory S. Kealey and Peter Warrian, eds., *Essays in Canadian Working-Class History*, 161–84. Toronto: McClelland and Stewart 1976.

– 'Coal Masters and Coal Miners: The 1922 Strike and the Roots of Class Conflict in the Cape Breton Coal Industry.' MA thesis, Dalhousie University 1974.

– 'Company Town/Labour Town: Local Government in the Cape Breton Coal Towns, 1917–1926.' *Histoire sociale/Social History* 27 (May 1981), 177–96.

– 'Contested Terrain: Workers' Control in the Cape Breton Coal Mines in the 1920s.' In Craig Heron and Robert Storey, eds., *On the Job: Confronting the*

Labour Process in Canada, 102–23. Kingston and Montreal: McGill-Queen's University Press 1986.

– 'The Miner's Financier: Women in the Cape Breton Coal Towns, 1917.' *Atlantis* 8, no. 2 (Spring 1983), 137–23.

– 'The 1920s: Class and Region, Resistance and Accommodation.' In E.R. Forbes and D.A. Muise, eds., *The Atlantic Provinces in Confederation*, 233–71. Toronto and Fredericton: University of Toronto Press and Acadiensis Press 1993.

– 'Tradition and Culture in the Cape Breton Mining Community in the Early Twentieth Century.' In Kenneth Donovan, ed. *Cape Breton at 200: Historical Essays in Honour of the Island's Bicentennial, 1785–1985*, 203–18. Sydney: University College of Cape Breton Press 1985.

– 'The Trial of J.B. McLachlan.' Canadian Historical Association. *Historical Papers* (1983), 208–25.

– 'Working-Class Politics: The Election of J.B. McLachlan, 1916–1935.' In Kenneth Donovan, ed., *The Island: New Perspectives on Cape Breton History, 1713–1990*, 187–219. Fredericton: Acadiensis Press 1990.

Frank, David, and Nolan Reilly. 'The Emergence of the Socialist Movement in the Maritimes, 1899–1916.' In Robert J. Brym and R.J. Sacouman, eds., *Underdevelopment and Social Movements in Atlantic Canada*, 81–106. Toronto: New Hogtown Press 1979.

Fraser, Dawn. *Echoes of Labor's War: Industrial Cape Breton in the 1920s*. Edited by David Frank and Don Macgillivray. Toronto: New Hogtown Press 1976.

Friesen, Gerald. 'Bob Russell's Political Thought: Socialism and Industrial Unionism in Winnipeg, 1914 to 1919.' In Gerald Friesen, *River Road: Essays on Manitoba and Prairie History*, 121–46. Winnipeg: University of Manitoba Press 1996.

– *The Canadian Prairies: A History*. Toronto: University of Toronto Press 1984.

– '"Yours in Revolt": Regionalism, Socialism, and the Western Canadian Labour Movement.' *Labour/Le Travailleur* 1 (1976), 139–57.

Fussell, Paul. *The Great War and Modern Memory*. New York: Oxford University Press 1975.

Gauvin, Michel. 'The Reformer and the Machine: Montreal Civic Politics from Raymond Préfontaine to Médéric Martin.' *Journal of Canadian Studies* 13, no. 2 (Summer 1978), 16–26.

Geary, Dick. *European Labour Protest, 1848–1939*. London: Methuen 1981.

– 'Radicalism and the German Worker: Metalworkers and Revolution, 1914–1923.' In Richard J. Evans, ed., *Society and Politics in Wilhelmine Germany*, 267–86. London: Croom Helm 1978.

Gerber, Larry G. 'The United States and Canadian National Industrial Conferences of 1919: A Comparative Analysis.' *Labor History* 32, no. 1 (Winter 1991), 42–65.

Gillespie, Bill. *A Class Act: An Illustrated History of the Labor Movement in Newfoundland and Labrador.* St John's: Newfoundland and Labrador Federation of Labour 1986.

Goeres, Michael. 'Disorder, Dependency and Fiscal Responsibility: Unemployment Relief in Winnipeg, 1907–1942.' MA thesis, University of Manitoba 1981.

Goodwyn, Lawrence. *The Populist Moment: A Short History of the Agrarian Revolt in America.* New York: Oxford University Press 1978.

Graham, Roger. *Arthur Meighen: A Biography.* Vol. 1, *The Door of Opportunity.* Toronto: Clarke Irwin 1960.

Gramsci, Antonio. *Selections from the Prison Notebooks.* Edited by Quinton Hoare and Geoffrey Nowell Smith. New York: International Publishers 1971.

Granatstein, J.L., and J.M. Hitsman. *Broken Promises: A History of Conscription in Canada.* Toronto: Oxford University Press 1977.

Grantham, R.G. 'Some Aspects of the Socialist Movement in British Columbia, 1898–1933.' MA thesis, University of British Columbia 1943.

Graves, Robert. *Goodbye to All That: An Autobiography.* London: Jonathan Cape 1929.

Gray, James H. *Booze: The Impact of Whiskey on the Prairie West.* Toronto: New American Library 1972.

– *The Boy from Winnipeg.* Toronto: Macmillan 1970.

Gray, Stephen. 'Woodworkers and Legitimacy: The IWA in Canada, 1937–1957.' PhD diss., Simon Fraser University 1989.

Grenke, Art. 'The German Community of Winnipeg and the English-Canadian Response to World War I.' *Canadian Ethnic Studies* 20, no. 1 (1988), 21–44.

Groupe de chercheurs de l'Université du Québec à Montréal sur l'histoire des travailleurs québécois. *L'Action politique des ouvriers québécois.*

Groupe de recherches sur l'histoire des mouvements politiques ouvriers de l'Université du Québec à Montréal. *Chronologie des mouvements politiques ouvriers de la fin du 19e siècle jusqu'à 1919.* Montreal 1976.

Haimson, Leopold H., and Charles Tilly, eds. *Strikes, Wars, and Revolutions in an International Perspective: Strike Waves in the Late Nineteenth and Early Twentieth Centuries.* Cambridge: Cambridge University Press 1989.

Hak, Gordon. 'British Columbia Loggers and the Lumber Workers Industrial Union, 1919–1922.' *Labour/Le Travail* 23 (Spring 1989), 67–90.

– 'On the Fringes: Capital and Labour in the Forest Economies of the Port Alberni and Prince George Districts, British Columbia, 1910–1939.' PhD diss., University of British Columbia 1986.

– 'The Socialist and Labourist Impulse in Small-Town British Columbia: Port Alberni and Prince George, 1911–1933.' *Canadian Historical Review* 70, no. 4 (December 1989), 519–42.

Hall, David. 'Times of Trouble: Labour Quiescence in Winnipeg, 1920–1929.' MA thesis, University of Manitoba 1983.

Hallowell, Gerald. *Prohibition in Ontario, 1919–1923*. Toronto: Ontario Historical Society 1972.

Hanebury, Derek. *Ginger Goodwin: Beyond the Forbidden Plateau*. Vancouver: Pulp Press 1986.

Hardy, René, and Normand Séguin. *Forêt et société en Mauricie: La formation de la région de Trois-Rivières, 1830–1930*. Montreal: Boréal Express 1984.

Harney, Robert F., ed. *Gathering Place: Peoples and Neighbourhoods of Toronto, 1834–1945*. Toronto: Multicultural History Society of Ontario 1985.

– *Italians in Canada*. Toronto: Multicultural History Society of Ontario 1978.

Harris, Richard. '"Canada's All Right": The Lives and Loyalties of Immigrant Families in a Toronto Suburb, 1900–1945.' *Canadian Geographer* 36, no. 1 (Spring 1992), 3–30.

Harris, Richard, and Matthew P. Sendbuehler. 'Hamilton's East End: The Early Working-Class Suburb.' *Canadian Geographer* 36, no. 4 (Winter 1992), 381–6.

Hart, John Edward. 'William Irvine and Radical Politics in Canada.' PhD diss., University of Guelph 1972.

Haydu, Jeffrey. *Between Craft and Class: Skilled Workers and Factory Politics in the United States and Britain, 1890–1922*. Berkeley: University of California Press 1988.

Heaps, Leo. *The Rebel in the House: The Life and Times of A.A. Heaps, M.P.* London: Niccolo Publishing 1970.

Heron, Craig. 'The Crisis of the Craftsman: Hamilton's Metal Workers in the Early Twentieth Century.' *Labour/Le Travailleur* 6 (Autumn 1980), 7–48.

– 'Daylight Savings Comes to Hamilton.' *Hamilton Spectator*, 26 October 1979.

– 'Frederick J. Flatman.' In *Dictionary of Hamilton Biography*. Vol. 3, *1925–1939*, 52–7. Hamilton: Dictionary of Hamilton Biography 1992.

– 'The Great War and Nova Scotia Steelworkers.' *Acadiensis* 16, no. 2 (Spring 1987), 2–34.

– 'The High School and the Household Economy in Working-Class Hamilton, 1890–1940.' *Historical Studies in Education* 7, no. 2 (Fall 1995), 217–59.

– 'Labourism and the Canadian Working Class. *Labour/Le Travail* 13 (Spring 1984), 45–76.

– 'Male Wage-Earners and the Canadian State.' In Michael Earle, ed., *Workers and the State in Twentieth-Century Nova Scotia*, 241–64. Fredericton: Acadiensis Press 1989.

– 'The Second Industrial Revolution in Canada, 1890–1930.' In Deian R. Hopkin and Gregory S. Kealey, eds., *Class, Community, and the Labour Movement: Wales*

and Canada, 1850–1930, 48–66. Aberystwyth, Wales: Llafur and Canadian Committee on Labour History 1989.
– 'Working-Class Hamilton, 1895–1930.' PhD diss., Dalhousie University 1981.
– *Working in Steel: The Early Years in Canada, 1883–1935*. Toronto: McClelland and Stewart 1988.
Heron, Craig, and George De Zwaan. 'Industrial Unionism in Eastern Ontario: Gananoque, 1918–1921.' *Ontario History* 77, no. 3 (September 1985), 159–82.
Heron, Craig, and Bryan D. Palmer. 'Through the Prism of the Strike: Industrial Conflict in Southern Ontario, 1901–1914.' *Canadian Historical Review* 58, no. 4 (December 1977), 423–58.
Hiebert, Daniel Joseph. 'Class, Ethnicity, and Residential Structure: The Social Geography of Winnipeg, 1901–1921.' *Journal of Historical Geography* 17, no. 1 (January 1991), 56–86.
– 'The Geography of Jewish Immigrants and the Garment Industry in Toronto, 1901–1931: A Study of Ethnic and Class Relations.' PhD diss., University of Toronto 1987.
Hinton, James. *The First Shop Stewards' Movement*. London: George Allen and Unwin 1973.
Hobsbawm, Eric. *Labouring Men*. London: Weidenfeld and Nicolson 1968.
Hoffman, J. David. 'The Farmer-Labour Government in Ontario.' MA thesis, University of Toronto 1959.
Hogan, Brian F. *Cobalt: Year of the Strike, 1919*. Cobalt, ON: Highway Book Shop 1978.
Holdsworth, Deryk W. 'House and Home in Vancouver: Images of West Coast Urbanism, 1886–1929.' In Gilbert A. Stelter and Alan F.J. Artibise, eds., *The Canadian City: Essays in Urban History*, 186–211. Toronto: McClelland and Stewart 1977.
Horn, Michiel. *The League for Social Reconstruction: Intellectual Origins of the Democratic Left in Canada, 1930–1942*. Toronto: University of Toronto Press 1980.
Horodyski, Mary. 'Women and the Winnipeg General Strike of 1919.' *Manitoba History* 11 (Spring 1986), 28–37.
Horrall, S.W. 'The Royal North-West Mounted Police and Labour Unrest in Western Canada, 1919.' *Canadian Historical Review* 61, no. 2 (June 1980), 169–90.
Hoskins, Ralph Ferland Harris. 'A Study of the Point St.-Charles Shops of the Grand Trunk Railway in Montreal, 1880–1917.' MA thesis, McGill University 1987.
Hovis, Logan W. 'The Origins of Modern Mining in the Western Cordillera, 1880–1930.' Paper presented to the B.C. Studies Conference, 1986.
– 'Technological Change and Mining Labour: Copper Mining and Milling Oper-

ations at the Britannia Mines, British Columbia, 1898–1937.' MA thesis, University of British Columbia 1986.

Howard, Irene. *The Struggle for Social Justice in British Columbia: Helena Gutteridge, the Unknown Reformer.* Vancouver: UBC Press 1992.

Hucul, J.G. 'Canada and the International Labour Organization.' MA thesis, University of Windsor 1984.

Hughes, Everett C. *French Canada in Transition.* Chicago: University of Chicago Press 1943.

Hunnicutt, Benjamin Kline. *Work without End: Abandoning Shorter Hours for the Right to Work.* Philadelphia: Temple University Press 1988.

Igartua, Jose E. 'Worker Persistence, Hiring Policies, and the Depression in the Aluminum Sector: The Saguenay Region, Quebec, 1925–1940.' *Histoire sociale/ Social History* 43 (May 1989), 9–34.

Industrial Workers of the World. *Founding Convention: Proceedings 1905.* New York: Merit Publishers 1969.

Irvine, Duncan Norman. 'Reform, War, and Industrial Crisis in Manitoba: F.J. Dixon and the Framework of Consensus.' MA thesis, University of Manitoba 1981.

Irvine, William. *The Farmers in Politics.* Toronto: McClelland and Stewart 1920.

Irving, Allan. 'The Development of a Provincial Welfare State: British Columbia, 1900–1939.' In Allan Moscovitch and Jim Albert, eds., *The 'Benevolent' State: The Growth of Welfare in Canada,* 155–74. Toronto: Garamond Press 1987.

Isbester, Frazer. 'A History of the National Catholic Unions in Quebec, 1901–1965.' PhD diss., Cornell University 1968.

Jamieson, Stuart Marshall. *Times of Trouble: Labour Unrest and Industrial Conflict in Canada, 1900–66.* Ottawa: Queen's Printer 1968.

Jensen, Vernon. *Nonferrous Metals Industry Unionism, 1932–1954: A Story of Leadership Controversy.* Ithaca: Cornell University 1954.

Johnson, A. Ernest. 'The Strikes in Winnipeg in May 1918: The Prelude to 1919?' MA thesis, University of Manitoba 1978.

Johnson, F. Henry. *A History of Public Education in British Columbia.* Vancouver: University of British Columbia 1964.

Johnson, Leo. 'Precapitalist Economic Formations and the Capitalist Labour Market in Canada, 1911–71.' In James E. Curtis and William G. Scott, eds., *Social Stratification: Canada,* 89–104. Scarborough: Prentice-Hall 1979.

Johnson, Ross A. 'No Compromise – No Political Trading: The Marxian Socialist Tradition in British Columbia.' PhD diss., University of British Columbia 1975.

Johnston, Charles M. *E.C. Drury: Agrarian Idealist.* Toronto: University of Toronto Press 1986.

Johnston, Hugh. *The Voyage of the Komagata Maru: The Sikh Challenge to Canada's Colour Bar.* Delhi: Oxford University Press 1979.

– ed. *The Pacific Province: A History of British Columbia*. Vancouver: Douglas and McIntyre 1996.

Jordon, Mary W. *Survival: The Trials and Tribulations of Canadian Labour*. Toronto: McDonald House 1976.

Kaplan, Temma. 'Women and Communal Strikes in the Crisis of 1917–1922.' In Renate Bridenthal et al., eds., *Becoming Visible: Women in European History*, 2nd ed., 429–50. Boston: Houghton Mifflin 1987.

Kaplan, William, ed. *Belonging: The Meaning and Future of Canadian Citizenship*. Kingston and Montreal: McGill-Queen's University Press 1993.

Kazymyra, Nadia O.M. 'Aspects of Ukrainian Opinion in Manitoba during World War I.' In M.L. Kovacs, ed., *Ethnic Canadians: Culture and Education*. Regina: Canadian Plains Research Center, University of Regina 1978.

Kealey, Gregory S. '1919: The Canadian Labour Revolt.' *Labour/Le Travail* 13 (Spring 1984), 11–44.

– 'The Parameters of Class Conflict: Strikes in Canada, 1891–1930.' In Deian R. Hopkin and Gregory S. Kealey, eds. *Class, Community, and the Labour Movement: Wales and Canada, 1850–1930*, 213–48. Aberystwyth, Wales: Llafur and Canadian Committee on Labour History 1989.

– 'The Royal Canadian Mounted Police, the Canadian Intelligence Service, the Public Archives of Canada, and Access to Information: A Curious Tale.' *Labour/Le Travail* 21 (Spring 1988), 199–226.

– 'The RCMP, the Special Branch, and the Early Days of the Communist Party of Canada: A Documentary Survey.' *Labour/Le Travail* 30 (Fall 1992), 169–204.

– 'The State, the Foreign Language Press, and the Canadian Labour Revolt of 1917–1920.' In Christine Harzig and Dirk Hoerder, eds., *The Press of Labour Migrants in Europe and North America, 1880s to 1930s*, 311–45. Bremen, Ger.: Labor Migration Project, Labor Newspaper Preservation Project, Universität Bremen 1985.

– 'State Repression of Labour and the Left in Canada, 1914–1920: The Impact of the First World War.' *Canadian Historical Review* 73, no. 3 (September 1992), 281–314.

– 'The Surveillance State: The Origins of Domestic Intelligence and Counter-Subversion in Canada.' *Intelligence and National Security* 7, no. 3 (1992), 172–210.

– *Toronto Workers Respond to Industrial Capitalism, 1867–1892*. Toronto: University of Toronto Press 1980.

Kealey, Gregory S., and Bryan D. Palmer. *Dreaming of What Might Be: The Knights of Labor in Ontario, 1880–1900*. New York: Cambridge University Press 1982.

Kealey, Gregory S., and Reg Whitaker, eds., *RCMP Security Bulletins: The Early Years, 1919–1929*. St John's: Canadian Committee on Labour History 1992.

Kealey, Linda. '"No Special Protection – No Sympathy": Women's Activism in the Canadian Labour Revolt of 1919.' In Deian R. Hopkin, and Gregory S. Kealey, eds., *Class, Community, and the Labour Movement: Wales and Canada, 1850–1930*, 134–59. Aberystwyth, Wales: Llafur and Canadian Committee on Labour History 1989.

– 'Prairie Socialist Women and World War I: The Urban West.' Paper presented to the Canadian Historical Association, Winnipeg 1986.

– 'Women and Labour during World War I: Women Workers and the Minimum Wage in Manitoba.' In Mary Kinnear, ed., *First Days, Fighting Days: Women in Manitoba History*, 76–99. Regina: Canadian Plains Research Center 1987.

– 'Women's Labour Militancy in Canada, 1900–20.' Paper presented to the Canadian Historical Association, Kingston 1991.

– ed. *A Not Unreasonable Claim: Women and Reform in Canada, 1880s–1920s*. Toronto: Women's Press 1979.

Kehler, Ken, and Alvin Esau. *Famous Manitoba Trials: The Winnipeg General Strike Trials: Research Source*. Winnipeg: Legal Research Institute, University of Manitoba 1990.

Kell, Robert. 'Winnipeg, 1919: A Portfolio.' *Labour/Le Travail* 20 (Fall 1987), 193–205.

Kerr, Don, and Stan Hanson. *Saskatoon, the First Half Century*. Edmonton: NeWest Publishers 1982.

Keshen, Jeff. 'All the News That Was Fit to Print: Ernest J. Chambers and Information Control in Canada, 1914–19.' *Canadian Historical Review* 73, no. 3 (September 1992), 315–43.

Keyfitz, Nathan. 'Population Problems.' In Jean-Claude Falardeau, ed., *Essais sur le Québec contemporain*. Quebec: Les Presses de l'Université Laval 1953.

King, William Lyon Mackenzie. *Industry and Humanity: A Study in the Principles Underlying Industrial Reconstruction*. Toronto: University of Toronto Press 1973 [1918].

Knight, Rolf. *Indians at Work: An Informal History of Native Labour in British Columbia, 1858–1930*. Vancouver: New Star Books 1978.

– *Stump Ranch Chronicles and Other Narratives*. Vancouver: New Star Books 1977.

Knight, Rolf, and Maya Koizumi, *A Man of Our Times: The Life History of a Japanese-Canadian Fisherman*. Vancouver: New Star Books 1976.

Kolasky, John. *Prophets and Proletarians: Documents on the History of the Rise and Decline of Ukrainian Communism in Canada*. Edmonton: Canadian Institute of Ukrainian Studies 1990.

– *The Shattered Illusion: The History of Ukrainian Pro-Communist Organizations in Canada*. Toronto: PMA Books 1979.

Krawchuk, Peter. *Matthew Popovich.* Toronto: Progress Books 1990.

– *The Ukrainian Socialist Movement in Canada, 1907–1918.* Toronto: Progress Books 1979.

Laine, Edward W. 'Finnish Canadian Radicalism and Canadian Politics: The First Forty Years, 1900–1940.' In Jorgen Dahlie and Tissa Fernando, eds., *Ethnicity, Power, and Politics in Canada,* 94–112. Toronto: Methuen 1981.

Lambly, Peter. 'Towards a Living Wage: The Minimum Wage Campaign for Women in Nova Scotia, 1920–1935.' BA Honours essay, Dalhousie University 1977.

– 'Working Conditions and Industrial Relations on Canada's Street Railways, 1900–1920.' MA thesis, Dalhousie University 1983.

Larivière, Claude. *Albert Saint-Martin, militant d'avant-garde (1865–1947).* Laval: Editions Albert Saint-Martin 1979.

Latta, Peter. 'A Labour Aristocracy: Skilled Labour in Amherst, Nova Scotia, 1891–1914.' MA thesis, St Mary's University 1991.

Lavigne, Marie, and Yolande Pinard, eds. *Travailleuses et féministes.* Montreal: Boréal Express 1983.

Lavoie, Louise B. *Les débuts du mouvement ouvrier à Sherbrooke, 1873–1919.* Sherbrooke: Groupe de recherche en histoire régionale, Université de Sherbrooke 1979.

Lavoie, Yolande. 'Les mouvements migratoires des Canadiens entre leur pays et les États-Unis au XIXe et XXe siècles.' In Hubert Charbonneau, ed., *La population au Québec: Études rétrospectives* Montreal: Boréal Express 1973, 73–89.

Leacock, Stephen. *The Unsolved Riddle of Social Justice.* London: J. Lane 1920.

Leblanc, Andre E. '*Le Monde ouvrier/The Labor World* (1916–1926): An Analysis of Thought and a Detailed Index.' DES thesis, University of Montreal 1971.

Leckow, Ross. 'Canadians in the Making: Icelandic Participation in the Great War and the Winnipeg General Strike.' Unpublished paper, University of Winnipeg 1979.

Lees, Elizabeth. 'Business Not as Usual: Shipbuilding in British Columbia, 1917–1920.' Paper presented to the Canadian Historical Association, June 1988.

– 'Problems of Pacification: Veterans' Groups in Vancouver, 1919–1922.' MA thesis, Simon Fraser University 1985.

Léger, Raymond. 'L'évolution des syndicats au Nouveau-Brunswick de 1910 à 1950.' *Égalité: revue acadienne d'analyse politique* 31 (Spring 1992), 19–40.

Leier, Mark. *Red Flags and Red Tape: The Making of a Labour Bureaucracy.* Toronto: University of Toronto Press 1995.

– 'Solidarity on Occasion: The Vancouver Free Speech Fights of 1909 and 1912.' *Labour/Le Travail* 23 (Spring 1989), 39–66.

– *Where the Fraser River Flows: The Industrial Workers of the World in British Columbia*. Vancouver: New Star Books 1990.

Levant, Victor. *Capital and Labour: Partners? Two Classes – Two Views*. Toronto: Steel Rail Press 1977.

Lévesque, Andrée. 'La citoyenne selon Eva Circé-Côté.' In Andrée Lévesque, *Résistance et transgression: Études en histoire des femmes au Québec*, 47–65. Montreal: Les Editions du Remue-ménage 1995.

Leyton, Miriam Judith. 'The Struggle for a Working-Class Consciousness: Jewish Garment Workers in Montreal, 1880–1920.' MA thesis, Carleton University 1987.

Lindstrom-Best, Varpu. *Defiant Sisters: A Social History of Finnish Immigrant Women in Canada*. Toronto: Multicultural History Society of Ontario 1988.

– 'Finnish Socialist Women in Canada, 1890–1930.' In Linda Kealey and Joan Sangster, eds., *Beyond the Vote: Canadian Women and Politics*, 196–216. Toronto: University of Toronto Press 1989.

Lindstrom-Best, Varpu, and Allen Seager. '*Toveritar* and Finnish Canadian Women, 1900–1930.' In Christianne Harzig and Dirk Hoerder, eds., *The Press of Labour Migrants in Europe and North America, 1880s to 1930s*, 243–64. Bremen, Ger.: Labor Migration Project, Labor Newspaper Preservation Project, Universität Bremen 1985.

Linteau, Paul-André, René Durocher, and Jean-Claude Robert. *Histoire du Québec contemporain: De la Confédération à la crise (1867–1929)*. Montreal: Boréal Express 1979.

Logan, H.A. *Trade Unions in Canada: Their Development and Functioning*. Toronto: Macmillan 1948.

Lorentsen, Edith, and Evelyn Woolner. 'Fifty Years of Labour Legislation in Canada.' In Aranka E. Kovaks, ed., *Readings in Canadian Labour Economics*, 92–36. Toronto: McGraw Hill 1961.

Lowe, Graham S. *Women in the Administrative Revolution: The Feminization of Clerical Work*. Toronto: University of Toronto 1987.

MacDowell, Laurel Sefton. 'The Formation of the Canadian Industrial Relations System during World War Two.' *Labour/Le Travailleur* 3 (1978), 175–96.

MacEwan, Paul. *Miners and Steelworkers: Labour in Cape Breton*. Toronto: Samuel Stevens Hakkert and Company 1976.

Macgillivray, Don. 'Industrial Unrest in Cape Breton, 1919–1925.' MA thesis, University of New Brunswick 1971.

– 'Military Aid to the Civil Power: The Cape Breton Experience in the 1920s.'

In Don Macgillivray and Brian Tennyson, eds., *Cape Breton Historical Essays*, 95–109. Sydney: University College of Cape Breton Press 1980.

Maciejko, Bill. 'Public Schools and the Workers' Struggle: Winnipeg, 1914–1921.' In Nancy M. Sheehan et al., eds., *Schools in the West: Essays in Canadian Educational History*, 213–37. Calgary: Detselig 1986.

MacIntosh, Robert. 'The Boys in the Nova Scotia Coal Mines, 1873–1923.' *Acadiensis* 3, no. 2 (Spring 1987), 35–50.

MacIver, R.M. *Labor in the Changing World*. Toronto: E.P. Dutton and Company 1919.

MacKenzie, Anthony. 'The Farmer-Labour Party in Nova Scotia.' MA thesis, Dalhousie University 1969.

Mackenzie, J.B. 'Section 98, Criminal Code, and Freedom of Expression in Canada.' *Queen's Law Journal* 1 (1972), 469–83.

MacLaren, Roy. *Canadians in Russia, 1918–1919*. Toronto: Macmillan 1976.

MacNeil, Robert J. 'The Origins and Development of the United Maritime Fishermen.' In *United Maritime Fishermen*. Antigonish, NS, 1945.

MacPherson, Ian. 'Creating Stability amid Degrees of Marginality: Divisions in the Struggle for Orderly Marketing in British Columbia, 1900–1940.' *Canadian Papers in Rural History* 7 (1990), 309–33.

– *Each for All: A History of the Co-operative Movement in English Canada, 1900–1945*. Toronto: McClelland and Stewart 1979.

Makahonuk, Glen. 'Class Conflict in a Prairie City: The Saskatoon Working-Class Response to Prairie Capitalism, 1906–19.' *Labour/Le Travail* 19 (Spring 1987), 89–124.

– 'Labour in a Prairie City: The Saskatoon Working-Class Experience and Response to Capitalism, 1906–1919.' In Harley H. Dickinson and Bob Russell, eds., *The Politics of Work in the West: Historical and Contemporary Perspectives*. Saskatoon: Social Research Unit, Department of Sociology, University of Saskatchewan 1985.

– 'Masters and Servants: Labour Relations in the Saskatchewan Civil Service, 1905–1945.' *Prairie Forum* 12, no. 2 (Fall 1987), 257–76.

– 'Painters, Decorators, and Paperhangers: A Case Study in Saskatchewan Labourism, 1906–1919.' *Prairie Forum* 10, no. 1 (Spring 1985), 189–204.

Makuch, Andrij. 'The Influence of the Ukrainian Revolution on Ukrainians in Canada, 1917–1922.' *Journal of Ukrainian Graduate Studies* 6 (1979), 42–61.

Maltais, M. Ludovic. *Les syndicats catholiques canadiens: Étude socioéconomique*. Washington: l'Université catholique d'Amérique 1925.

Manley, John. 'Communists and Canadian Autoworkers: The Struggle for

Industrial Unionism in the Canadian Automobile Industry, 1925–1936.' *Labour/Le Travail* 17 (Spring 1986), 105–34.

– 'Communists and the Canadian Labour Movement during a Period of Retreat: The 1920s.' Unpublished paper, Department of History, Dalhousie University 1979.

– 'Preaching the Red Stuff: J.B. McLachlan, Communism, and the Cape Breton Miners, 1922–1935.' *Labour/Le Travail* 30 (Fall 1992), 65–114.

Mardiros, Anthony. *William Irvine: The Life of a Prairie Radical*. Toronto: James Lorimer 1979.

Marine Workers and Boilermakers Industrial Union, Local No.1, Marine Retirees Association. *A History of Shipbuilding in British Columbia*. Vancouver: Marine Retirees Association 1977.

Maroney, Paul. '"The Great Adventure": The Context and Ideology of Recruiting in Ontario, 1914–1917.' *Canadian Historical Review* 77, no. 1 (March 1996), 62–98.

Marquis, Greg. 'The History of Policing in the Maritime Provinces: Themes and Perspectives.' *Urban History Review* 19, no. 1 (October 1990), 84–99.

– 'Police Unionism in Early-Twentieth-Century Toronto.' *Ontario History* 81, no. 2 (June 1989), 109–28.

Marshall, Herbert, Frank Southard, Jr., and Kenneth W. Taylor. *Canadian–American Industry: A Study in International Investment*. Toronto: McClelland and Stewart 1976 [1936].

Marshall, T.H., and Tom Bottomore. *Citizenship and Social Class*. London: Pluto Press 1992.

Martynowych, Orest T. 'The Ukrainian Socialist Movement in Canada, 1900–1918.' *Journal of Ukrainian Graduate Studies* 1, no. 1 (Fall 1976), 27–44; 2, no. 1 (Spring 1977), 22–31.

Martynowych, Orest T., and Nadia Kazymyra. 'Political Activity in Western Canada, 1896–1923.' In Manoly R. Lupul, ed., *A Heritage in Transition: Essays in the History of Ukrainians in Canada*, 85–107. Toronto: McClelland and Stewart 1982.

Marwick, Arthur. *War and Social Change in the Twentieth Century: A Comparative Study of Britain, France, Germany, Russia, and the United States*. London: Macmillan 1974.

Masters, D.C. *The Winnipeg General Strike*. Toronto: University of Toronto Press 1950.

Matters, Diane. 'Public Welfare Vancouver Style, 1910–1920.' *Journal of Canadian Studies* 14 (Spring 1979), 3–15.

Mayse, Susan. *Ginger: The Life and Death of Albert Goodwin*. Madeira Park, BC: Harbour Publishing 1990.

McCallum, Margaret. 'Corporate Welfarism in Canada, 1919–1939.' *Canadian Historical Review* 71, no. 1 (March 1990), 46–79.
– 'Keeping Women in Their Place: The Minimum Wage in Canada, 1910–1925.' *Labour/Le Travail* 17 (Spring 1986), 29–59.
McCormack, A. Ross. 'Cloth Caps and Jobs: The Ethnicity of English Immigrants in Canada, 1900–1914.' In J.M. Bumsted, ed., *Interpreting Canada's Past*. Vol. 2, *After Confederation*, 175–91. Toronto: Oxford University Press 1986.
– 'Networks among British Immigrants and Accommodation to Canadian Society, 1900–1914.' *Histoire sociale/Social History* 34 (November 1984), 357–74.
– *Reformers, Rebels, and Revolutionaries: The Western Canadian Radical Movement, 1899–1919*. Toronto: University of Toronto Press 1977.
– 'The Western Working-Class Experience.' In W.J.C. Cherwinski and G.S. Kealey, eds., *Lectures in Canadian Labour and Working-Class History*, 115–26. St John's: Committee on Canadian Labour History 1985.
McDonald, Ian. 'Class Conflict and Political Factionalism: A History of Local 213 of the International Brotherhood of Electrical Workers, 1901–1961.' MA thesis, Simon Fraser University 1986.
McDonald, Ian D.H. *'To Each His Own': William Coaker and the Fishermen's Protective Union in Newfoundland Politics, 1908–1925*. St John's: ISER Books 1987.
McDonald, Robert J. 'Working-Class Vancouver, 1886–1914: Urbanism and Class in British Columbia.' In Patricia E. Roy, ed., *A History of British Columbia: Selected Readings*, 324–53. Toronto: Copp Clark Pitman 1989.
McEwen, Tom. *He Wrote for Us: The Story of Bill Bennett, Pioneer Socialist Journalist*. Vancouver: Tribune Publishing Company 1951.
McGregor, F.A. *The Fall and Rise of Mackenzie King, 1911–1919*. Toronto: Macmillan 1962.
McInnis, Peter. 'All Solid along the Line: The Reid Newfoundland Strike of 1918.' *Labour/Le Travail* 26 (Fall 1990), 61–84.
– 'Newfoundland Labour and World War I: The Emergence of the Newfoundland Industrial Workers' Association.' MA thesis, Memorial University of Newfoundland 1987.
McKay, Ian. '"By Wisdom, Wile or War": The Provincial Workmen's Association and the Struggle for Working-Class Independence in Nova Scotia, 1879–1997.' *Labour/Le Travail* 18 (Fall 1986), 13–62.
– *The Craft Transformed: An Essay on the Carpenters of Halifax, 1885–1985*. Halifax: Holdfast Press 1985.
– 'Industry, Work, and Community in the Cumberland Coalfields, 1848–1927.' PhD diss., Dalhousie University 1983.
– 'The 1910s: The Stillborn Triumph of Progressive Reform.' In E.R. Forbes and

D.A. Muise, eds. *The Atlantic Provinces in Confederation,* 192–229. Toronto and Fredericton: University of Toronto Press and Acadiensis Press 1993.

– 'The Provincial Workmen's Association.' In W.J.C. Cherwinski and Gregory S. Kealey, eds., *Lectures in Canadian Labour and Working-Class History,* 127–34. St John's: Committee on Canadian Labour History 1985.

– 'The Realm of Uncertainty: The Experience of Work in the Cumberland Coal Mines, 1873–1927.' *Acadiensis* 16, no. 1 (Autumn 1986), 3–57.

– 'Strikes in the Maritimes, 1901–1914.' *Acadiensis* 13 (1983), 3–46.

– ed., *For a Working-Class Culture in Canada: A Selection of Colin McKay's Writings on Political Economy and Sociology, 1897–1939.* St John's: Canadian Committee on Labour History 1996.

McKillop, A. Brian. 'Citizen and Socialist: The Ethos of Political Winnipeg, 1919–1935.' MA thesis, University of Manitoba 1970.

McLean, Bruce. *'A Union amongst Government Employees': A History of the B.C. Government Employees' Union, 1919–1979.* N.p. 1979.

McMenemy, John M. 'Lion in a Den of Daniels: A Study of Sam Lawrence, Labour in Politics.' MA thesis, McMaster University 1965.

McMillan, C.J. 'Trade Unionism in District 18, 1900–1925: A Case Study.' MBA thesis, University of Alberta 1969.

McNaught, Kenneth. 'Political Trials and the Canadian Political Tradition.' In M.L. Friedland, ed., *Courts and Trials: A Multidisciplinary Approach,* 137–61. Toronto: University of Toronto Press 1975.

– *A Prophet in Politics: A Biography of J.S. Woodsworth.* Toronto: University of Toronto Press 1959.

McNaught, Kenneth, and David Bercuson. *The Winnipeg General Strike.* Don Mills, Ont.: Longman 1974.

Mellor, John. *The Company Store: John Bryson McLachlan and the Cape Breton Coal Miners, 1900–1925.* Toronto: Doubleday 1983.

Melnycky, Peter. 'A Political History of the Ukrainian Community in Manitoba, 1899–1922.' MA thesis, University of Manitoba 1979.

Miliband, Ralph. 'State Power and Class Interests.' *New Left Review* 138 (March–April 1983), 57–68.

Milkman, Ruth, ed. *Women, Work, and Protest: A Century of U.S. Women's Labor History.* Boston: Routledge and Kegan Paul 1985.

Millar, David. 'The Winnipeg General Strike, 1919: A Reinterpretation in the Light of Oral History and Pictorial Evidence.' MA thesis, Carleton University 1970.

Miller, J.O., ed. *The New Era in Canada: Essays Dealing with the Upbuilding of the Canadian Commonwealth.* Toronto: J.M. Dent and Sons 1917.

Mills, Allen. '*The Canadian Forum* and Socialism, 1920–1934.' *Journal of Canadian Studies* 13, no. 4 (Winter 1978–79), 11–27.

– *A Fool for Christ: The Political Thought of J.S. Woodsworth*. Toronto: University of Toronto Press 1991.

– 'Single Tax, Socialism, and the Independent Labour Party of Manitoba: The Political Ideas of F.J. Dixon and S.J. Farmer.' *Labour/Le Travailleur*, 5 (1980), 33–56.

Minville, Esdras. *Syndicalisme, législation ourvière et régime social au Québec avant 1940*. Montreal: Fides 1986.

Mitchell, Tom. 'Brandon 1919: Labour Relations in the Wheat City in the Year of the General Strike.' *Manitoba History* 17 (Spring 1989), 2–13.

– 'From the Social Gospel to "The Plain Bread of Leninism": A.E. Smith's Journey to the Left in the Epoch of Reaction after World War I.' *Labour/Le Travail* 33 (Spring 1994), 125–51.

– '"The Manufacture of Souls of Good Quality": Winnipeg's 1919 Conference on Canadian Citizenship, English-Canadian Nationalism, and the New Order after the Great War.' *Journal of Canadian Studies* 31, no. 4 (Winter 1996–97), 5–28.

– '"Repressive Measures": A.J. Andrews, the Committee of 1,000, and the Campaign against Radicalism after the Winnipeg General Strike.' *Left History* 3, no. 2/4, no. 1 (Fall 1995/Spring 1996), 133–67.

– '"A Square Deal for All and No Railroading": Labour and Politics in Brandon, 1900–1920.' *Prairie Forum* 15, no. 1 (Spring 1990), 46–65.

– '"To Reach the Leadership of This Revolutionary Movement": A.J. Andrews, the Canadian State, and the Suppression of the Winnipeg General Strike.' *Prairie Forum* 18, no. 2 (Fall 1993), 239–55.

Molnar, Donald. 'The Winnipeg General Strike: Class, Ethnicity, and Class Formation in Canada.' MA thesis, McGill University 1987.

Montague, John Tait. 'Trade Unionism in the Canadian Meatpacking Industry.' PhD diss., University of Toronto 1950.

Montgomery, David. *The Fall of the House of Labor: The Workplace, the State, and American Labor Activism, 1865–1925*. New York: Cambridge University Press 1987.

– 'Immigrants, Industrial Unions, and Social Reconstruction in the United States, 1916–1923.' *Labour/Le Travail* 13 (Spring 1984), 101–15.

– 'New Tendencies in Union Struggles and Strategies in Europe and the United States, 1916–1922.' In James A. Cronin and Carmen Sirianni, eds., *Work, Community, and Power: The Experience of Labor in Europe and America, 1900–1925*, 88–116. Philadelphia: Temple University Press 1983.

Morris, Peter. *Embattled Shadows: A History of Canadian Cinema, 1895–1939*. Montreal: McGill-Queen's University Press 1978.

Morris, Philip A., ed. *The Canadian Patriotic Fund: A Record of Its Activities from 1914 to 1919*. Ottawa: Canadian Patriotic Fund, n.d.

Morton, Desmond. 'Aid to the Civil Power: The Canadian Militia in Support of Social Order, 1867–1914.' In Michiel Horn and Ronald Sabourin, eds., *Studies in Canadian Social History*, 417–34. Toronto: McClelland and Stewart 1974.

– *Canada and War: A Military and Political History.* Toronto: Butterworths 1981.

– *The Canadian General: Sir William Otter.* Toronto: Hakkert 1974.

– *When Your Number's Up: The Canadian Soldier in the First World War.* Toronto: Random House 1993.

Morton, Desmond, with Terry Copp. *Working People: An Illustrated History of the Canadian Labour Movement.* Ottawa: Deneau 1984.

Morton, Desmond, and J.L. Granatstein. *Marching to Armageddon: Canadians and the Great War.* Toronto: Lester and Orpen Dennys 1989.

Morton, Desmond, and Glenn Wright. *Winning the Second Battle: Canadian Veterans and the Return to Civilian Life, 1915–1930.* Toronto: University of Toronto Press 1987.

Morton, Suzanne. *Ideal Surroundings: Domestic Life in a Working-Class Suburb in the 1920s.* Toronto: University of Toronto Press 1995.

– 'Labourism and Economic Action: The Halifax Shipyards Strike of 1920.' *Labour/Le Travail* 22 (Fall 1988), 67–98.

– 'Labourism and Independent Labour Politics in Halifax, 1919–1926.' MA thesis, Dalhousie University 1986.

– 'Women on Their Own: Single Mothers in Working-Class Halifax in the 1920s.' *Acadiensis* 21, no. 2 (Spring 1992), 90–107.

Morton, W.L. *The Progressive Party in Canada.* Toronto: University of Toronto Press 1950.

Mott, Morris Kenneth. 'The Foreign Peril: Nativism in Winnipeg, 1916–1923.' MA thesis, University of Manitoba 1970.

Mouat, Jeremy. 'The Genesis of Western Exceptionalism: British Columbia's Hard Rock Miners, 1895–1903.' *Canadian Historical Review* 71, no. 3 (September 1990), 317–45.

– *Roaring Days: Rossland's Mines and the History of British Columbia.* Vancouver: UBC Press 1995.

Muir, James. 'The Demand for British Justice: Protest and Culture during the Winnipeg General Strike Trials.' *Canadian Legal History Project Working Paper Series.* Winnipeg: Legal Research Institute, University of Manitoba 1993.

Muise, Del. 'The Making of an Industrial Community: Cape Breton Coal Towns, 1867–1900.' In Don Macgillivray and Brian Tennyson, eds., *Cape Breton Historical Essays*, 76–94. Sydney: University College of Cape Breton Press 1980.

Murray, Robert K. *Red Scare: A Study in National Hysteria, 1919–1920.* New York: McGraw Hill 1964.

Nagant, Francine. 'La politique municipale à Montréal de 1910 à 1914: L'échec des reformistes et le triomphe de Médéric Martin.' MA thesis, Université de Montréal 1982.

National Conference on Character in Relation to Canadian Citizenship. *Report of the Proceedings*. Winnipeg: n.p. 1919.

Naylor, James. *The New Democracy: Challenging the Industrial Order in Industrial Ontario*. Toronto: University of Toronto Press 1991.

– 'Ontario Workers and the Decline of Labourism.' In Roger Hall et al., eds., *Patterns of the Past: Interpreting Ontario's History*, 278–300. Toronto: Dundurn Press 1988.

– 'Toronto 1919.' Canadian Historical Association. *Historical Papers* (1986), 33–55.

– 'Workers and the State: Experiments in Corporatism after World War One.' *Studies in Political Economy* 42 (Autumn 1993), 81–111.

Naylor, R.T. 'The Canadian State, the Accumulation of Capital, and the Great War.' In R.T. Naylor, ed., *Dominion of Debt: Centre, Periphery and the International Economic Order*, 61–108. Montreal: Black Rose Books 1985.

– *The History of Canadian Business, 1867–1914*. 2 vols. Toronto: James Lorimer 1975.

Nelles, H.V., and Christopher Armstrong. 'The Great Fight for Clean Government.' *Urban History Review* 2-76 (October 1976), 50–66.

Nelson, Sten Sparre. 'Labour Insurgency in Norway: The Crisis of 1917–1920.' *Social Science History* 5, no. 4 (Fall 1981), 393–416.

Norcross, Elizabeth. 'Mary Ellen Smith: The Right Woman in the Right Place at the Right Time.' In Barbara Latham and Roberta J. Pazdro, eds., *Not Just Pin Money*, 357–64. Victoria: Camosun College 1984.

Norrie, Kenneth, and Douglas Owram. *A History of the Canadian Economy*. Toronto: Harcourt Brace Jovanovitch 1991.

Norris, John. 'The Vancouver Island Coal Mines, 1912–1914: A Study of an Organizational Strike.' *BC Studies* 45 (Spring 1980), 56–72.

O'Connor, Harvey. *Revolution in Seattle: A Memoir*. New York: Monthly Review Press 1964.

Oliver, Peter. 'Sir William Hearst and the Collapse of the Ontario Conservative Party.' In Peter Oliver, ed., *Public and Private Persons: The Ontario Political Culture, 1914–1934*, 16–43. Toronto: Clarke Irwin 1975.

One Big Union. *Origin of the One Big Union: A Verbatim Report of the Calgary Conference*. Winnipeg: One Big Union 1919.

Orlikow, L.G. 'A Survey of the Reform Movement in Manitoba, 1910 to 1920.' MA thesis, University of Manitoba 1955.

Osborne, Kenneth. *R.B. Russell and the Labour Movement*. Agincourt, Ont.: Book Society of Canada 1978.

Owram, Doug. *The Government Generation: Canadian Intellectuals and the State, 1900–1945.* Toronto: University of Toronto Press 1986.

Palmer, Bryan D. *A Culture in Conflict: Skilled Workers and Industrial Capitalism in Hamilton, Ontario, 1860–1914.* Kingston and Montreal: McGill-Queen's University Press 1979.

– '"Give Us the Road and We Will Run It": The Social and Cultural Matrix of an Emerging Labour Movement.' In Gregory S. Kealey and Peter Warrian, eds., *Essays in Canadian Working-Class History,* 106–24. Toronto: McClelland and Stewart 1976.

– *Working-Class Experience: Rethinking the History of Canadian Labour, 1800–1991.* Toronto: McClelland and Stewart 1992.

– *Working-Class Experience: The Rise and Reconstitution of Canadian Labour, 1800–1980.* Toronto: Butterworths 1983.

Palmer, Howard. 'William Irvine and the Emergence of Political Radicalism in Calgary, 1916–1921.' *Fort Calgary Quarterly* 7, no. 2 (1987), 2–19.

Parenteau, Bill. 'The Woods Transformed: The Emergence of the Pulp and Paper Industry in New Brunswick, 1918–1931.' *Acadiensis* 22, no. 1 (Autumn 1992), 5–43.

Parisé, Robert. *Le fondateur du syndicalisme catholique au Québec: Mgr Eugène Lapointe* Montreal: Les Presses de l'Université du Québec 1978.

Pariseau, J.J.B. *Disorders, Strikes, and Disasters: Military Aid to the Civil Power in Canada, 1867–1933.* Ottawa: Directorate of History, National Defence Headquarters 1973.

Parr, Joy. *The Gender of Breadwinners: Women, Men, and Change in Two Industrial Towns, 1880–1950.* Toronto: University of Toronto Press 1990.

– 'Hired Men: Ontario Agricultural Wage Labour in Historical Perspective.' *Labour/Le Travail* 15 (Spring 1985), 91–103.

Peitchinis, Stephen G. *Labour–Management Relations in the Railway Industry.* Ottawa: Queen's Printer 1971.

Penfold, Steven. '"Have You No Manhood in You?": Gender and Class in the Cape Breton Coal Towns, 1920–1926.' *Acadiensis* 23 (Spring 1994), 21–44.

Penner, Jacob. 'Recollections of the Early Socialist Movement in Winnipeg,' *Marxist Quarterly* 2 (Summer 1962), 29–30.

Penner, Norman. *Canadian Communism: The Stalin Years and Beyond.* Toronto: Methuen 1988.

– *The Canadian Left: A Critical Analysis.* Scarborough: Prentice Hall 1977.

– ed. 'Jacob Penner's Recollections.' *Histoire sociale/Social History* 14 (November 1974), 366–78.

– *Winnipeg 1919: The Strikers' Own History of the Winnipeg General Strike.* Toronto: James Lorimer 1973.

Pentland, H. Clare. 'Fifty Years After.' *Canadian Dimension* 6, no. 2 (July 1969), 14–17.
– *A Study of the Changing Social, Economic, and Political Background of the Canadian System of Industrial Relations*. Ottawa: Queen's Printer 1968.
– 'The Western Canadian Labour Movement, 1897–1919.' *Canadian Journal of Political and Social Theory* 3, no. 2 (Spring–Summer 1979), 53–78.
Peterson, Larry. 'The One Big Union in International Perspective: Revolutionary Industrial Unionism, 1900–1925.' *Labour/Le Travailleur* 7 (Spring 1981), 41–66.
– 'Revolutionary Socialism and Industrial Unrest in the Era of the Winnipeg General Strike: The Origins of Communist Labour Unionism in Europe and North America.' *Labour/Le Travail* 13 (Spring 1984), 115–32.
Peterson, T. 'Ethnic and Class Politics in Manitoba.' In Martin Robin, ed., *Canadian Provincial Politics*, 81–6. Scarborough: Prentice-Hall 1978.
Petryshyn, Jaroslav. 'From Clergyman to Communist: The Radicalization of Albert Edward Smith.' *Journal of Canadian Studies* 13 no. 4 (Winter 1978–79), 61–71.
Phillips, Paul. 'The National Policy and the Development of the Western Canadian Labour Movement.' In A.W. Rasporich and H.C. Klassen, eds., *Prairie Perspectives*, 2, 41–62. Toronto: Holt, Rinehart and Winston 1973.
– *No Power Greater: A Century of Labour in BC*. Vancouver: British Columbia Federation of Labour 1967.
– 'Power Politics: Municipal Affairs and Seymour James Farmer, 1909–1924.' In A.R. McCormack and Ian Macpherson, eds., *Cities in the West: Papers of the Western Canada Urban History Conference*, 159–80. Ottawa: National Museum of Man 1975.
Pitsula, James. 'The Emergence of Social Work in Toronto.' *Journal of Canadian Studies* 14, no. 1 (Spring 1979), 35–42.
Piva, Michael J. *The Condition of the Working Class in Toronto, 1900–1921*. Ottawa: University of Ottawa Press 1978.
– 'The Toronto District Labour Council and Independent Political Action: Factionalism and Frustration, 1900–1921.' *Labour/Le Travailleur*, 4 (1979), 115–30.
– 'Workers and Tories: The Collapse of the Conservative Party in Urban Ontario, 1908–1919.' *Urban History Review* 3–76 (1977), 23–9.
Pond, Douglas Daaman. *The History of Marysville, New Brunswick*. Fredericton: D.D. Pond 1983.
Pratt, Douglas Frederick. 'William Ivens, M.A., B.D., and the Winnipeg Labour Church.' BD thesis, St Andrew's College, Saskatoon 1962.
Price, Enid M. 'Changes in the Industrial Occupations of Women in the Environment of Montreal during the Period of the War, 1914–1918.' MA thesis, McGill University 1919.

Pringle, Jim. *United We Stand: A History of Winnipeg's Civic Workers*. Winnipeg: Manitoba Labour Education Centre 1991.

Provencher, Jean. *Québec sous la loi des mesures de guerre*. Montreal: Boréal Express 1971.

Pue, Wesley. 'Lawyers and the Constitution of Political Society: Containing Radicalism and Maintaining Order in Prairies Canada, 1900–1930.' *Canadian Legal History Project Working Paper Series*. Winnipeg: Legal Research Institute, University of Manitoba 1993.

– 'A Profession in Defence of Capital?' *Canadian Journal of Law and Society* 7, no. 2 (Fall 1992), 267–84.

Radeki, Henry, with Benedykt Heydenkorn. *A Member of a Distinguished Family: The Polish Group in Canada*. Toronto: McClelland and Stewart 1976.

Radforth, Ian. *Bushworkers and Bosses: Logging in Northern Ontario, 1900–1980*. Toronto: University of Toronto Press 1987.

– 'Finnish Lumber Workers in Ontario, 1919–1946.' *Polyphony* 3 (Fall 1981), 23–34.

Rajala, Richard. 'Managerial Crisis: The Emergence and Role of the West Coast Logging Engineer, 1900–1930.' In Peter Baskerville, ed., *Canadian Papers in Business History*, 101–27. Victoria: Public History Group 1989.

– 'The Rude Science: A Social History of West Coast Logging, 1890–1930.' MA thesis, University of Victoria 1987.

Ramirez, Bruno. 'Brief Encounters: Italian Immigrant Workers and the CPR, 1900–1930.' *Labour/Le Travail* 17 (Spring 1986), 9–28.

– *On the Move: French-Canadian and Italian Migrants in the North Atlantic Economy, 1860–1914*. Toronto: McClelland and Stewart 1991.

– 'Workers without a Cause: Italian Immigrant Labour in Montreal, 1880–1930.' In Roberto Perin and Franc Sturino, eds., *Arrangiarsi: The Italian Immigrant Experience in Canada*, 119–34. Montreal: Guernica 1992.

Ramkhalawansingh, Ceta. 'Women during the Great War.' In Janice Acton et al., eds., *Women at Work: Ontario, 1850–1930*, 261–307. Toronto: Women's Press 1974.

Rasporich, Anthony W. *For a Better Life: A History of the Croatians in Canada*. Toronto: McClelland and Stewart 1982.

Rawlyk, G.A. 'The Farmer-Labour Movement and the Failure of Socialism in Nova Scotia.' In Laurier LaPierre et al., eds., *Essays on the Left*, 31–41. Toronto: McClelland and Stewart 1971.

Ray, Arthur J. *The Canadian Fur Trade in the Industrial Age*. Toronto: University of Toronto Press 1990.

Rea, J.E. 'The Politics of Class: Winnipeg City Council, 1919–45.' In Carl Berger and Ramsay Cook, eds., *The West and the Nation: Essays in Honour of W.L. Morton*, 232–49. Toronto: McClelland and Stewart 1976.

– 'The Politics of Conscience: Winnipeg after the Strike.' Canadian Historical Association. *Historical Papers* (1971), 276–88.

– *The Winnipeg General Strike*. Toronto: Holt, Rinehart and Winston 1973.

Read, Daphne, ed. *The Great War and Canadian Society: An Oral History*. Toronto: New Hogtown Press 1978.

Reid, David J. 'Company Mergers in the Fraser River Salmon Canning Industry.' In W. Peter Ward and R.A.J. McDonald, eds., *British Columbia: Historical Readings*, 306–27. Vancouver: Douglas and McIntyre 1981.

Reilly, Nolan. 'The Emergence of Class Consciousness in Industrial Nova Scotia: A Study of Amherst, 1891–1925.' PhD diss., Dalhousie University 1983.

– 'The General Strike in Amherst, Nova Scotia, 1919.' *Acadiensis* 9 (1980), 56–77.

Reilly, Sharon. 'Robert Kell and the Art of the Winnipeg General Strike.' *Labour/Le Travail* 20 (Fall 1987), 185–92.

Reimer, Chad. 'War, Nationhood, and Working-Class Entitlement: The Counter-hegemonic Challenge of the 1919 Winnipeg General Strike.' *Prairie Forum* 18, no. 2 (Fall 1993), 219–37.

Reynolds, Lloyd G. *The British Immigrant: His Social and Economic Adjustment in Canada*. Toronto: Oxford University Press 1935.

Rhodes, D. Berkeley. 'The Star and the New Radicalism, 1917–1926.' MA thesis, University of Toronto 1955.

Rider, Peter. 'The Imperial Munitions Board and Its Relationship to Government, Business and Labour, 1914–1920.' PhD diss., University of Toronto 1974.

Roback, Leo. 'Quebec Workers in the Twentieth Century.' In W.J.C. Cherwinski and G.S. Kealey, eds., *Lectures in Canadian Working-Class History*, 165–82. St John's: Committee on Canadian Working Class History 1985.

Robb, Andrew. 'Third Party Experience on the Island.' In V. Smitheram et al., eds., *The Garden Transformed: Prince Edward Island, 1945–1980*. Charlottetown: Ragweed Press 1982.

Roberts, Barbara. *Whence They Came: Deportation from Canada, 1900–1935*. Ottawa: University of Ottawa Press 1988.

Roberts, Wayne. 'Studies in the Toronto Labour Movement, 1896–1914.' PhD diss., University of Toronto 1978.

– 'Toronto Metal Workers and the Second Industrial Revolution, 1889–1914.' *Labour/Le Travailleur* 6 (Autumn 1980), 49–72.

Robin, Martin. *Radical Politics and Canadian Labour, 1880–1930*. Kingston: Industrial Relations Centre, Queen's University 1968.

– 'Registration, Conscription, and Independent Labour Politics, 1916–1917.' *Canadian Historical Review* 47, no. 2 (June 1966), 101–18.

– *The Rush for Spoils: The Company Province, 1871–1933*. Toronto: McClelland and Stewart 1972.

Roby, Yves. *Les Francos-Américains de la Nouvelle-Angleterre, 1776–1930*. Quebec: Septentrion 1990.

– *Les Québécois et les investissements américains (1918–1929)*. Quebec: Les Presses de l'Université Laval 1976.

Roche, Maurice. 'Citizenship, Social Theory, and Social Change.' *Theory and Society* 16, no. 3 (May 1987), 363–99.

Rodney, Williams. 'Broken Journey: Trotsky in Canada, 1917.' *Queen's Quarterly* 74 (1967), 649–65.

– *Soldiers of the International: A History of the Communist Party of Canada, 1919–1929*. Toronto: University of Toronto Press 1968.

Roediger, David R., and Philip S. Foner. *Our Own Time: A History of American Labor and the Working Day*. New York: Verso 1989.

Roome, Patricia. 'Amelia Turner and Calgary Labour Women, 1919–1935.' In Linda Kealey and Joan Sangster, eds., *Beyond the Vote: Canadian Women and Politics*, 89–117. Toronto: University of Toronto Press 1989.

Rose, Clifford. *Four Years with the Demon Rum, 1925–1929: The Autobiography and Diary of Temperance Inspector Clifford Rose*. Fredericton: Acadiensis Press 1980.

Rosenberg, Louis. *Canada's Jews: A Social and Economic Study of the Jews in Canada*. Montreal: Bureau of Social and Economic Research, Canadian Jewish Congress 1939.

Rosenfeld, Mark. '"It Was a Hard Life": Class and Gender in the Work and Family Rhythms of a Railway Town, 1920–1950.' Canadian Historical Association. *Historical Papers* (1988), 237–79.

Roth, David M. 'A Union on the Hill: The International Union of Mine, Mill and Smelter Workers and the Organization of Trail Smelter and Chemical Workers.' MA thesis, Simon Fraser University 1991.

Rouillard, Jacques. 'L'action politique ouvrière, 1899–1915.' In Fernand Dumont et al., eds., *Idéologies au Canada français, 1900–1929*, 267–312. Quebec: Les Presses de l'Université Laval 1974.

– *Ah Les Etats! Les travailleurs canadiennes français dans l'industrie textile de la Nouvelle-Angleterre d'après le témoignage des derniers migrants*. Montreal: Boréal Express 1985.

– 'Les écrits d'Alfred Charpentier, 1920–1945.' In Fernand Dumont, Jean Hamelin, and Jean-Pierre Montminy, eds., *Idéologies au Canada français, 1940–1976*, 295–316. Quebec: Les Presses de l'Université Laval 1981.

– *Histoire de la CSN (1921–1981)*. Montreal: Confédération des syndicats nationaux 1981.

– *Histoire du syndicalisme québécois: Des origines à nos jours*. Montreal: Boréal 1989.

– 'Le Québec et le congrès de Berlin, 1902.' *Labour/Le Travailleur* 1 (1976), 69–91.

– *Les syndicats nationaux au Québec de 1900 à 1930*. Quebec: Les Presses de l'Université Laval 1979.
– *Les travailleurs du coton au Québec, 1900–1915*. Montreal: Les Presses de l'Université du Québec 1974.
– 'Les travailleurs juifs de la confection à Montreal (1910–1980).' *Labour/Le Travailleur* 8/9 (Autumn/Spring 1981–82), 253–9.
Roy, Patricia. *Vancouver: An Illustrated History* Vancouver: James Lorimer 1980.
– 'Vancouver: "The Mecca of the Unemployed," 1907–1929.' In Alan Artibise, ed., *Town and City: Aspects of Western Canadian Urban Development*, 393–413. Regina: Canadian Plains Research Center 1981.
– *A White Man's Province: British Columbia Politicians and Chinese and Japanese Immigrants, 1858–1914*. Vancouver: UBC Press 1989.
Roy, William. 'The French–English Division of Labour in the Province of Quebec.' MA thesis, McGill University 1935.
Rudin, Ronald. *The Forgotten Quebecers: A History of English-Speaking Quebec, 1759–1980*. Quebec: Institute québécois de recherche sur la culture 1985.
Rumilly, Robert. *Histoire de Montréal*. 5 vols. Montreal: Fides 1970–75.
– *Histoire de la Province de Québec*. 35 vols. Montreal: various publishers 1940–69.
Russell, Bob. *Back to Work? Labour, State, and Industrial Relations in Canada*. Scarborough: Nelson 1990.
Ryder, Walter Scott. 'Canada's Industrial Crisis of 1919.' MA thesis, University of British Columbia 1920.
Sacouman, James. 'Semi-Proletarianization and Rural Underdevelopment in the Maritimes.' *Canadian Review of Sociology and Anthropology* 17 (1980), 232–45.
Sammons, J. Douglas. 'Desperate Unions: Co-operation between the United Farmers of Ontario and the Independent Labor Party in the Election of 1919.' MA thesis, University of Waterloo 1973.
Samson, Daniel, ed. *Contested Countryside: Rural Workers and Modern Society in Atlantic Canada, 1800–1950*. Fredericton: Acadiensis Press 1994.
Samuels, Elliott. 'The Red Scare in Ontario: The Reaction of the Ontario Press to the Internal and External Threat of Bolshevism, 1917–1919.' MA thesis, Queen's University 1971.
Sandberg, L. Anders. 'The Deindustrialization of Pictou County, Nova Scotia: Capital, Labour, and the Process of Regional Decline, 1881–1921.' PhD diss., McGill University 1985.
– 'Dependent Development, Labour, and the Trenton Steel Works, Nova Scotia, c.1900–1943.' *Labour/Le Travail* 27 (Spring 1991), 127–62.
Sangster, Joan. *Dreams of Equality: Women on the Canadian Left, 1920–1950*. Toronto: McClelland and Stewart 1989.

– 'The 1907 Bell Telephone Strike: Organizing Women Workers.' *Labour/Le Travailleur* 3 (1978), 109–30.

Savage, Candace. *Our Nell: A Scrapbook Biography of Nellie McClung*. Saskatoon: Prairie Books 1979.

Saywell, J.T. 'Labour and Socialism in British Columbia.' *BC Historical Quarterly* 65 (1953), 129–50.

Scarrow, Howard A. *Canada Votes: A Handbook of Federal and Provincial Election Data*. New Orleans: Hauser Press 1962.

Schonning, Gil. 'Union–Management Relations in the Pulp and Paper Industry in Ontario and Quebec, 1914–1950.' PhD diss., University of Toronto 1955.

Schulze, David. 'The Industrial Workers of the World and the Unemployed in Edmonton and Calgary in the Depression of 1913–1915.' *Labour/Le Travail* 25 (Spring 1990), 47–76.

Schwantes, Carlos. *The Pacific Northwest: An Interpretive History*. Lincoln: University of Nebraska Press 1989.

– *Radical Heritage: Labor, Socialism, and Reform in Washington and British Columbia, 1885–1917*. Seattle: University of Washington Press 1970.

Scott, Bruce. '"A Place in the Sun": The Industrial Council at Massey-Harris, 1919–1929.' *Labour/Le Travailleur* 1 (1976), 158–92.

Scott, Stanley. 'A Profusion of Issues: Immigrant Labour, the World War, and the Cominco Strike of 1917.' *Labour/Le Travail* 2 (1977), 54–78.

Seager, Allen. 'Class, Ethnicity, and Politics in the Alberta Coalfields, 1905–1945.' In Dirk Hoerder, ed., *'Struggle a Hard Battle': Essays on Working-Class Immigrants*, 304–24. De Kalb: Northern Illinois University Press 1986.

– 'Finnish Canadians and the Ontario Miners' Movement.' *Polyphony* 3 (Fall 1981), 35–45.

– 'Miners' Struggles in Western Canada, 1890–1930.' In Deian R. Hopkin and Gregory S. Kealey, eds., *Class, Community, and the Labour Movement: Wales and Canada, 1850–1930*, 160–98. Aberystwyth, Wales: Llafur and Canadian Committee on Labour History 1989.

– 'Minto, New Brunswick: A Study of Class Relations between the Wars.' *Labour/Le Travailleur* 5 (Spring 1980), 81–132.

– 'A New Era for Labour? Canadian National Railways and the Railway Worker, 1919–1929.' Canadian Historical Association. *Journal* (1992), 171–96.

– 'Nineteen Nineteen: Year of Revolt.' *Journal of the West* 23, no. 4 (1984), 40–7.

– 'A Proletariat in Wild Rose Country: The Alberta Coal Miners, 1905–1945.' PhD diss., York University 1981.

– 'Socialists and Workers: The Western Canadian Coal Miners, 1900–1921.' *Labour/Le Travail* 16 (Fall 1985), 23–59.

– 'Workers, Class, and Industrial Conflict in New Westminster, 1900–1930.' In

Rennie Warburton and David Coburn, eds., *Workers, Capital, and the State in British Columbia: Selected Papers,* 117–40. Vancouver: UBC Press 1988.

Séguin, Normand. 'L'économie agro-forestière: Genèse du développement au Saguenay au 19e siècle.' In Normand Séguin, ed., *Agriculture et colonisation au Québec: Aspects historiques,* 159–64. Montreal: Boréal Express 1980.

Selekman, Ben M. *Postponing Strikes: A Study of the Industrial Disputes Investigation Act of Canada.* New York: 1927.

Sephton, Shaun. 'The Soldier Problem and 1919: The Case of Winnipeg.' Paper presented to the Manitoba History Conference, Winnipeg 1995.

Shilliday, Gregg, ed. *Manitoba 125: A History.* Vol. 2, *Gateway to the West.* Winnipeg: Great Plains Publications 1993.

Shorter, Edward, and Charles Tilly. *Strikes in France, 1830–1968.* London: Cambridge University Press 1974.

Shortt, Adam. 'The Economic Effects of War upon Canada.' Royal Society of Canada. *Transactions,* 3rd ser., 10 (1916), 65–74.

Shrum, G.M. 'Among Canada's West Coast Fishermen.' *Journal of Adult Education* (October 1940).

Siemiatycki, Myer. 'Labour Contained: The Defeat of a Rank and File Workers' Movement in Canada, 1914–1921.' PhD diss., York University 1986.

– 'Munitions and Labour Militancy: The 1916 Hamilton Machinists' Strike.' *Labour/Le Travailleur* 3 (1978), 131–52.

Sirianni, Carmen. *Workers' Control and Socialist Democracy: The Soviet Experience.* London: Verso 1982.

Sisu, Skari Tokoi. *'Even through a Stone Wall': The Autobiography of the First Premier of Finland.* New York 1957.

Skelton, O.D. 'The Western Strikes.' *Queen's Quarterly* 27, no. 1 (July–Sept. 1919), 121–8.

Smillie, Christine. 'The Invisible Workforce: Women Workers in Saskatchewan from 1905 to World War II.' *Saskatchewan History* 29, no. 2 (Spring 1986), 62–79.

Smith, A.E. *All My Life: An Autobiography.* Toronto: Progress Books 1949.

Smith, David Edward. 'Emergency Government in Canada.' *Canadian Historical Review* 50, no. 4 (December 1969), 429–48.

Smith, Doug. *Joe Zuken: Citizen and Socialist.* Toronto: James Lorimer 1990.

– *Let Us Rise! An Illustrated History of the Manitoba Labour Movement.* Vancouver: New Star Books 1985.

Smith, S.A. *Red Petrograd: Revolution in the Factories, 1917–1918.* Cambridge: Cambridge University Press 1983.

Socknat, Thomas P. *Witness against War: Pacificism in Canada, 1900–1945.* Toronto: University of Toronto Press 1987.

Spence, R.E. *Prohibition in Canada*. Toronto: Ontario Branch of the Dominion Alliance 1919.
Stacey, Duncan. *Sockeye and Tinplate: Technological Change in the Fraser River Canning Industry, 1871–1912*. Victoria: British Columbia Provincial Museum 1982.
Steedman, Mercedes Wells. 'Female Participation in the Canadian Clothing Industry, 1890 to 1940.' PhD diss., University of London 1990.
– 'Skill and Gender in the Canadian Clothing Industry, 1890–1940.' In Craig Heron and Robert Storey, eds., *On the Job: Confronting the Labour Process in Canada*, 152–76. Kingston and Montreal: McGill-Queens' University Press 1986.
Steeves, Dorothy G. *The Compassionate Rebel: Ernest Winch and the Growth of Socialism in Western Canada*. Vancouver: J.J. Douglas 1960.
Steinhart, Allan L. *Civil Censorship in Canada during World War I*. Toronto: Unitrade Press 1986.
Stevens, Francis Graham. 'A History of Radical Political Movements in Essex County and Windsor, 1919–1945.' MA thesis, University of Western Ontario 1948.
Strong, Anna Louise. *I Change Worlds: The Remaking of an American*. New York: H. Holt and Company 1935.
Strong-Boag, Veronica. 'The Girl of the New Day: Canadian Working Women in the 1920s.' *Labour/Le Travailleur* 4 (1979), 131–64.
– 'Wages for Housework: Mothers' Allowances and the Beginnings of Social Security in Canada.' *Journal of Canadian Studies* 14, no. 1 (Spring 1979), 24–34.
Struthers, James. *No Fault of Their Own: Unemployment and the Canadian Welfare State, 1914–1941*. Toronto: University of Toronto Press 1983.
– 'A Profession in Crisis: Charlotte Whitton and Canadian Social Work in the 1930s.' *Canadian Historical Review* 62, no. 2 (June 1981), 169–85.
Stubbs, Roy St. George. *Prairie Portraits*. Toronto: McClelland and Stewart 1954.
Sutcliffe, Joseph Harry. 'The Economic Background of the Winnipeg Strike: Wages and Working Conditions.' MA thesis, University of Manitoba 1972.
Sutcliffe, Joseph Harry, and Paul Phillips. 'Real Wages and the Winnipeg General Strike: An Empirical Investigation.' Unpublished paper.
Sutherland, Neil. *Children in English-Canadian Society: Framing the Twentieth-Century Consensus*. Toronto: University of Toronto Press 1976.
Swankey, Ben, and Jean Evans Shiels. *'Work and Wages': A Semi-Documentary Account of the Life and Times of Arthur H. Slim Evans*. Vancouver: Trade Union Research Bureau 1977.
Sweatman, Margaret. *Fox*. Winnipeg: Turnstone Press 1990.
Swettenham, John. *Allied Intervention in Russia, 1918–1919, and the Part Played by Canada*. Toronto: Ryerson Press 1967.
Swyripa, Frances, and John Herd Thompson, eds. *Loyalties in Conflict: Ukrainians*

during the Great War. Edmonton: Canadian Institute of Ukrainian Studies, University of Alberta 1983.

Synge, Jane. 'Self-Help and Neighbourliness: Patterns of Life in Hamilton.' In Irving Abella and David Millar, eds., *The Canadian Worker in the Twentieth Century,* 97–104. Toronto: Oxford University Press 1978.

– 'The Transition from School to Work: Growing Up Working Class in Early Twentieth Century Hamilton, Ontario.' In K. Ishwaran, ed., *Childhood and Adolescence in Canada,* 249–69. Toronto: McGraw-Hill Ryerson 1979.

Taraska, Elizabeth Ann. 'The Calgary Craft Union Movement, 1900–20.' MA thesis, University of Calgary 1975.

Taylor, G.W. *The Railway Contractors: The Story of John W. Stewart, His Enterprises and Associates.* Victoria: Morris Publishing 1988.

– *Timber: History of the Forest Industry in B.C.* Vancouver: J.J. Douglas 1975.

Taylor, John. 'Sources of Political Conflict in the 1930s: Welfare Policy and the Geography of Need.' In Allan Moscovitch and Jim Albert, ed., *The 'Benevolent' State: The Growth of Welfare in Canada,* 144–154. Toronto: Garamond Press 1987.

Tennant, Paul. *Aboriginal Peoples and Politics: The Indian Land Question in British Columbia, 1849–1889.* Vancouver: UBC Press 1990.

Têtu, Michel. 'Les premiers syndicats catholiques canadiens (1900–1921).' PhD diss., Université Laval 1964.

Thistle, Mel. *The Inner Ring: The Early History of the National Research Council of Canada.* Toronto: University of Toronto Press 1966.

Thomas, Lillian Jean. 'A Test of Social Conflict Theory: The Case of the Winnipeg General Strike.' MA thesis, University of Manitoba 1977.

Thompson, Fred. 'A Rebel Voice: Fred Thompson Remembers Halifax, 1919–1920.' *This Magazine* 12 (1978), 8–9.

Thompson, John Herd. '"The Beginning of Our Regeneration": The Great War and Western Canadian Reform Movements.' Canadian Historical Association. *Historical Papers* (1972), 227–45.

– 'Bringing in the Sheaves: The Harvest Excursionists, 1890–1929.' *Canadian Historical Review* 59, no. 4 (December 1978), 467–89.

– 'The Enemy Alien and the Canadian General Election of 1917.' In Frances Swyripa and John Herd Thompson, eds., *Loyalties in Conflict: Ukrainians during the Great War,* 25–46. Edmonton: Canadian Institute of Ukrainian Studies, University of Alberta 1983.

– *The Harvests of War: The Prairie West, 1914–1918.* Toronto: McClelland and Stewart 1978.

Thompson, John Herd, and Allen Seager, *Canada, 1922–1939: Decades of Discord.* Toronto: McClelland and Stewart 1985.

Thomson, Anthony. '"The Large and Generous View": The Debate on Labour

Affiliation in the Canadian Civil Service, 1918–1928.' *Labour/Le Travailleur* 2 (1977), 108–36.

Thornton, Patricia A. 'The Problem of Out-Migration from Atlantic Canada, 1871–1920: A New Look.' *Acadiensis* 15, no. 1 (Autumn 1985), 3–34.

Thwaites, James. 'La grève au Québec: Une analyse quantitative exploratoire portant sur la période 1896–1915.' *Labour/Le Travail* 10 (Fall 1984), 183–204.

Tipping, Fred. 'Religion and the Making of a Labour Leader.' In Richard Allen, ed., *The Social Gospel in Canada*, 63–65. Ottawa: National Museum of Man 1975.

Trachtenberg, Henry. 'The Winnipeg General Strike, the Arrested Aliens, and the Winnipeg Jewish Commuity, 1919: "Adapt to the Institutions and Manners of this Country and Become Loyal Canadian Citizens."' Paper presented to the Canadian Jewish Historical Society, 1993.

– 'The Winnipeg Jewish Community and Politics: The Inter-War Years, 1919–1939.' Historical and Scientific Society of Manitoba. *Transactions*, 3rd ser., nos. 34–35 (1977–78 and 1978–79), 115–53.

Tranfield, Pam. 'Girl Strikers.' *NeWest* 14, no. 5 (June/July 1989).

Traves, Tom. *The State and Enterprise: Canadian Manufacturers and the Federal Government, 1917–1931*. Toronto: University of Toronto Press 1979.

Trofimenkoff, Susan Mann. 'Henri Bourassa and "The Woman Question."' In Susan Mann Trofimenkoff and Alison Prentice, eds., *The Neglected Majority*, 104–15. Toronto: McClelland and Stewart 1977.

Troop, G.R.F. 'Socialism in Canada.' MA thesis, McGill University 1924.

Trueman, Allan. 'New Brunswick and the 1921 Federal Election.' MA thesis, University of New Brunswick 1975.

Tuck, Hugh. 'Union Authority, Corporate Obstinacy, and the Grand Trunk Strike of 1910.' Canadian Historical Association. *Historical Papers* (1976), 175–92.

Tucker, Eric. *Administering Danger in the Workplace: The Law and Politics of Occupational Health and Safety Regulation in Ontario, 1850–1914*. Toronto: University of Toronto Press 1990.

– 'World War I and the Post-War Labour Revolt.' Unpublished paper, Osgoode Law School 1996.

Tulchinsky, Gerald. 'The Contours of Canadian Jewish History.' *Journal of Canadian Studies* 17, no. 4 (Winter 1982–3), 46–56.

– *Taking Root: The Origins of the Canadian Jewish Community*. Toronto: Lester 1992.

– 'The Third Solitude: A.M. Klein's Jewish Montreal.' *Journal of Canadian Studies* 19, no. 2 (Summer 1984), 96–112.

Tuttle, William M. *Race Riot: Chicago in the Red Summer of 1919*. New York: Atheneum 1970.

Ursel, Jane. 'The State and the Maintenance of Patriarchy: A Case Study of Family, Labour and Welfare Legislation in Canada.' In James Dickinson and Bob Russell, eds., *Family, Economy and State: The Social Reproduction Process under Capitalism*, 150–91. Toronto: Garamond Press 1986.

Usiskin, Roseline. 'Toward a Theoretical Reformulation of the Relationship between Political Ideology, Social Class, and Ethnicity: A Case Study of the Winnipeg Jewish Radical Community, 1905–1920.' MA thesis, University of Manitoba 1978.

– 'The Winnipeg Jewish Radical Community: Its Early Formation, 1905–1918.' In Jewish Historical Society of Western Canada, *Jewish Life and Times: A Collection of Essays*, 155–68. Winnipeg: Jewish Historical Society of Western Canada 1983.

Valentine, Jaime. 'The Call of Iron in "New Ontario": Steelworkers in Sault Ste. Marie, Ontario, 1900–1921.' MA thesis, Queen's University 1986.

Vanasse, Gilbert. *Histoire de la fédération des travailleurs du papier et de la forêt*. Vol. 1, *1907–1958*. Montreal: Editions Saint-Martin 1986.

Vance, Catherine. *Not by Gods, But by People: The Story of Bella Hall Gauld*. Toronto: Progress Books 1968.

Van Dieren, Karen. 'The Response of the WMS to the Immigration of Asian Women, 1888–1942.' In Barbara Latham and Roberta J. Pazdro, eds., *Not Just Pin Money*, 79–95. Victoria: Camosun College 1984.

Wade, Susan. 'Helena Gutteridge: Votes for Women and Trade Unions.' In Barbara Latham and Cathy Kess, eds., *In Her Own Right: Selected Essays on Women's History in B.C.*, 187–204. Victoria: Camosun College 1980.

Ward, W. Peter. 'Class and Race in the Social Structure of British Columbia.' *BC Studies* 45 (Spring 1980), 17–35.

Warrian, Peter. 'The Challenge of the One Big Union in Canada, 1919–21.' MA thesis, University of Waterloo 1971.

Watson, Louise. *She Was Never Afraid: The Biography of Annie Buller*. Toronto: Progress Books 1976.

Watson, Margaret. 'The United Farmers of Ontario and Political Co-operation with the Independent Labour Party, 1919–1923.' Unpublished paper, York University 1984.

Watt, Frank William. 'Radicalism in English-Canadian Literature since Confederation.' PhD diss., University of Toronto 1957.

Webber, Jeremy. 'The Malaise of Compulsory Conciliation: Strike Prevention in Canada during World War II.' *Labour/Le Travail* 15 (Spring 1985), 57–90.

Whitaker, Reginald. 'The Liberal Corporatist Ideas of Mackenzie King.' *Labour/Le Travailleur* 2 (1977), 137–69.

Wichern, P.H. 'Historical Influences on Contemporary Local Politics: The Case of Winnipeg.' *Urban History Review* 12, no. 1 (June 1983), 39–45.

Wickberg, Edgar, ed. *From China to Canada: A History of the Chinese Communities in Canada*. Toronto: McClelland and Stewart 1982.

Williams, C. Brian. 'International Trade Unionism: The United Mine Workers in Eastern Canada, 1900–1920.' *Relations industrielles/Industrial Relations* 41, no. 3 (1986), 519–40.

Williams, Gwyn A. *Proletarian Order: Antonio Gramsci, Factory Councils, and the Origins of Communism in Italy, 1911–1921*. London: Pluto Books 1975.

Wilson, Barbara M. *Ontario and the First World War, 1914–1918*. Toronto: University of Toronto Press 1977.

Winsor, Fred. '"Solving a Problem": Privatizing Workers' Compensation for Nova Scotia's Offshore Fishermen, 1926–1928.' In Michael Earle, ed., *The Worker and the State in Twentieth-Century Nova Scotia*, 68–84. Fredericton: Acadiensis Press 1989.

Winter, J.M. *The Great War and the British People*. Cambridge: Harvard University Press 1987.

Wiseman, Adele. *Crackpot*. Toronto: McClelland and Stewart 1974.

Wood, Louis Aubrey. *A History of Farmers' Movements in Canada*. Toronto: Ryerson Press 1924.

Working Lives Collective. *Working Lives: Vancouver, 1886–1986*. Vancouver: New Star Books 1985.

Wormsbecker, Kathleen O'Gorman. 'The Rise and Fall of the Labour Political Movement in Manitoba, 1919–1927.' MA thesis, Queen's University 1977.

Woywitka, Anne. 'Drumheller Strike of 1919.' *Alberta Historical Review* 21 no. 1 (Winter 1973), 1–7.

Wrigley, Chris, ed. *Challenges of Labour: Central and Western Europe, 1917–1920*. London: Routledge 1993.

Yarmie, Andrew. 'The Right to Manage: Vancouver Employers' Associations, 1900–1923.' *BC Studies* 90 (1991), 40–74.

Yeo, David Patrick. 'An Alliance Unrealized: Farmers, Labour, and the 1919 Winnipeg General Strike.' MA thesis, University of Calgary 1986.

– 'Rural Manitoba Views the Winnipeg General Strike.' *Prairie Forum* 14, no. 1 (Spring 1989), 23–36.

Young, Walter. *The Anatomy of a Party: The National CCF, 1932–1961*. Toronto: University of Toronto Press 1969.

– 'Ideology, Personality, and the Origin of the CCF in British Columbia.' In W. Peter Ward and Robert A.J. McDonald, eds., *British Columbia: Historical Readings*, 555–77. Vancouver: Douglas and McIntyre 1981.

Young, W.R. 'Conscription, Rural Depopulation, and the Farmers of Ontario, 1917–1919.' *Canadian Historical Review* 53, no. 3 (September 1972), 289–320.
Zerker, Sally. *The Rise and Fall of the Toronto Typographical Union, 1832–1972: A Case Study of Foreign Domination*. Toronto: University of Toronto Press 1982.
Zucchi, John E. *Italians in Toronto: Development of a National Identity, 1875–1935*. Kingston and Montreal: McGill-Queen's University Press 1988.

Illustration Credits

Beaton Institute, University College of Cape Breton: steelworkers in Trenton, 77-150-284

The Boag Foundation: James Watters

City of Toronto Archives, James Collection: men waiting to enlist, 735A; Earlscourt, a workers' suburb, 727; CPR employees, 737; Toronto women, 858; angry machinists, 851; unidentified Toronto workers, 2543; Toronto veterans, 903

Glenbow Archives, Calgary, Alberta: garment workers in Edmonton, NC 6-3270

***Halifax Herald*:** J.B. McLachlan cartoon

National Archives of Canada: protests after the arrest of Winnipeg strike leaders, C37329

Provincial Archives of Manitoba: the government's 'special' constables, N12335; 'Bloody Saturday,' N12316

Public Archives of Nova Scotia: 'Canadian Labor Will Crush Bolshevism'

University of British Columbia, Frank Sherman Collection: miners of Fernie cartoon

Western Canadian Pictorial Index: crowds in Winnipeg's Victoria Park, photograph by Lewis Foote, 1293-38716; Citizens' Committee banquet, 1293-38699

***Western Labor News*, courtesy Manitoba Museum of Man and Nature:** 'Labor Church;' 'No Need to Hunger'

Contributors

Geoffrey Ewen teaches history at Glendon College, York University.

Craig Heron teaches social science and history at York University.

Ian McKay teaches history at Queen's University.

Tom Mitchell works at Brandon University.

Suzanne Morton teaches history at McGill University.

James Naylor teaches history at Brandon University.

David Roth works for the British Columbia Union of Indian Chiefs.

Allen Seager teaches history at Simon Fraser University.

Myer Siemiatycki teaches politics at Ryerson Polytechnic University.

Index

absenteeism 19
Acadians 44, 45
African-Canadian workers 44, 61, 271
agricultural workers 15, 241
Aikens, J.A.M. 213
Ainey, Joseph 92, 122, 123, 124, 126–7, 128
Alberta 20, 181, 191, 232; *see also* Calgary; Drumheller; Edmonton
Albert County, New Brunswick 55
Alien Investigation Board 184
Almavoff, Moses 210
Amalgamated Association of Iron, Steel and Tin Workers 57, 148; *see also* steelworkers
Amalgamated Association of Street and Electric Railway Employees 255; *see also* street railway workers
Amalgamated Clothing Workers (ACW) 93, 99, 100, 105, 106, 114, 130, 147; *see also* clothing workers
Amalgamated Meat Cutters and Butcher Workmen 148; *see also* packinghouse workers
Amalgamated Mine Workers of Nova Scotia (AMW) 49
Amalgamated Society of Engineers (ASE) 90, 93, 110, 114, 146, 152, 154, 171; *see also* machinists
amalgamation of craft unions 129, 153, 154, 155, 168, 193, 195, 292
American Federation of Labor: Canadian membership of 28, 49, 52, 87, 90, 93, 132, 133, 148, 290, 293; craft-unionist policies of 99, 152, 167, 251, 258, 292, 296; officials of 123, 198; and war 123, 160
American Federation of Teachers 117
Amherst, Nova Scotia 4, 51, 52, 53, 54, 57, 64, 82, 302
Amherst Federation of Labor 52, 53, 54
Amherst general strike. *See* general strikes
anarchism 180
Anderson, Ed 228
Anderson, Perry 216
Andrews, A.J. 203, 204, 205, 206, 207, 208, 209, 210, 211, 212, 224, 225, 227, 228
Anglo-Celtic workers 23, 44, 89, 90, 112, 121, 183, 184, 309; *see also* ethnic conflict

Angus shops. *See* Canadian Pacific Railway
Antigonish, Nova Scotia 77
Anti-Loafing Act 14, 33
Anyox, British Columbia 251
Arbeiter Ring 179
arbitration of labour disputes 103–4, 195, 278
Arcand, Narcisse 98, 122
Armstrong, George 209, 215
Armstrong, Helen 185, 273
Armstrong, W.H. 246
Asbestos Corporation 98
Australia 4, 21, 26
Austria-Hungary 4, 23, 34
Austrian workers 98, 183

Bainbridge, Isaac 149, 153
Bank of Montreal 102
barbers 93, 111, 242
Barrett, Silby 50
Bathurst, New Brunswick 45
Baugh, William 111, 116
Baxter, Robert 50, 68
BC Federationist 249, 252, 258
BC Fishermen's Protective Association 256
BC Loggers' Union 251, 259
BC Mills, Timber, and Trading Company 237
BC Miners' Association 259
BC Packers' Association 235
BC Provincial Service Association 302
Beatty, F.M. 223
Beck, Sir Adam 164
Bercovitch, Peter 100
Bercuson, David 5, 9, 217, 219, 220, 227, 230, 258
Berg, Carl 200
Bernier, Alphonse 121, 124
Besco. *See* British Empire Steel Corporation
Binette, Ulrike 124, 128
Bishop, Gordon 273
blacklisting 28, 51, 56, 73, 75, 247, 259, 261, 287
blacks. *See* African-Canadian workers
'blanketstiffs.' *See* labourers, unskilled
Bliss, Michael 171
'Bloody Saturday' (Winnipeg) 198, 211 256; *see also* Winnipeg General Strike, repression of
'Bloody Sunday' (Sydney) 73, 74
Blumenberg, Samuel 181, 183, 210, 215
Board of Commerce 15
Board of Grain Supervisors 15
boilermakers 51, 111, 114, 149, 199, 251
Bolshevism 26, 51, 53, 81, 112, 182, 192, 212, 231, 249, 285, 294, 305, 311; business and state fears of 35, 73, 74, 118, 182, 203–15, 253, 260, 306; *see also* Communism in Canada; Red Scare
boot and shoe workers 88, 89, 90, 91, 94, 107, 117, 118, 119, 122, 245
Borden, Sir Robert 5, 12, 21, 24, 29, 30, 31, 32, 33, 34–7, 152, 209, 229, 249, 290
Bouchard, Emma 109
Bourassa, Henri 13, 130, 132
box makers 57
Braithwaite, Louis 149
Brandon, Manitoba 190, 196, 215
Brandon Trades and Labor Council 190, 191, 196, 222
Brantford, Ontario 163, 164
Bray, R.E. 209

breadwinning 53, 78, 107, 130, 161, 191, 273, 280, 283, 301
Breeze, W. 217
bricklayers 114, 192
Bright, David 196, 199, 220, 221, 223
British Columbia, economy of 232–7, 243–5
British Columbia Federation of Labor 18, 238, 247, 249, 250, 254, 258
British Columbia Telephone 257
British Empire Steel Corporation 68, 73, 74, 75, 76
Broatch, Andrew G. 190, 194
Brotherhood of Locomotive Trainmen 58; *see also* railway workers
Brotherhood of Railway Carmen, 122–3; *see also* railway workers
Bruce, John 36, 37
Bruchesi, Archbishop 103
Buctouche, New Brunswick 48
Buhay, Becky 59, 128, 130
Buhay, Michael 128, 129
Builders' Exchange 114, 116
building trades councils 51, 111, 113, 114, 116, 154, 191, 199
building trades workers 278; in British Columbia 237, 238, 245; in Maritimes 47, 52; in Prairie provinces 177, 189, 198; in Quebec 90, 109, 114, 116, 117; *see also* bricklayers; carpenters; electricians; iron workers; labourers, building; painters; plumbers; roofers; stonecutters
Buller, Annie 59, 128, 130, 294
Bund 179
Bungalow Building and Finance Company 237
bureaucratization 50, 73, 75, 79, 293, 296
business agents 94, 98, 104, 108, 293
Businessmen's Strike Relief Committee 100
business unionism 66, 112; *see also* bureaucratization; craft unionism; international unionism
butchers 245, 252
butcher workers. *See* packinghouse workers
Butt, Michael 187

Cahan, C.H. 25, 204
Caiserman, Hananiah Meir 93
Caldwell, T.W. 61
Caledonia, Nova Scotia 75
Calgary 24, 145, 153, 177, 181–2, 183, 188, 189, 190, 191, 193, 194, 196, 198–200, 203, 209, 223, 250, 259, 273, 276, 291
Calgary Conference. *See* Western Labour Conference
Calgary Federation of Civic Employees 199
Calgary Trades and Labor Council 190, 191, 194, 196, 198, 199
Cameron, D.S. 242
Campbell, F.A. 65, 66
Campbell, Peter 178, 217, 218, 219
Canada Western Lumber Company 236
Canadian Brotherhood of Railway Employees 52
Canadian Car and Foundry 51, 54, 114, 116, 117
Canadian Catholic Confederation of Labour 119; *see also* Catholic unionism
Canadian Consolidated Rubber 111
Canadian Cotton Company 65
Canadian Expeditionary Force 12, 38
Canadian Jewish Congress 93

Canadian Labor News 289, 292
Canadian Labor Party 32, 123, 274, 294, 295; *see also* Ontario Section; Quebec Section
Canadian Manufacturers' Association 36, 203, 291
Canadian National Railways 15, 63, 197
Canadian Northern Railway 238, 256
Canadian Pacific Railway 104, 181–2, 185, 235, 246, 253, 257, 271; Angus shops 89, 104, 120, 125; Ogden shops 190, 195–6, 199; strike-breaking activities of 102, 115
Canadian Patriotic Fund 13, 18, 245, 265
Canadian Reconstruction Association 214, 289
Canadian Union of Ex-Servicemen 275
Canadian Vickers 89, 95, 97, 110–11, 113, 116, 117
Canadian Wool Commission 15
canning industry, salmon 235
Cap-de-la-Madeleine, Quebec 90, 117
Cape Breton 33, 45, 47, 54, 56, 57, 59, 65, 66, 70, 73, 77, 81, 272, 279, 287, 294, 297, 308
Cape Breton Independent Labor Party 276
Carleton Place, Ontario 304
carpenters 94, 98, 106, 108, 114, 122, 123, 147, 150, 152, 153, 154, 162, 191, 192, 239, 290
carriage makers 140
car workers 51, 53, 114, 116, 117
Cascaden, Gordon 155
Cassidy, Annie 162
Cassidy, Tom 26, 122, 273
Catholic unionism 28, 289; in Maritimes 45; in Quebec 87, 89, 91, 94, 98, 101, 118–21, 133, 140, 309
cereal workers 251
Charitinoff, Michael 210
Charlottetown 57, 64
Charpentier, Alfred 96, 134
Chatham, New Brunswick 52, 64
check-off of union dues 49, 50, 76
Cherwinski, W.J.C. 190, 222
Chicoutimi, Quebec 90
Chilliwack, British Columbia 251
Chinese Canadian Labour Union 252
Chinese Shingle Weavers' Union 252, 271
Chinese workers 148, 191, 232, 235, 240, 241, 245, 252, 259
Chippewa, Ontario 166
Christophers, Phillip M. 261, 273
Churchill, Winston 206
cigarmakers 90, 105, 107, 126
Circé-Côté, Eva 130, 131
Citizen (Halifax) 56, 59, 86
Citizen (Winnipeg) 182, 184, 219, 306
Citizens' Committee (Calgary) 202
Citizens' Committee of 100 (Winnipeg) 181
Citizens' Committee of 1000 (Winnipeg) 182, 184, 202, 203, 205, 208, 210, 211, 212, 213, 214, 215, 219, 225, 228
citizenship 184, 190, 228; bourgeois definition of 211, 213–14, 290; labour definition of 184, 211, 277
Citizen's League (Vancouver) 256, 257
Citizens' Protective Association, Committee of Public Safety (Montreal) 103
civic workers. *See* municipal workers
Clarke, Joe 201

clerical workers 50, 57, 108, 191, 241, 271, 311
closed shop 117, 119, 239, 245, 259; *see also* open shop; union recognition
Clothing Manufacturers' Association (Montreal) 99, 100
clothing workers 12, 22, 28, 269, 292, 296; in British Columbia 241, 245; in Ontario 147, 148, 152, 271; in Prairie provinces 185, 200; in Quebec 88, 89, 90, 93, 94, 97, 99–100, 104, 105–6, 107, 108, 110, 111, 114, 117, 129, 271, 278; *see also* tailors
Club Libéral des Femmes 143
Coaker, William 286
Coal Controller 15, 246
coal industry 15, 23, 44, 46
Cobalt, Ontario 20
Cody, Henry 290
collective bargaining 33, 36, 48, 49, 72, 79, 100, 101, 112, 182, 186, 206, 209, 227, 255, 278, 279, 293, 307; *see also* industrial legality
Colorado Plan 279
Columbus Rubber Company 111
Cominco 19
Committee of 350 202
Communism in Canada 7, 57, 59, 66, 70, 76, 128–9, 169, 193, 293, 295, 307; opposition to 71, 75; *see also* Bolshevism; Communist Party of Canada; Workers' Party of Canada
Communist International 129, 261, 294
Communist Party of Canada 7, 59, 66, 128, 230, 259, 261, 294
community unionism 51–2, 272
company unionism 65; *see also* industrial councils
conciliation, boards of. *See* Industrial Disputes Investigation Act
confectionery workers 57, 88, 185
Congdon, H.S. 78
Conley, James 239
conscription, military 16, 21, 24, 47, 157; labour responses to 31, 150, 190, 249, 250, 274, 290; resistance to 24, 103, 121–3, 309
conscription of wealth 21, 31, 122
Conseil central national des métiers du district de Québec 125
Conservative Party 296; in British Columbia 260, 267; and federal government 12, 15–16, 21, 159; in Maritimes 62, 63, 75, 77, 83; in Ontario 156, 163, 167, 289, 310; in Prairie provinces 201, 242; in Quebec 128, 129
Consolidated Mining and Smelting Company 235, 247
construction workers 12, 46, 89; *see also* building trades workers
consumer spending, working-class 12, 18, 19, 74, 311
contracts. *See* industrial legality
Cooks and Waiters' Union 240; *see also* hotel and restaurant workers; waitresses
Co-operative Commonwealth Federation 170, 259, 261, 275, 295
cooperative movement 124; Antigonish 77
cooperative stores 22
coopers 147
Corrigan, Philip 213
Cosmos Cotton Mill 63
cost of living 15, 20–1, 22, 31, 33, 53, 146, 245
Cost of Living Commissioner 15

courts and labour 61, 66, 74, 105, 117, 118, 119, 169, 204–11, 228; *see also* sedition

Coyne, J.C. 203, 228

craft unionism 27–8, 29, 91, 99, 113, 114, 121, 155, 198, 202, 206, 232, 270, 272, 296, 307; changes in during war 148, 155, 177, 191, 272 (*see also* amalgamation of craft unions; joint bargaining); opposition to industrial unionism 113, 121, 125, 132, 258, 291, 292, 293; opposition to radicalism 291, 292, 294; *see also* American Federation of Labor; Trades and Labor Congress of Canada; trades and labour councils

craftworkers 22, 50, 100, 235; relations with less skilled 44, 51, 146, 183, 189; *see also* craft unionism; 'dilution' of labour; joint bargaining

Cranbrook, British Columbia 248, 260

Creese, Gillian 240

Criminal Code 206; Section 98 35, 207, 211, 226, 289

crowds, working-class 36, 48, 59, 61, 74–5, 96, 102–3, 109–10, 121, 122, 131, 184, 208, 220, 240, 281

Crow's Nest Pass 233, 246, 251, 253, 258, 259, 260, 273

Cruikshank, Douglas 237, 269

Cumberland County Labor Party 55

Dane, Clifford C. 50, 51, 81, 273

Dartmouth, Nova Scotia 51, 78

Davis, William 75

'Daylight Saving' 14

Décary, Ernest 102, 115

democracy, as labour goal 25–6, 27, 30, 50, 145, 158, 276, 277, 296, 307, 312

democratic management. *See* industrial democracy

Department of Justice, federal 204, 212, 225

Department of Labour, British Columbia 232, 263

Department of Labour, federal 30, 32, 47, 64, 66, 73, 81, 100, 108, 119, 147, 157, 238, 270, 278, 288

deportation. *See* immigrants

detectives, private 104, 288; *see also* special police; strike-breaking

Detroit Auto Workers' News 155

Dickie, Charles 113

'dilution' of labour 22, 106, 146, 148, 172, 237

Director of Public Information 14

Director of Public Safety 204

district councils 272; *see also* trades and labour councils

Dixon, Frederick J. 211, 212, 215, 229

dockers. *See* longshoremen

Doherty, C.J. 212, 213

domestic servants 58, 147, 162, 191, 277

Domestic Workers' Association 277

Dominion, Nova Scotia 48, 75

Dominion Coal Company 57, 58

Dominion Express Company 104

Dominion Iron and Steel Company 57

Dominion Labor Party 188, 201, 215

Dominion Police 14, 35, 122, 250

Dominion Textile 104, 113, 116

Donaldson, Bertha 58

Donnacona, Quebec 95

Doyle, Henry 235

Draper, P.M. (Paddy) 29

Drolet, Benjamin 105, 112

Drumheller, Alberta 24

Drummond, Robert 50

Drummondville, Quebec 88
Drury, E.C. 164
Duncan, James A. 195
Dunsmuir family 239

Eastern Federationist (New Glasgow) 50, 56, 86
Eastern Townships 88, 89
economic depressions: post-war 22, 63, 116, 120, 183, 215, 295, 307, 308, 311; pre-war 11–12, 18, 29, 244
Edmonton 26, 188, 190, 200–2, 273, 291
Edmonton Free Press 292
Edmonton Trades and Labor Council 195, 200, 201, 202, 291
education 59, 118, 157, 311; and citizenship 213–14, 290; francophone 16; socialist 178, 214, 273, 276, 294; for workers 56, 128, 129, 161, 194, 274–5, 281
elections, federal: by-elections 61–2, 131, 162, 164; (1917) 16, 32, 54, 122, 124, 160, 189, 193, 194, 249, 275; (1921) 65, 131, 170, 200, 215, 261, 290, 294
elections, municipal 54, 55, 56, 93, 124, 126, 128, 142, 149, 156–7, 159, 188, 215, 218, 230, 275
elections, provincial: in British Columbia 248, 249, 260, 275; in Manitoba 215, 275; in New Brunswick 55, 61–3, 275; in Nova Scotia 54, 59, 62, 275; in Ontario, 144, 155, 163–4, 167, 275; in Prairie provinces 190–1, 215, 261; in Quebec 125, 128, 131, 275
electoral workers 33
electrical parts workers 88, 106
electricians 111, 114, 197, 255
Employers' Association of Toronto 151, 154
employers' associations 36, 99, 100, 103, 114, 116, 120, 151, 154, 181, 202, 203, 236, 238, 256, 257, 259; *see also* Citizens' Committee of 1000
Employment Service of Canada 15
'enemy aliens' 13, 14, 19, 23, 98, 179, 182, 183, 184, 284, 301; internment of 14, 35, 179
English, John 16
ethnic conflict 28, 214; and Asians 24, 240, 241, 252, 284, 310; and eastern European 'enemy aliens' 13, 16, 23, 24, 37, 148, 284, 301; and Germans 13, 37, 98, 99; and French Canadians 16; and Jewish immigrants 99
ethnic divisions in working class 87, 93, 96–7, 98, 112, 129, 148, 284, 286; efforts to overcome 98, 184, 240, 284
Ex-Soldiers' and Sailors' Labor Party 215

Fairhurst, James 261
fair wage clause 97
family economies, working-class 19, 20, 53, 94, 107, 283, 306, 308, 311; *see also* consumer spending, working-class; cost of living; housing, working-class
family wage 107, 161, 163, 273, 280, 301
Farmer, S.J. 215
Farmer-Labour government 144, 163–7, 170, 275, 294, 309
Farmer-Labour parties 55, 62, 63, 65, 165, 275
farmers 44, 57, 60, 213; alliances with labour 54, 61–3, 65, 77, 84, 92, 125, 144, 159, 164, 165, 275, 285, 307;

organizations of 17, 61–2, 125, 159, 164, 165, 287; protests of 26, 61, 310
Farmilo, Alfred 122, 195, 200, 291
federal labour unions 87, 101, 149, 154, 155, 191, 200; *see also* federations of labour
Federal Workers' Union (Calgary) 191
Federated Labor Party 249, 260–1
Fédération des clubs ouvriers municipaux de Montréal 92, 94, 96, 97, 100, 104, 122, 123, 124
federations of labour, in Maritimes 51, 53, 57
Fermiers unis du Québec 125
Fernie, British Columbia 248, 259, 260, 291, 294
Ferro-Concrete Construction Company 237
Fillmore, Roscoe 53
Finnish workers 26, 271
firefighters 90, 101, 102–3, 104, 113, 118, 147, 185, 191, 201
First World War: casualties in 13; military preparations for 12–13; *see also* conscription, military; recruitment, military; war economy
Fishermen's Protective Union of Newfoundland 286
fishers 286; in British Columbia 235, 238, 239, 256; in Maritimes 45, 57, 60, 61, 62
Flatman, Frederick 153, 155, 161, 273, 294, 304
Flavelle, Sir Joseph 21, 24, 146, 171
Foley, Welsh and Stewart 236
Food Board 15
Fortier, Adélard 96, 104
Foster, J.T. 91, 98, 105, 112, 113, 116
Foster, William Z. 161
Fowler Amendment 180, 181
franchise: and property qualifications 157, 159; restrictions on for immigrants 16, 159, 174; for women 16, 17, 54, 129, 130, 156, 161, 174, 243, 280
Francq, Gustave 91, 105, 110, 122, 123, 126, 127, 128
Frank, David 72
Fraser River Valley, British Columbia 232, 238
French-Canadian workers 55, 89, 90, 91, 92, 95, 96, 100, 102, 106, 108, 115, 122, 126, 129, 284, 293, 309; aversion to socialism 93, 112, 126, 129, 132; nationalism of 91, 297
Fredericton 57, 64
Fredericton Trades and Labor Council 52
'Free Speech Fight' 238
free trade. *See* tariff
freight handlers 181, 193, 195–6, 204
Friesen, Gerald 217
fruit packers 239
Fuel Controller 246
Furniture Manufacturers' Association 154
furniture workers 88, 106, 154
fur workers 99, 105, 107

Gale, R.H. 257
Gananoque, Ontario 4, 269, 273
Gartshore, W.M. 155
Gastonier, Anita 108
gas workers 104
Gauthier, Joseph 127, 128
general strikes 178, 184, 188, 190, 195, 207, 249, 272, 292; Amherst 47, 54, 57, 58, 82, 115, 272, 274; Brandon 196–7; Calgary 191, 195–6, 198–200; Montreal 110–13, 114, 115–16, 130,

131, 132, 133; Moose Jaw 222; New Westminster 255, 256; Prince Rupert 255; Regina 192, 197–8; Saskatoon 197; Seattle 4, 195; Toronto 111, 114, 144, 150–2, 153, 155, 164; Vancouver 24–5, 36, 239, 250, 254–8; Victoria 250, 255–6; Winnipeg 180–1, 182, 195; *see also* sympathy strikes; Winnipeg General Strike
German workers 13, 37, 98
Gillis, J.A. 48
Glace Bay, Nova Scotia 47, 48, 54
glassworkers 111
Gompers, Samuel 32, 33, 81, 123, 160, 272, 292
Goodwin, Albert ('Ginger') 25, 250
Gouin, Jean-Lomer 102, 103, 115, 128, 141
Gramsci, Antonio 206, 226, 306
Granby, Quebec 88, 104, 113, 120
Grand Forks, British Columbia 248
Grand-Mère, Quebec 90
Grand Trunk Pacific Railway 238
Gray, C.F. 207, 215
Greater Toronto Labor Party 159, 301
Great Shadow, The 289
Great War. *See* First World War
Great War Veterans' Association 17, 48, 183; *see also* veterans
Greenwood, British Columbia 248
Guelph, Ontario 150, 163, 294
Guelph Independent Labor Party 165
Guthrie, Sam 260
Gutteridge, Helena 243, 273
gypsum quarrymen 46, 47, 61

Hak, Gordon 237
Halcrow, George 166
Halifax 4, 24, 47, 48, 51, 52, 55, 56, 57, 58, 64, 65, 66, 78, 81, 294
Halifax Labor Party 59, 65, 66
Halifax Trades and Labor Council 52, 53, 66
Halifax Workers' Party 59
Hall, Bella 124, 128, 130
Hall, Grant 103
Hamilton 3, 20, 98, 144, 145, 146, 147, 148, 152, 154, 155, 157, 160, 165, 165, 166, 273, 293, 294, 299, 304
Hamilton Women's Independent Labor Party 161, 162, 163
Hanson, Stanley 197
Hants County, Nova Scotia 47, 60
Harrington, John D. 261
Hawthornthwaite, J.H. 243, 249
Heaps, A.A. 209, 215
Hearst, William 164
Heenan, Peter 261
Henderson, Rose 59, 124, 126, 130, 131, 273
Herald (London), 162
Herman, Neil 86
Heseltine, Ralph 192, 198
Hobsbawm, Eric 218
Holt, Herbert 253
Hooley, J.S. 194, 198
Horodyski, Mary 185
Hotel and Restaurant Employees International Alliance, Local 599 277
hotel and restaurant workers 191, 245, 252, 277; *see also* waitresses
Houde, Camillien 128
hours of labour 54, 58, 64, 94, 102, 107, 116, 138, 158, 279–80, 288, 301; double shifts 246; eight-hour day 36, 49, 54, 57, 58, 84, 109, 110, 111, 119, 165, 166, 199, 245, 247, 260, 279, 285, 287;

forty-four-hour week 112; forty-hour week 3; nine-hour day 20, 60, 120, 157; overtime 235; six-hour day 216, 251, 255, 279; ten-hour day 64
housewives 21, 45, 78, 83, 107, 185; organizations among 45, 58, 108, 162–3, 280
housing, working-class 19, 20, 23, 56, 146, 233
Houston, J.O. 271
Hughes, Sam 12, 16
Hull, Quebec 88, 89, 113, 117
Humphrey, Levi 261
Hungarian workers 178, 183
Hyatt, Fred 53

immigrants: American 89, 233; Asian 6, 148, 240, 252, 284 (*see also* Chinese workers; Japanese workers; South Asian workers); British, 18, 89, 93, 121, 232, 233, 234, 243, 263; deportation of 35, 207, 210; European 6, 13, 14, 16, 19, 23, 35, 89, 93, 112, 121, 132, 148, 150, 179, 184, 233, 280, 284, 309; and job opportunities during war 23; and Russian Revolution 26, 112, 274, 292, 294; *see also* ethnic conflict
Immigration Act, amendments to 35, 184, 205, 206, 207, 211, 226, 284, 289
Imperial Munitions Board 14, 19, 23, 24, 25, 31, 97, 145, 151, 157, 244, 245–6; and fair wage clause 30, 97
Imperial Oil 65, 149
'Imperoyal' 65
income tax 15, 21
independent commodity producers 44, 62, 285; *see also* farmers; fishers
Independent Labor Alliance 51
Independent Labor Party of Nova Scotia 54, 55, 62
Independent Labor Party of Ontario 124, 156, 159, 160, 161, 163–9, 309
independent labour parties 274, 281, 294, 306; in British Columbia 249, 260–1; in New Brunswick 55, 65; in Nova Scotia 53, 54, 55–6, 62, 65, 66, 276; in Ontario 156, 159, 160, 161, 163–9, 309; in Prairie provinces 188, 201, 215; in Quebec 124
Industrial Banner (Toronto) 144, 157, 158, 159, 162
industrial councils 36, 65, 73, 279
industrial democracy 5–6, 55, 105, 250–1, 276, 277, 278, 288; *see also* workers' councils
Industrial Disputes Investigation Act (IDIA) 14, 24, 100, 101, 117, 269, 278; labour opposition to 30
industrial legality 28, 33, 46, 48, 50, 61, 67, 69–76, 94, 110, 112, 117, 123, 137, 257, 278, 293, 296, 309
industrial spies 28, 73, 288; *see also* detectives, private; secret service
industrial unionism 27–28, 51–2, 54, 97, 99, 114, 121, 129, 130, 145, 148, 149, 151, 153, 168, 190, 191, 193, 238, 250, 272, 274, 293, 296, 309; *see also* amalgamation of crafts; Industrial Workers of the World; One Big Union
Industrial Workers of the World (IWW) 28, 187, 198, 238, 248, 255, 259, 260
inflation. *See* cost of living
intellectuals 17, 26, 44, 57; *see also* middle class
International Association of Machinists 114, 193; *see also* machinists

International Brotherhood of Electrical Workers 255; *see also* electricians
International Labour Organization 36
International Ladies' Garment Workers Union (ILGWU) 93, 99, 104, 106, 108, 129; *see also* clothing workers
International Molders' Journal 164
International Typographical Union 123, 127; *see also* printers
international unionism 28, 50, 73, 87, 90, 91, 94, 97, 98, 100, 101, 111, 112, 113, 114, 116, 118, 119, 120, 123, 125, 128, 130, 147, 180, 250, 272, 290, 291, 292, 294, 306
International Union of Mine, Mill and Smelter Workers 247; *see also* miners, metalliferous; smelter workers; Western Federation of Miners
Inverness County, Nova Scotia 49, 51
iron workers 95, 117, 237
Irvine, William 189, 200, 223, 261, 275
Italian workers 89, 90, 96, 98, 99, 100, 148, 233, 238, 271
Ivens, William 155, 187, 209, 211, 215, 275

Jacobs, Lyon W. 100
James Pender and Company 76
Japanese Camp and Mill Workers' Union 271
Japanese workers 232, 240, 259
Jewish Federation of Charities 100
Jewish workers 26, 89, 90, 91, 92, 93, 96, 99, 100, 105, 106, 129, 132, 148, 179–80, 210, 271, 284
jingoism. *See* patriotism
John Inglis Company 19
Johns, R.J. 111, 153, 178, 209
Johnston-Knight, Sarah 195, 200, 273
joint bargaining 51, 52, 97, 100, 114, 131, 154, 155, 189
Jonquière, Quebec 90, 117
Joy, John 50
Julien, Henri 93, 115

'Kaiserism' 13, 25, 278
Kavanagh, Jack 194, 256, 261, 262, 273
Kealey, Gregory S. 5, 205, 269, 302
Kénogami, Quebec 90, 117
Kerr, Donald 197
Ketchen, General H.D.B. 207, 209, 210, 226
King, William Lyon Mackenzie 241, 261, 279, 297
Kingsley, E.T. 247, 249
Kinsella, Fred 198
Kirwin, Harry 111
Kitchener, Ontario 3, 149
Komagata Maru 240
Kootenays, British Columbia 238, 258
Knight, Joseph 153, 200, 273
Knights of Labor 147, 150, 263
Ku Klux Klan 86

Labor Church 187, 188, 215
Labor Leader (Sydney) 56
Labor News (Hamilton) 45, 148, 164
Labor Temples 110, 184, 187, 209, 250, 251, 257, 258
labour clubs 91, 92, 94, 96, 97, 100, 104, 109, 115, 121, 122, 123, 124, 125, 128
Labour College 128
Labour Day 52, 122, 278
labourers, building 147, 148, 179, 197, 238
labourers, unskilled 44, 89, 90, 106, 233, 237, 238, 256, 271
labourism 28–9, 275, 276, 286, 300; in

British Columbia 248; in Maritimes 46, 54, 55, 56, 58, 59, 65, 68, 75, 76, 77–8; in Ontario 156, 159, 164–70; in Prairie provinces 218; in Quebec 91, 92, 93, 94, 121, 125, 126, 127, 129, 131, 132, 133; *see also* independent labour parties
labour newspapers 25, 27, 272, 273, 298, 306; in British Columbia 249, 252, 258; in Maritimes 50, 56, 59, 74, 83, 86; in Ontario 144, 148, 153, 155, 157, 158, 159, 161, 162, 164, 289, 292, 304; in Prairie provinces 182, 184, 187, 195, 196, 197, 211, 215, 218, 221, 278, 292; in Quebec 91, 98, 110, 112, 123, 125
Labour Open Forums 56
Labour Party, Australian 26
Labour Party, British 3, 26, 161, 168, 275
labour representation: in federal Parliament 31, 32, 102, 123, 146, 164, 170, 215, 261, 295, 299; in municipal councils 29, 54, 56, 92, 123, 157, 201, 215, 275, 295, 311; in provincial legislatures 29, 54–5, 62–3, 125, 127–8, 156, 163–4, 166, 190–1, 215, 243, 248, 249, 260–1, 275, 295
labour shortages 14, 15, 18–19, 278
labour turnover 19–20
Lachine, Quebec 120
Lacombe, Aurèle 125, 127, 128
Ladies' Clothing Manufacturers' Association 100
Lakehead, Ontario 154
Lambert, Alfred 104
Landers, Samuel 299
Lanouette, Adélard 124
Larocque, Mrs S. 130
laundry workers 104, 191, 241, 245, 252
Laurendeau, Adélard 125, 127, 128
Laurier, Sir Wilfrid 13, 124, 141, 201, 249, 275
Lauzon, Quebec 101, 116
Lavergne, Armand 121
Law and Order League 202
layoffs. *See* unemployment
leather workers 88
Lefeaux, Wallis 257
Lenin, V.I. 206, 231, 258
letter carriers. *See* postal workers
Lévis, Quebec 100, 101, 113, 119, 123, 138
Lewis, John L. 71, 72, 75
Liberal–Labour cooperation 55, 121, 126, 127, 128, 131, 224, 249, 275, 299, 309
Liberal Party, 13, 16, 296; in British Columbia 242, 243, 260, 261, 266–7, 290, 296; in Maritimes 55, 57, 63, 82; in Ontario 156, 167; in Prairie provinces 184, 201; in Quebec 115, 123, 124, 125, 126, 127, 131, 141
Lib-Labism. *See* Liberal–Labour cooperation
Liebknecht, Karl 178, 183, 206
Ligue auxiliaire des femmes d'unionistes 109, 131, 132
Lindsay Arsenal 23
Livingston, Dan 50, 68, 71, 72, 73, 74
Lloyd George, David 206
loggers 44, 61, 271, 286, 292; in British Columbia 236–7, 244, 251, 257, 259–60, 273; in New Brunswick 52; in Ontario 167; in Quebec 89
London, Ontario 3, 147, 149, 150, 155, 157, 158, 162, 163, 170
longshoremen 3, 28, 270; in British

Columbia 239, 256; in Maritimes 45, 52, 60, 86; in Quebec 90
Longueil Labor Club 92
Longuet, Jean 161
Lortie, E.A. 125
Louisbourg, Nova Scotia 49
lumber industry 44, 60; *see also* loggers; sawmill workers
Lumber Workers' Industrial Union 167, 259–60, 286
Lunn, C.W. 86
Luxemburg, Rosa 183, 206
Lyall, Mayor 208

MacBride, M.M. 164, 166
McBride, Sir Richard 242
MacCallum, J.O. 223
machinists 22, 48, 54, 90, 93, 98, 100, 104, 110, 114, 122, 146, 148, 150, 152, 154, 160, 180, 182, 190, 200, 271, 283
McClary Manufacturing Company 155
McClung, Nellie 285
McCormack, A. Ross 220, 237
McCreath, R. 200
McDonald, Angus 164
MacDonald, Daniel 192
MacDonald, John (Jack) 159, 168, 273, 294
McGill, Helen Gregory 242
McGrath, C.A. 246
McInnis, Angus 261
McKay, A.A. 68
McKay, A.T. 57
McKay, Colin 53, 83
McLachlan, J.B. 48, 49, 50, 51, 58, 65, 67, 68, 70, 71, 72, 73, 74, 81, 83, 273, 294
MacLean, Neil 161
McNab, Mary 162, 273
McNaught, Kenneth 203, 227
McVety, James H. 18, 249, 291, 299
Magog, Quebec 104, 113
Maisonneuve, Quebec 123, 125
Maisonneuve Labor Club 125
management 40, 235, 237, 287; scientific 102, 115, 192, 234–5, 236, 237, 311; in wartime 19, 22, 146; *see also* industrial democracy
Marine Trades Federation: in Maritimes 51; in Ontario 154; in Quebec 100, 101, 111, 114, 119
Maritime Labor Herald 74, 83
Maritime Progressive Workmen's Association 78
Maritime Rights movement 45, 46, 57, 76–7, 86, 289, 297, 309
Maritimes, economy of 12, 44, 46, 60, 63–4
Marks, Joseph 144, 157, 158, 159, 161, 170
Martel, Gédéon 122, 124
Martin, Médéric 92, 95, 96, 97, 100, 102, 122, 126–7
Marxism 247, 248, 261, 276, 286; *see also* Communism in Canada; socialism in Canada
Marysville, New Brunswick 65
masculinity, working-class 59, 78, 83, 87, 130, 161, 163, 191, 273, 280, 282, 283
Master Plumbers' Association (Montreal) 120
Masters, D.C. 178, 220, 227, 228
maternal feminism 58, 167, 280
Mathers, T.G. 36
Mathers Commission. *See* Royal Commission on Industrial Relations

Mathieu, Alfred 93, 115, 124, 128, 129, 141–2
Mathieu, Alphétus 127
May Day 110, 130, 159
meat packers. *See* packinghouse workers
Meighen, Arthur 35, 203, 204, 206, 207, 208, 209, 212, 225, 228
Mendelssohn, Mrs Ray 130
metal trades councils: in British Columbia 245, 252, 253; in Maritimes 51, 52; in Montreal 114, 116, 117; in Ontario 152, 153, 154, 159; in Prairie provinces 114, 177, 182, 186, 199, 209
metalworkers 12, 22, 50, 88, 90, 97, 115, 146, 155, 190, 199, 218, 269, 270, 287, 310; *see also* boilermakers; machinists; moulders; pattern makers
Methodist Church of Canada 17, 187
Métivier, Joseph 108, 124
middle class 58, 236; alliance with labour 57, 92, 123, 275, 279, 285, 307; fear of labour 206, 285; *see also* intellectuals
Midgley, Victor 250
migration: from Maritimes 61, 64, 65; in Quebec 90, 95, 116
Miliband, Ralph 203
militancy. *See* strikes
military, use of in strikes 35, 42, 68, 113, 116, 119, 152, 169, 188, 197, 207–11, 226, 254, 257, 279, 289
Military Service Act. *See* conscription, military
Military Voters Act 174
Mills, Walt 223
miners, asbestos 20, 88, 89, 97, 98, 271
miners, coal 3, 20, 28, 29, 269, 270, 292; in Alberta 37, 232, 233, 246, 251, 253, 265, 278, 281, 287, 299, 310; in British Columbia 232, 246, 251, 258, 260, 310; in New Brunswick 49; in Nova Scotia 36, 45, 46, 48, 49, 50, 53, 54, 58, 59, 63, 64, 67–76, 278, 281, 287, 299, 308; *see also* United Mine Workers of America
miners, metalliferous 233, 235, 236, 239, 258
miners, silver 20
minimum wage, female 58, 129–30, 167, 242, 261, 290
Minto, New Brunswick 49, 50
Miramichi district, unions in 51, 64
Moffatt, John 50, 299
Moncton, New Brunswick 51, 52, 55, 56, 62, 63, 65
Moncton Amalgamated Central Labor Union 53
Moncton Labor Party 55, 86
Moncton Trades and Labor Council 52, 57
Monde ouvrier/Labor World 91, 98, 110, 112, 125, 126, 130
Mongeau, Paul-Émile 121, 141
Montgomery, David 234
Montmorency, Quebec 104, 113, 116
Montreal 4, 20, 26, 87, 88, 89, 90, 92, 93, 99, 100, 101–3, 111, 113, 114, 115, 116, 117, 118, 125, 209, 271, 273, 278, 284, 291, 294, 309
Montreal Agreement 67
Montreal Board of Trade 103
Montreal Catholic School Commission 118, 140
Montreal Labor Party 124, 125–6, 129, 130
Montreal Light, Heat and Power Company 104

Montreal Trades and Labor Council 91, 93, 94, 97, 98, 101, 103, 104, 105, 106, 107, 108, 109, 110, 111, 115, 117, 118, 121, 122, 123, 125, 126, 127, 128, 131, 132, 135
Moore, Tom 36, 150, 155, 167, 199, 290, 291
Moose Jaw, Saskatchewan 189, 195
Moose Jaw Trades and Labor Council 181, 190, 195, 222
Morden, Manitoba 213
Morrison, Frank 33
mothers' allowance legislation 58, 129, 166, 167, 261, 277, 290
Mould, Arthur 170
moulders 64, 82, 114, 146, 164
municipal reform movement 92
municipal workers 50, 89, 101, 102–4, 108, 112, 114, 115, 116, 118, 120, 128, 132, 147, 151, 157, 180–1, 191, 193, 195, 196, 199, 200, 203, 225, 271
munitions industries 12, 13, 15, 18, 20, 23, 94
munitions workers 22, 30, 97, 105–6, 107, 146, 270, 278, 283; strikes of 13, 20, 95, 144, 146
Murdoch, James 261
Murray, Philip 72
musicians 200

Nanaimo, British Columbia 239, 248, 261
National Conference on Character Education 213, 214, 290
National Council of Women 162
National Industrial Conference 36, 279, 289, 291
nationalization. *See* public ownership
National Research Council 15
National Service Board 14, 31, 249
National Steel Car 20
national unions 91, 94, 114, 118, 119
native peoples 44, 235, 239, 240, 286
Naturalization Act, amendments to 211, 226
Natural Resources Commission 15
Neagle, Armand 122
Nearing, Scott 234, 259
Neelands, Harry 261
Nelson, British Columbia 261
New Aberdeen, Nova Scotia 75
New Brunswick 44, 48, 49, 50, 51, 52, 55
New Brunswick Federation of Labor 52
Newcastle, British Columbia 248, 249, 260
Newcastle, New Brunswick 52, 55, 56, 60
New Democracy (Hamilton) 153, 161, 292, 304
Newfoundland 8
New Glasgow, Nova Scotia 56, 57
New Waterford, Nova Scotia 47, 54, 75
New Westminster, British Columbia 237, 248
New Westminster Trades and Labor Council 242, 255
New Zealand 4, 21
Niagara District Trades Federation 155, 166
Nichols, Clifford 276
Norris, T.C. 184
northern Ontario 8, 20, 24, 271
Nova Scotia 44
Nova Scotia Federation of Labor 50, 52, 54, 81

Nova Scotia Steel Company 51
nurses 56, 241

Ogden shops. *See* Canadian Pacific Railway
old-age pensions 166, 277, 297
Oliver, Frank 201
Oliver, John 260
One Big Union (OBU) 6, 50, 51, 52, 53, 73, 144, 152, 177, 178, 183, 186, 189, 193, 194, 198, 199, 201, 214, 215, 217, 229, 234, 250–1, 252, 255, 258, 259, 261, 262, 274, 279, 291, 293, 310; in Australia 26; in Montreal 110, 111, 112, 113, 116, 121, 124, 125–6, 128, 130, 132, 304; in Nova Scotia 54, 81; in Ontario 152–3, 155, 304; organizational structure of 299; *see also* Western Labour Conference
Ontario Labor News (Toronto) 153, 155
Ontario Section of the Canadian Labor Party 168
On to Ottawa Trek 43
open shop 64, 120, 236, 239, 258, 288; *see also* closed shop; union recognition
operating engineers 191, 256
Order of Railroad Telegraphers 32
Orillia, Ontario 149
Ottawa 150, 160

Pacific Construction Company 257
pacifism 13, 30, 149, 248
packinghouse workers 104, 107, 111, 117, 148, 149, 151, 183, 189, 241, 271, 278
Pagé, L.G.N. 93
painters 106, 107, 125, 154, 253
papermakers 95, 117, 251
parades 52–3, 61, 110, 122, 205, 211, 250, 257, 278, 281, 305
Parr, Joy 301
partyism 156, 164, 165, 166
paternalism 44, 63, 65, 309
patriotism 12, 16, 18, 46, 53, 146, 214, 245, 248, 275; labour's version of 30, 278
patronage 16, 45, 76, 117, 144, 159, 164, 165
pattern makers 114
Patterson, Albert 253
peace treaty. *See* Treaty of Versailles
Penfold, Steven 59
Penner, Jacob 179
Penner, Norman 5
People's Church 215
Peterborough, Ontario 157, 278
Pettipiece, R.P. (Parm) 239
Pictou County, Nova Scotia 49, 50, 51, 52, 55, 57, 63, 81, 273
Pictou County Independent Labor Party 55, 59, 61
Pictou County Trades and Labor Council 51, 52
Pinkerton Detective Agency 288
Pitbaldo, Isaac 203, 228, 229
plumbers 53, 64, 114, 120, 140
Poale Zion (Labour Zionists) 93, 179, 180
police: provincial, and labour 73; special 28, 35, 208–11; unions 50, 53, 90, 101, 118, 191, 196, 207
Polish workers 96, 178
Port Arthur 24
postal workers 34, 50, 181, 182, 191, 192, 193, 197, 199, 200, 203, 204, 225, 250, 254–5, 256, 271, 276
Powell River, British Columbia 251
Prenter, Harriet 162

press censorship 13, 35, 98, 144, 150, 197, 258
Prince Edward Island 44, 57, 62
Prince Rupert, British Columbia 255
printers 89, 90, 123, 198, 200, 239, 240, 255, 256, 261, 278, 279, 287
Pritchard, William A. 209, 230, 261, 268
profiteering 21, 24, 37, 58, 109, 144, 146, 158–9, 160, 170, 190, 192, 224
profit sharing 65
prohibition 14, 17, 24, 61
propaganda, pro-war 13, 14, 25, 48, 145, 148, 157, 180
property qualifications for electoral candidates 277
proportional representation 55, 159, 277
prostitution 241, 264
protectionism. *See* tariff
Protestant Ministerial Association of the Lower Mainland 243
provincial federations of labour 18, 50, 52–3, 54, 81, 238, 249, 250, 254, 258, 281
provincial governments and labour: legislation 106–7, 115, 290; repression 36, 126
Provincial Workmen's Association (PWA) 48, 49
Prudential Investment Company 237
public ownership 21, 124, 246, 249, 255, 265, 276, 277
public-sector workers 33, 117, 155, 190, 271, 285, 302, 311; *see also* firefighters; municipal workers; police; postal workers; teachers
public space, control of 35, 36, 238, 281, 284, 306; *see also* parades
Public Utilities Council 155
pulp and paper workers, 278; in Maritimes 45, 50, 52, 60, 64; in Quebec 88, 89
Puttee, Arthur 187, 221, 299

Quebec, economy of 88, 94, 95
Quebec City 88, 89, 90, 91, 100, 101, 116, 117, 120, 122, 123, 140, 302
Quebec Labor Party 91, 92, 94, 97, 102, 110, 121, 123, 124, 125
Quebec Section of the Canadian Labor Party (QSCLP) 124, 125, 126, 128, 130
Queen, John 209, 215

racism. *See* ethnic conflict
Railway Brotherhoods. *See* railway workers, running trades
Railway Employees Department, Division 4 111, 113, 114, 193
railways 15, 23, 63
railway workers: running trades 3, 29, 32, 58, 82, 90, 192, 197, 205, 207, 208, 209, 227, 255, 256, 261; semiskilled 52; in shops 33, 101, 106, 107, 111, 113, 114, 117, 120, 122–3, 129, 181, 189, 190, 192, 198, 200, 257, 292, 310; *see also* freight handlers; labourers, unskilled; sleeping-car porters
Rea, J.E. 230
reconstruction 17, 157–8; federal government and 32, 34–5; labour views of 158–9, 160, 301
Reconstruction and Development Committee, Labour Sub-Committee of 32
recruitment, military 13, 18, 245; *see also* conscription, military

Red International of Trade Unions 70, 71
Red Scare 5, 36, 42, 65, 166, 184, 206, 288, 294, 302, 311
Rees, David 291, 299
Regina 37, 188, 190, 198, 200, 221
Regina Builders' Exchange 191
Regina Trades and Labor Council 21, 181, 190, 191–2, 197, 198, 222, 273
registration of manpower 14, 31, 32, 157, 190, 249
Reimer, Chad 184, 211
relief 18, 30
religion. *See* Labor Church; Methodist Church of Canada; People's Church; Roman Catholic Church; social gospel
Reserve, Nova Scotia 75
retail workers 78, 147, 185, 190, 191, 241
returned soldiers. *See* veterans
Revelstoke, British Columbia 248
Rigg, R.A. 189
Riordan, John 238
Rivers Inlet, British Columbia 238
Roback, Leo 123
Robertson, Gideon 32, 33, 144, 170, 181, 182, 195, 204, 207, 208, 209, 227, 259
Robin, Martin 194
Robinson, Ernest 181, 291
Robochyi narod (Winnipeg) 179, 210
Rogers, Robert 16
Roman Catholic Church 28, 77, 118, 133, 289
Rompré, Mme 108
roofers 140
Ross, Alex 190, 198, 199, 291
Rossland, British Columbia 233, 246
Rotary Clubs 181, 214
Rouillard, Jacques 134, 140
Rowell, Alberta Jean 162
Royal Canadian Mounted Police 66
Royal Commission on Industrial Relations 36, 37, 81, 158, 192, 193–4, 197, 199, 202, 223, 224, 253, 276, 279, 287, 289, 307
Royal Commission on Labour Conditions in British Columbia 242
royal commissions: on Nova Scotia coal industry 49, 75; and workers 30, 81, 101, 115, 278, 300
Royal North-West Mounted Police (RNWMP) 14, 35, 198, 205, 206, 207, 209, 210, 211, 215, 253, 305
rubber workers 88, 104, 106, 107, 108, 111, 113, 116, 119, 147, 149, 278
rum-running 61
rural workers 224, 285–6, 311; in Maritimes 44, 51–2, 60, 62, 76, 309; in Quebec 90
Russell, R.B. 178, 179, 182, 209, 211, 212, 213, 217, 219, 273
Russian Revolution 3, 4, 5, 34, 206; impact on Canada 26, 53, 110, 177, 178, 192, 217, 271, 274; *see also* Bolshevism; Communism in Canada; socialism in Canada
Russian workers 26, 96, 98

Sackville, New Brunswick 55, 82
Saguenay region, Quebec 88, 90
sailors 104
St Catharines, Ontario 157, 160–1, 162
Sainte-Marie, Quebec 127
Sainte-Marie Labor Club 93, 125, 128
Saint-Hyacinthe, Quebec 120
St Jérôme, Quebec 104, 113
Saint John 47, 48, 50, 53, 55, 64, 65, 66, 76

Saint John Trades and Labor Council 52, 53, 65
Saint-Louis, Quebec 100, 129
Saint-Louis Labor Club 92, 93, 129
Saint-Martin, Albert 93, 129
Sambrook, Joseph 192, 198, 273
Sangster, George 122, 199
Sangster, Joan 58
sanitorium workers 190
Sarnia, Ontario 149
Saskatchewan 195; *see also* Moose Jaw; Regina; Saskatoon
Saskatoon, Saskatchewan 188, 197
Saskatoon Trades and Labor Council 181, 197, 223
Sault Ste Marie, Ontario 164
sawmill workers 45, 48, 52, 60
Sayer, Derek 213
scandals, political 16, 21, 24
Schoppelrei, Oscar 210
Schubert, Joseph 93, 124, 129
Seattle, Washington 231, 246, 254
Seattle Plan 195
Second Industrial Revolution 22, 40; *see also* management
secret service 35, 253, 289; *see also* industrial spies
sedition 35, 204, 209, 213
Senate, abolition of 277
sexual harassment 130
Shawinigan, Quebec 90, 122
sheet metal workers 200
Shell Committee 15, 16
Sherbrooke, Quebec 88, 95, 101, 120
shingle weavers 245, 252
shipyard workers 12, 20, 33, 189, 269, 270, 287, 289; in British Columbia 33, 231, 244–5, 246, 251, 254, 256, 257; in Nova Scotia 45, 56, 58, 63, 66; in Quebec 89, 95, 97, 100–1, 110, 113, 114, 116, 117, 119, 138
shop stewards, British 26, 310
Siemiatycki, Myer 9, 195
Simpson, James 149, 153, 154, 168, 274, 293
single tax 165, 276
Slavic workers 233
sleeping-car porters 271
Slocan, British Columbia 248
smelter workers 235, 246, 251, 271
Smith, A.E. 215, 275
Smith, Mary Ellen 260–1
Smith, Ralph 260–1
Smith Butchering Machine 235
social democracy 7, 56, 277, 307; *see also* Co-operative Commonwealth Federation
Social Democratic Party 276, 293; in British Columbia 248; in Ontario 149, 160, 168; in Prairie provinces 179, 180, 215, 218; in Quebec 93, 96, 124, 128, 129, 130, 135; and women 162, 179
social gospel 17, 243, 285
socialism in Canada 26, 29, 55, 56, 74, 90, 93, 97, 110, 124, 132, 145, 149, 155, 165, 167–9, 177, 183, 187, 193, 194, 214, 216, 248, 253, 273, 292, 294, 311; and alliance with labourism 156, 160, 215, 249, 260, 276, 294; Catholic opposition to 91; and ethnic groups 93, 94, 96, 126, 150, 179, 180, 183, 284; splits in 293–4; state repression of 14, 25, 33, 35, 42, 150, 179, 180, 204, 207, 294; and unions 48, 49, 110, 112, 151, 152, 155, 177, 182, 194, 221, 250, 273, 274, 291; and war 14, 121, 248; and women 59,

130–1, 162, 242–3, 284; and workers' revolt 6, 9
Socialist League 56
socialist newspapers 14, 25, 26, 153, 155, 161, 179, 210, 242, 261
Socialist Party of Canada 294; in British Columbia 194, 247–8, 249, 257, 259, 260, 261; in Maritimes 53, 54, 56; in Prairie provinces 177, 178, 179, 180, 181, 182, 183, 185, 199, 202, 214, 215, 217, 218, 221; in Quebec 93, 96, 128
Socialist Party of North America 168
Somerville, James 189, 193–4
Sorel, Quebec 100, 142
South Asian workers 232, 240, 259
Soviet, The 26
Soviet Union, Canadian invasion of 27, 216
special police 28, 35, 208–11
Springhill, Nova Scotia 47, 49, 53, 54, 58, 71
Starnes, C. 209
state and labour: conciliation 32, 36, 166; legislation 14; repression 5, 14, 25, 150, 289, 311; *see also* courts and labour; Industrial Disputes Investigation Act; royal commissions; Royal North-West Mounted Police; secret service
Steel Company of Canada 117
steel industry 23; in Nova Scotia 46, 51, 63
steelworkers 22, 189, 278; in Nova Scotia 23, 36, 45, 48, 50, 53, 64, 73, 271, 287, 307; in Ontario 148; in Quebec 89, 116, 117
Stewart, F.W. 104
stonecutters 108, 191
Stratford, Ontario 150
street railway workers 65, 66, 90, 101, 120, 125, 150, 151, 152, 155, 191, 195, 200, 201, 255, 256, 257, 261, 270
strike-breaking 28, 34, 35, 48, 53, 61, 66, 98, 102, 104, 110, 115, 127, 150, 179, 181, 185, 201, 203–11, 240, 257, 288
Strike Bulletin (Brandon) 196, 197
strike-on-the-job strategy 68
strikes 269–70, 281, 287, 297; in Alberta 20; ban on 14, 24, 25, 33, 47, 101, 150, 182, 195, 279, 306; in British Columbia 238, 239, 241, 245–7, 251–2, 259, 269; causes of 24; community support for 97, 102–3, 104, 109–10, 120; impact of patriotism on 46; labour leaders and 33, 34; in Maritimes 47, 48, 53, 64–5, 66, 67–8, 73–5, 82, 269; in Ontario 20, 147, 155, 269; in Prairie provinces 269; pre-war 48, 49, 94–5, 238–9; in Quebec 20, 94–5, 97–104, 108, 110–17, 119, 269; state constraints on 30, 33; violence in 53, 61, 103, 211; *see also* general strikes; munitions workers; sympathy strikes; women workers
Strong, Anna Louise 231
Stuart, H.H. 56
Studholme, Allan 156
Sudbury, Ontario 24
sugar workers 64
Sussex, New Brunswick 53
Sweatman, Travers 203, 204
Sydney, Nova Scotia 25, 36, 47, 48, 50, 54, 58, 64, 73, 271, 287
Sydney Mines, Nova Scotia 51, 63, 75
Sydney Trades and Labor Council 52
sympathy strikes 34, 279, 287, 292; in Maritimes 47, 66, 73; in Ontario 147,

152, 153, 154; in Quebec 95; in Prairie provinces 180, 195–6, 310; *see also* general strikes; Winnipeg General Strike
syndicalism 6, 9, 180, 194, 218, 239, 248, 260, 273

tailors 64, 95, 99, 122, 240
Tallon, R.J. 190, 191, 273
Taraska, Elizabeth Ann 221
tariff 17, 165–6, 286–7, 289, 297, 308, 310
Taschereau, Louis-Alexandre 125, 127
Taylor, F.W. 237
teachers 50, 57, 117–8, 140, 241, 252, 285, 311
teamsters 104, 110, 112, 116, 120, 147, 185, 191, 195, 251, 270
technological change 235, 236, 237, 239
telephone operators 108, 147–8, 185, 191, 225, 241, 251, 257, 258
Temiskaming, Ontario 164
temperance, working-class 56, 58, 83; *see also* prohibition
Terris, Archie 54
textile workers 28, 269, 278; in Maritimes 57, 64, 65, 81; in Quebec 88, 89, 90, 104, 107, 108, 111, 116
Thetford, Quebec 20, 88, 98, 120, 142, 271
Thiel Detective Agency 288
Third International. *See* Communist International
Thompson, John Herd 189
Thompson, Phillips 150
Thorburn, Nova Scotia 50
Tighe, James 86
Tipping, Fred 182
tobacco workers 88, 89, 90, 108
Toronto 4, 19, 25, 144, 148, 149, 150–2, 157, 162, 163, 164, 165, 168, 271, 273, 278, 293
Toronto Building Trades League 154
Toronto District Labor Council 30, 150, 151, 152, 158, 168
Toveritar 243
Trades and Labor Congress of Canada 28, 91, 148, 150, 168, 190, 216, 251, 279, 290, 294; affiliates of 52, 87, 90, 118, 302; conventions of 122, 144, 178, 290–1, 298, 302; and independent labour politics 32, 55, 123, 126, 167, 292; lobbying efforts of 21, 29–34, 91, 147, 157, 178; officers of 29, 36, 102, 155, 198, 199, 274, 293; secession from 50–1, 145, 153–5, 177, 193, 195, 198, 202, 250, 291, 293, 294 (*see also* One Big Union; Western Labour Conference); support for war of 13, 30–1, 33, 122, 249
trades and labour councils 28, 52, 91, 153, 156, 157, 181, 183, 190, 212, 254, 272, 294
Trade Union Educational League (TUEL) 128
Trail, British Columbia 235, 246, 271
tramway workers. *See* street railway workers
Treaty of Versailles 26, 48, 206
Triple Alliance 3, 26
Trites, A.E. 65
Trois-Rivières, Quebec 88, 89, 90, 100, 101, 113, 119, 138
Trotsky, Leon 206
Trotter, W.R. 299
Truro, Nova Scotia 57, 58, 68
Turner, Amelia 273
typographers. *See* printers

Ukrainian Social Democratic Party 179; newspaper of 179
Ukrainian workers 14, 26, 135, 178, 179
unemployed workers: demonstrations of 18, 93, 95–6, 130, 135, 179; organizations of 78, 129
unemployment 11–12, 18, 22, 29, 30, 279, 285, 288, 311; in British Columbia 244, 246, 254, 257, 259; in Maritimes 63–4, 66, 68, 69, 76; in Ontario 151, 160, 166, 168; in Quebec 93, 94–6, 106, 116, 120, 127; in Prairie provinces 183
unemployment insurance 277
Union Advocate (Newcastle) 56
Union Bus Company 65, 66
Union government 16, 24, 25, 159, 189, 275
l'Unioniste (Quebec City) 123
union label 109, 131
union membership 18, 29, 64, 238, 246, 257, 270, 281, 288, 296, 297, 302, 306
union recognition 24, 33, 47, 48, 49, 53, 54, 100, 114, 191, 201, 245, 250, 270, 278
Union Worker (Saint John) 56
United Brotherhood of Carpenters and Joiners 98, 135, 147
United Farmers of New Brunswick 61–2
United Farmers of Nova Scotia 62
United Farmers of Ontario 159, 163, 164, 166
United Mine Workers of America 259, 296; (District 18) 37, 200, 246, 258, 261, 265; (District 26) 48, 49, 50, 57, 65, 67–76; (District 28) 239
United Women's Educational Federation of Ontario 162
United Workmen of Nova Scotia 78
l'Université ouvrière 129
unorganized workers, strikes of 48, 57, 60, 95, 146, 149, 185
Uphill, Tom 260

Vancouver 4, 18, 24, 25, 230, 231, 237, 238, 240, 241, 244, 245, 252, 256, 257, 258, 260, 273, 291, 299
Vancouver Citizen 257
Vancouver Island 233, 236, 239, 240, 260, 310
Vancouver Master Builders' Association 238
Vancouver Trades and Labor Council 18, 181, 217, 239, 240, 243, 249, 250, 251, 253, 259
Verdun Labor Club 93
Verenchuck, Mike 210
Verville, Alphonse 102, 123, 299
veterans 13, 15, 17, 23, 26, 47, 205, 254, 277, 311; alliances with labour 47–8, 54–5, 61, 160, 184, 186, 210, 211, 215, 220, 255, 274, 275, 277–8; attacks on 'enemy aliens' 183, 284; attacks on labour groups 183, 186, 190, 208, 250
Victoria 181, 245, 248, 251, 252, 253, 255, 279
Victoria-Carleton, New Brunswick 61
Victoria Trades and Labor Council 249, 250, 253, 302
violence against women 58
Voice (Winnipeg) 187, 221
voter turnout 128, 201, 296

wages: decline of real 20–1; higher, as union/strike demand 48, 52, 57, 60,

67, 95, 102, 199, 245, 247, 252; increases in 19, 20, 23, 23, 49; reductions of 63, 64, 67, 69, 71, 74, 75, 94, 95, 116, 117, 252, 259, 287, 288
waitresses 58, 107, 185, 241, 245; *see also* hotel and restaurant workers
Walker Theatre 178, 179, 187, 213
Wallace, Joe 57
war bonds 18, 19, 245
war economy 11–12, 18–19, 95, 96, 144, 244; regional inequities in 12
War Measures Act 13, 30, 150, 212; *see also* state and labour, repression
war profit tax 15
Wartime Elections Act 16, 174
War Trade Board 15
Waterloo, Ontario 163
Watters, James 29, 31, 32, 33
welfarism, corporate 65, 288, 289; *see also* industrial councils
Welland, Ontario 157, 163
Wells, A.S. 258
Welsh, F.W. 252, 253
Western Clarion 242, 261
Western Federation of Miners (WFM): in British Columbia 236, 238; in Quebec 98, 114, 120, 142
Western Fuel 239
Western Labor News 187, 195, 221; *Special Strike Edition* 182, 184, 211, 215, 218, 278
Western Labour Conference 35, 145, 153, 177, 178, 183, 188, 192, 193, 194–5, 198, 200, 222, 250, 291
Westville, Nova Scotia 50
White, Thomas 254
Whitley Committee 279
Wilkinson, J.R. 238
Williams, E.K. 228
Williams, Parker 243
Willison, Sir John 289
Winch, Ernest 217, 259
Windsor, Nova Scotia 61, 150, 163
Winning, James 179
Winnipeg 24, 25, 26, 111, 127, 176, 189, 193, 200, 201, 215, 273, 291, 297, 299
Winnipeg Board of Trade 181, 203
Winnipeg Citizens' League 214, 215, 229
Winnipeg General Strike 4, 24, 37, 43, 103, 114, 116, 144, 151, 176–88, 195, 197, 203–13, 217, 272, 278, 284, 285, 287; constructed as 'revolution' 5, 182, 184, 204, 219; historiography of 5, 176, 206, 216; in novels 4, 9; protests against repression of 113, 201, 215, 229, 256, 273; provincial inquiry into 211; repression of 35, 152, 198, 205–11, 212, 269, 279; strike committees of 186, 187, 188, 209, 210, 227; support in eastern Canada for 111, 112; women in 185
Winnipeg Industrial Bureau 208, 214
Winnipeg Real Estate Board 181
Winnipeg Trades and Labor Council 177, 178, 179, 180, 181, 182, 184, 186, 187, 215, 217
Winsor, Fred 60
Wolfe, Carolyn 108
Wolvin, Roy 66, 73
women candidates in elections 58–9, 83, 131
women's auxiliaries 58, 59, 108–9, 162, 163
women's independent labour parties 161–3, 280
Women's Labor Leagues 59, 109, 162, 185, 191, 212, 221–2, 280
women's organizations, middle-class 26, 130, 131, 162, 242, 260

Women's Social Democratic League 162, 179
women's suffrage. *See* franchise, for women
Women's Trade Union Label League of the United States and Canada 109
women voters 16, 17, 54, 129, 130, 156, 161
women workers 57, 78, 89, 148, 235, 241, 283; male unionists' attitudes towards 106, 107, 132, 161, 241, 252, 283, 309; in munitions 19, 22, 106, 146, 148, 283; on strike 99, 106, 108, 185–6, 251; in unions 7, 57–8, 105–7, 108, 148, 185, 191, 271, 280; in war economy 13, 19, 106, 107, 148; *see also* housewives
Woodsworth, J.S. 7, 127, 129, 170, 200, 211, 215, 251, 261, 275, 285, 297
Woodward, M.S. 253
Worker (Toronto) 170, 259, 260
workers' compensation 55, 60, 157, 260
workers' councils 4, 274, 279
Workers' International Industrial Union 155
Workers' Party of Canada 59, 66, 68, 128, 129, 168, 169, 294
workers' revolt: in British Columbia and mining west 310; causes of 18–27; defeat of 7, 307–9; extent of 306–7; goals of 307; historiography of 4–7, 9, 87, 144, 189, 194; in Maritimes 308–9; outside Canada 3–4, 177, 189, 206, 217; in Prairie provinces 310; in Quebec 309; radicalism in 6, 144, 189; regionalism in 6, 7, 87, 144, 189, 231, 282, 283, 299, 308; in southern Ontario 309
Workers' Weekly (Stellarton) 56
Working Women's Association 256
Workmen's Compensation Act (Ontario) 157
Wrigley, G. Weston 247

Yarmouth, Nova Scotia 65
Yates, William 255
Ymir, British Columbia 248

www.ingramcontent.com/pod-product-compliance
Lightning Source LLC
La Vergne TN
LVHW040756070826
844660LV00025B/1157

9780802080820